THE SEVEN DEADLY SINS

nakaba suzuki presents

32

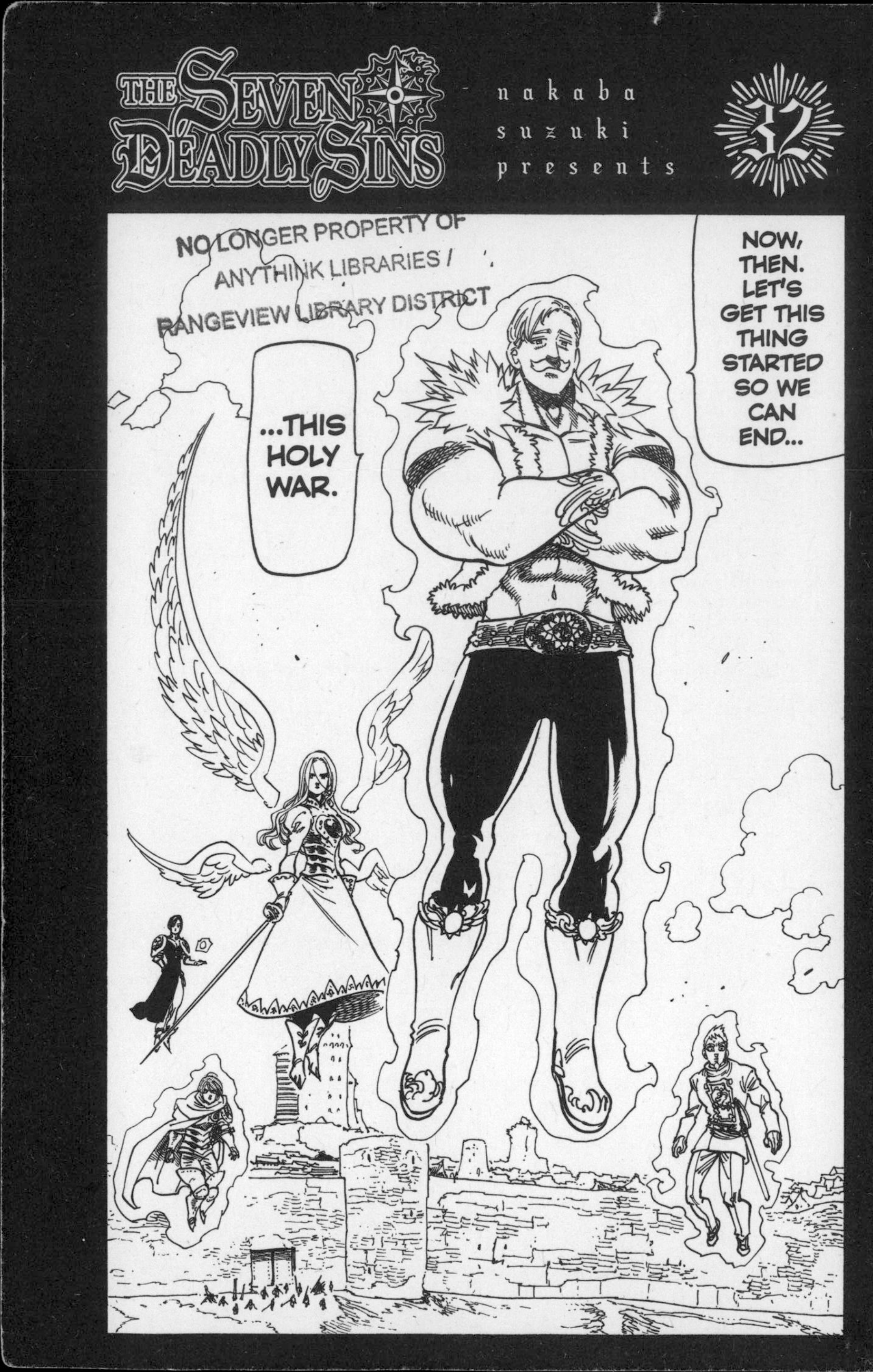
NOW, THEN. LET'S GET THIS THING STARTED SO WE CAN END...
...THIS HOLY WAR.

CONTENTS

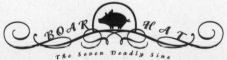

BOAR HAT

The Seven Deadly Sins

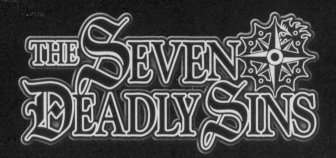

THE SEVEN DEADLY SINS

Chapter 259 - War-Ravaged Britannia

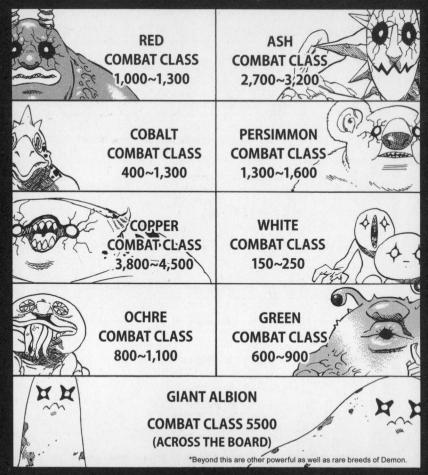

RED COMBAT CLASS 1,000~1,300	**ASH** COMBAT CLASS 2,700~3,200
COBALT COMBAT CLASS 400~1,300	**PERSIMMON** COMBAT CLASS 1,300~1,600
COPPER COMBAT CLASS 3,800~4,500	**WHITE** COMBAT CLASS 150~250
OCHRE COMBAT CLASS 800~1,100	**GREEN** COMBAT CLASS 600~900

GIANT ALBION

COMBAT CLASS 5500 (ACROSS THE BOARD)

*Beyond this are other powerful as well as rare breeds of Demon.

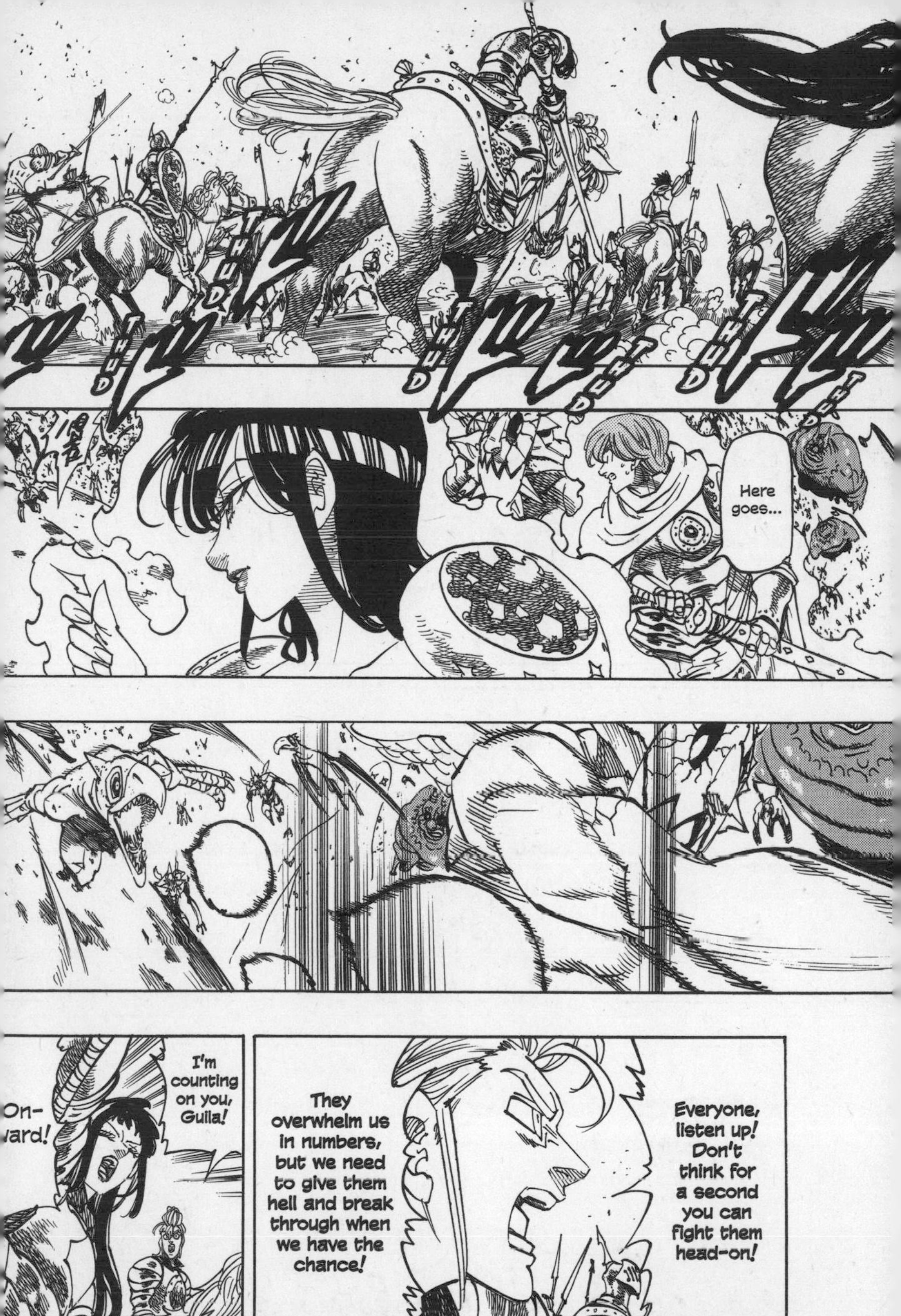
THUD
THUD
THUD
THUD
THUD
THUD
Here goes...
Everyone, listen up! Don't think for a second you can fight them head-on!
They overwhelm us in numbers, but we need to give them hell and break through when we have the chance!
I'm counting on you, Guila!
On-ward!

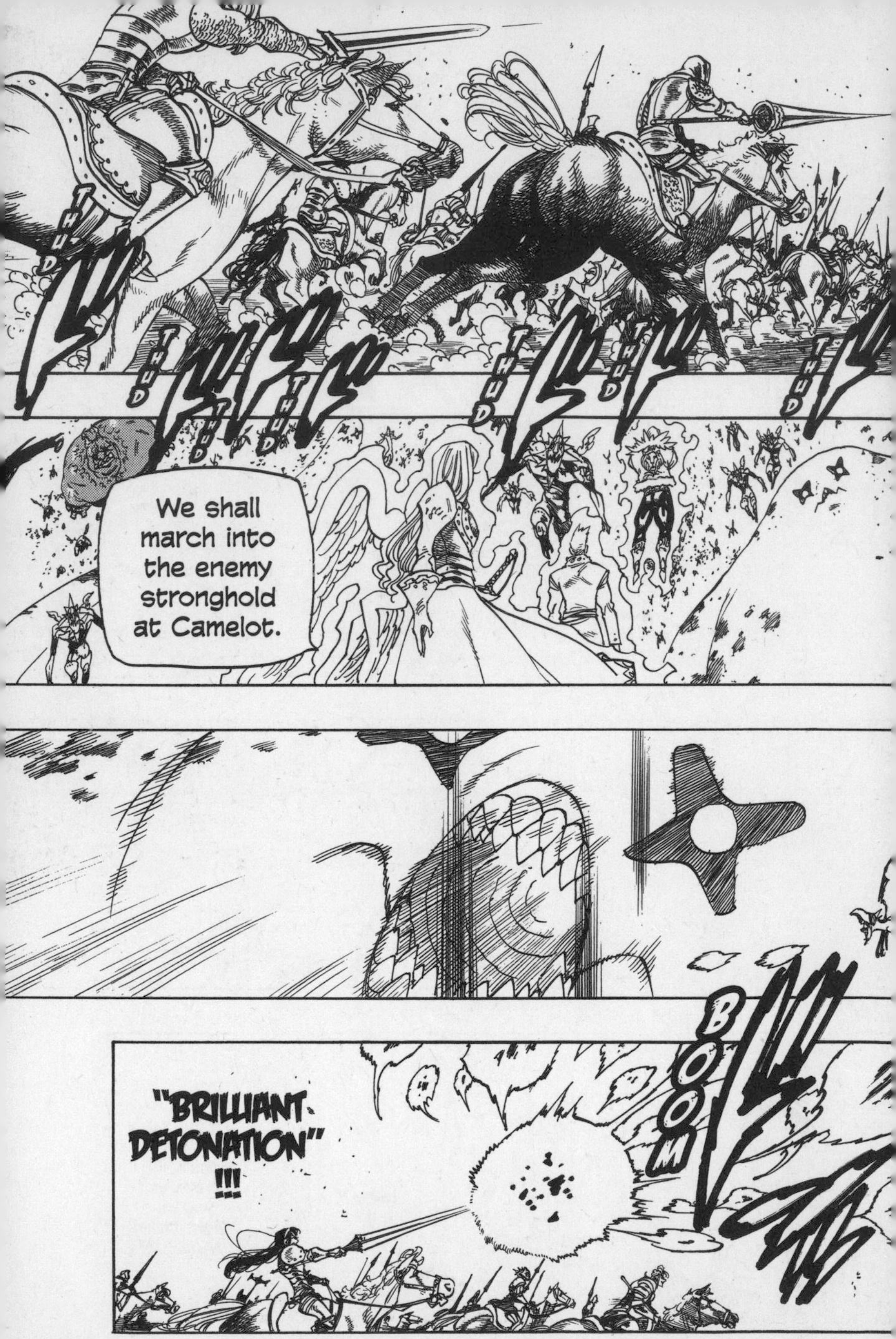
THUD
THUD
THUD
THUD
THUD
THUD
THUD
We shall march into the enemy stronghold at Camelot.
BOOM
"BRILLIANT DETONATION" !!!

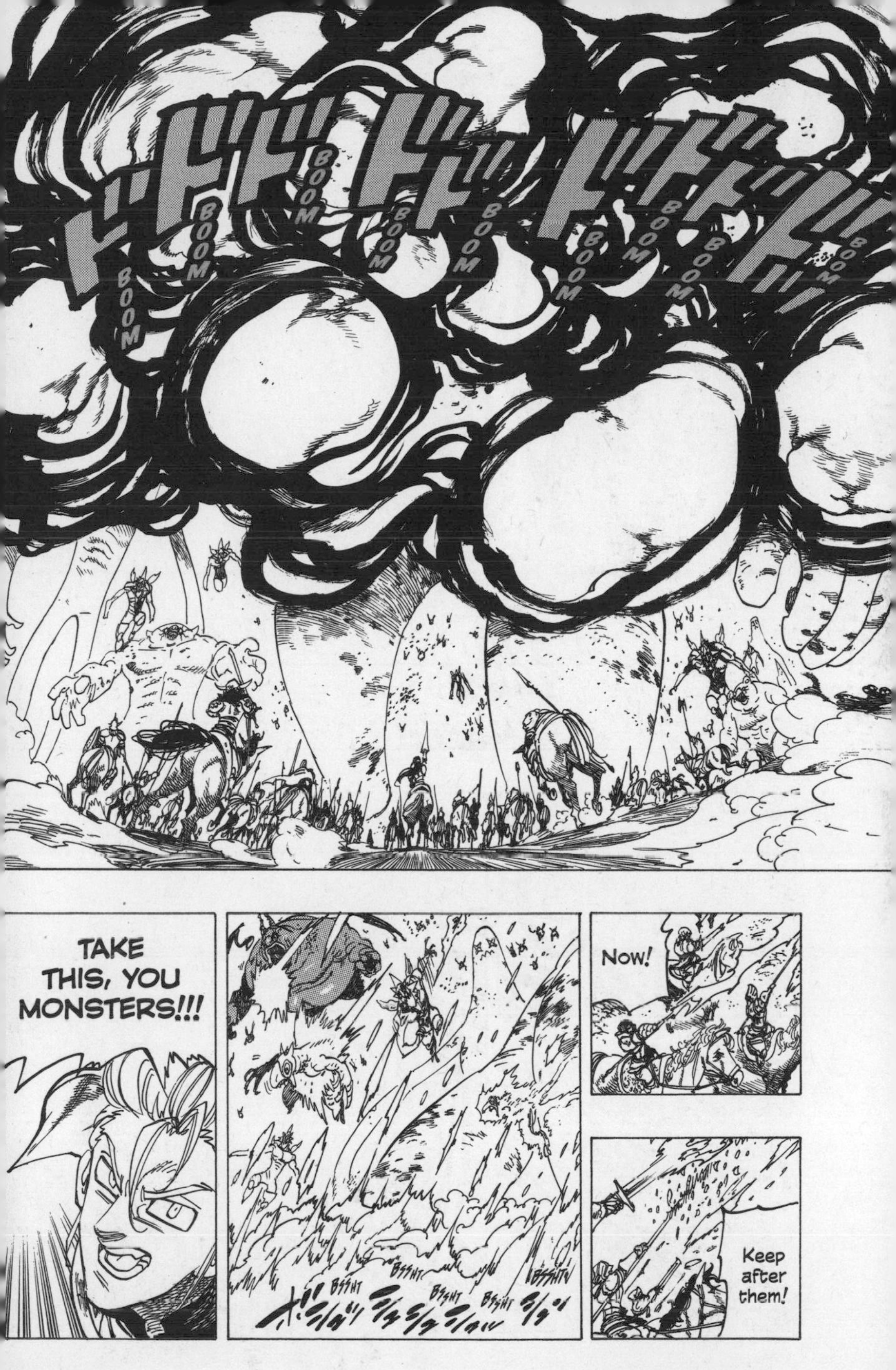
BOOM
BOOM
BOOM
BOOM
BOOM
BOOM
BOOM
BOOM
BOOM
Now!
Keep after them!
BSSHT
BSSHT
BSSHT
BSSHT
BSSHT
TAKE THIS, YOU MONSTERS!!!

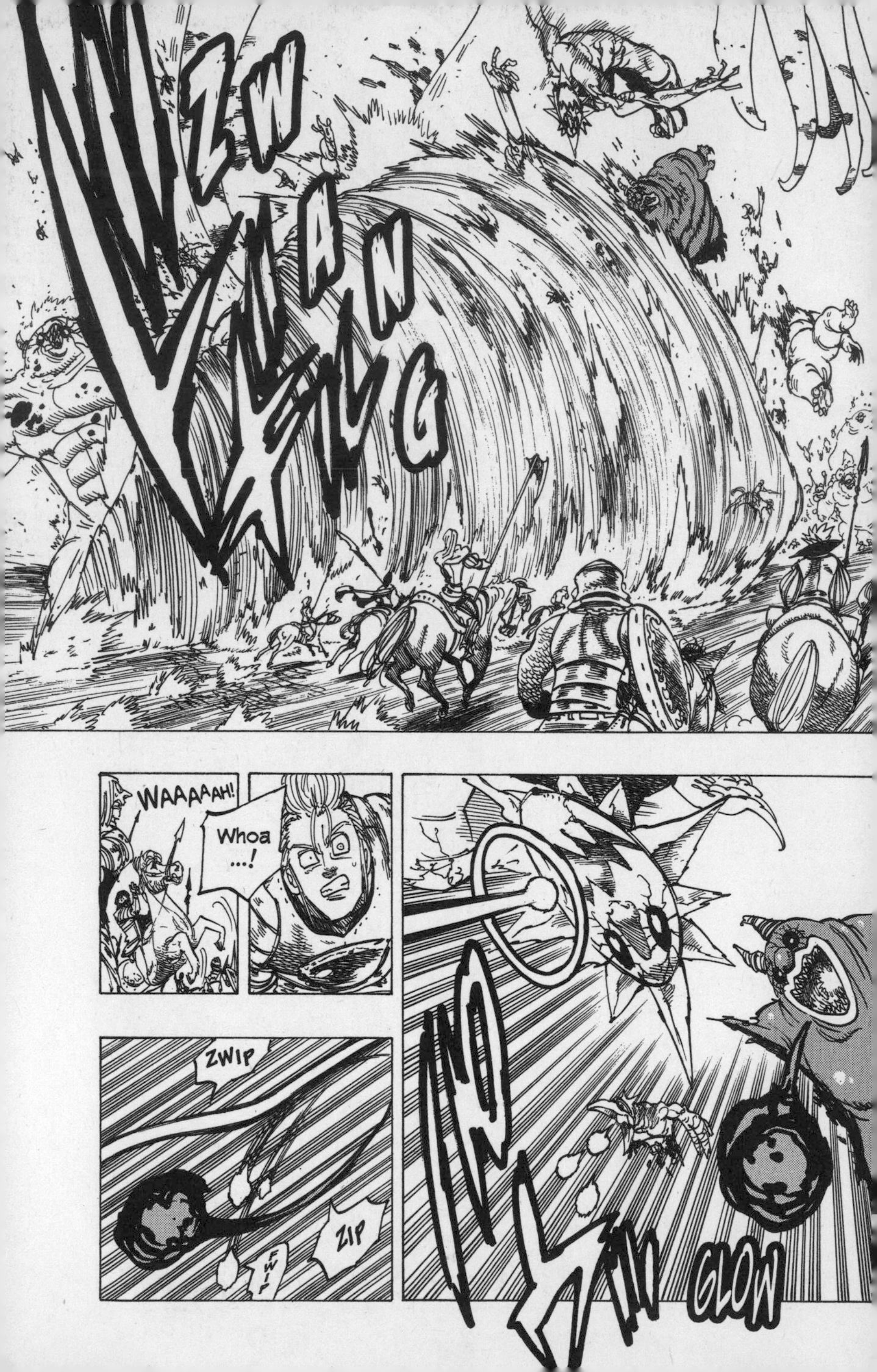
GLOW
Whoa
...!
WAAAAAH!
ZWIP
ZIP
FWIP

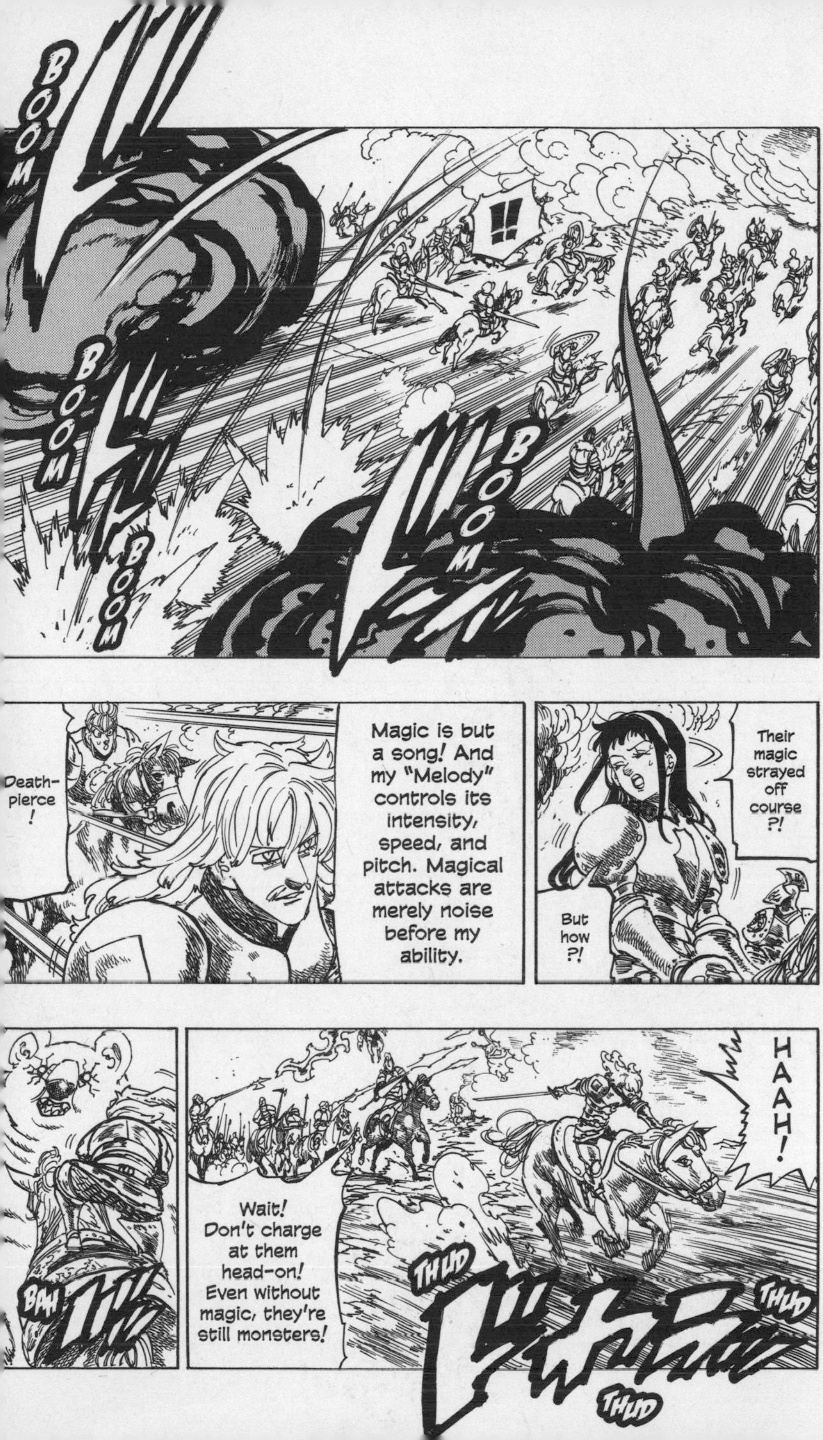
BOOM
BOOM
BOOM
BOOM
Their magic strayed off course?!
But how?!
Magic is but a song! And my "Melody" controls its intensity, speed, and pitch. Magical attacks are merely noise before my ability.
Death-pierce!
HAAH!
Wait! Don't charge at them head-on! Even without magic, they're still monsters!
THUD
THUD
THUD
BAH

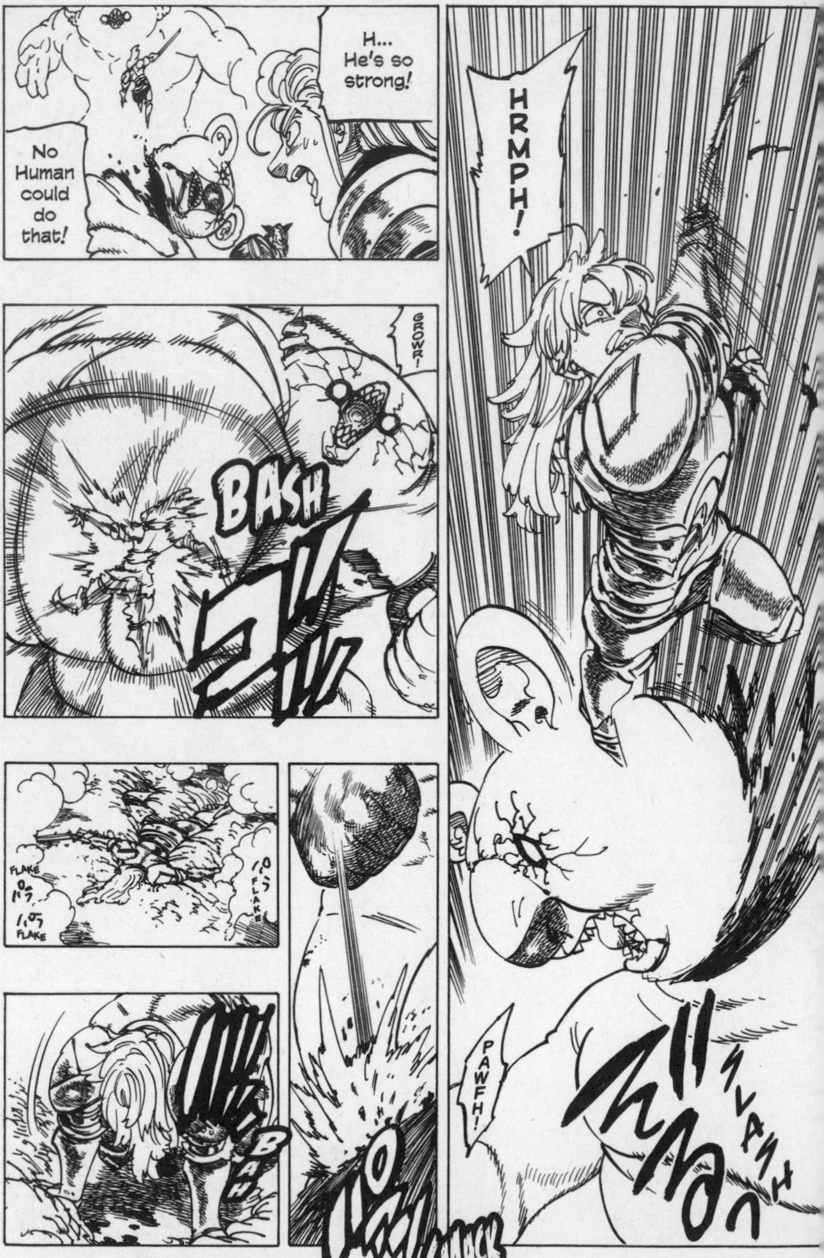
HRMPH!
PAWFH!
SLASH
H... He's so strong!
No Human could do that!
GROWR!
BASH
SMACK
FLAKE
FLAKE
FLAKE
BAH

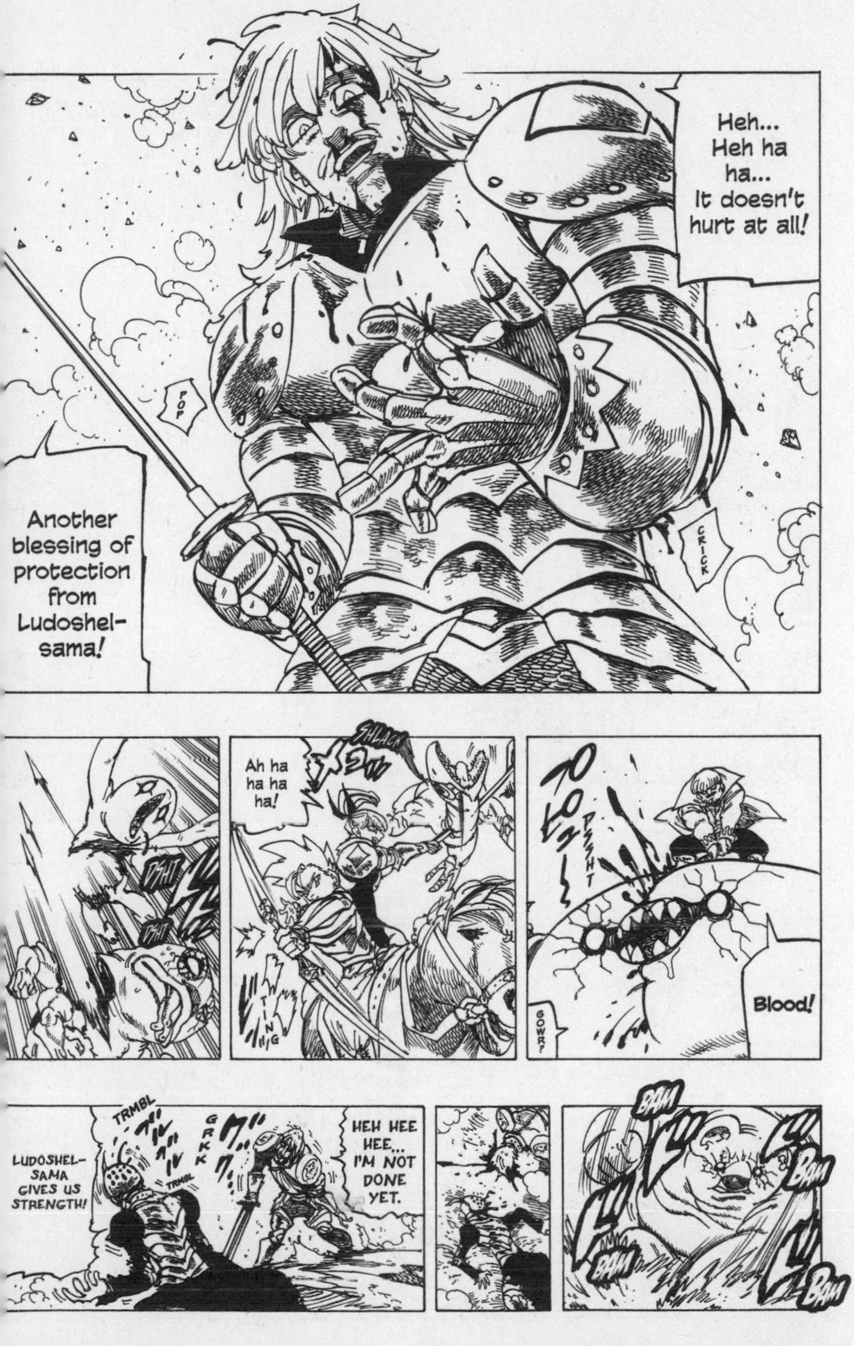
Heh... Heh ha ha... It doesn't hurt at all!
CRICK
POP
Another blessing of protection from Ludoshel-sama!
PSSHT
Blood!
GOWR?
SHLACK
Ah ha ha ha ha!
TING
DSHT
DSHT
BAM
BAM
BAM
BAM
BAM
HEH HEE HEE... I'M NOT DONE YET.
GRKK
TRMBL
TRMBL
LUDOSHEL-SAMA GIVES US STRENGTH!

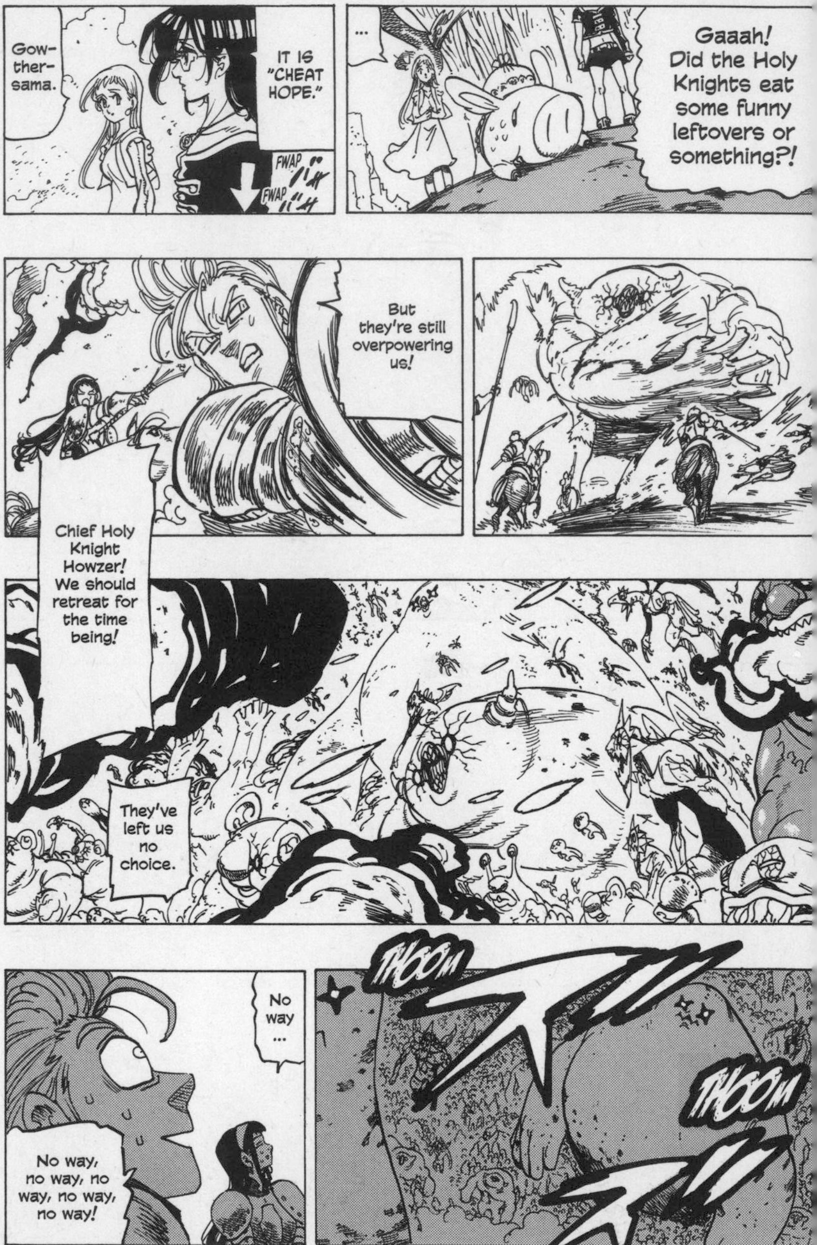

Gaaah! Did the Holy Knights eat some funny leftovers or something?!
...
Gow-ther-sama.
IT IS "CHEAT HOPE."
FWAP FWAP
But they're still overpowering us!
Chief Holy Knight Howzer! We should retreat for the time being!
They've left us no choice.
THOOM
THOOM
No way ...
No way, no way, no way, no way, no way!

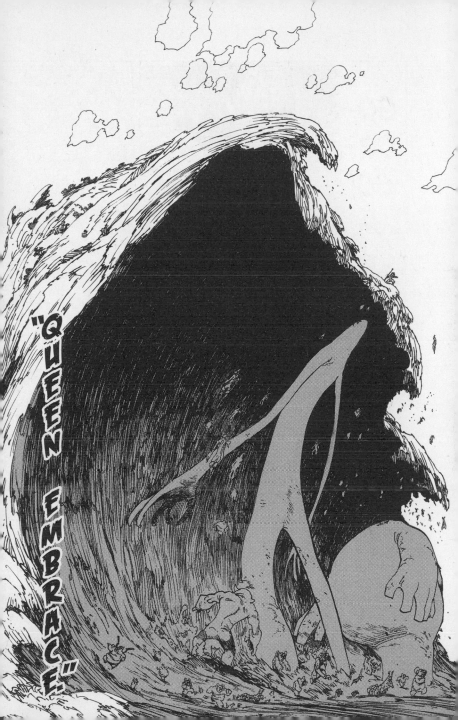

"QUEEN EMBRACE"

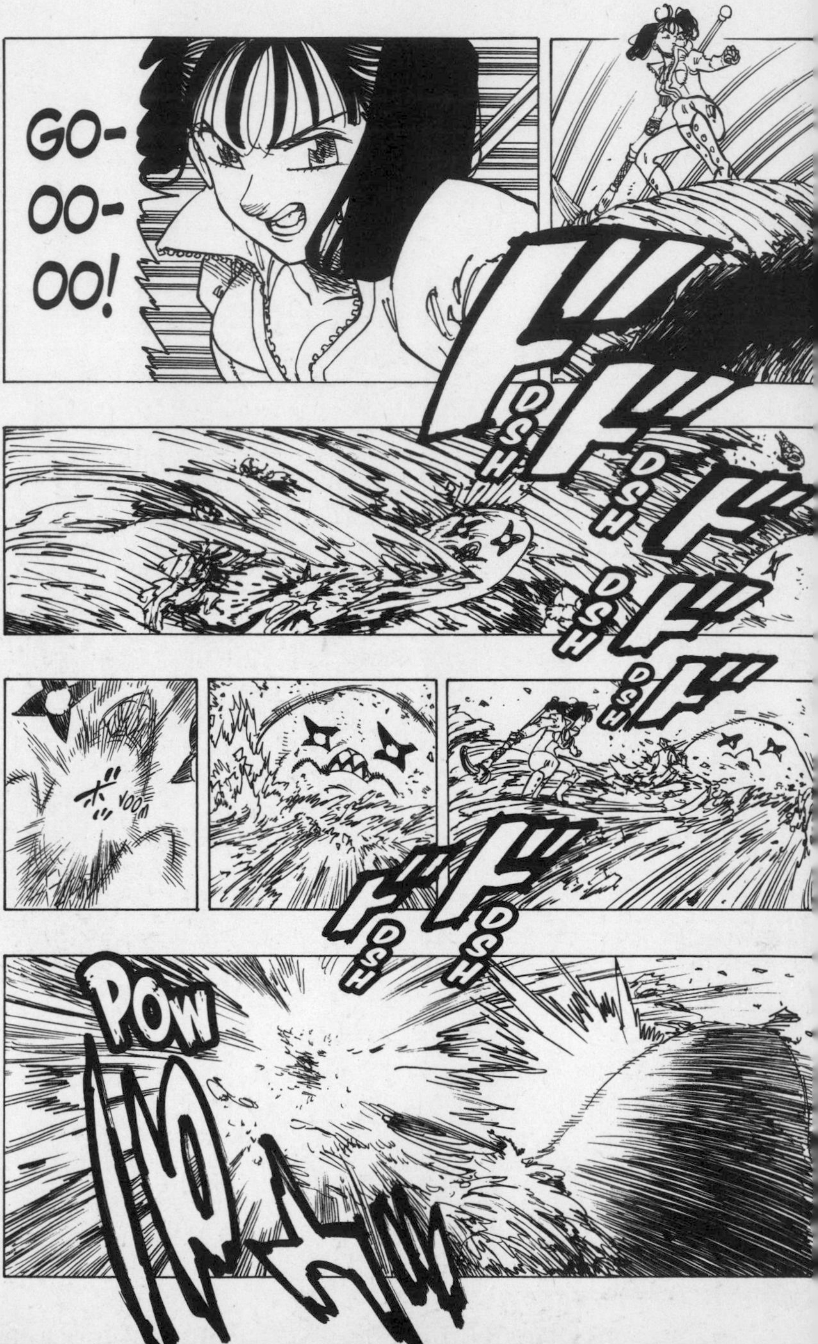
GO-OO-OO!
DSH
DSH
DSH
DSH
ボッ
VOOM
DSH
DSH
POW

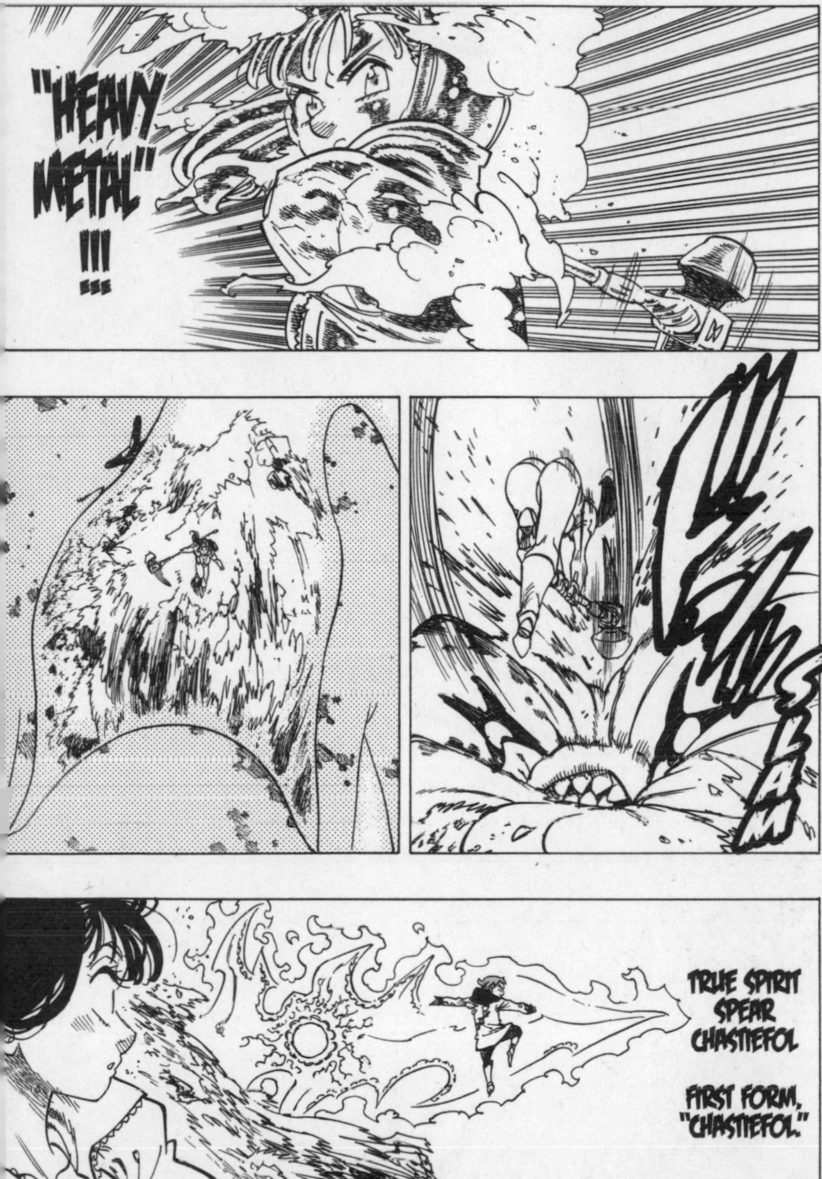
"HEAVY METAL"!!!
SLAM
TRUE SPIRIT SPEAR CHASTIEFOL
FIRST FORM, "CHASTIEFOL."

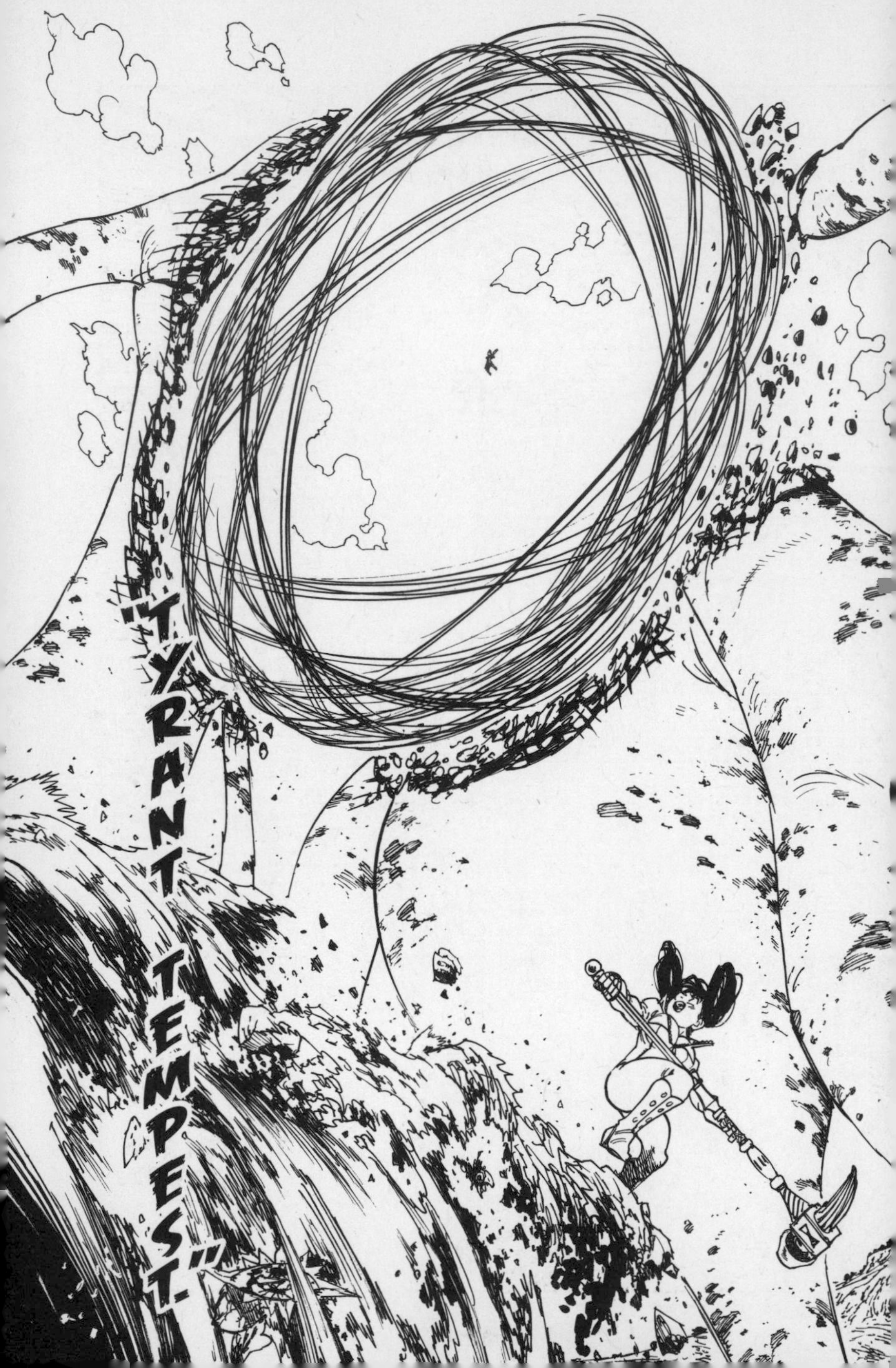
"TYRANT TEMPEST..."

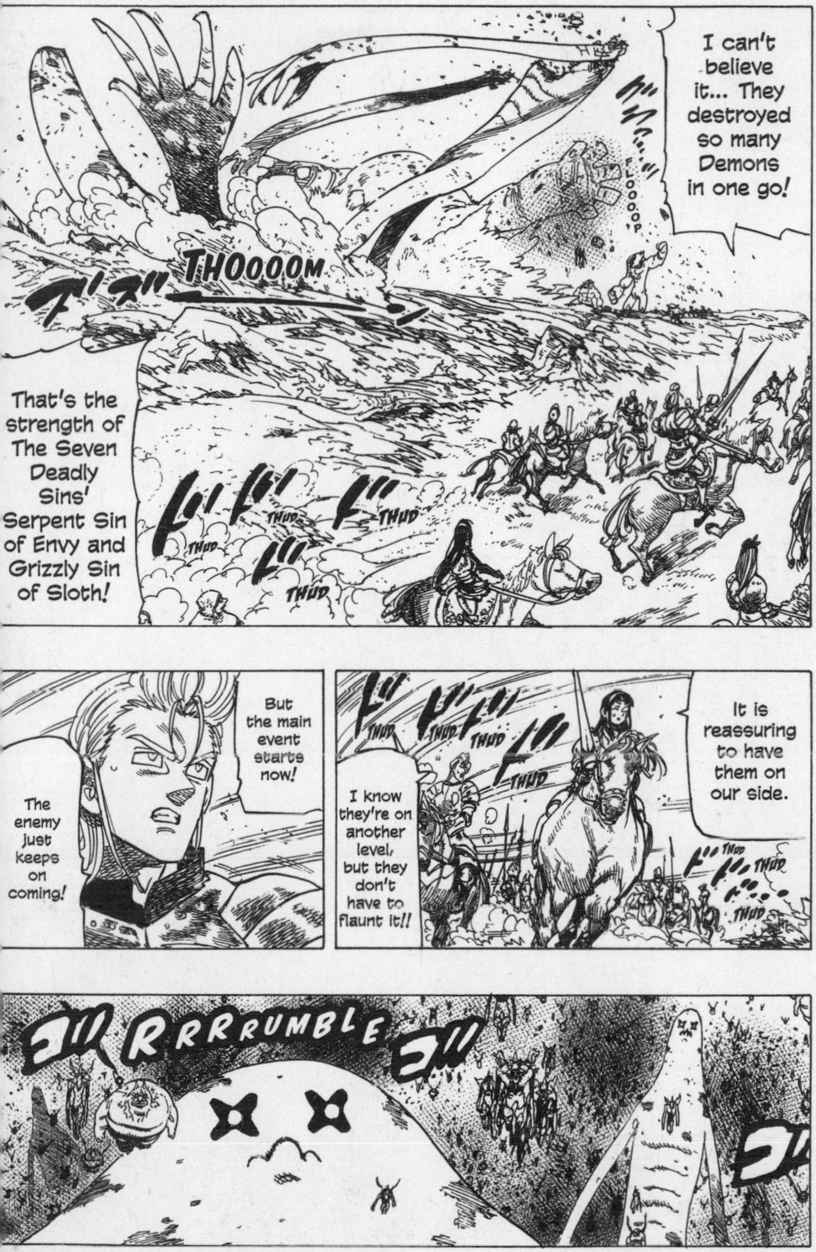
I can't believe it... They destroyed so many Demons in one go!
FLOOOOP
THOOOOM
That's the strength of The Seven Deadly Sins' Serpent Sin of Envy and Grizzly Sin of Sloth!
THUD
THUD
THUD
THUD
It is reassuring to have them on our side.
THUD
THUD
THUD
THUD
I know they're on another level, but they don't have to flaunt it!!
THUD
THUD
THUD
But the main event starts now!
The enemy just keeps on coming!
RRRRUMBLE

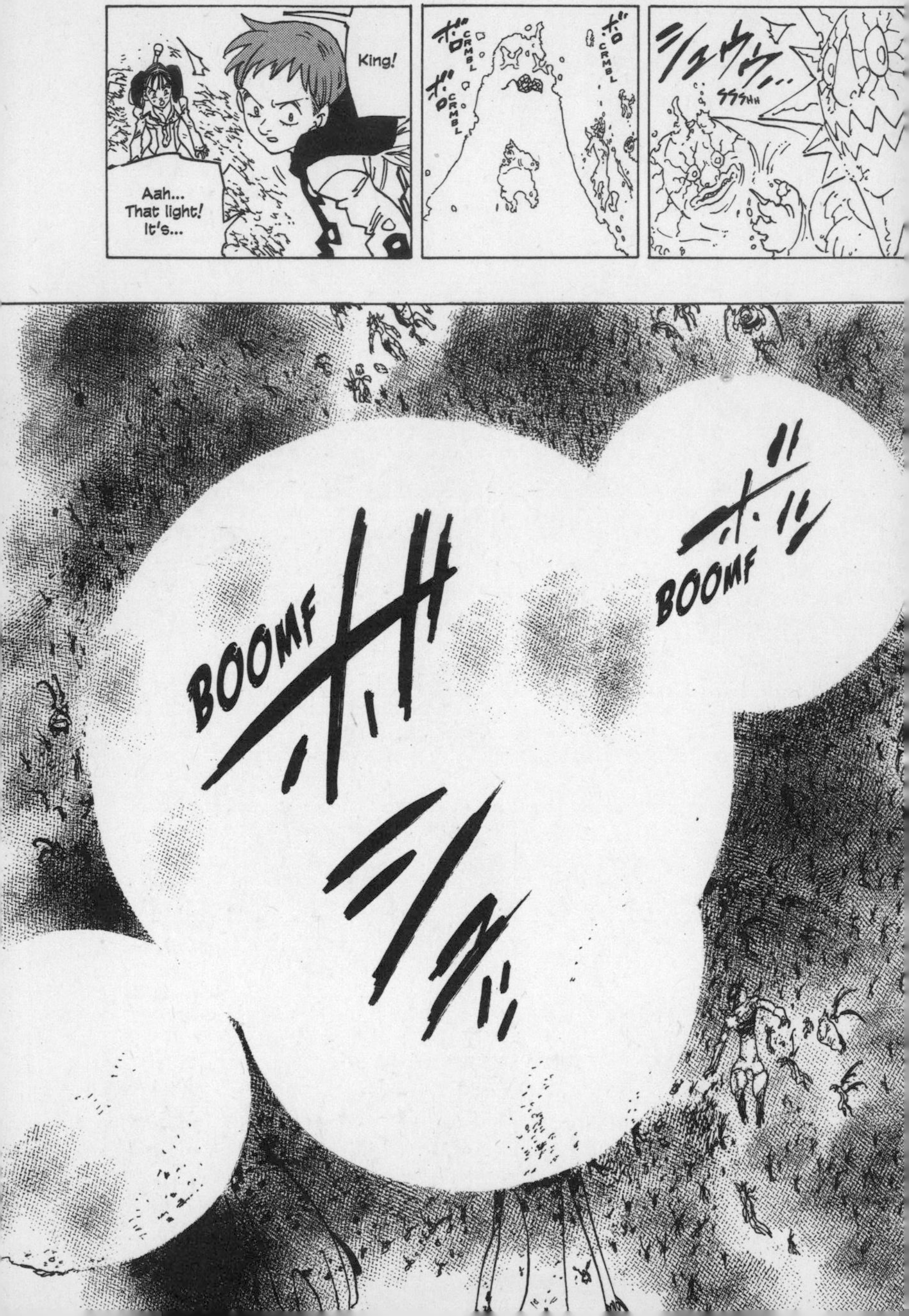
SSSHH
CRMBL
CRMBL
CRMBL
King!
Aah... That light! It's...
BOOMF
BOOMF

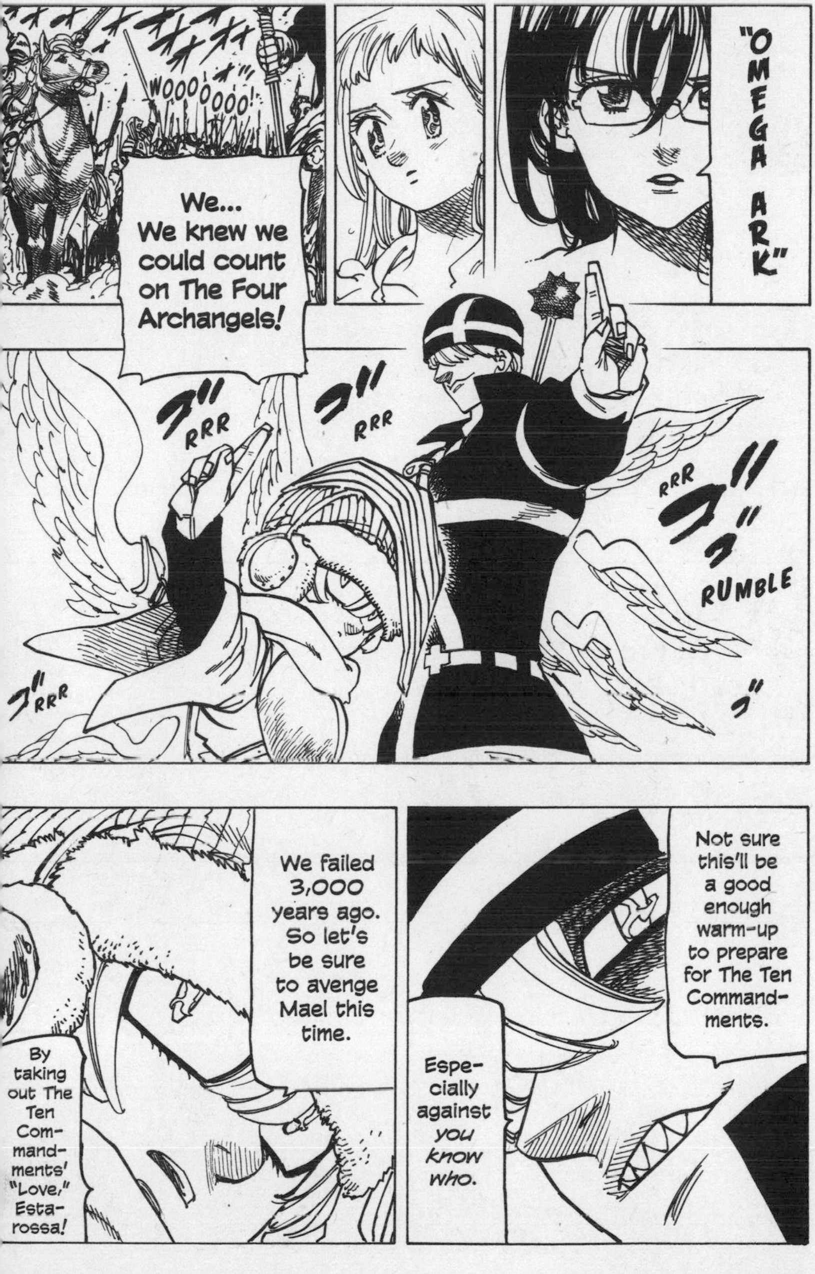
"OMEGA ARK"
WOOOOOOOO!
We... We knew we could count on The Four Archangels!
RRR
RUMBLE
RRR
RRR
RRR
Not sure this'll be a good enough warm-up to prepare for The Ten Commandments.
Especially against *you know who*.
We failed 3,000 years ago. So let's be sure to avenge Mael this time.
By taking out The Ten Commandments' "Love," Estarossa!

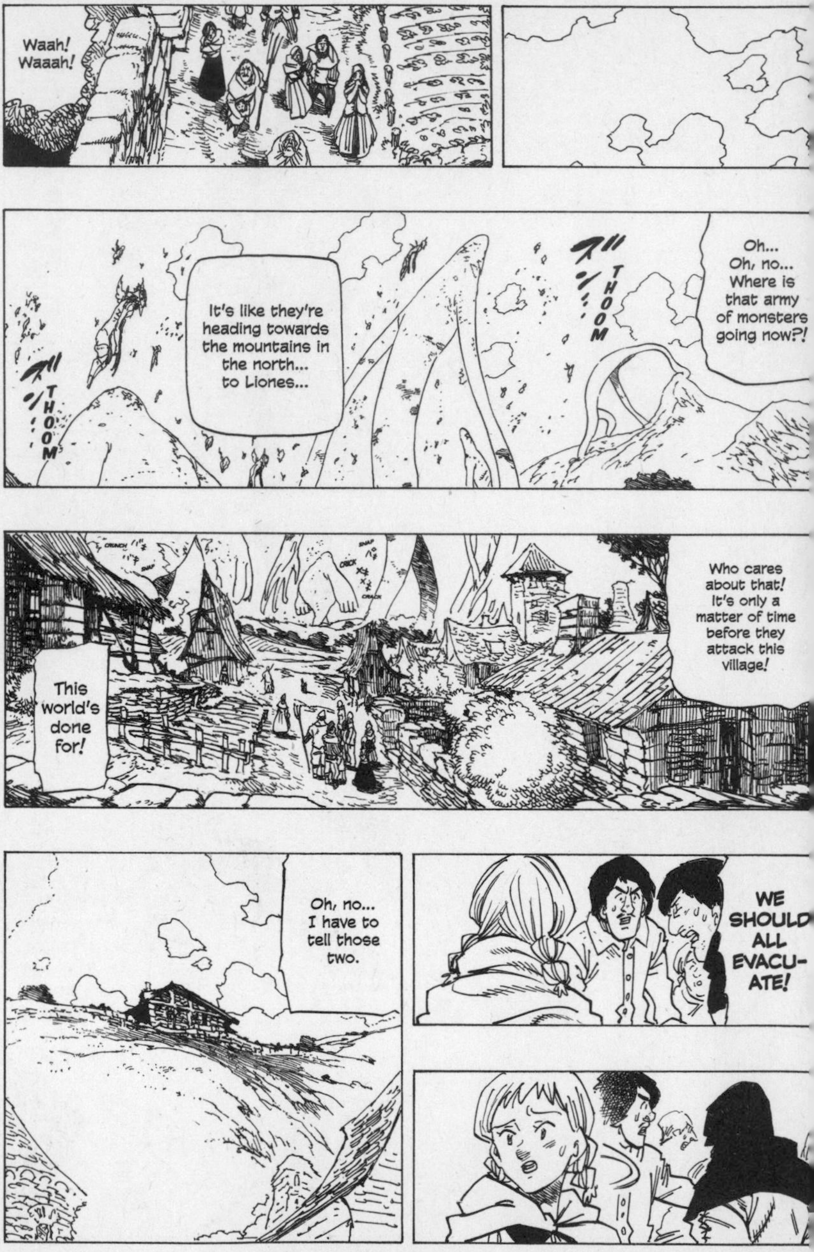
Waah! Waaah!
Oh... Oh, no... Where is that army of monsters going now?!
THOOM
It's like they're heading towards the mountains in the north... to Liones...
THOOM
Who cares about that! It's only a matter of time before they attack this village!
This world's done for!
WE SHOULD ALL EVACU-ATE!
Oh, no... I have to tell those two.

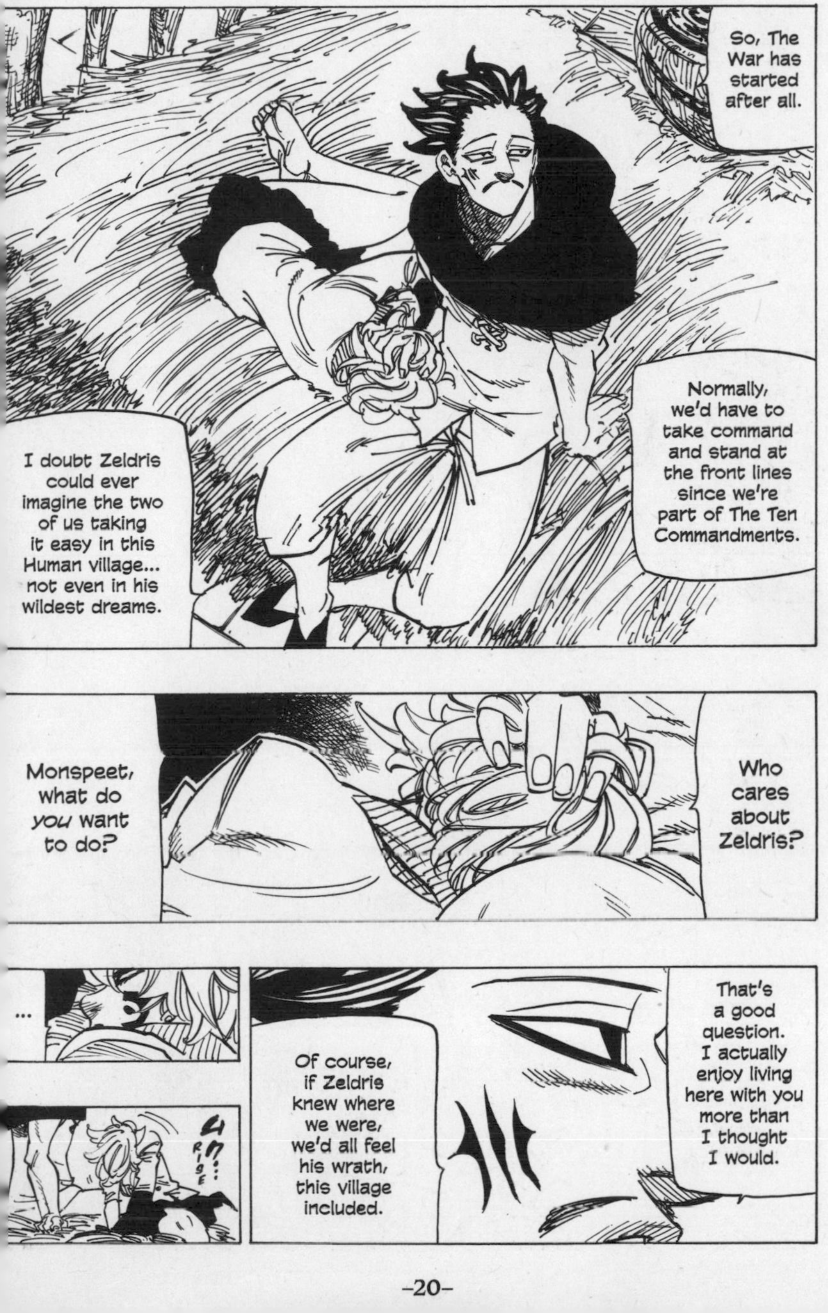
So, The War has started after all.
Normally, we'd have to take command and stand at the front lines since we're part of The Ten Commandments.
I doubt Zeldris could ever imagine the two of us taking it easy in this Human village... not even in his wildest dreams.
Who cares about Zeldris?
Monspeet, what do *you* want to do?
That's a good question. I actually enjoy living here with you more than I thought I would.
Of course, if Zeldris knew where we were, we'd all feel his wrath, this village included.
...
RISE

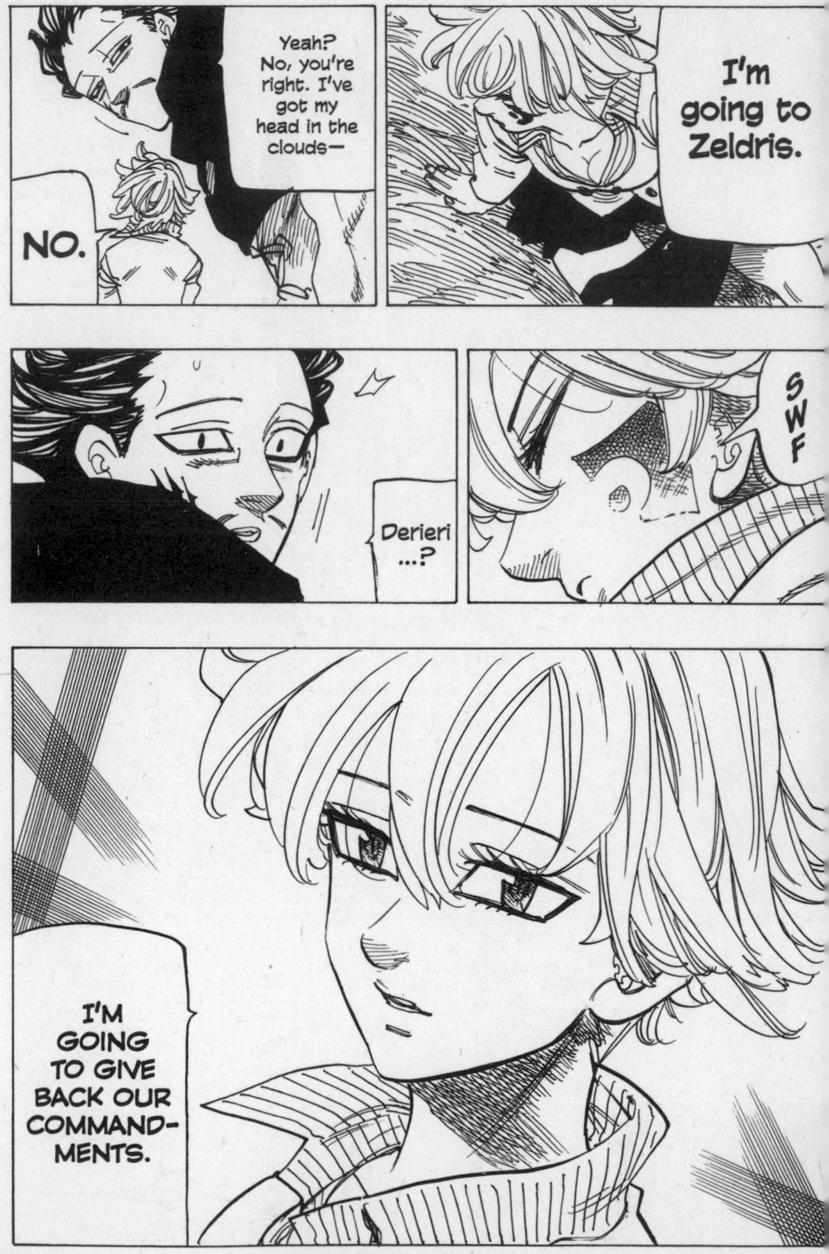
I'm going to Zeldris.
Yeah? No, you're right. I've got my head in the clouds—
NO.
SWF
Derieri ...?
I'M GOING TO GIVE BACK OUR COMMAND-MENTS.

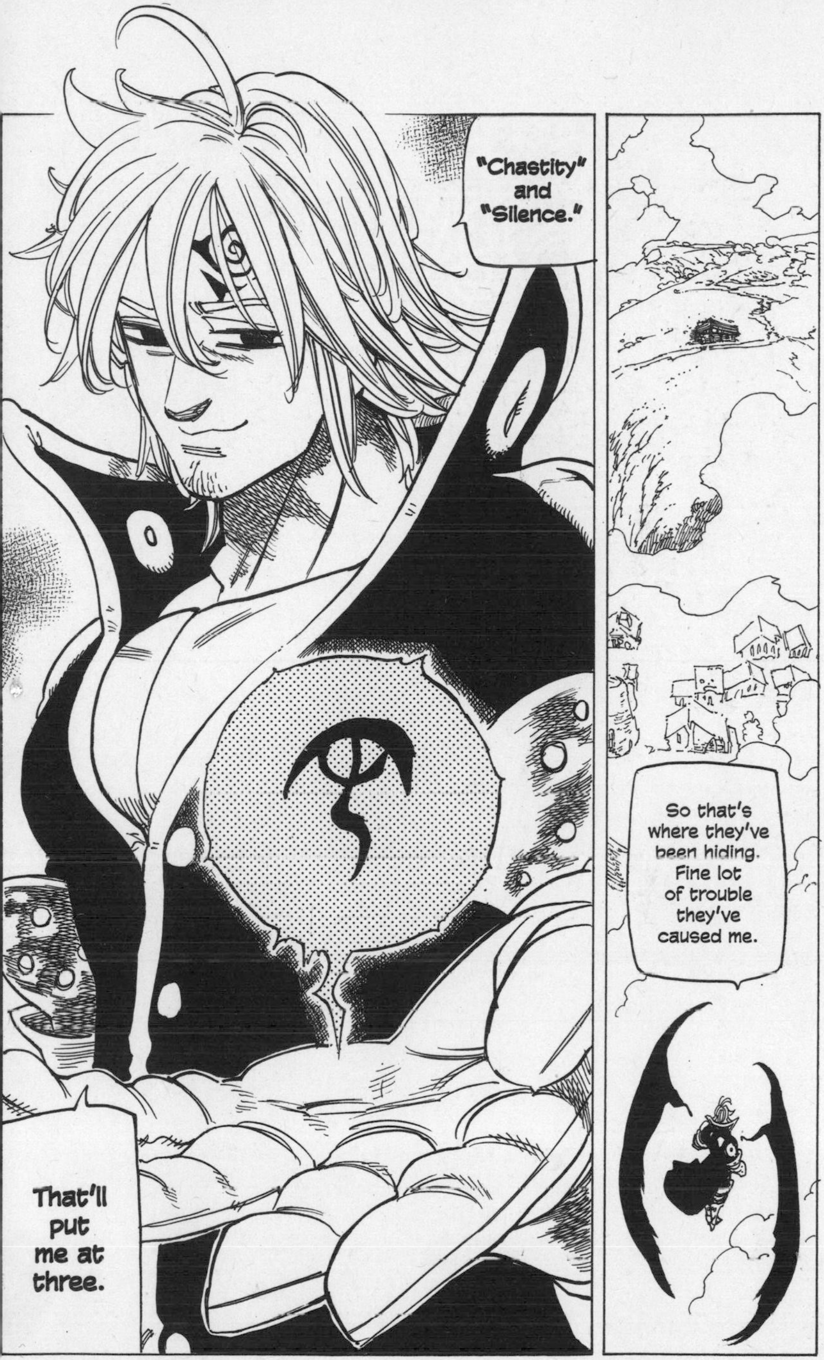
So that's where they've been hiding. Fine lot of trouble they've caused me.
"Chastity" and "Silence."
That'll put me at three.

THE SEVEN DEADLY SINS

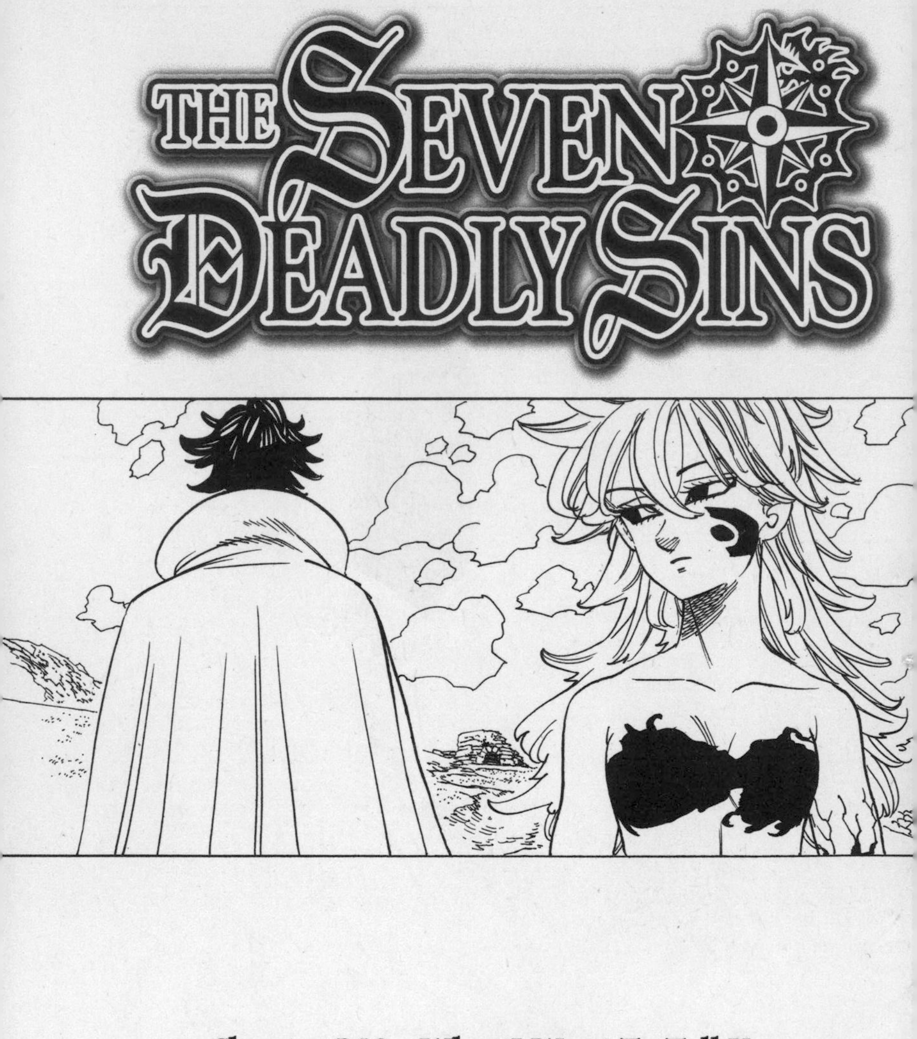

Chapter 260 - What I Want To Tell You

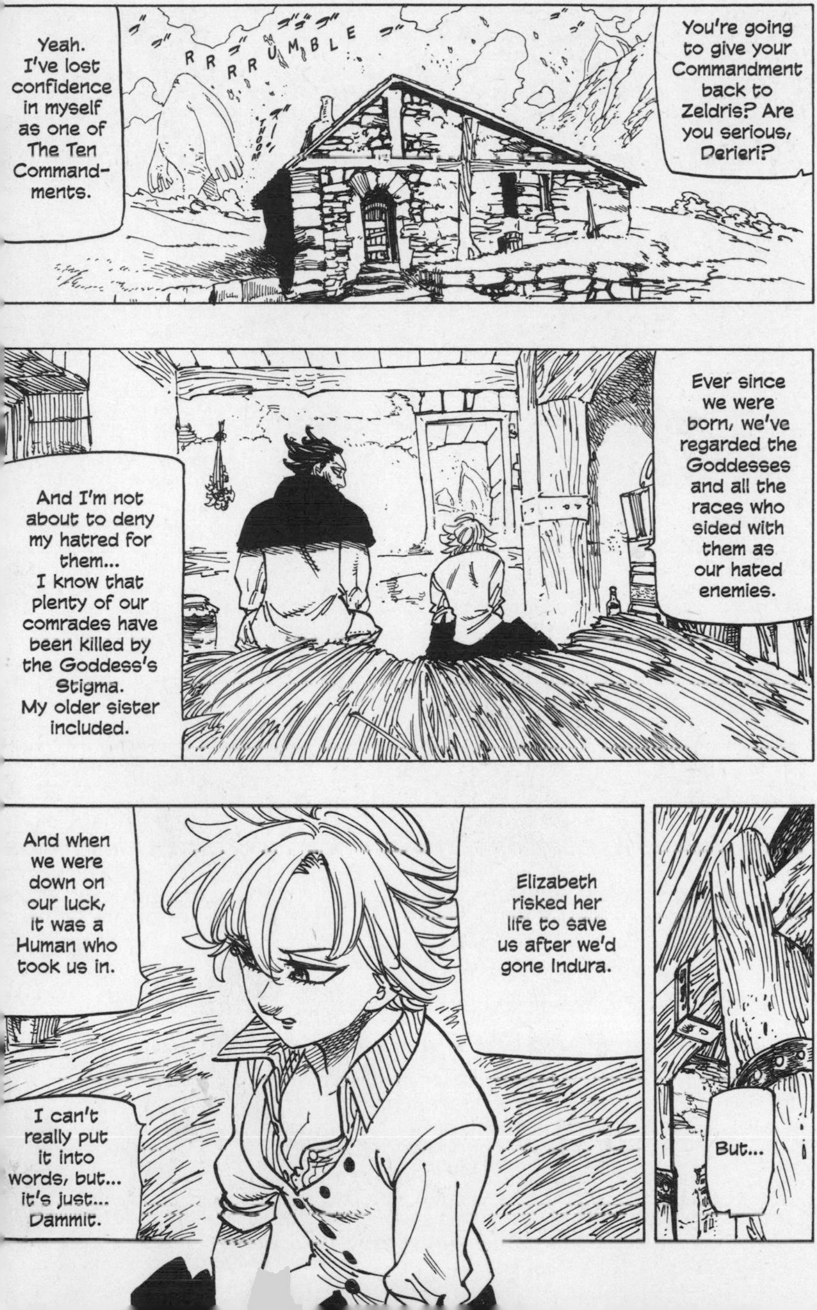
You're going to give your Commandment back to Zeldris? Are you serious, Derieri?
RRRRUMBLE
THOOM
Yeah. I've lost confidence in myself as one of The Ten Command-ments.
Ever since we were born, we've regarded the Goddesses and all the races who sided with them as our hated enemies.
And I'm not about to deny my hatred for them... I know that plenty of our comrades have been killed by the Goddess's Stigma. My older sister included.
But...
Elizabeth risked her life to save us after we'd gone Indura.
And when we were down on our luck, it was a Human who took us in.
I can't really put it into words, but... it's just... Dammit.

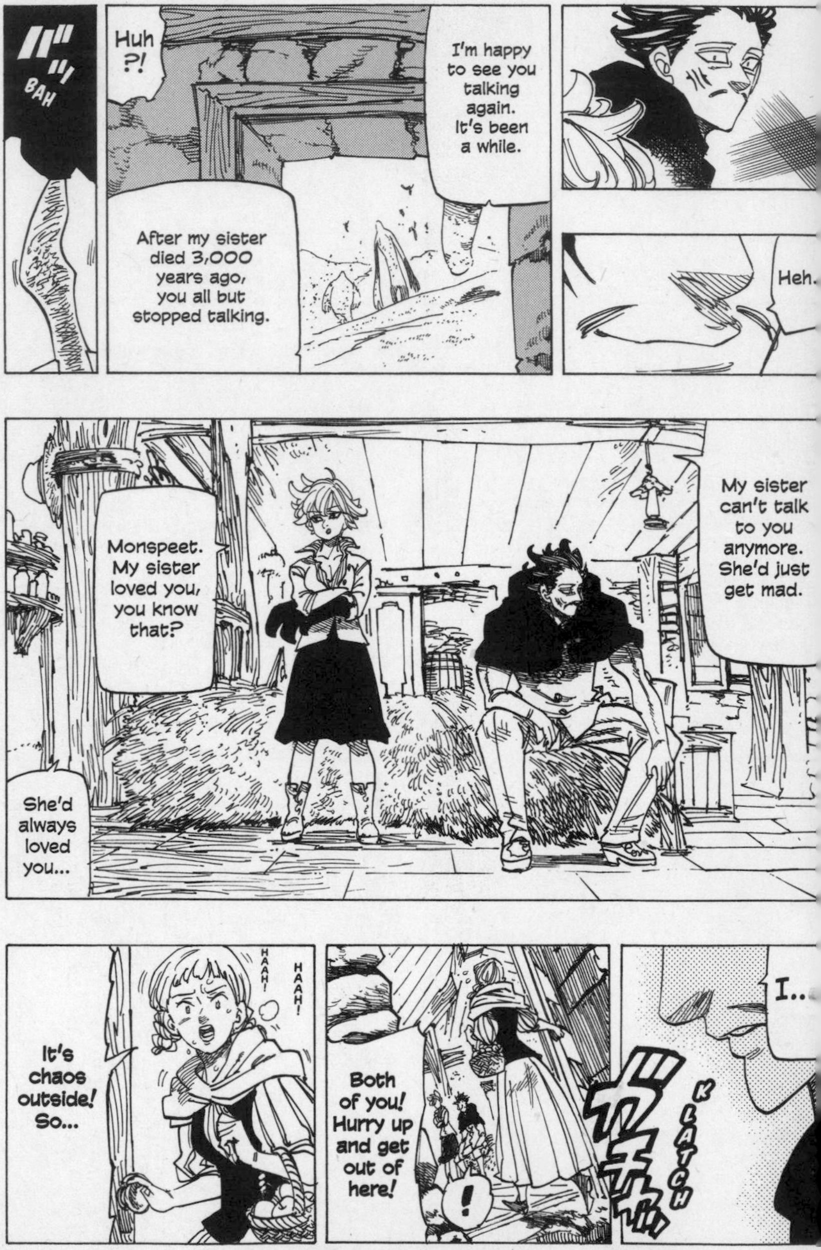
Heh.
I'm happy to see you talking again. It's been a while.
Huh?!
After my sister died 3,000 years ago, you all but stopped talking.
BAH
My sister can't talk to you anymore. She'd just get mad.
Monspeet. My sister loved you, you know that?
She'd always loved you...
I...
KLATCH
Both of you! Hurry up and get out of here!
HAAH! HAAH!
It's chaos outside! So...

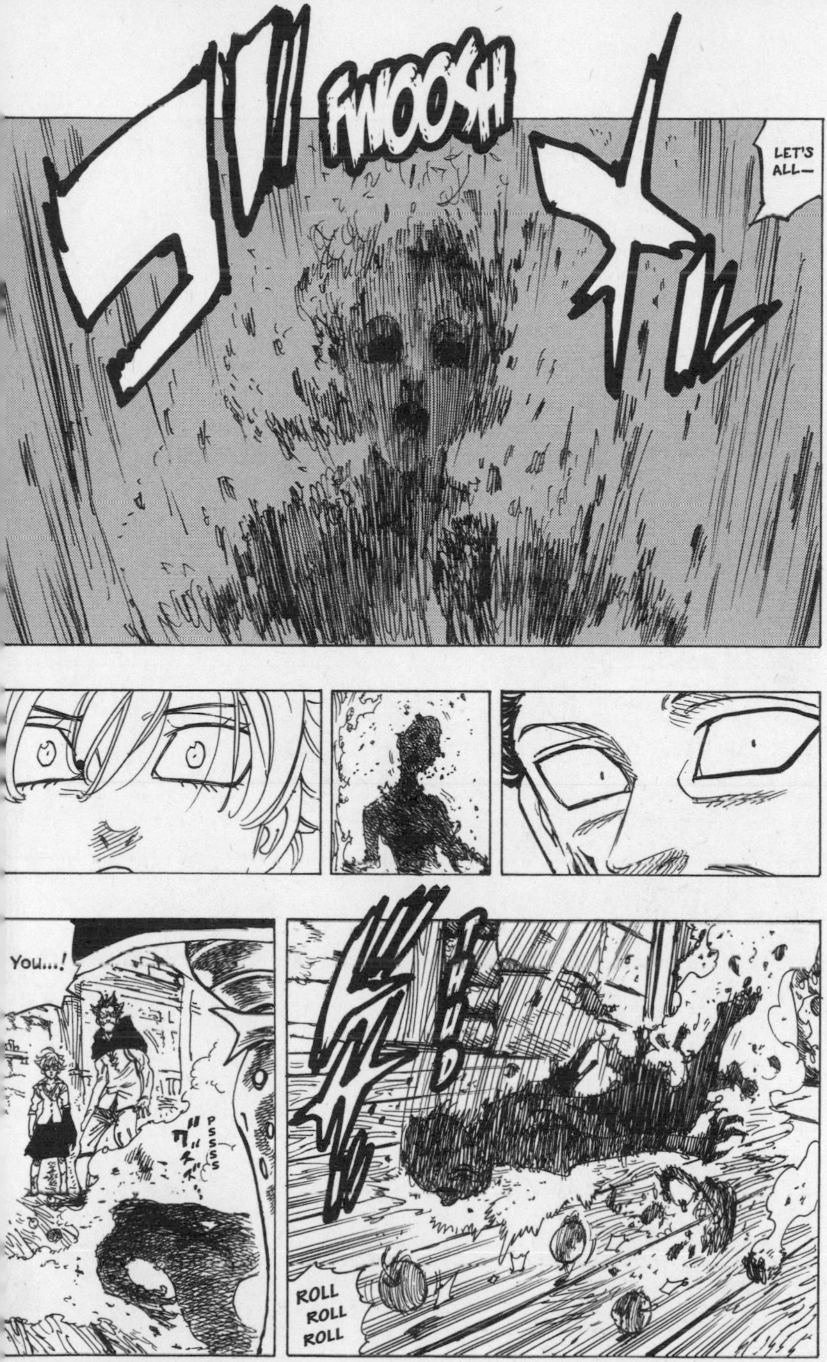
FWOOSH
LET'S ALL—
THUD
ROLL
ROLL
ROLL
You...!
PSSSS

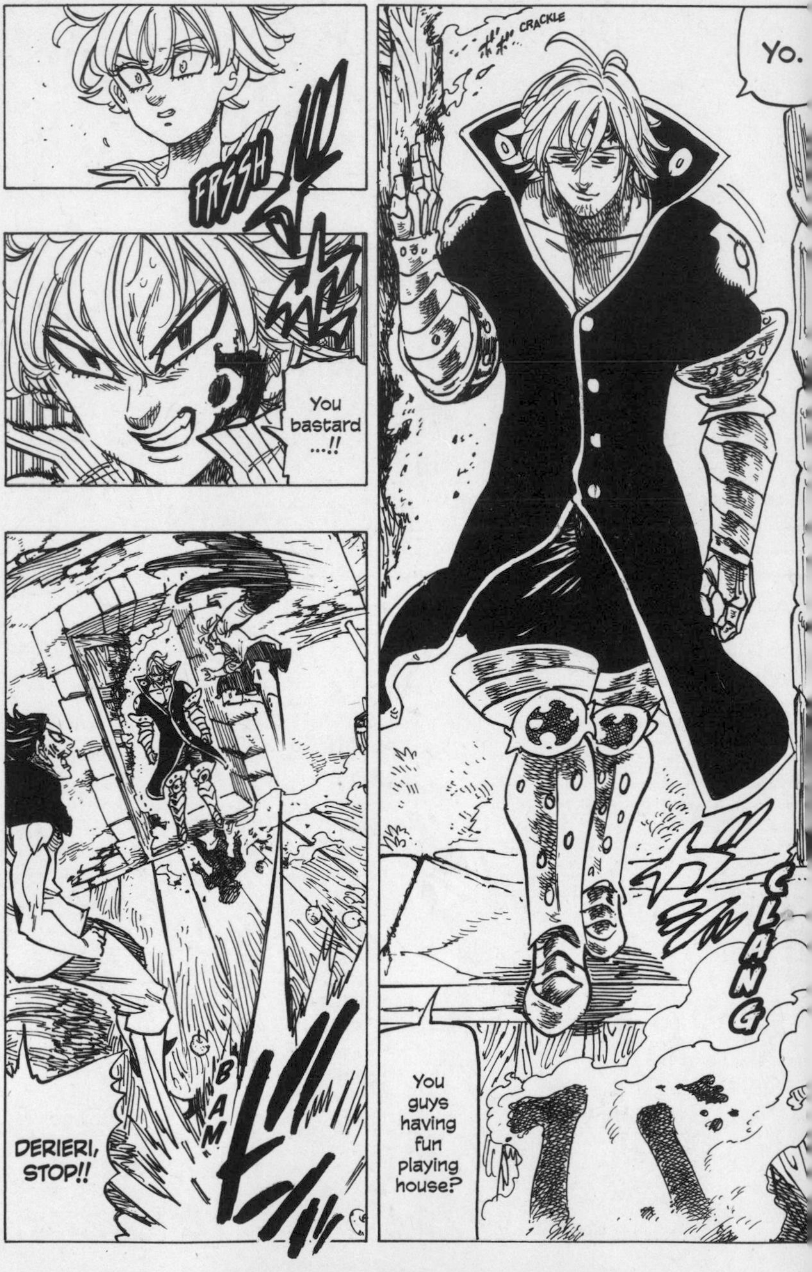
Yo.
CRACKLE
CLANG
You guys having fun playing house?
FRSSH
You bastard ...!!
DERIERI, STOP!!
BAM

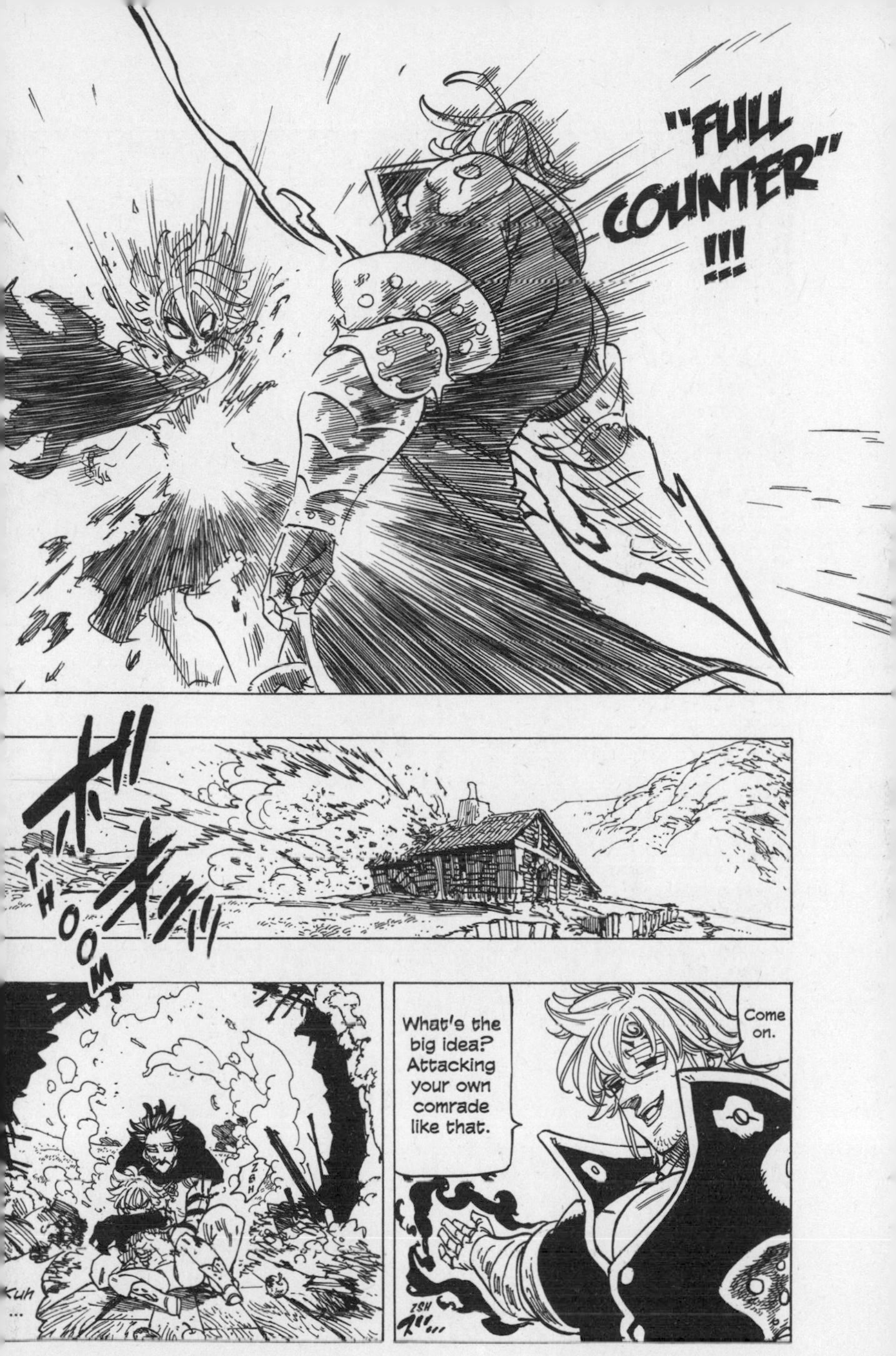
"FULL COUNTER"!!!
THOOOM
Come on.
What's the big idea? Attacking your own comrade like that.
ZSH
ZSH
Kuh...

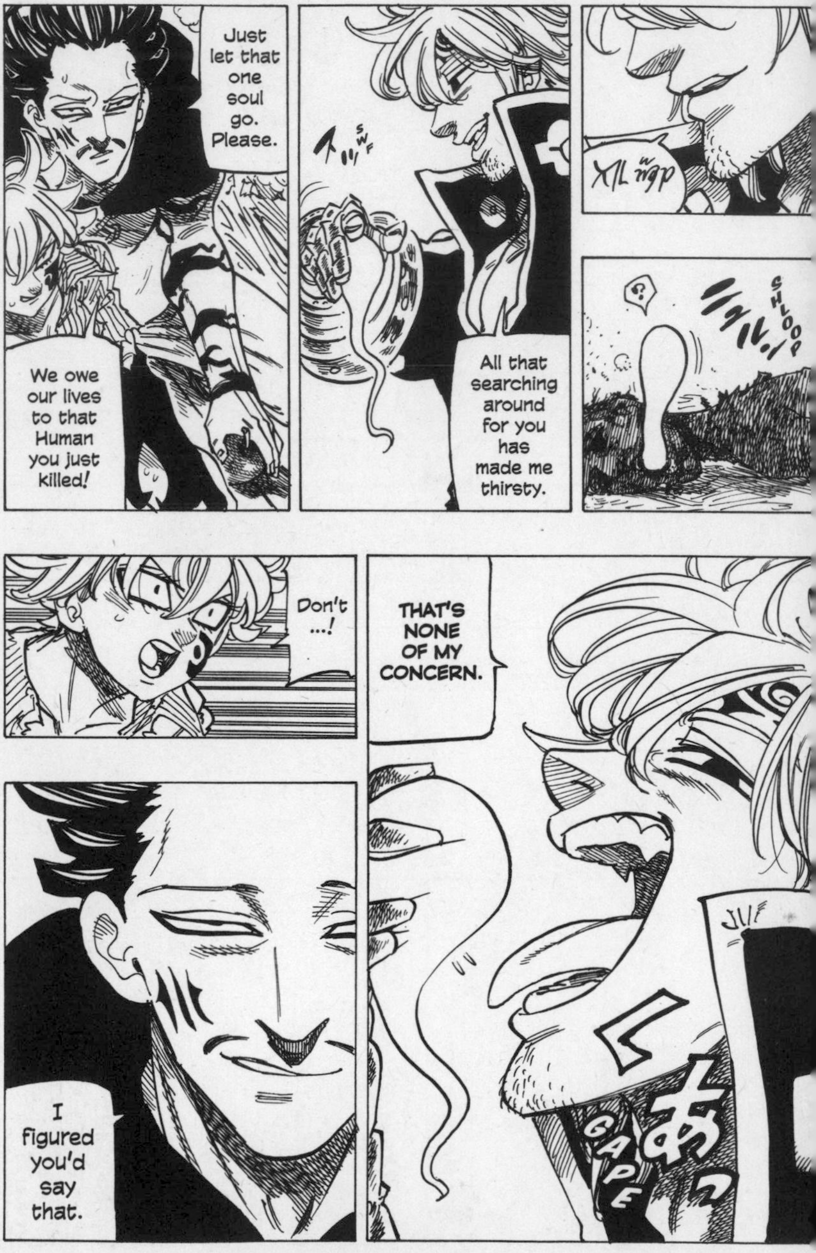
gulp
SHLOOP
SWF
All that searching around for you has made me thirsty.
Just let that one soul go. Please.
We owe our lives to that Human you just killed!
THAT'S NONE OF MY CONCERN.
GAPE
Don't ...!
I figured you'd say that.

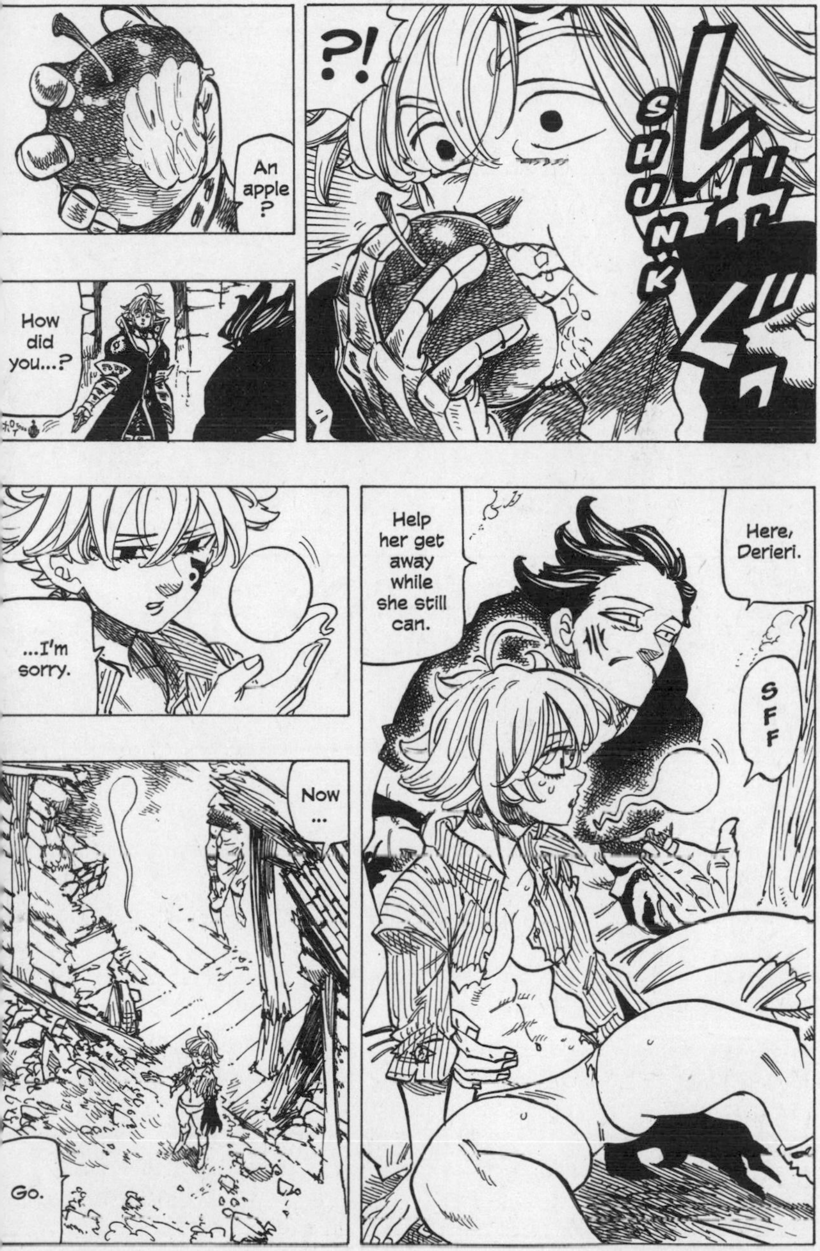
?!
SHUNK
An apple?
How did you...?
Here, Derieri.
Help her get away while she still can.
SFF
...I'm sorry.
Now ...
Go.

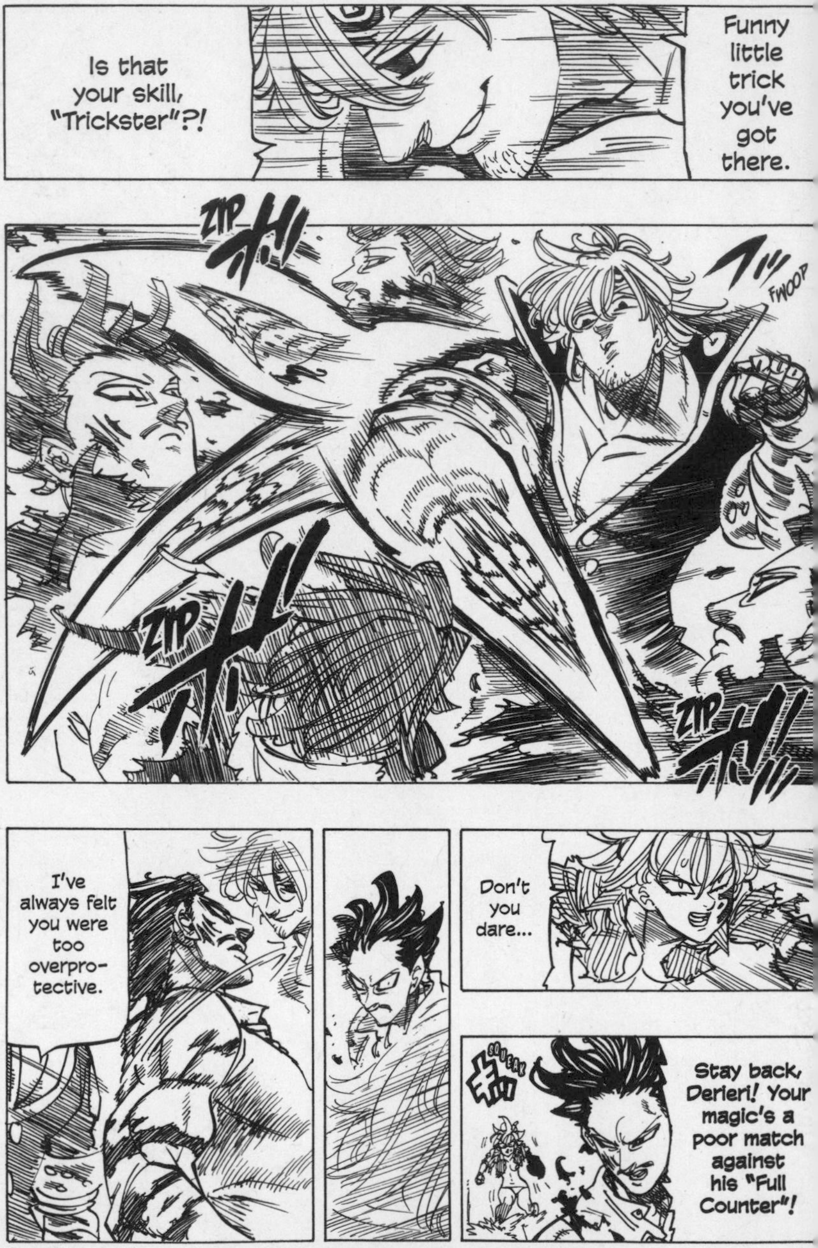
Funny little trick you've got there.
Is that your skill, "Trickster"?!
FWOOP
ZIP
ZIP
ZIP
Don't you dare...
SQUEAK
Stay back, Derieri! Your magic's a poor match against his "Full Counter"!
I've always felt you were too overpro-tective.

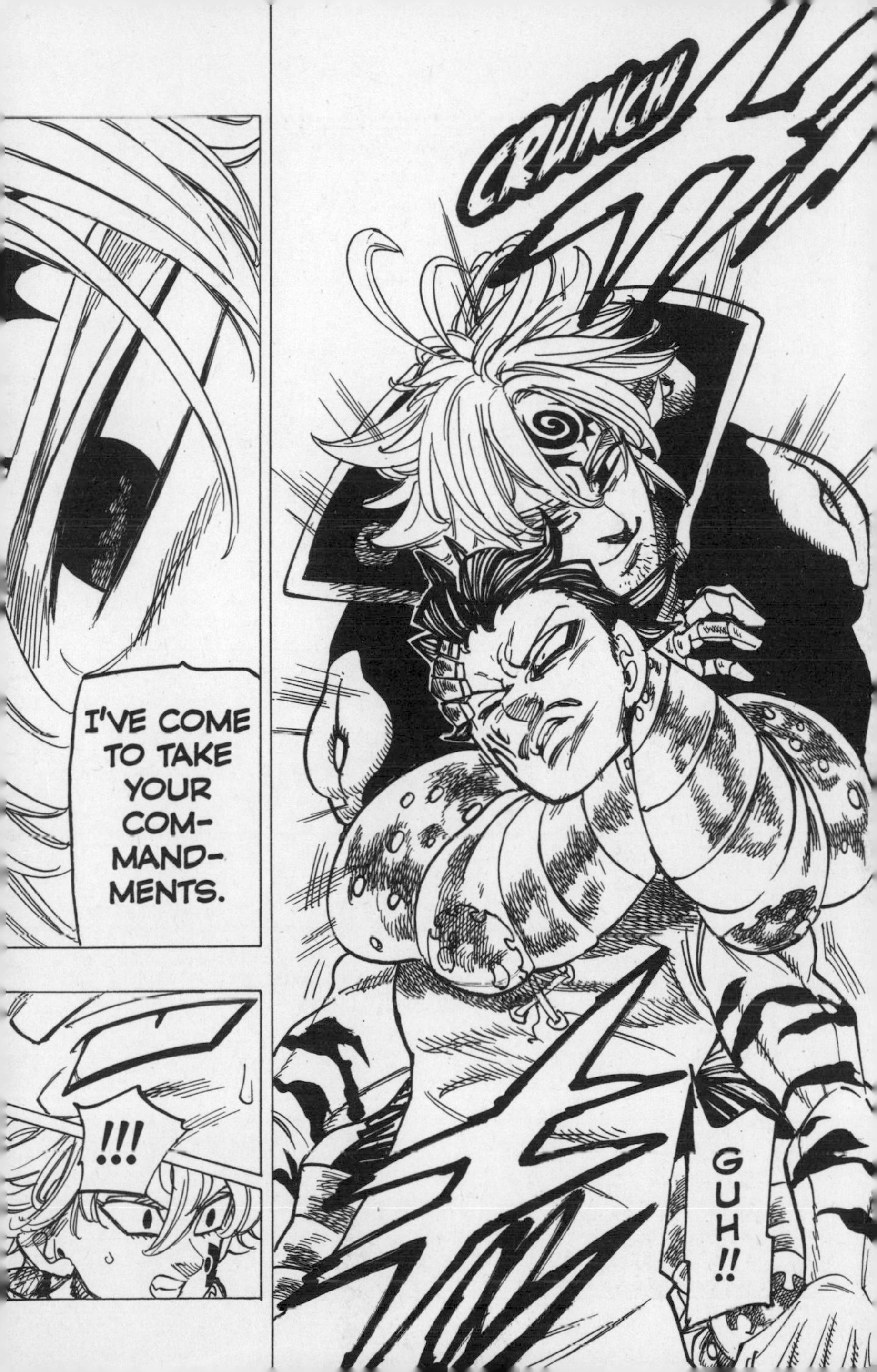
CRUNCH
GUH!!
I'VE COME TO TAKE YOUR COM-MAND-MENTS.
!!!

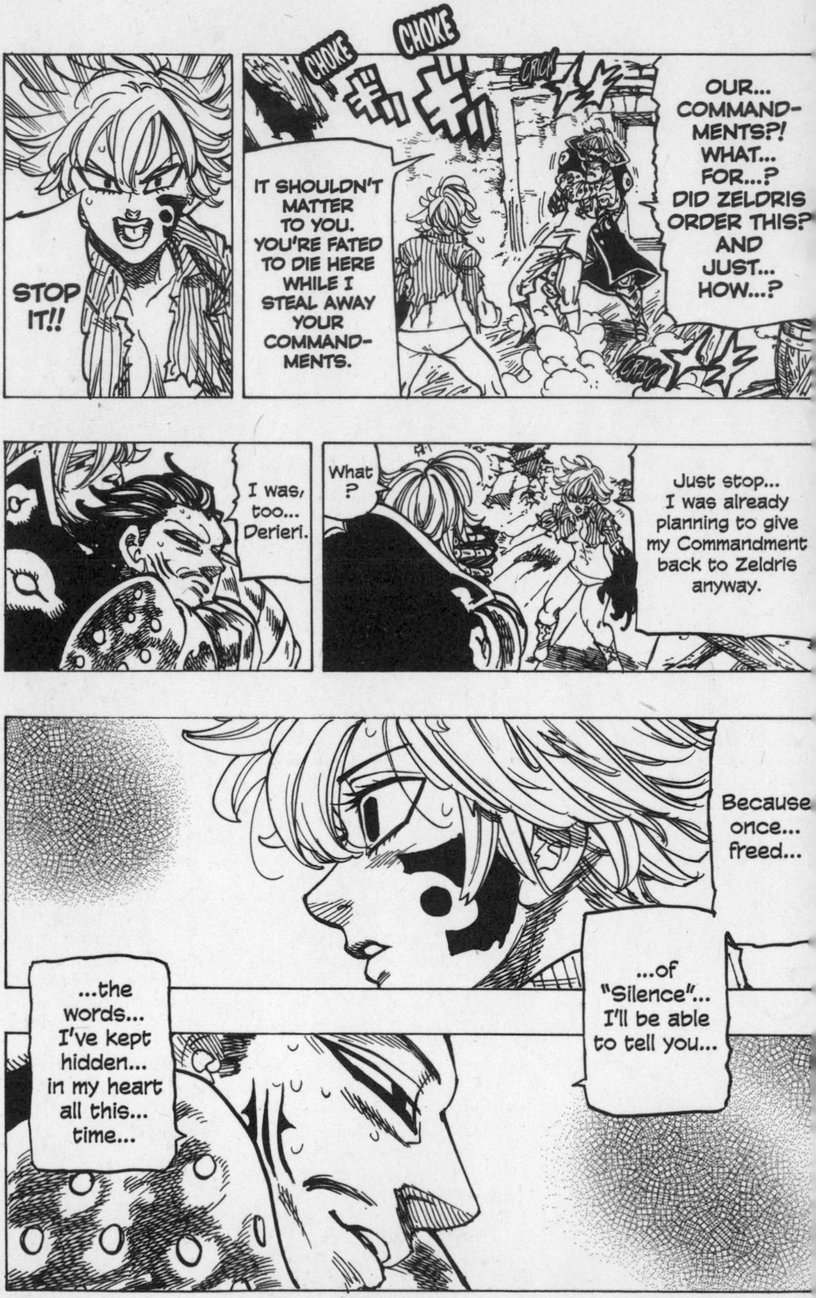
CHOKE
CHOKE
CRICK
OUR... COMMANDMENTS?! WHAT... FOR...? DID ZELDRIS ORDER THIS? AND JUST... HOW...?
CRACK
IT SHOULDN'T MATTER TO YOU. YOU'RE FATED TO DIE HERE WHILE I STEAL AWAY YOUR COMMANDMENTS.
STOP IT!!
Just stop... I was already planning to give my Commandment back to Zeldris anyway.
What?
I was, too... Derieri.
Because once... freed...
...of "Silence"... I'll be able to tell you...
...the words... I've kept hidden... in my heart all this... time...

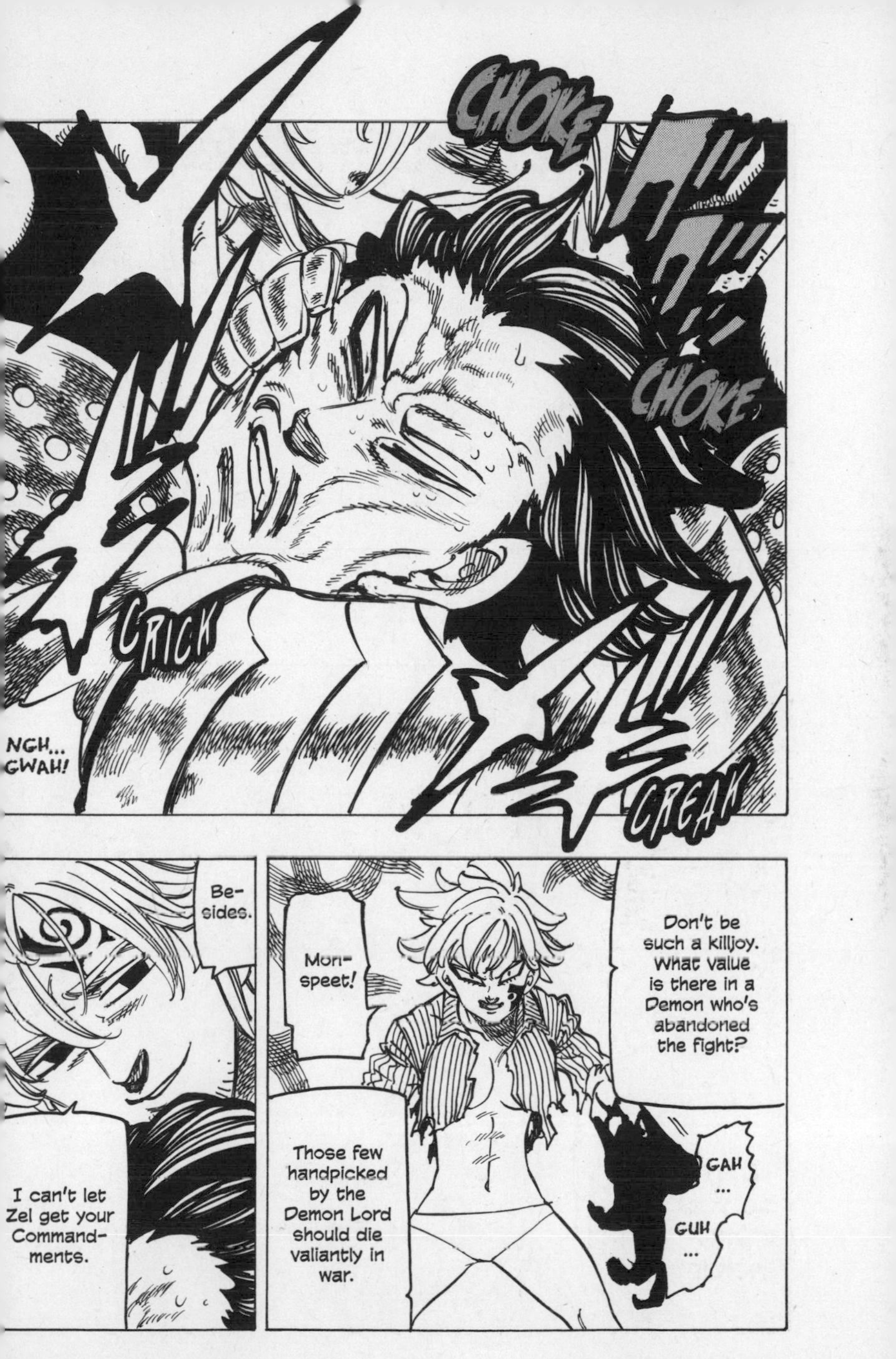
CHOKE
CHOKE
CRICK
CREAK
NGH... GWAH!
Don't be such a killjoy. What value is there in a Demon who's abandoned the fight?
Mon-speet!
GAH ... GUH ...
Those few handpicked by the Demon Lord should die valiantly in war.
Be-sides.
I can't let Zel get your Command-ments.

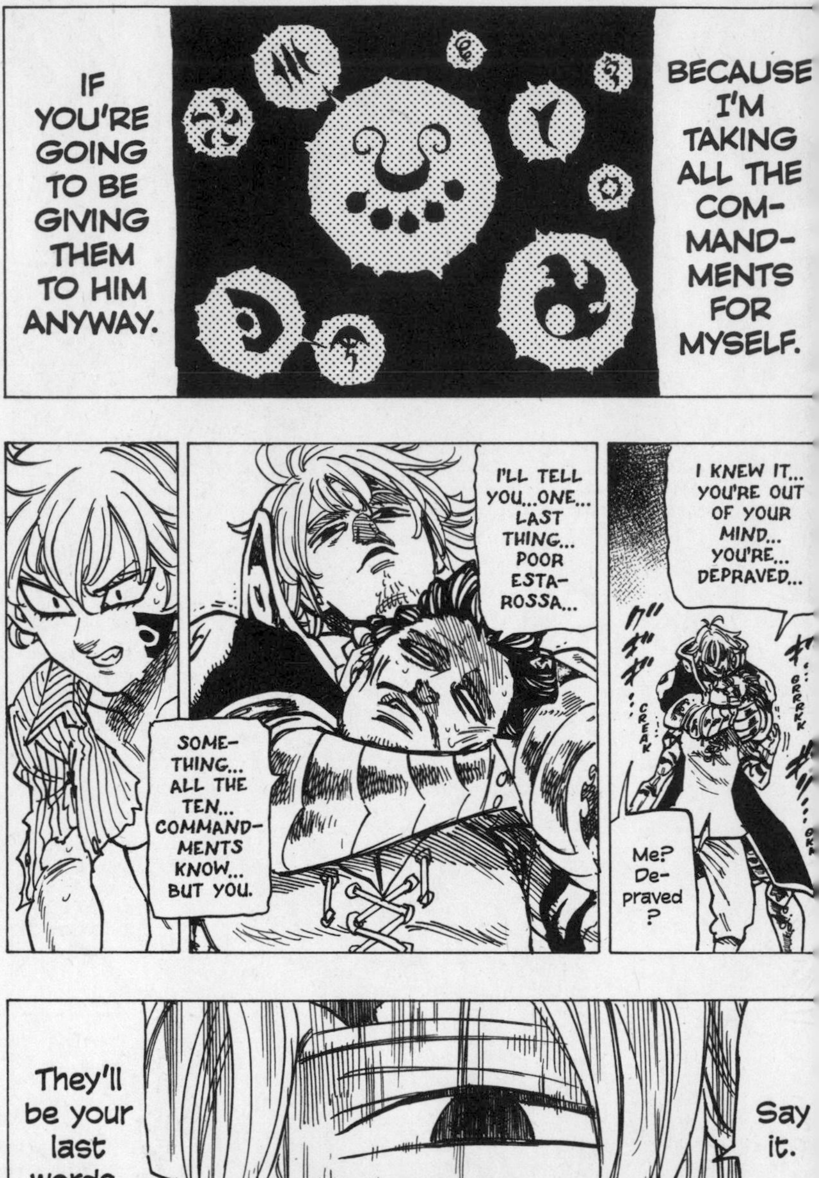
BECAUSE I'M TAKING ALL THE COM-MAND-MENTS FOR MYSELF.
IF YOU'RE GOING TO BE GIVING THEM TO HIM ANYWAY.
I KNEW IT... YOU'RE OUT OF YOUR MIND... YOU'RE... DEPRAVED...
GRRRKK
CREAK
Me? De-praved?
I'LL TELL YOU...ONE... LAST THING... POOR ESTA-ROSSA...
SOME-THING... ALL THE TEN... COMMAND-MENTS KNOW... BUT YOU.
Say it.
They'll be your last words.

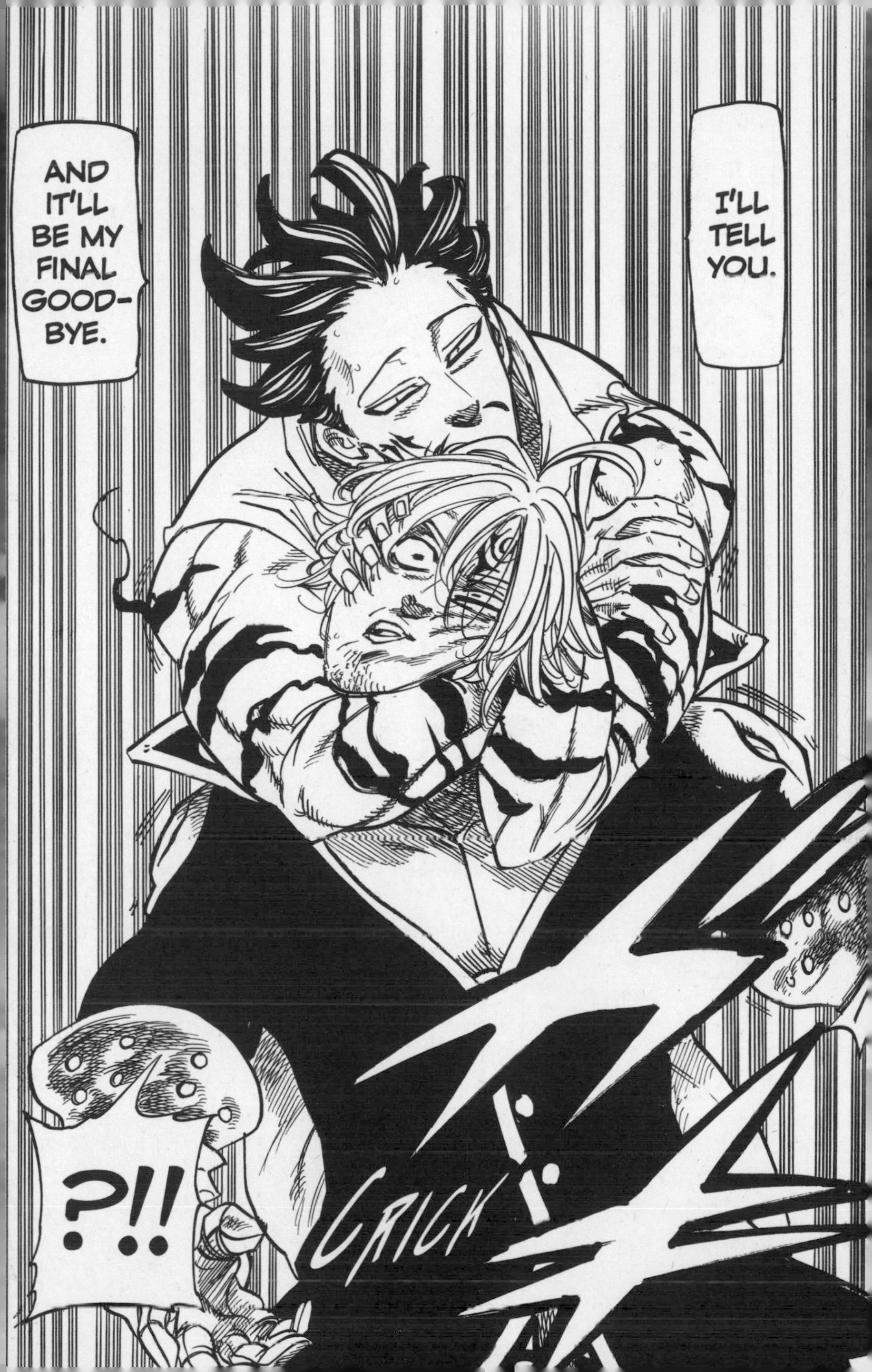
I'LL TELL YOU.
AND IT'LL BE MY FINAL GOOD-BYE.
CRICK
?!!

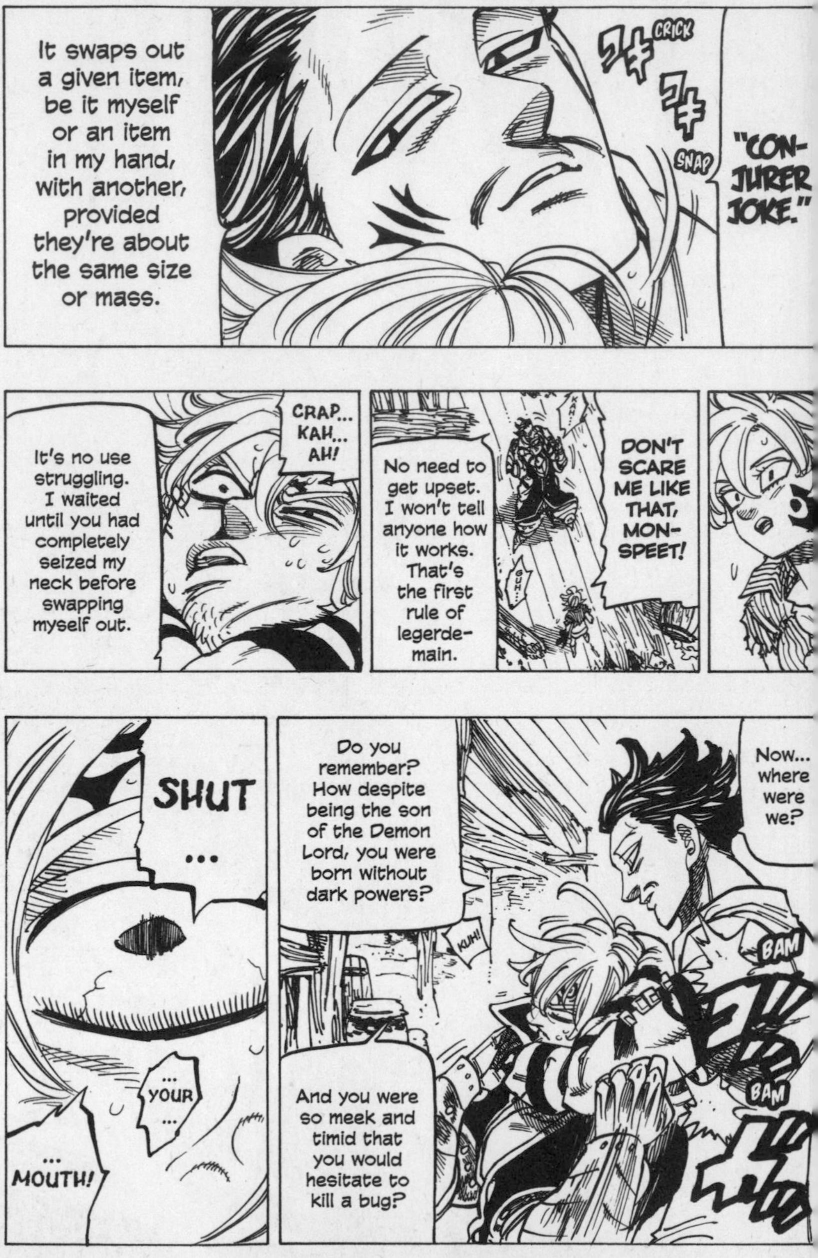
"CON-JURER JOKE."
CRICK
SNAP
It swaps out a given item, be it myself or an item in my hand, with another, provided they're about the same size or mass.
DON'T SCARE ME LIKE THAT, MONSPEET!
KAH...
SUH...
No need to get upset. I won't tell anyone how it works. That's the first rule of legerdemain.
CRAP... KAH... AH!
It's no use struggling. I waited until you had completely seized my neck before swapping myself out.
Now... where were we?
BAM
Do you remember? How despite being the son of the Demon Lord, you were born without dark powers?
KUH!
BAM
And you were so meek and timid that you would hesitate to kill a bug?
SHUT
...
... YOUR ...
... MOUTH!

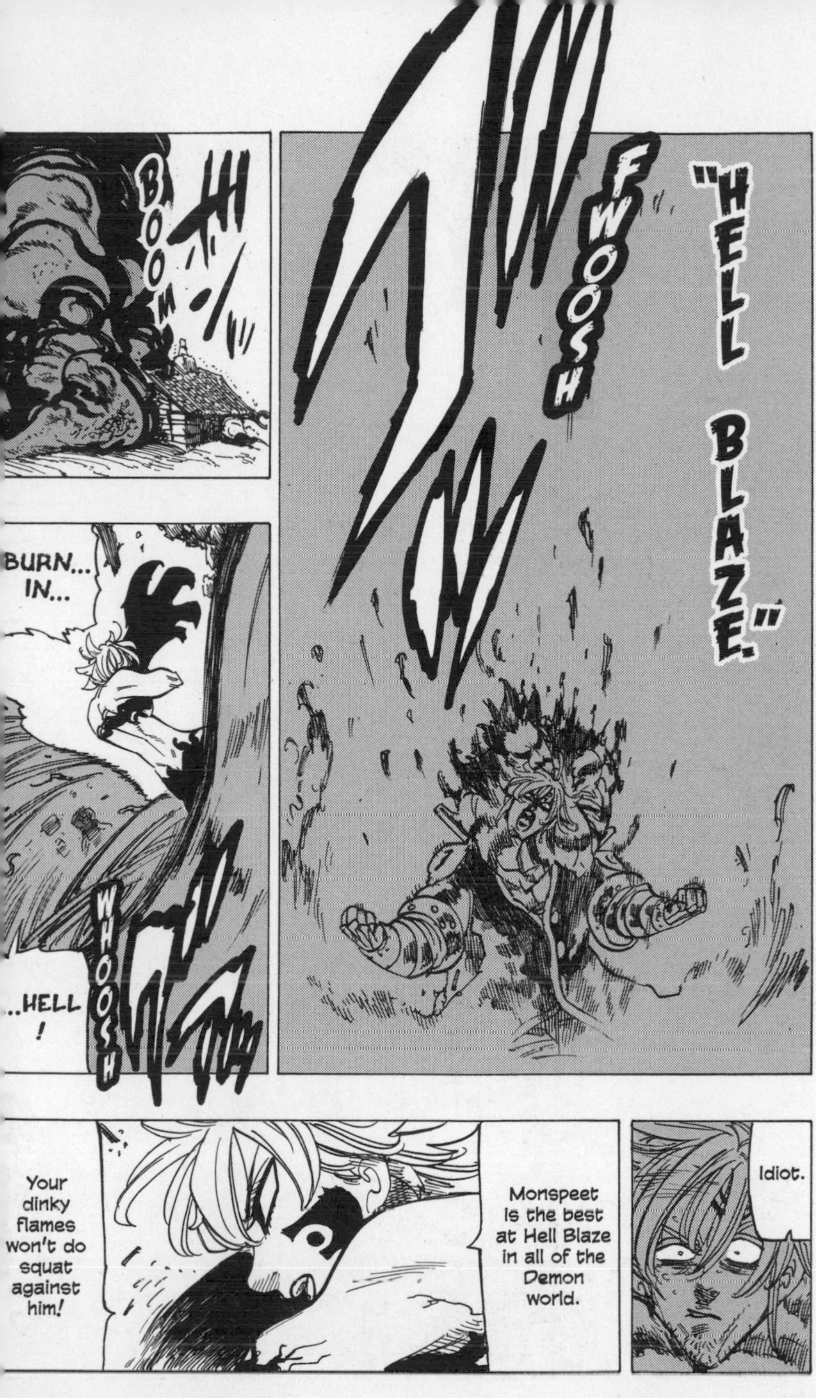
"HELL BLAZE."
FWOOSH
BOOOM
BURN... IN...
...HELL!
WHOOSH
Idiot.
Monspeet is the best at Hell Blaze in all of the Demon world.
Your dinky flames won't do squat against him!

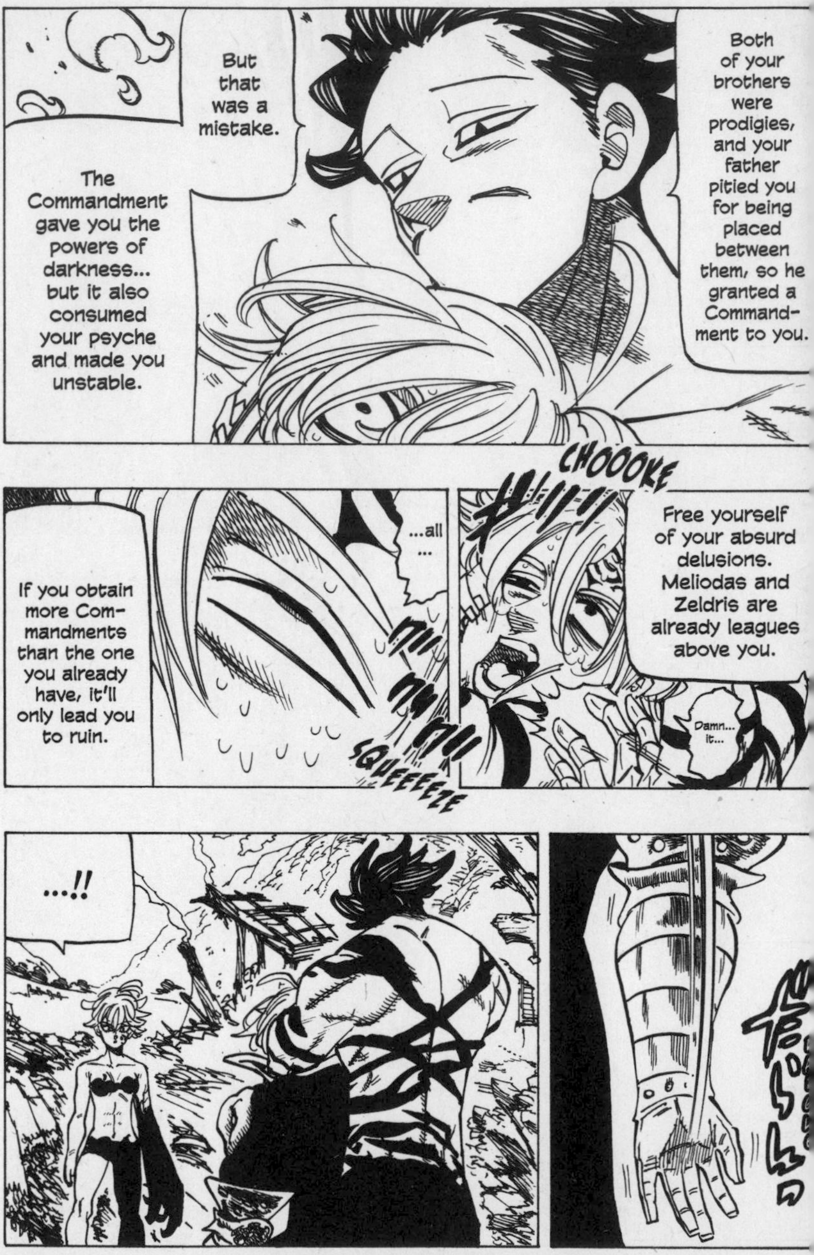
Both of your brothers were prodigies, and your father pitied you for being placed between them, so he granted a Commandment to you.
But that was a mistake.
The Commandment gave you the powers of darkness... but it also consumed your psyche and made you unstable.
CHOOOKE
Free yourself of your absurd delusions. Meliodas and Zeldris are already leagues above you.
Damn... it...
...all ...
If you obtain more Commandments than the one you already have, it'll only lead you to ruin.
SQUEEEEZE
...!!

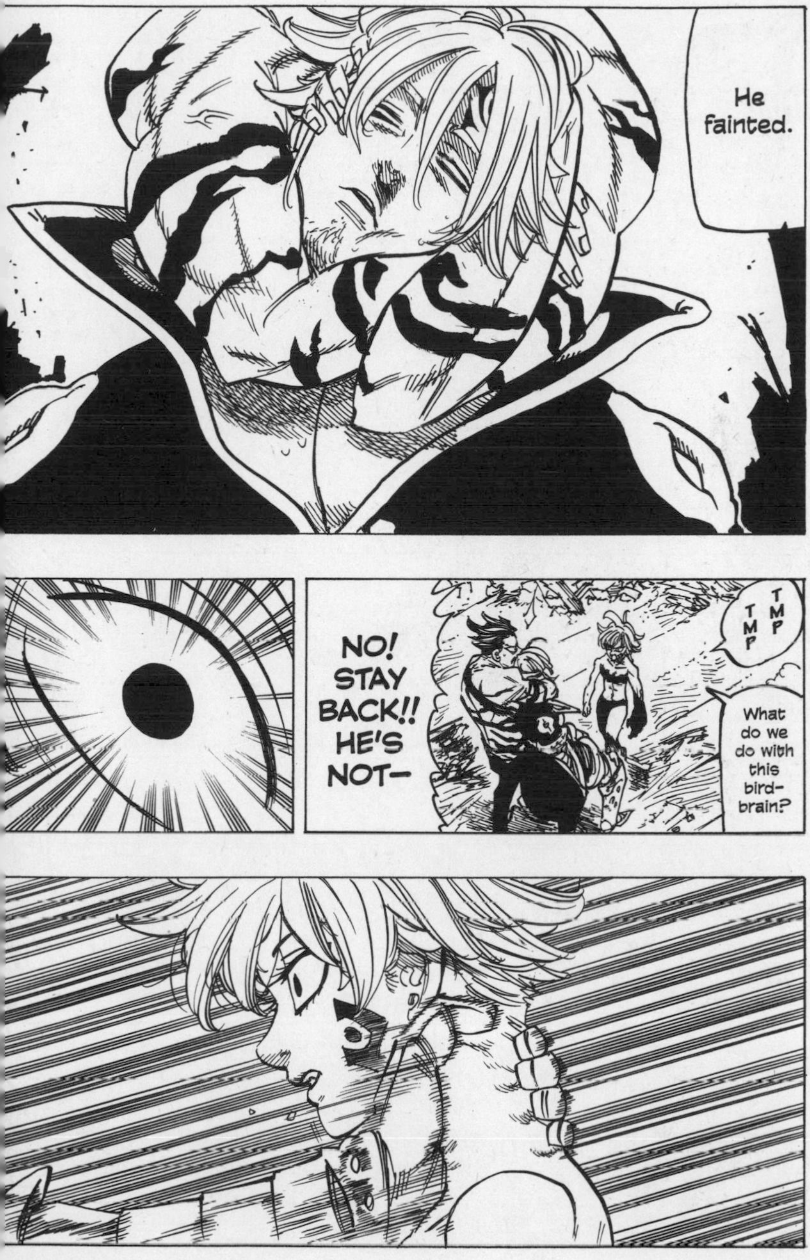
He fainted.
TMP TMP
What do we do with this bird-brain?
NO! STAY BACK!! HE'S NOT—

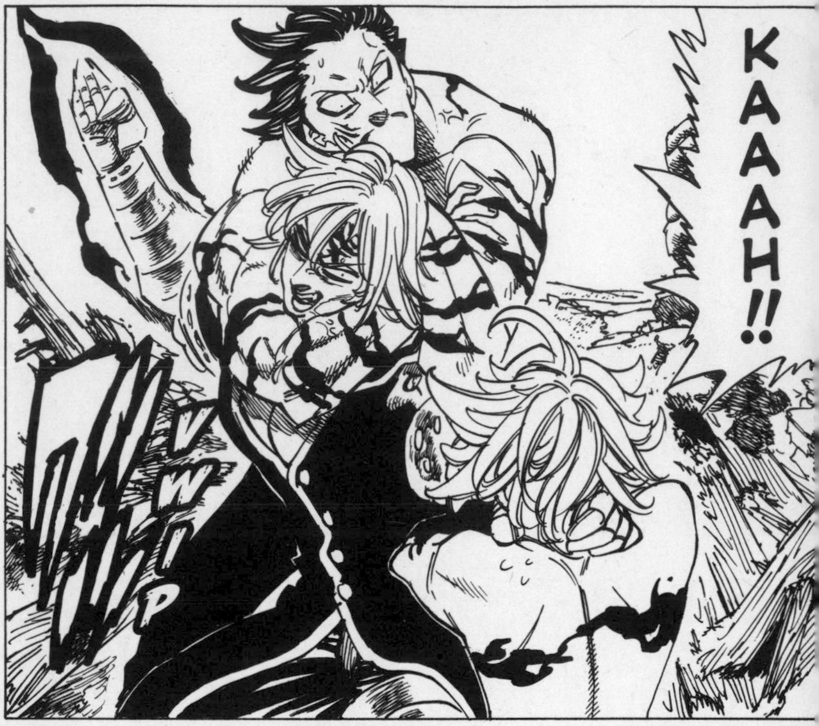
KAAAH!!
VWIP

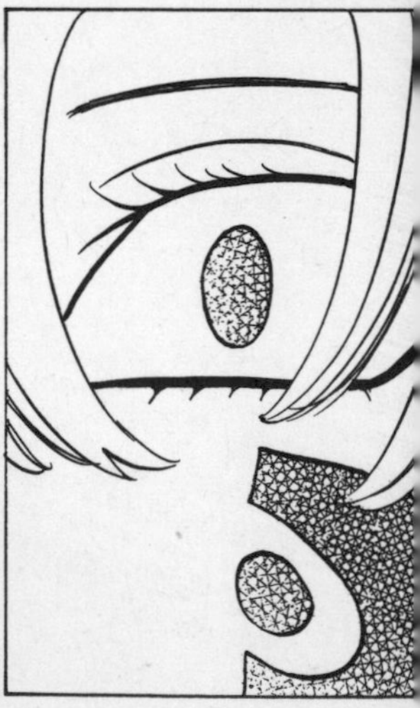

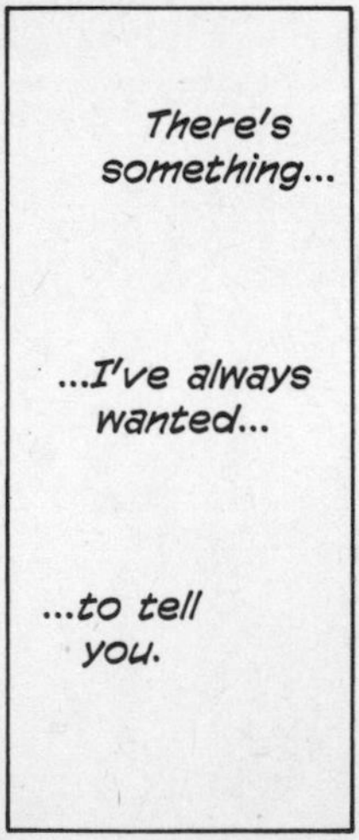
There's something...
...I've always wanted...
...to tell you.

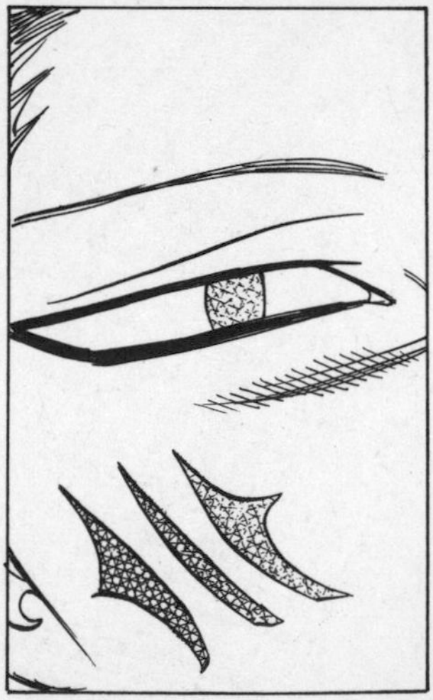

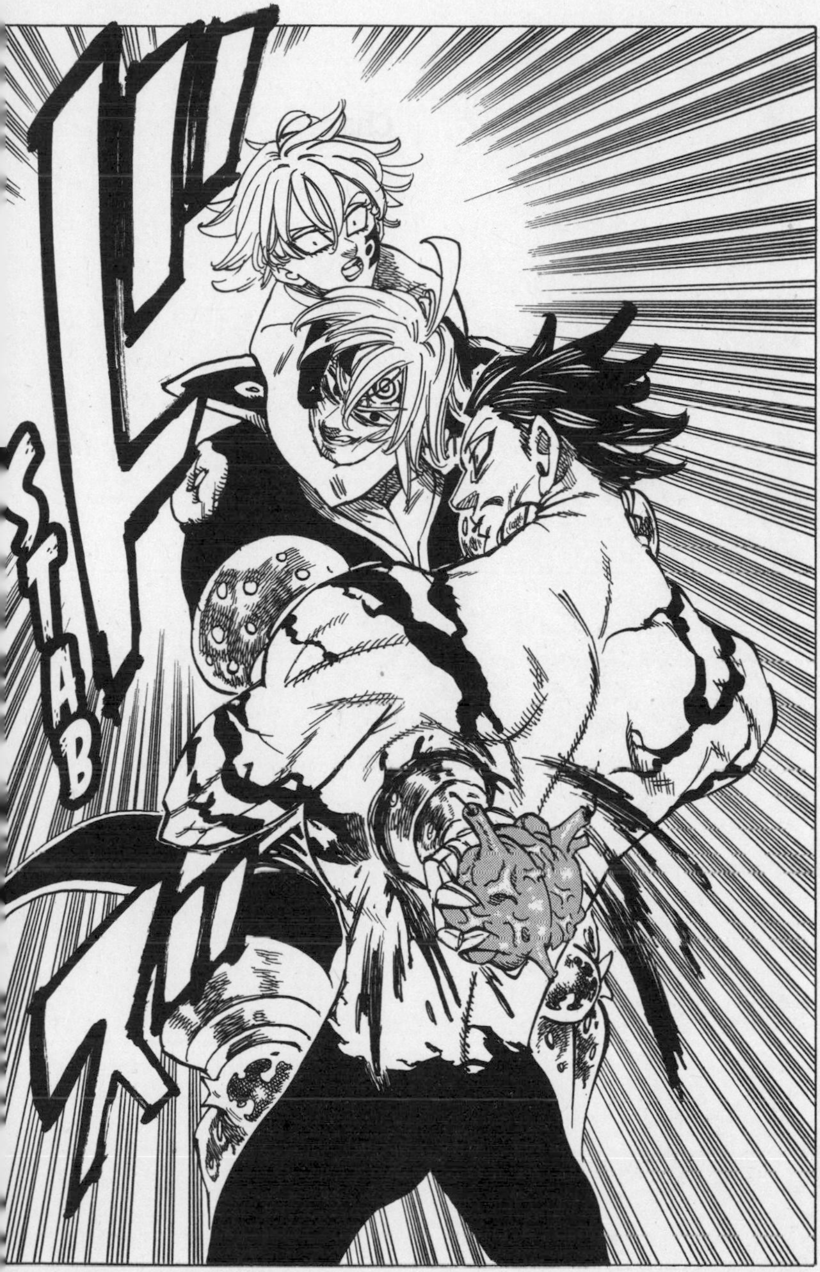
STAB

Chapter 261 - Lost Cat

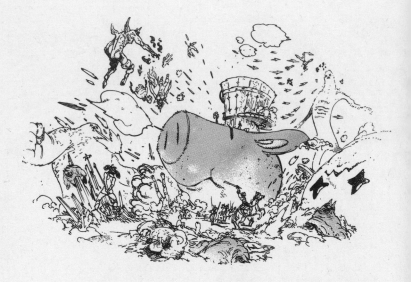

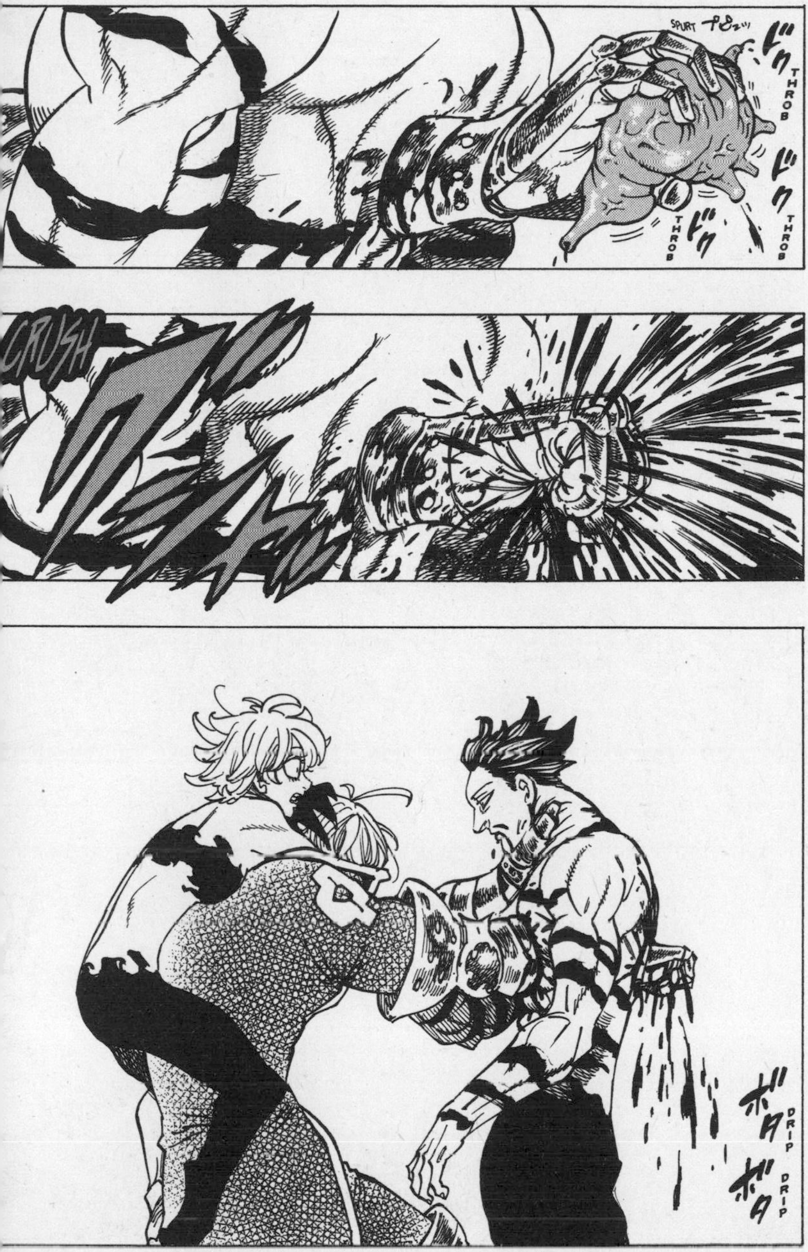
SPURT
THROB
THROB
THROB
CRUSH
DRIP
DRIP

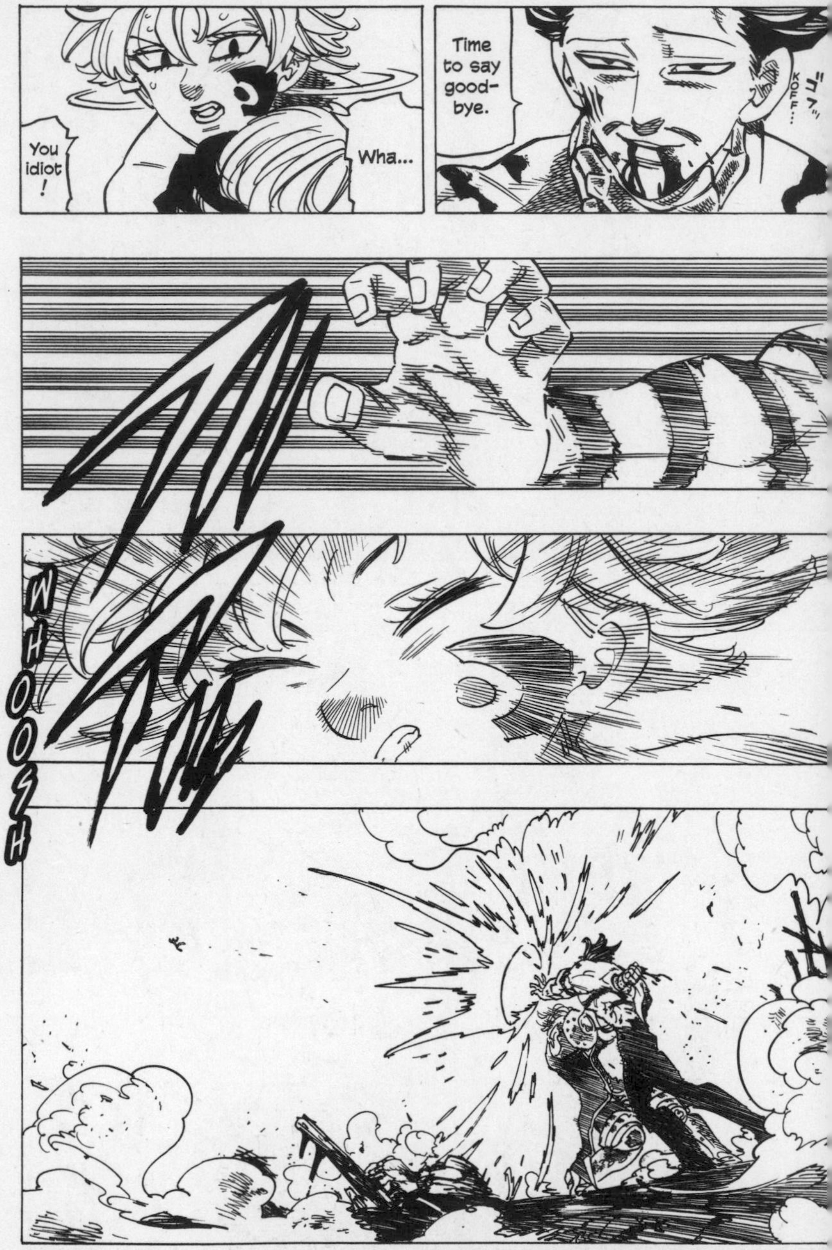
Time to say good-bye.
KOFF...
Wha...
You idiot!
WHOOOSH

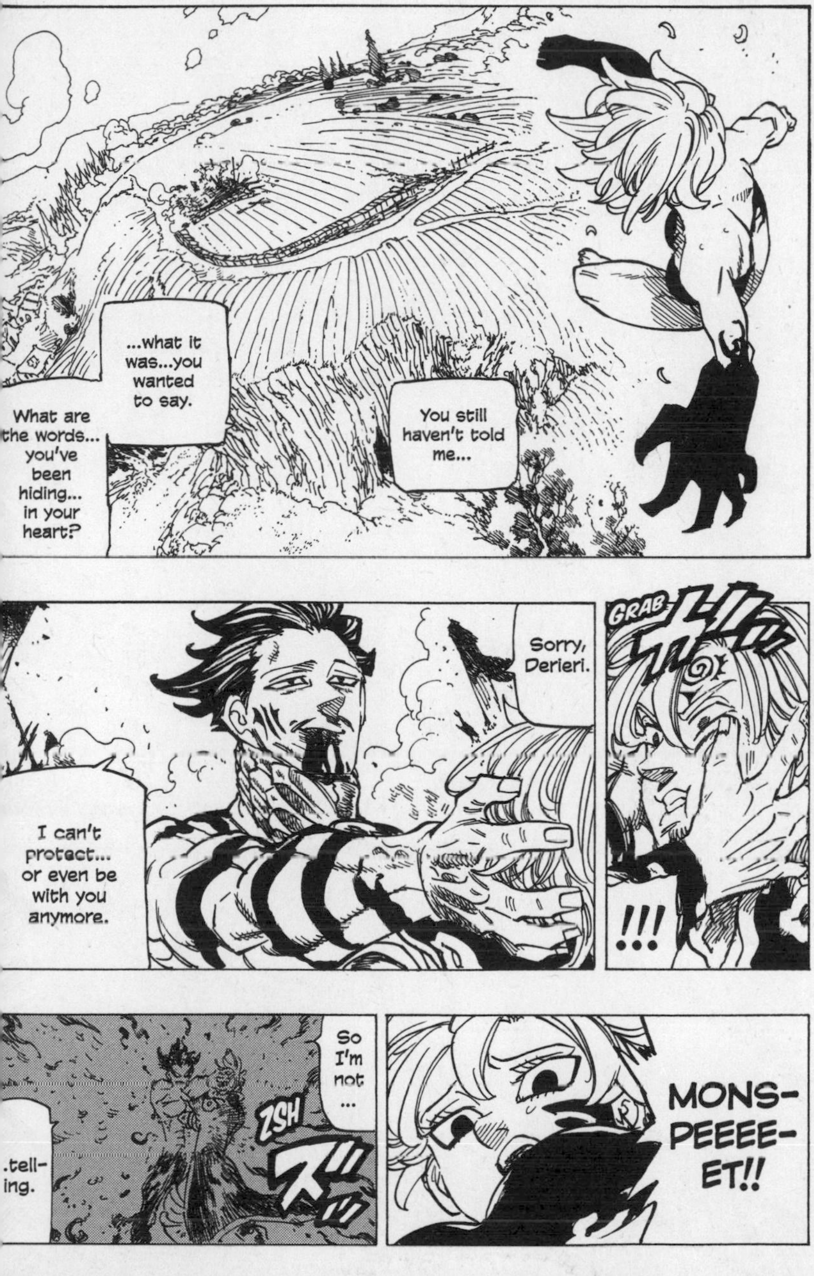
You still haven't told me...
...what it was...you wanted to say.
What are the words... you've been hiding... in your heart?
GRAB
!!!
Sorry, Derieri.
I can't protect... or even be with you anymore.
MONS-PEEEEE-ET!!
So I'm not ...
ZSH
.tell-ing.

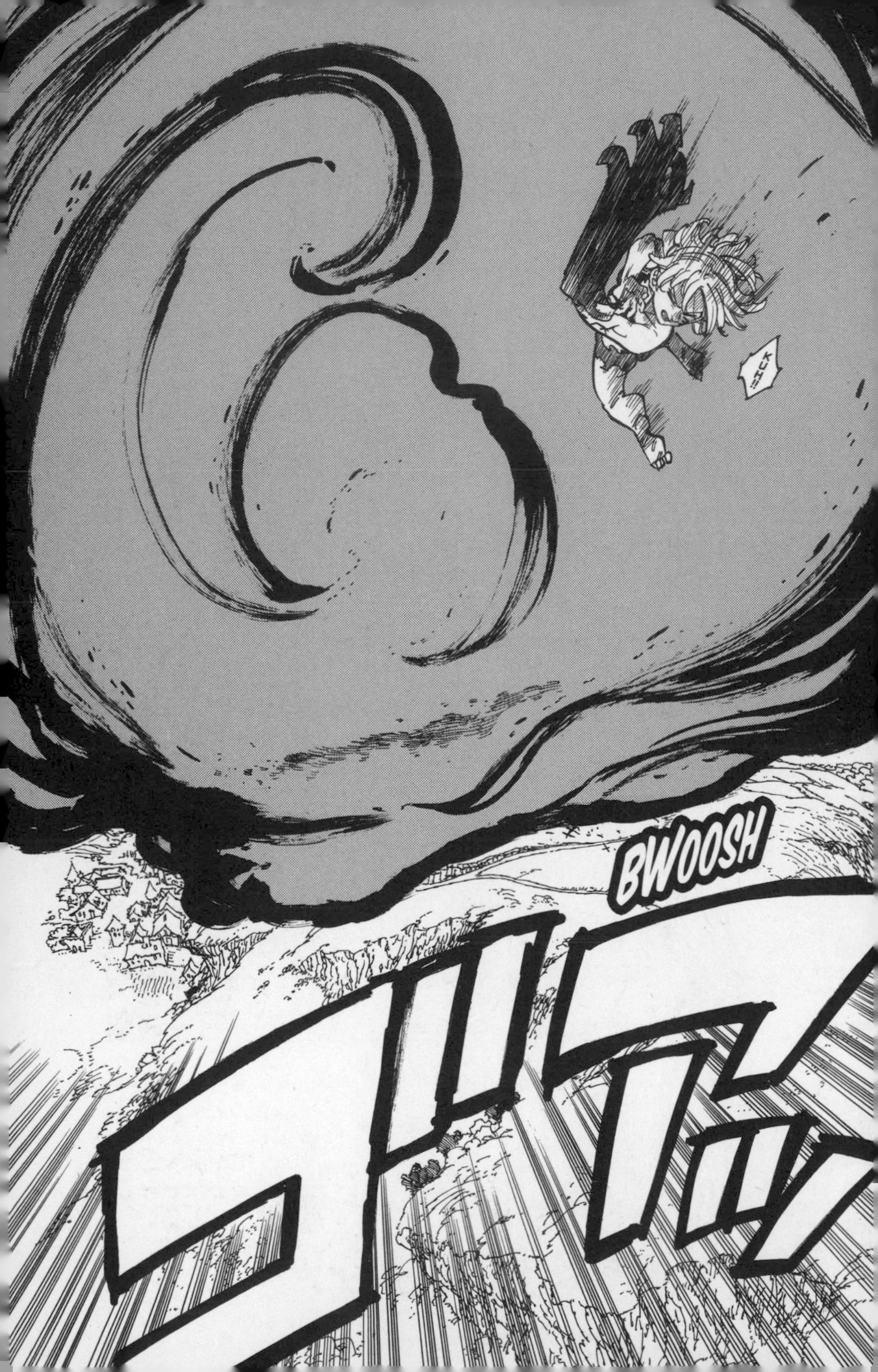
KUH!!
BWOOSH

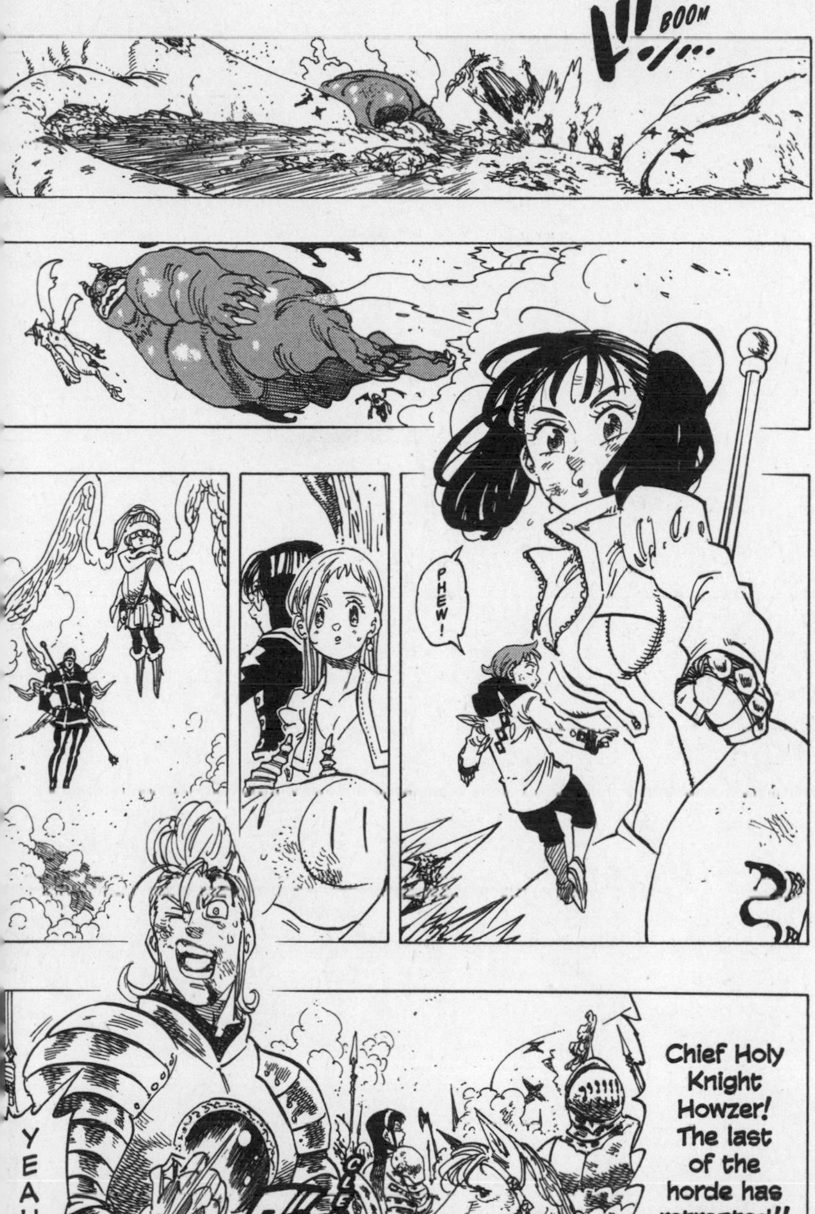
BOOM
PHEW!
Chief Holy Knight Howzer! The last of the horde has retreated!!
CLENCH
YEAH!!

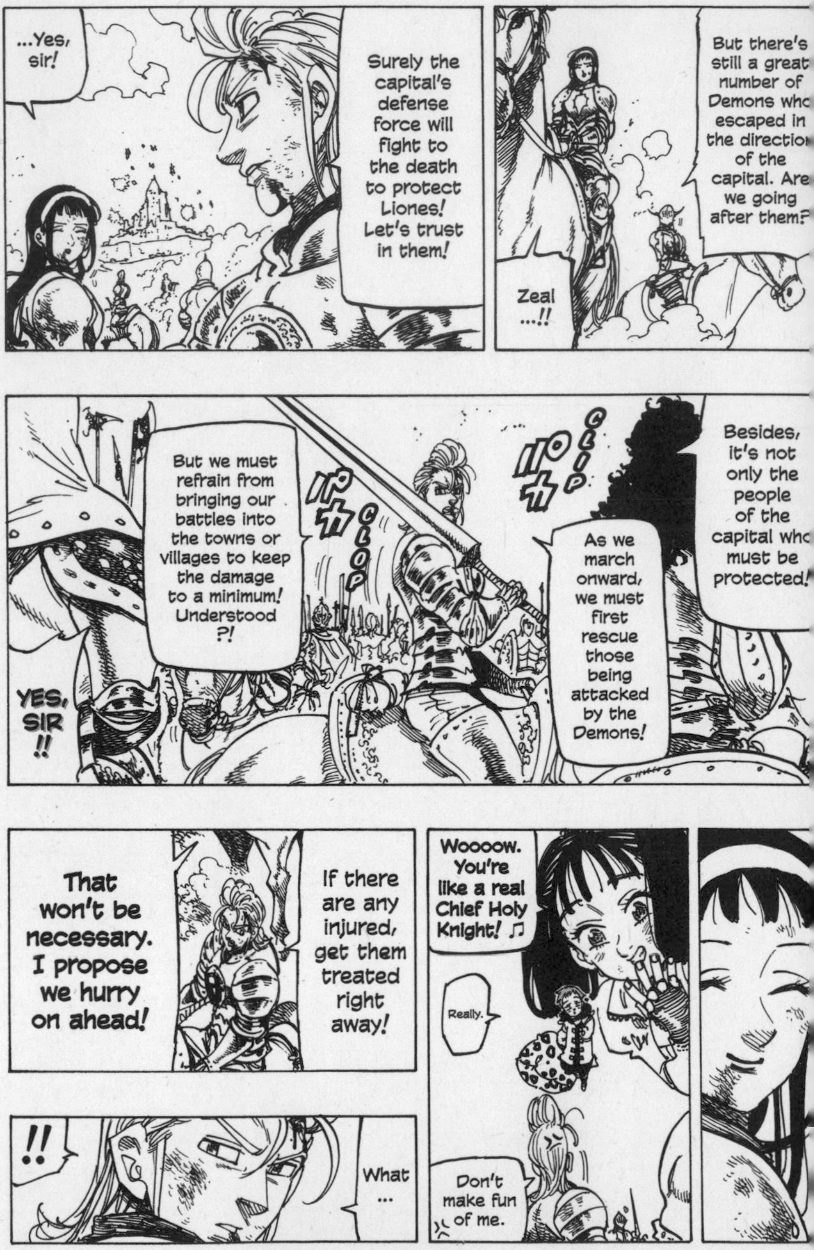

But there's still a great number of Demons who escaped in the direction of the capital. Are we going after them?
Zeal ...!!
Surely the capital's defense force will fight to the death to protect Liones! Let's trust in them!
...Yes, sir!
Besides, it's not only the people of the capital who must be protected!
パカ CLIP
As we march onward, we must first rescue those being attacked by the Demons!
パカ CLOP
But we must refrain from bringing our battles into the towns or villages to keep the damage to a minimum! Understood ?!
YES, SIR !!
Wooow. You're like a real Chief Holy Knight! ♫
Really.
Don't make fun of me.
If there are any injured, get them treated right away!
That won't be necessary. I propose we hurry on ahead!
What ...
!!

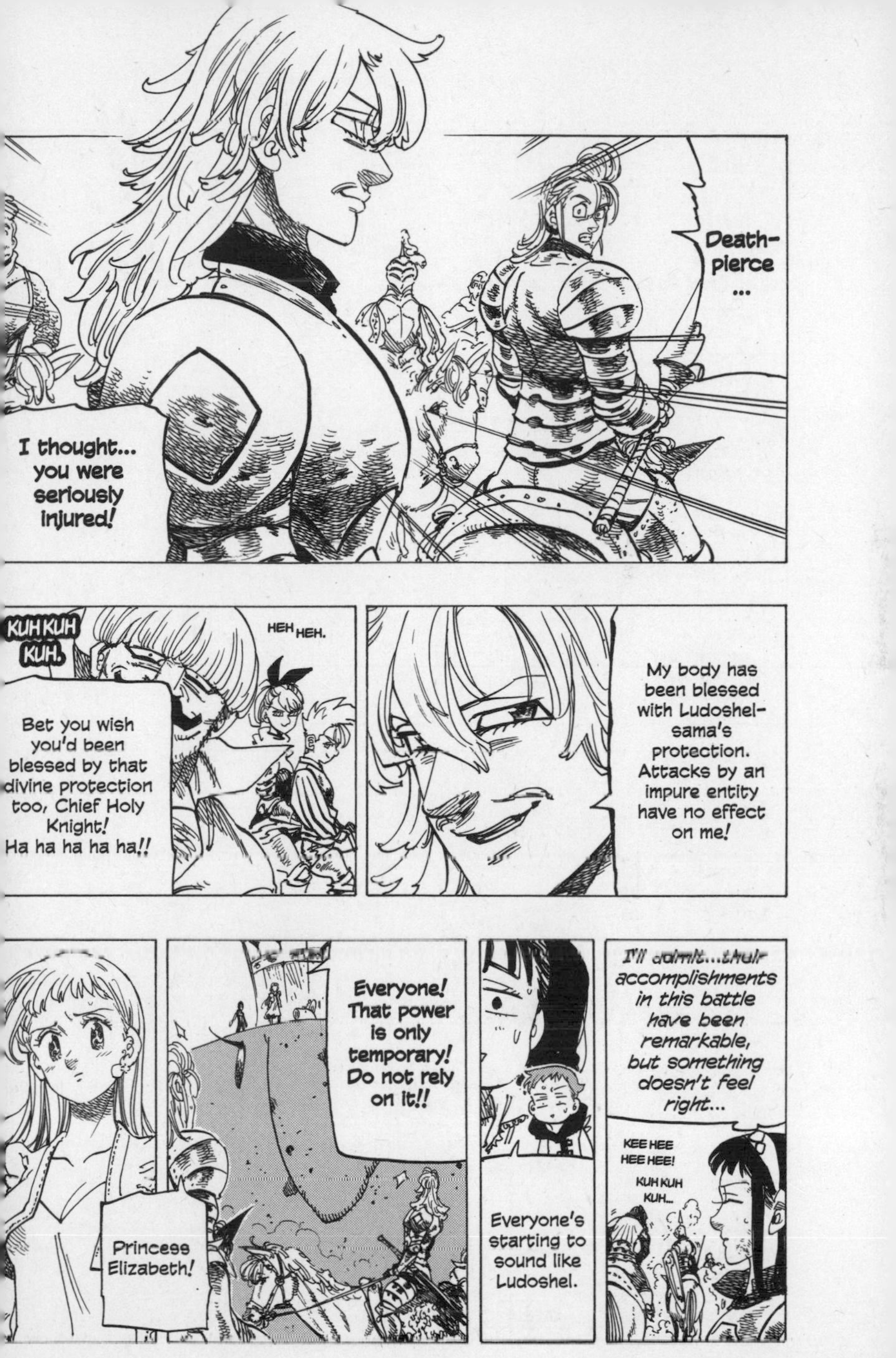
Death-pierce...
I thought... you were seriously injured!
My body has been blessed with Ludoshel-sama's protection. Attacks by an impure entity have no effect on me!
HEH HEH.
KUH KUH KUH.
Bet you wish you'd been blessed by that divine protection too, Chief Holy Knight! Ha ha ha ha ha!!
I'll admit...their accomplishments in this battle have been remarkable, but something doesn't feel right...
KEE HEE HEE HEE!
KUH KUH KUH...
Everyone's starting to sound like Ludoshel.
Everyone! That power is only temporary! Do not rely on it!!
Princess Elizabeth!

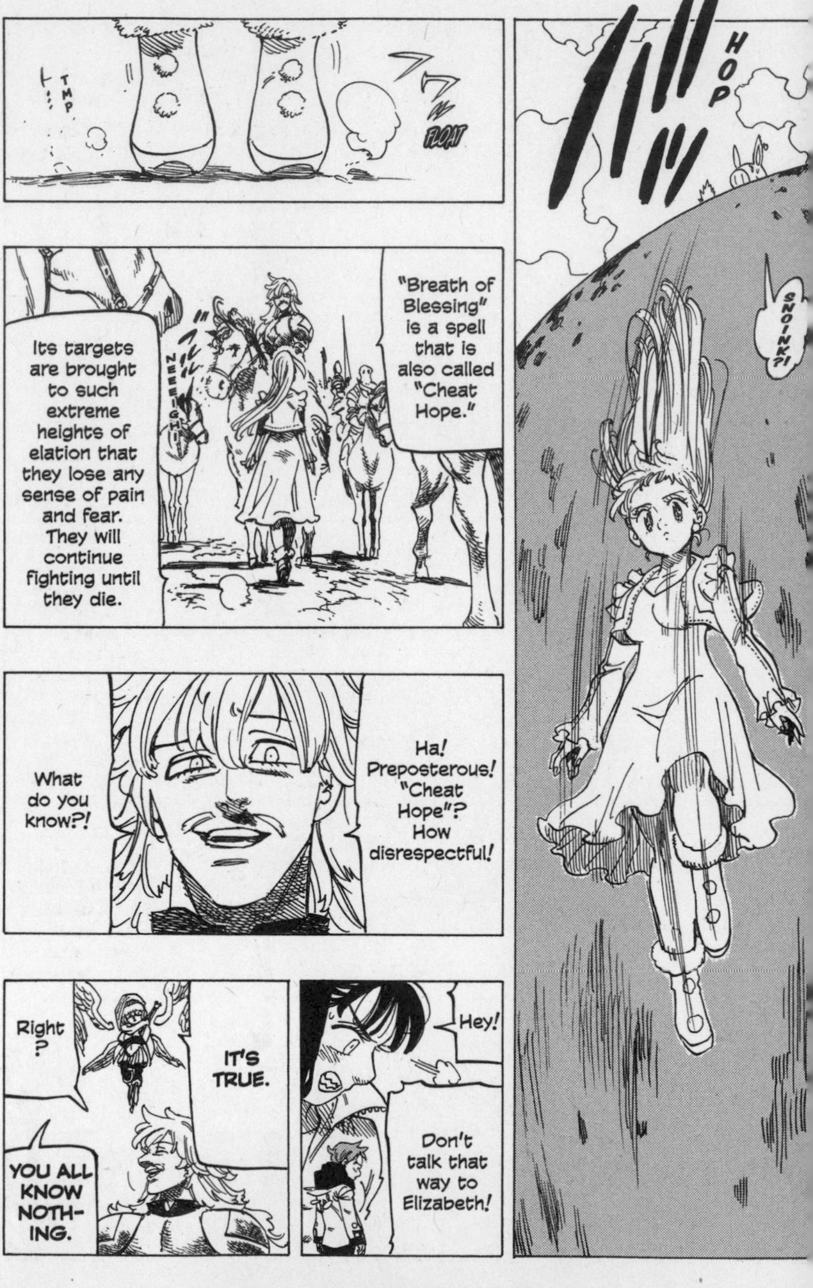
HOP
SNOINK?!
TMP
FLOAT
"Breath of Blessing" is a spell that is also called "Cheat Hope."
NEEEIGH!
Its targets are brought to such extreme heights of elation that they lose any sense of pain and fear. They will continue fighting until they die.
Ha! Preposterous! "Cheat Hope"? How disrespectful!
What do you know?!
Hey!
Don't talk that way to Elizabeth!
IT'S TRUE.
Right?
YOU ALL KNOW NOTH-ING.

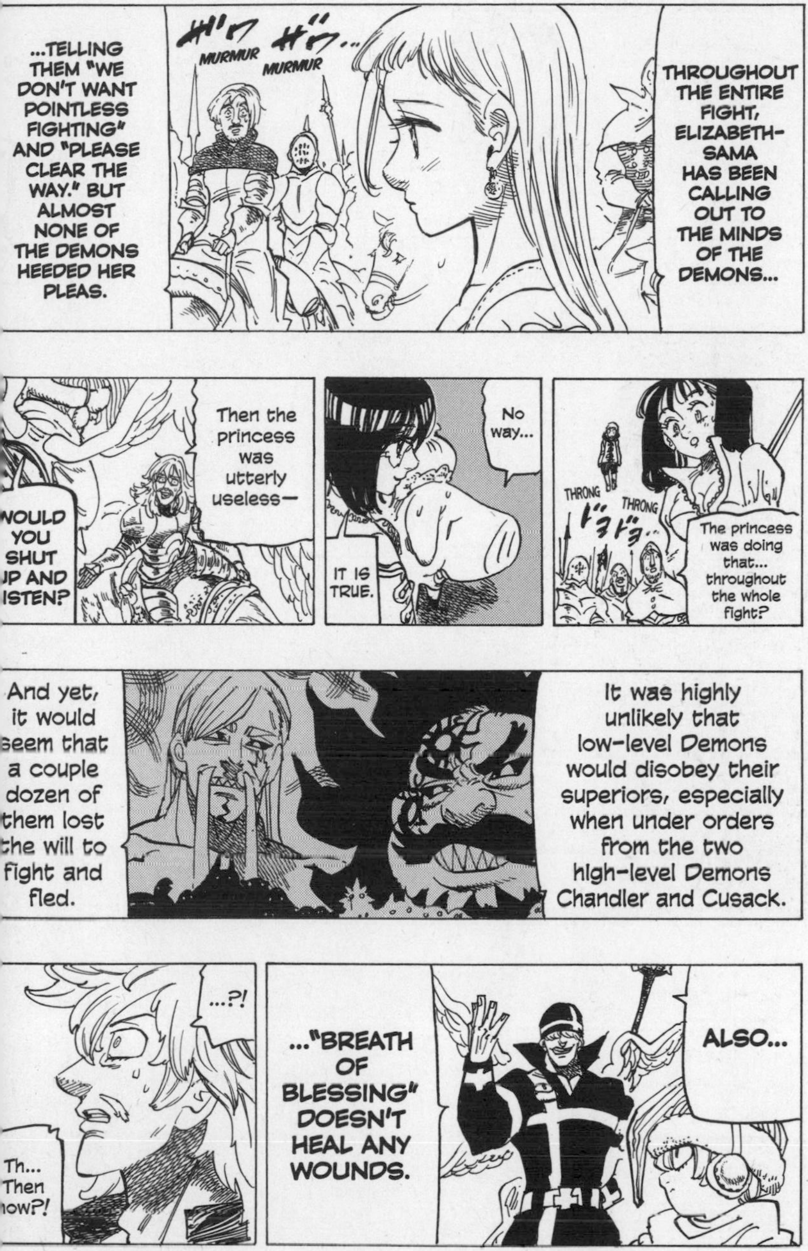
THROUGHOUT THE ENTIRE FIGHT, ELIZABETH-SAMA HAS BEEN CALLING OUT TO THE MINDS OF THE DEMONS...
MURMUR
MURMUR
...TELLING THEM "WE DON'T WANT POINTLESS FIGHTING" AND "PLEASE CLEAR THE WAY." BUT ALMOST NONE OF THE DEMONS HEEDED HER PLEAS.
THRONG
THRONG
The princess was doing that... throughout the whole fight?
No way...
IT IS TRUE.
Then the princess was utterly useless—
WOULD YOU SHUT UP AND LISTEN?
It was highly unlikely that low-level Demons would disobey their superiors, especially when under orders from the two high-level Demons Chandler and Cusack.
And yet, it would seem that a couple dozen of them lost the will to fight and fled.
ALSO...
..."BREATH OF BLESSING" DOESN'T HEAL ANY WOUNDS.
...?!
Th... Then how?!

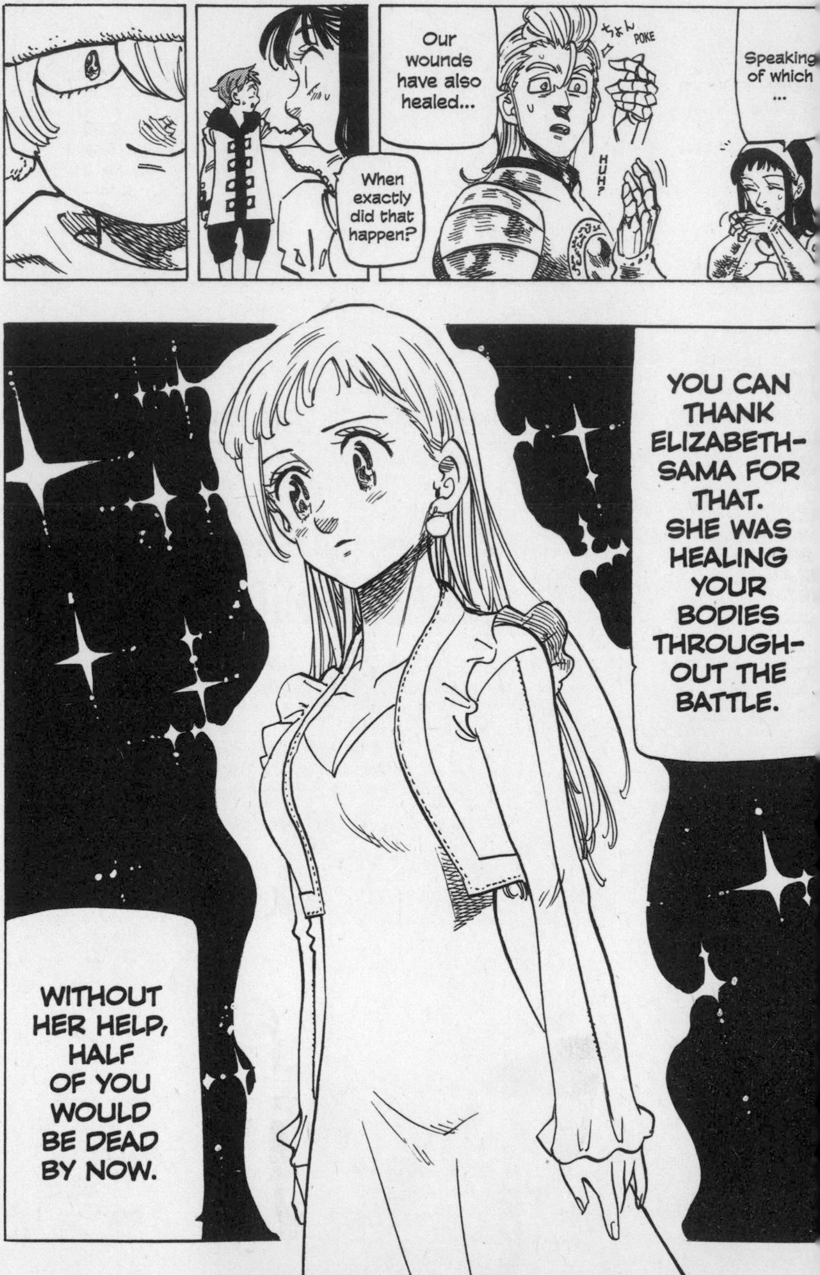
Speaking of which ...
Our wounds have also healed...
ちょん POKE
HUH?
When exactly did that happen?
YOU CAN THANK ELIZABETH-SAMA FOR THAT. SHE WAS HEALING YOUR BODIES THROUGH-OUT THE BATTLE.
WITHOUT HER HELP, HALF OF YOU WOULD BE DEAD BY NOW.

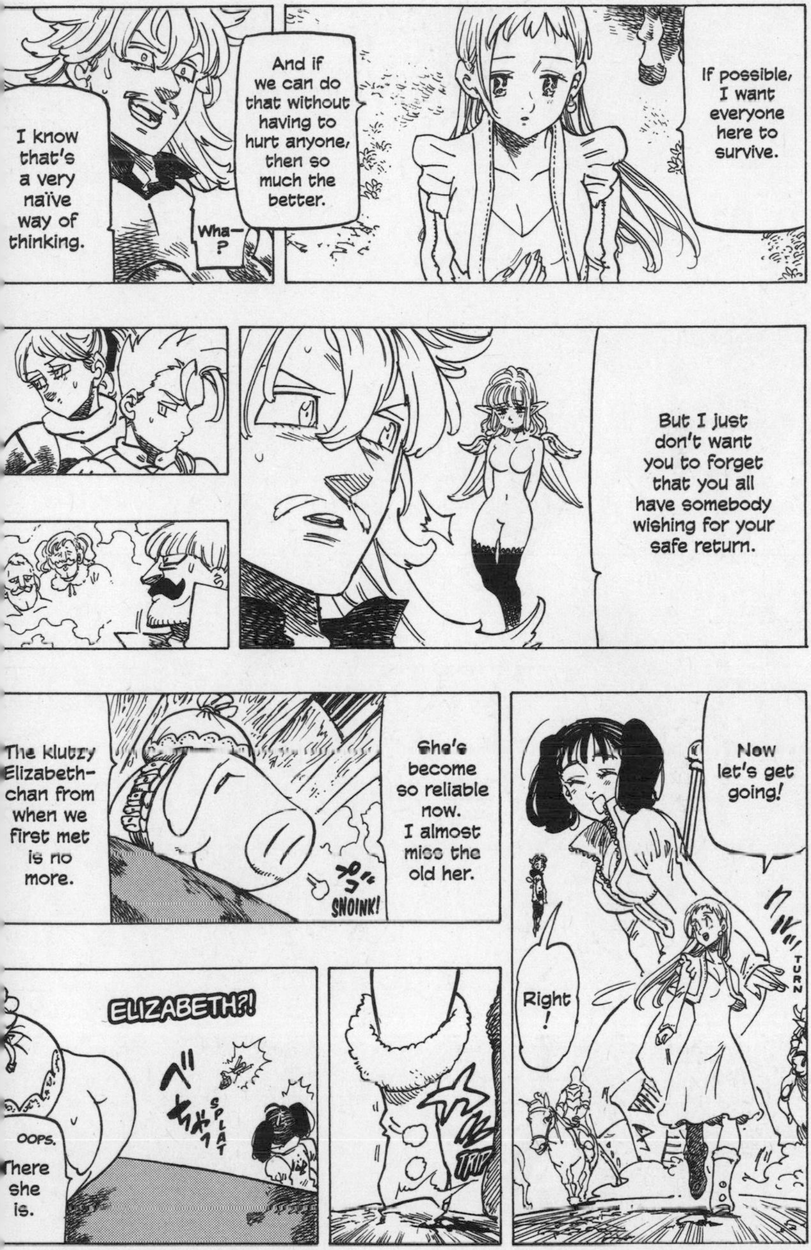
If possible, I want everyone here to survive.
And if we can do that without having to hurt anyone, then so much the better.
Wha-?
I know that's a very naïve way of thinking.
But I just don't want you to forget that you all have somebody wishing for your safe return.
Now let's get going!
TURN
Right!
She's become so reliable now. I almost miss the old her.
SNOINK!
The klutzy Elizabeth-chan from when we first met is no more.
TRIP
ELIZABETH?!
SPLAT
OOPS.
There she is.

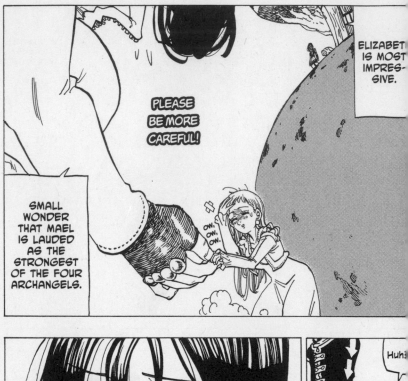

ELIZABETH IS MOST IMPRESSIVE.

PLEASE BE MORE CAREFUL!

OW, OW, OW.

SMALL WONDER THAT MAEL IS LAUDED AS THE STRONGEST OF THE FOUR ARCHANGELS.

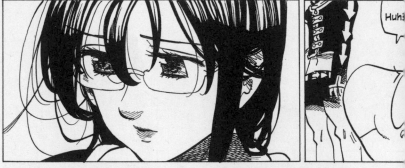

Huh?

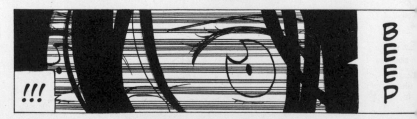

!!!

BEEP

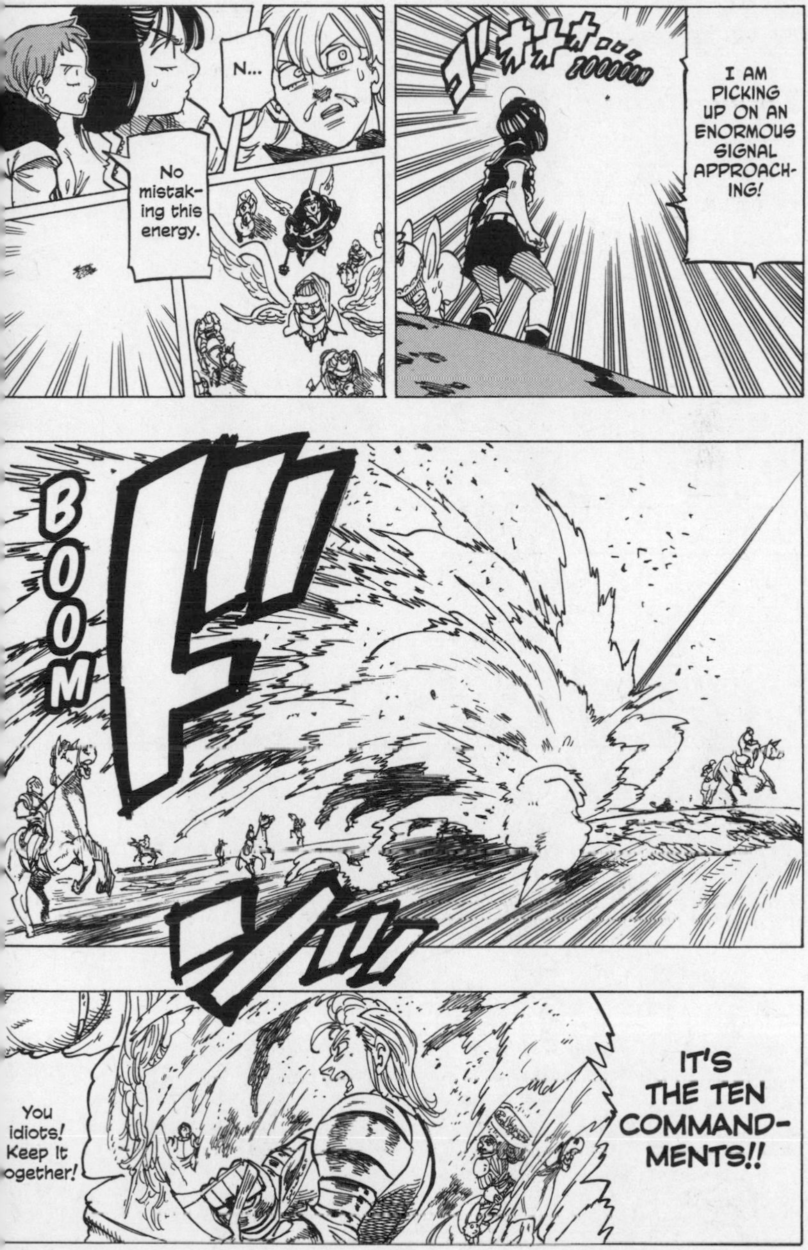
ZOOOOOM
I AM PICKING UP ON AN ENORMOUS SIGNAL APPROACHING!
N...
No mistaking this energy.
BOOM
IT'S THE TEN COMMANDMENTS!!
You idiots! Keep it
ogether!

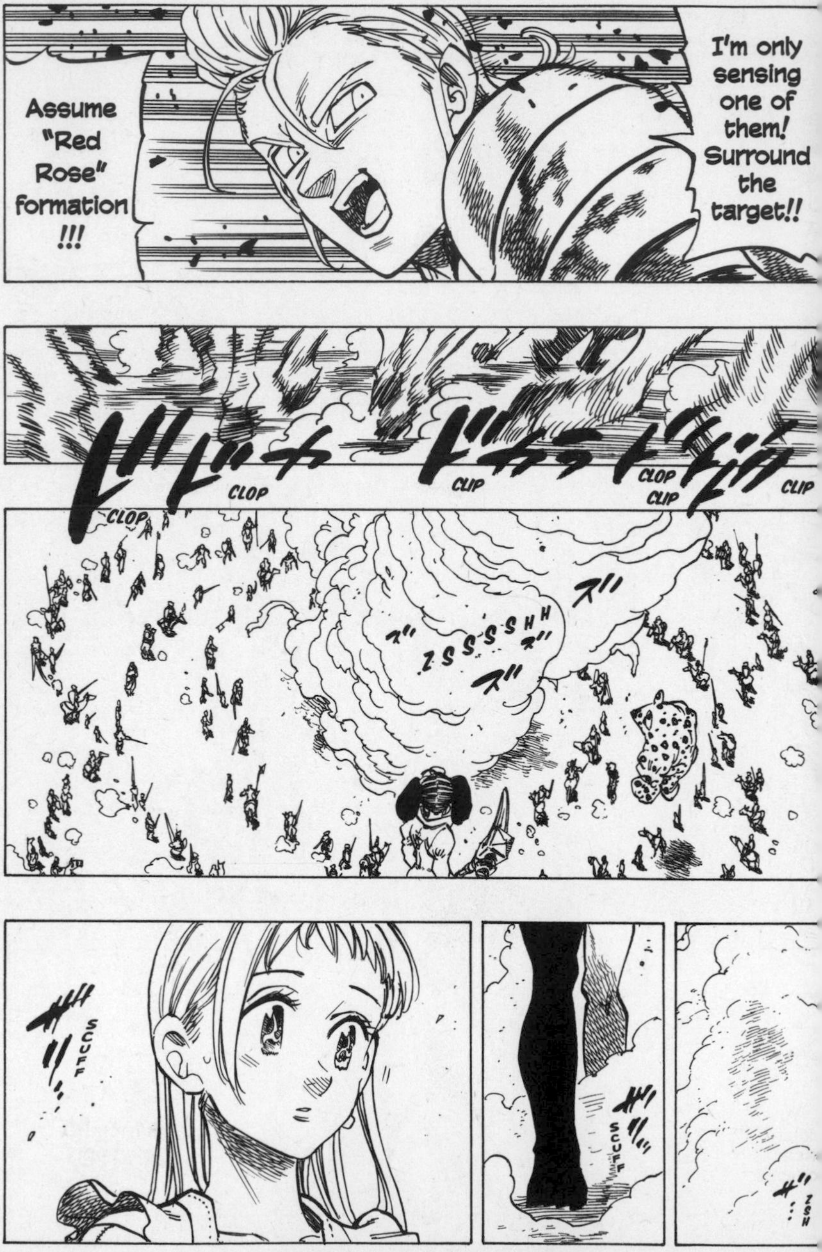
I'm only sensing one of them! Surround the target!!
Assume "Red Rose" formation!!!
CLIP
CLOP
CLIP
CLIP
CLOP
CLOP
ZSSSSSHH
ZSH
SCUFF
SCUFF

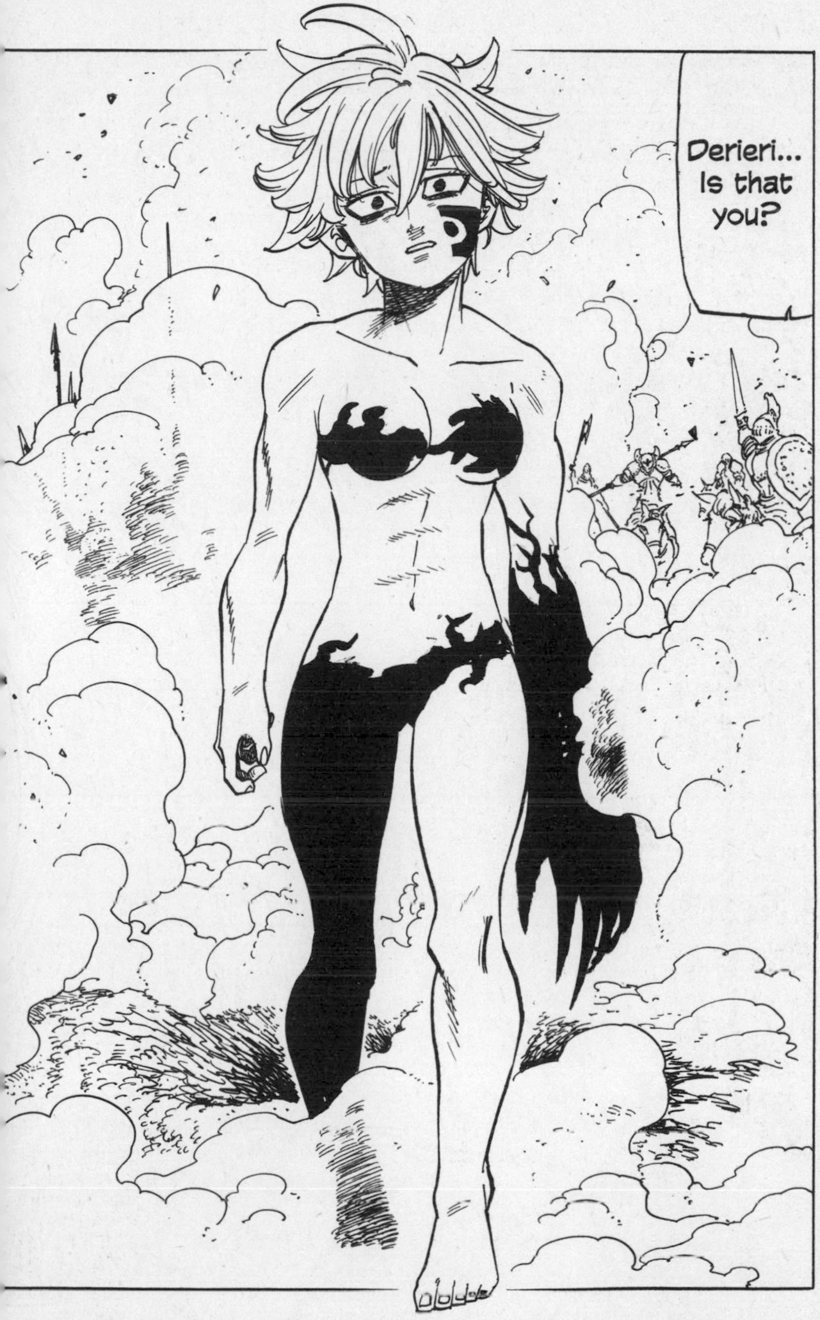
Derieri... Is that you?

Chapter 262 - The One Warped by Darkness

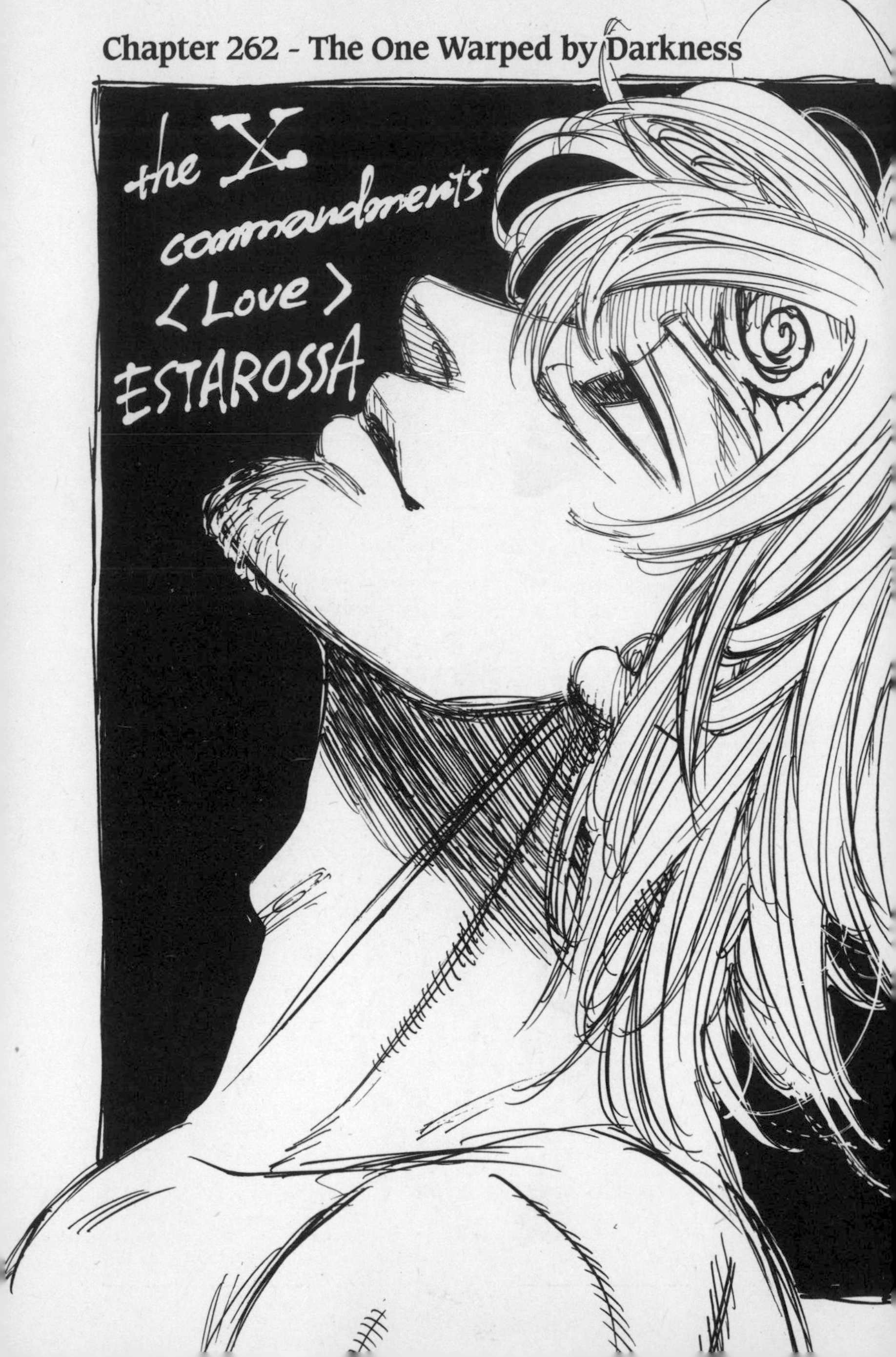
the X commandments
<Love>
ESTAROSSA

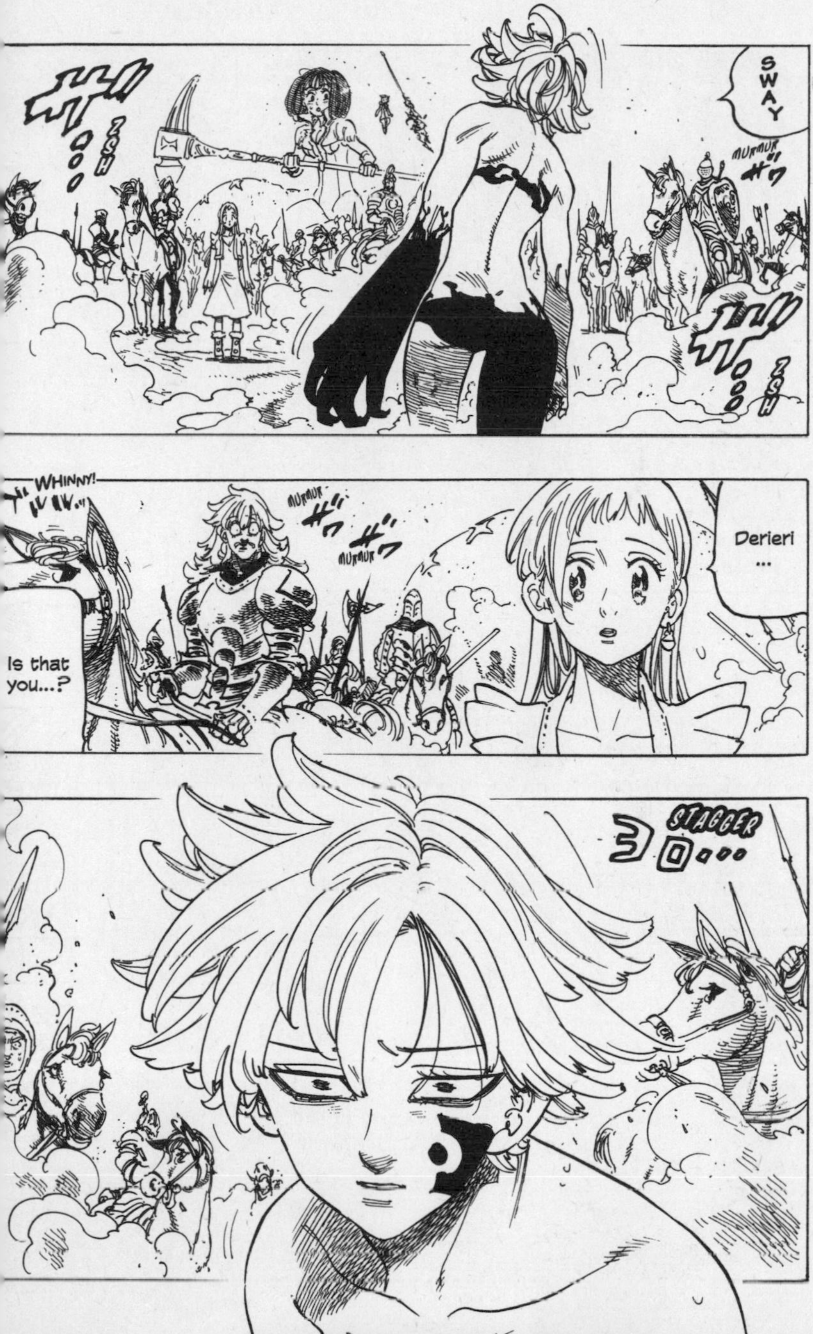
SWAY
MURMUR
ZSH
ZSH
Derieri ...
MURMUR
MURMUR
WHINNY!
Is that you...?
STAGGER

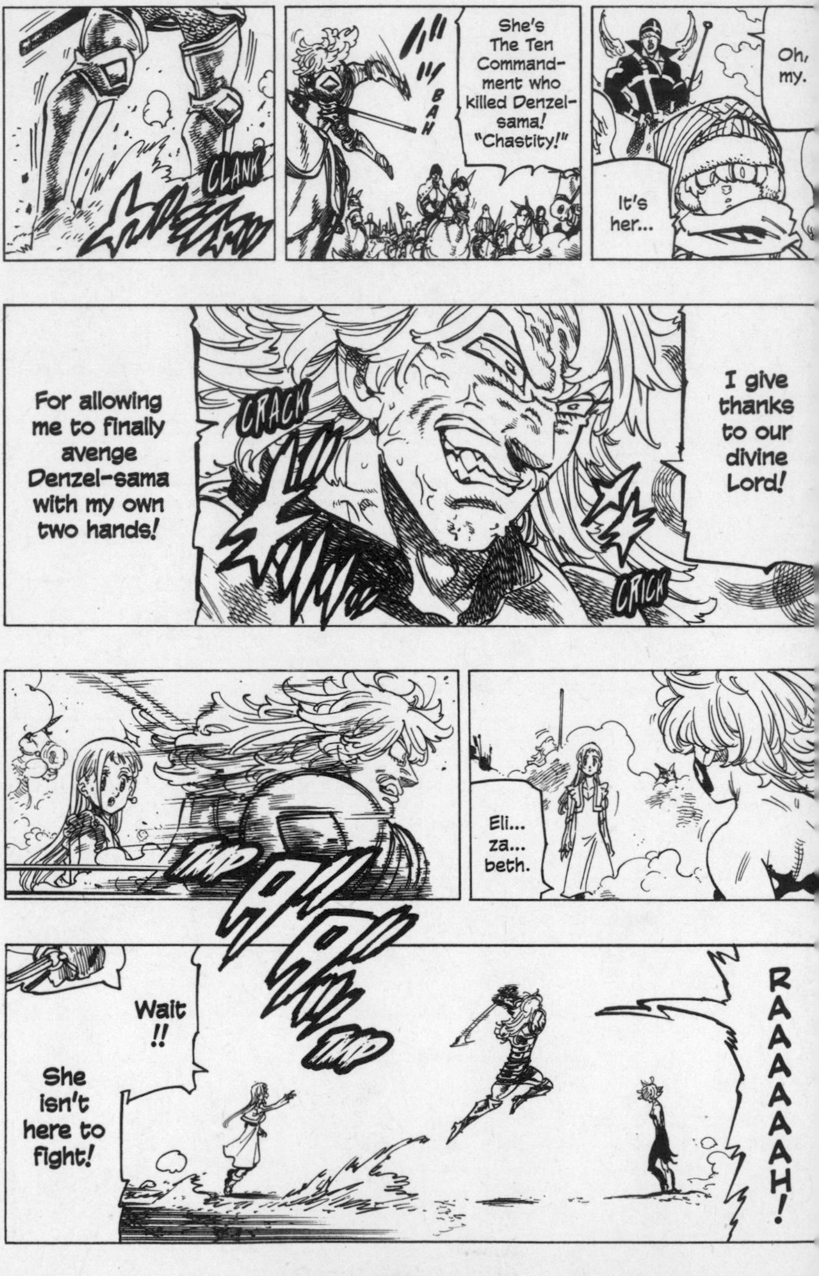
Oh, my.
It's her...
She's The Ten Commandment who killed Denzel-sama! "Chastity!"
BAH
CLANK
I give thanks to our divine Lord!
CRICK
For allowing me to finally avenge Denzel-sama with my own two hands!
CRACK
Eli... za... beth.
TMP
RAAAAAAH!
Wait!!
She isn't here to fight!
TMP

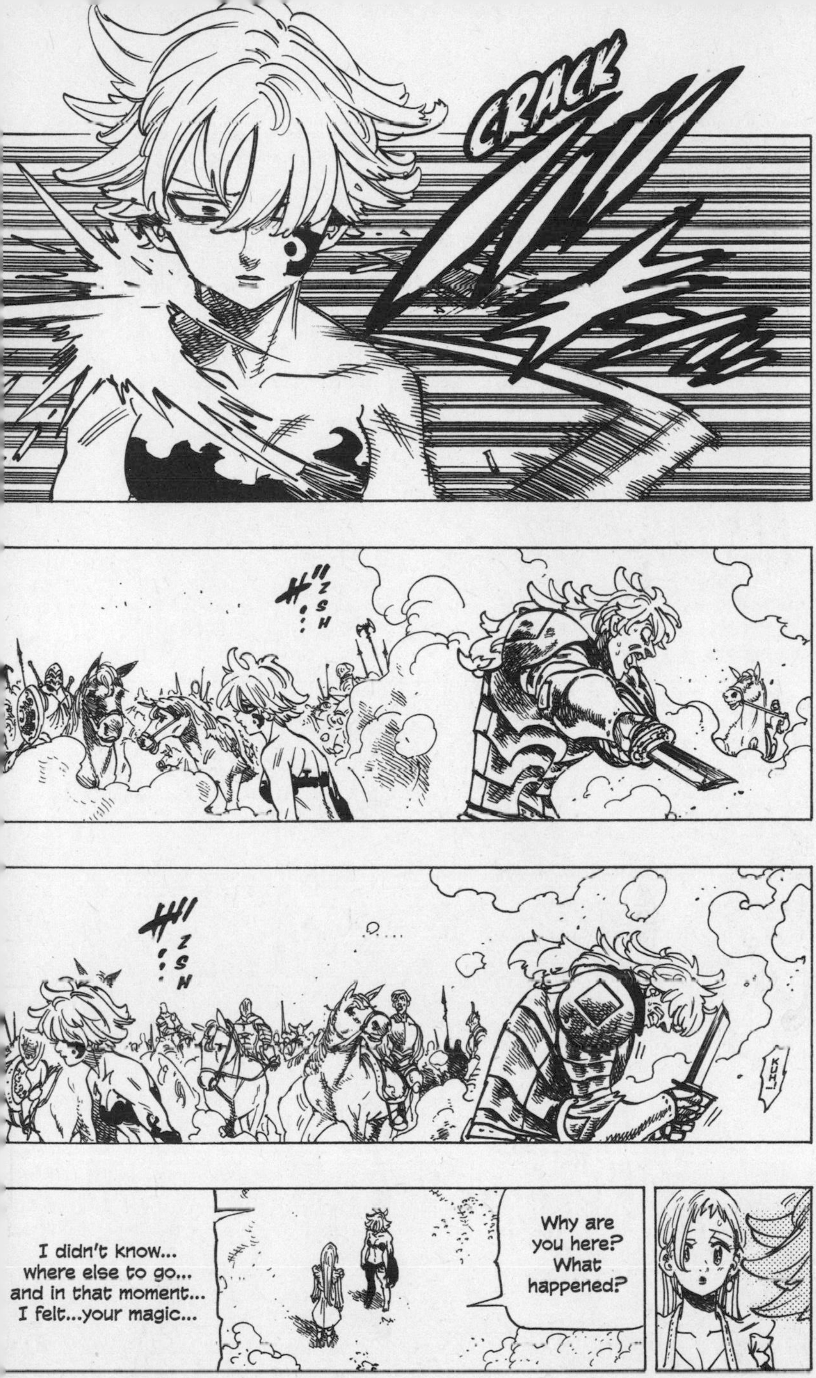
CRACK
ZSH!!
ZSH!!
KUH...!
Why are you here? What happened?
I didn't know... where else to go... and in that moment... I felt...your magic...

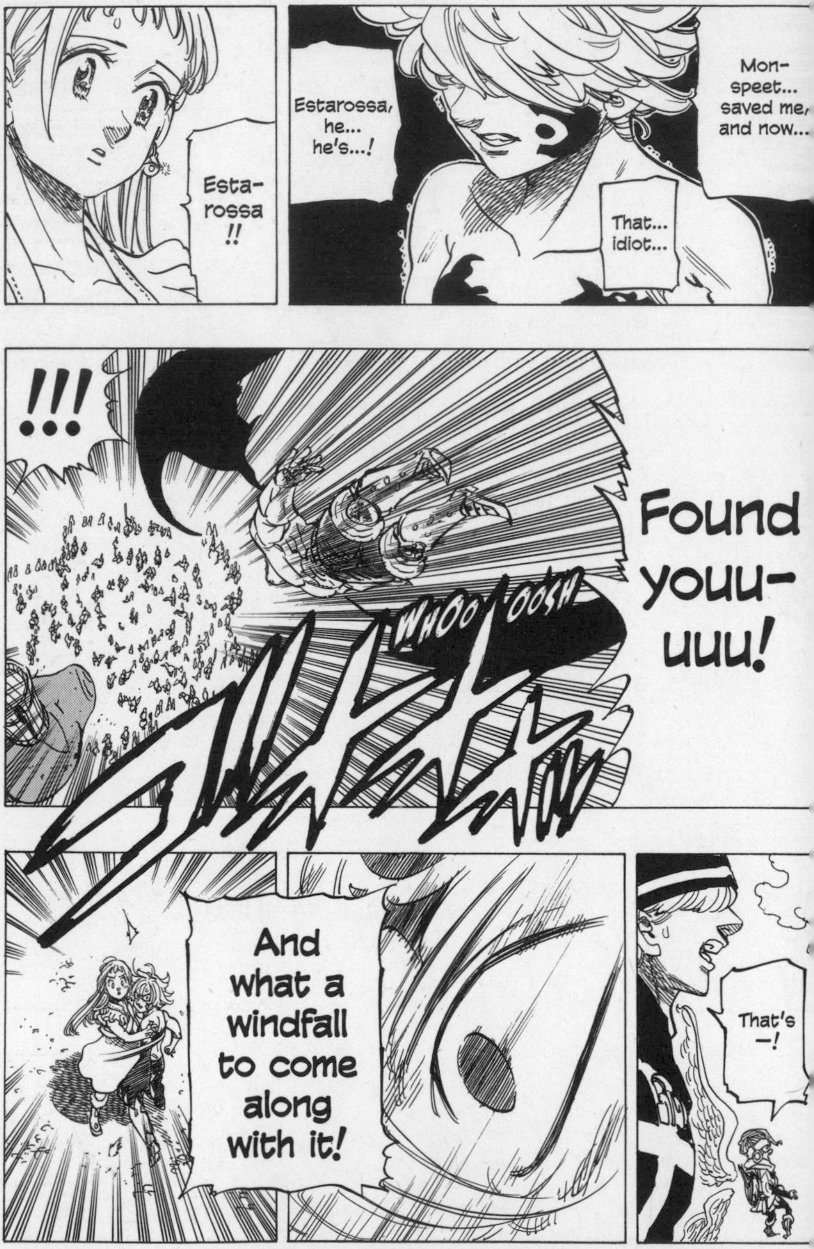
Mon-speet... saved me, and now...
Estarossa, he... he's...!
That... idiot...
Esta-rossa!!
Found youu-uuu!
WHOOOOSH
!!!
That's—!
And what a windfall to come along with it!

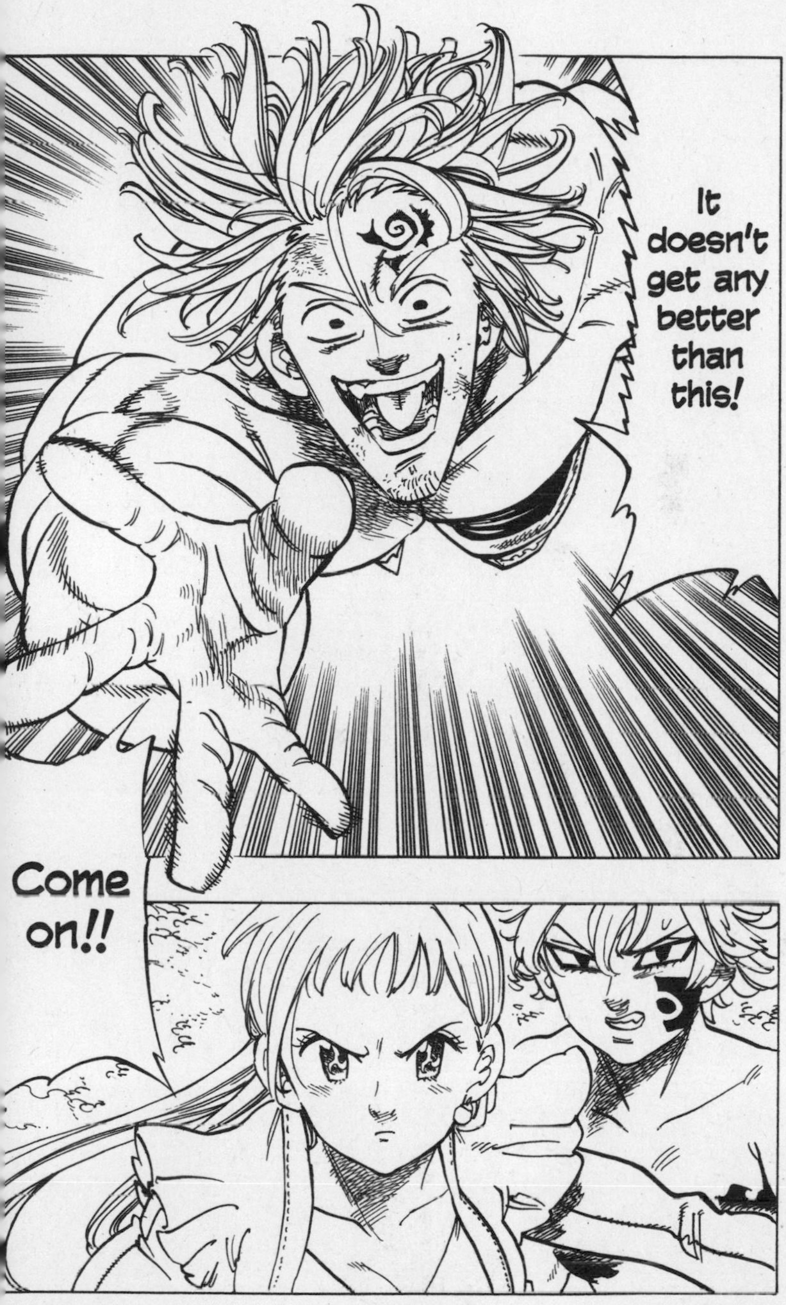
It doesn't get any better than this!
Come on!!

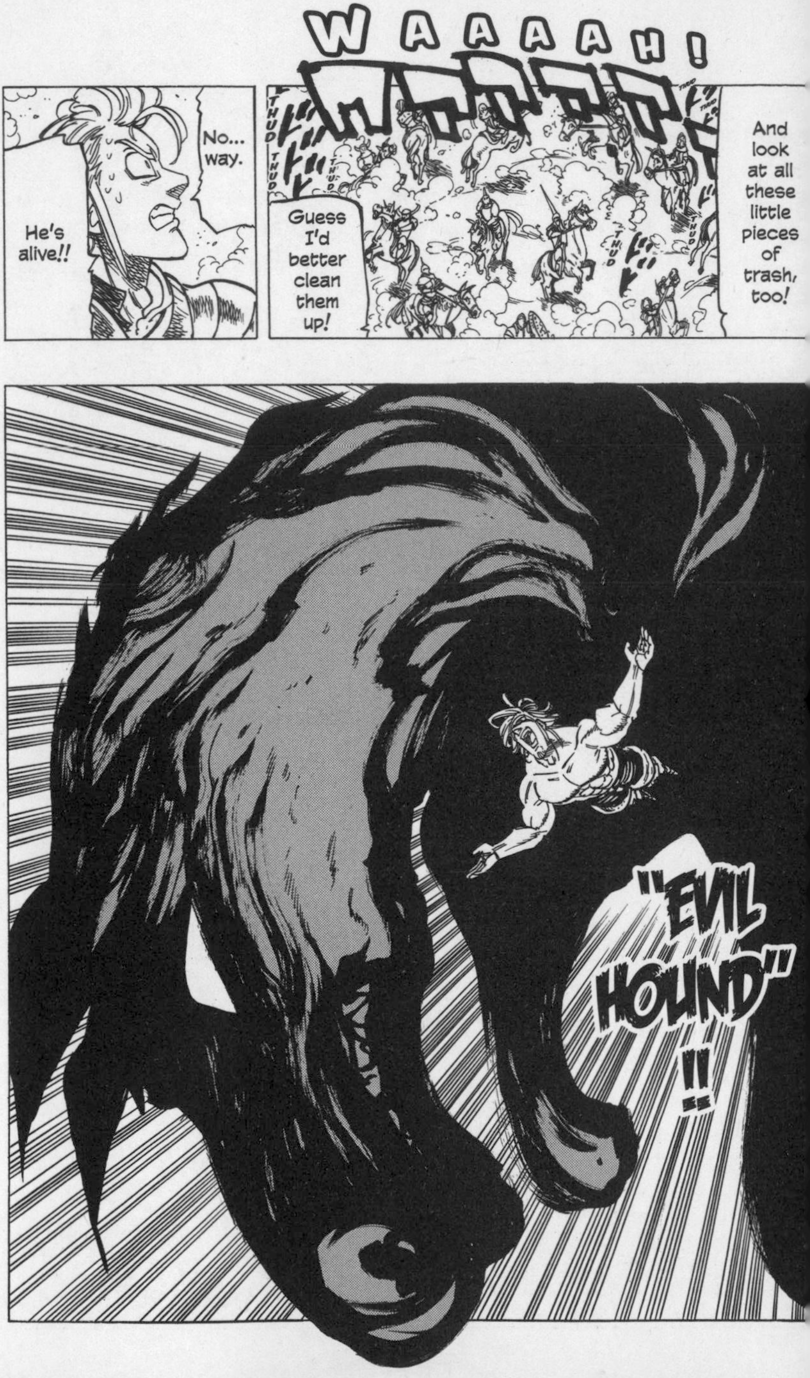
WAAAAAH!
And look at all these little pieces of trash, too!
Guess I'd better clean them up!
THUD THUD
No... way.
He's alive!!
"EVIL HOUND"!!

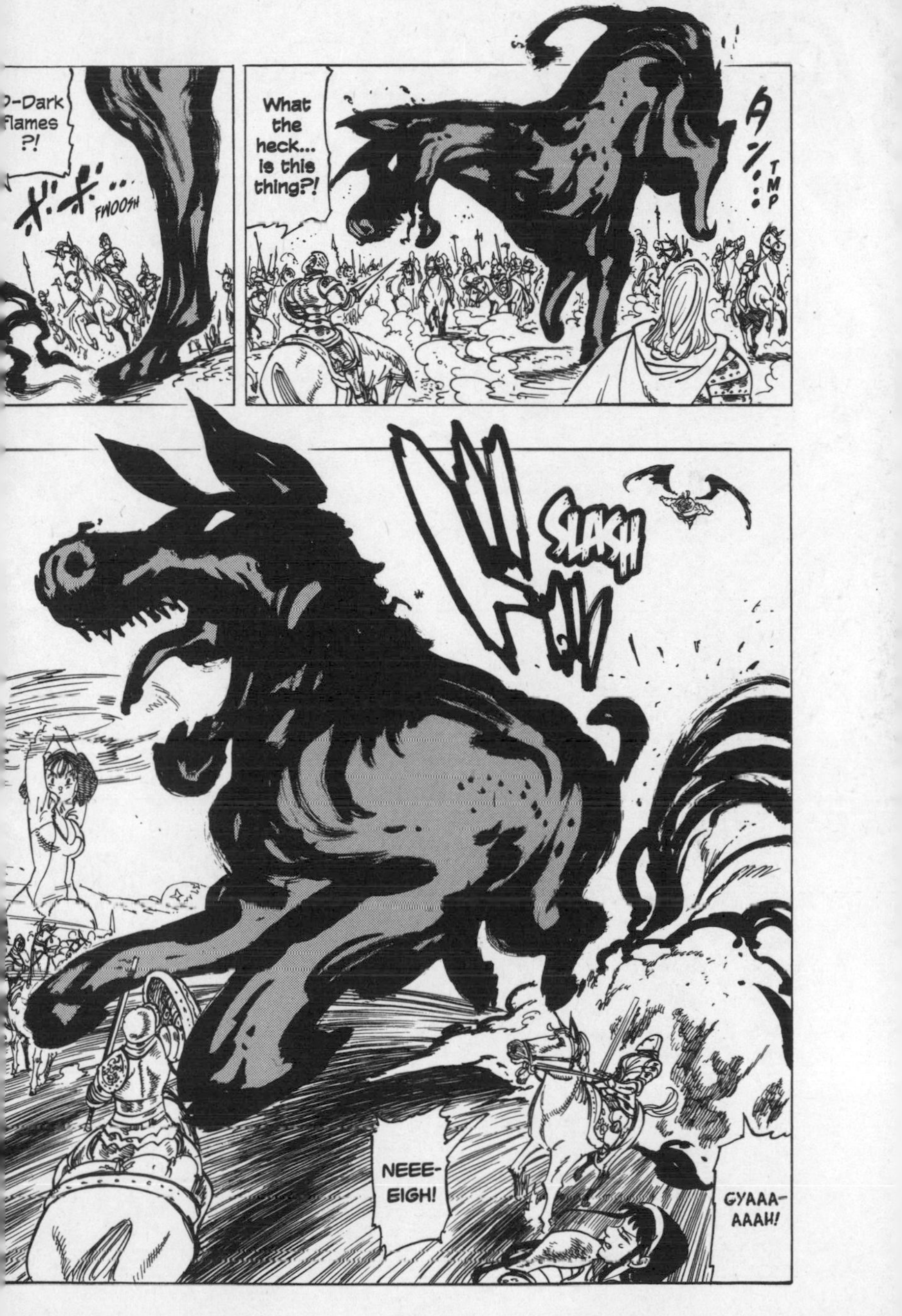

What the heck... is this thing?!
TMP
D-Dark flames?!
FWOOSH
SLASH
GYAAA-AAAH!
NEEE-EIGH!

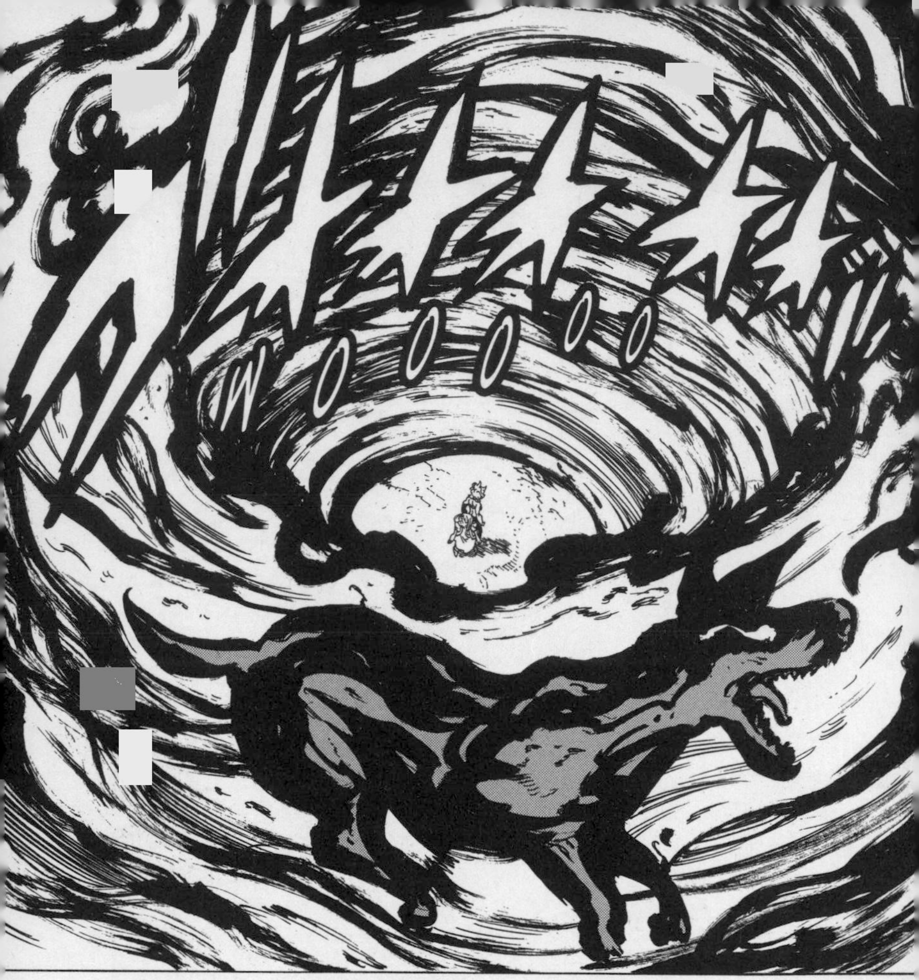
WOOOOOO
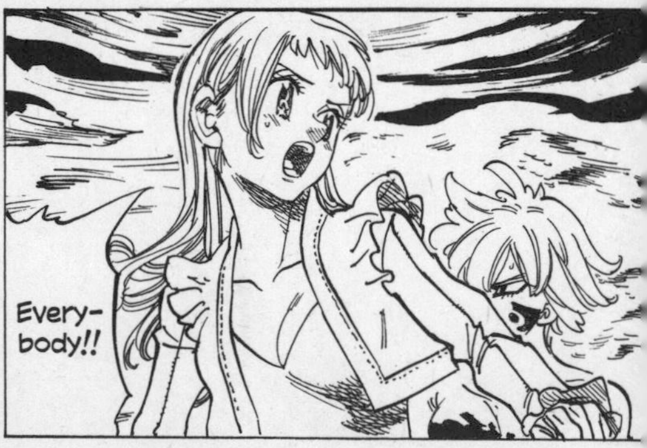
Every-
body!!
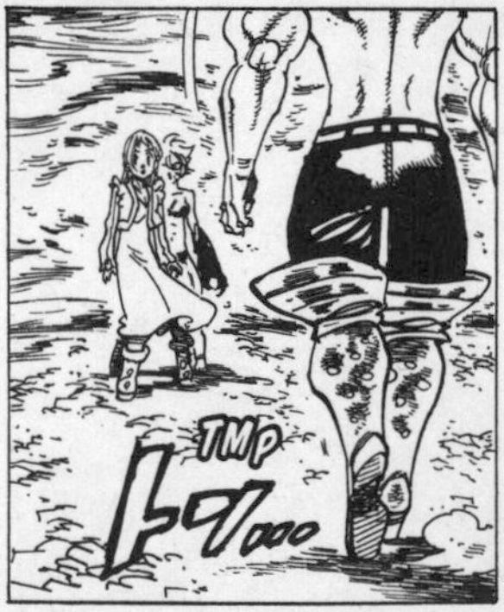
TMP

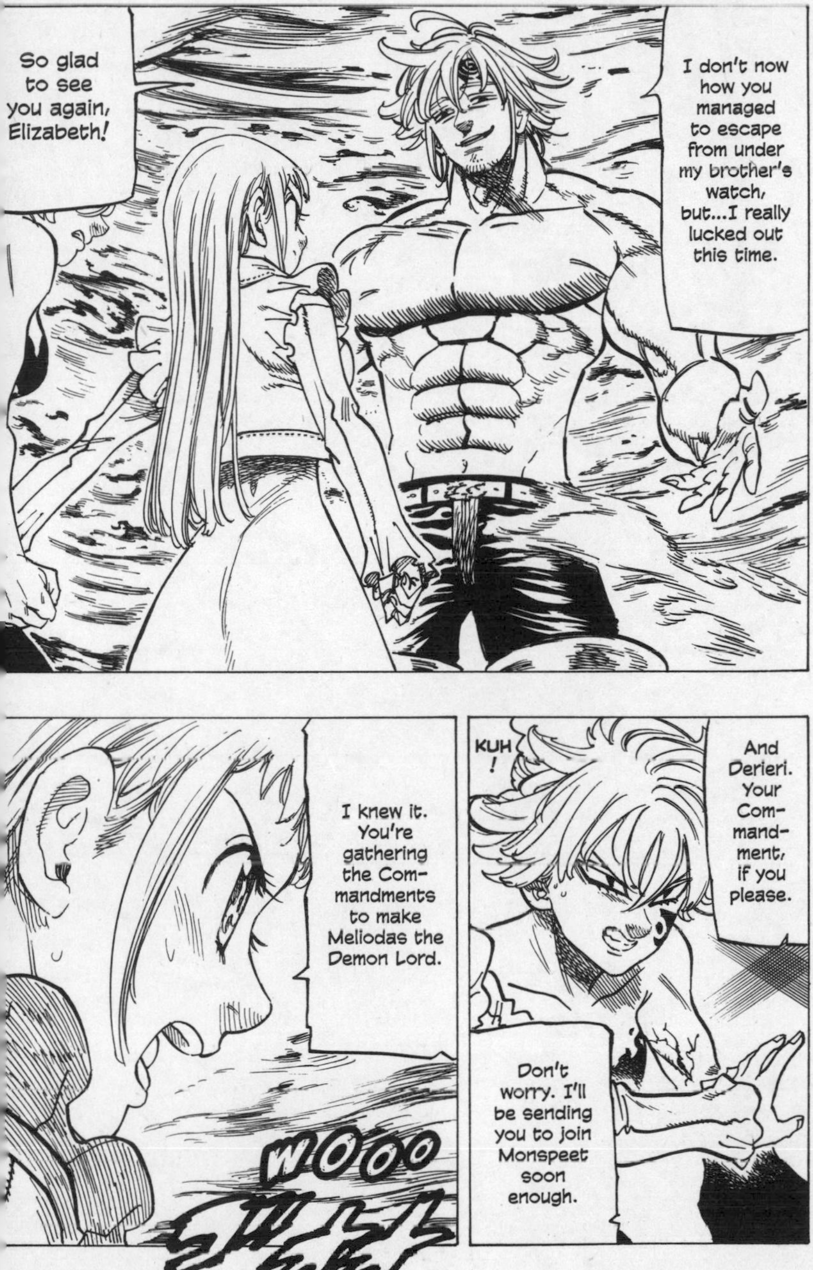

I don't now how you managed to escape from under my brother's watch, but...I really lucked out this time.
So glad to see you again, Elizabeth!
And Derieri. Your Commandment, if you please.
KUH!
Don't worry. I'll be sending you to join Monspeet soon enough.
I knew it. You're gathering the Commandments to make Meliodas the Demon Lord.
WOOO

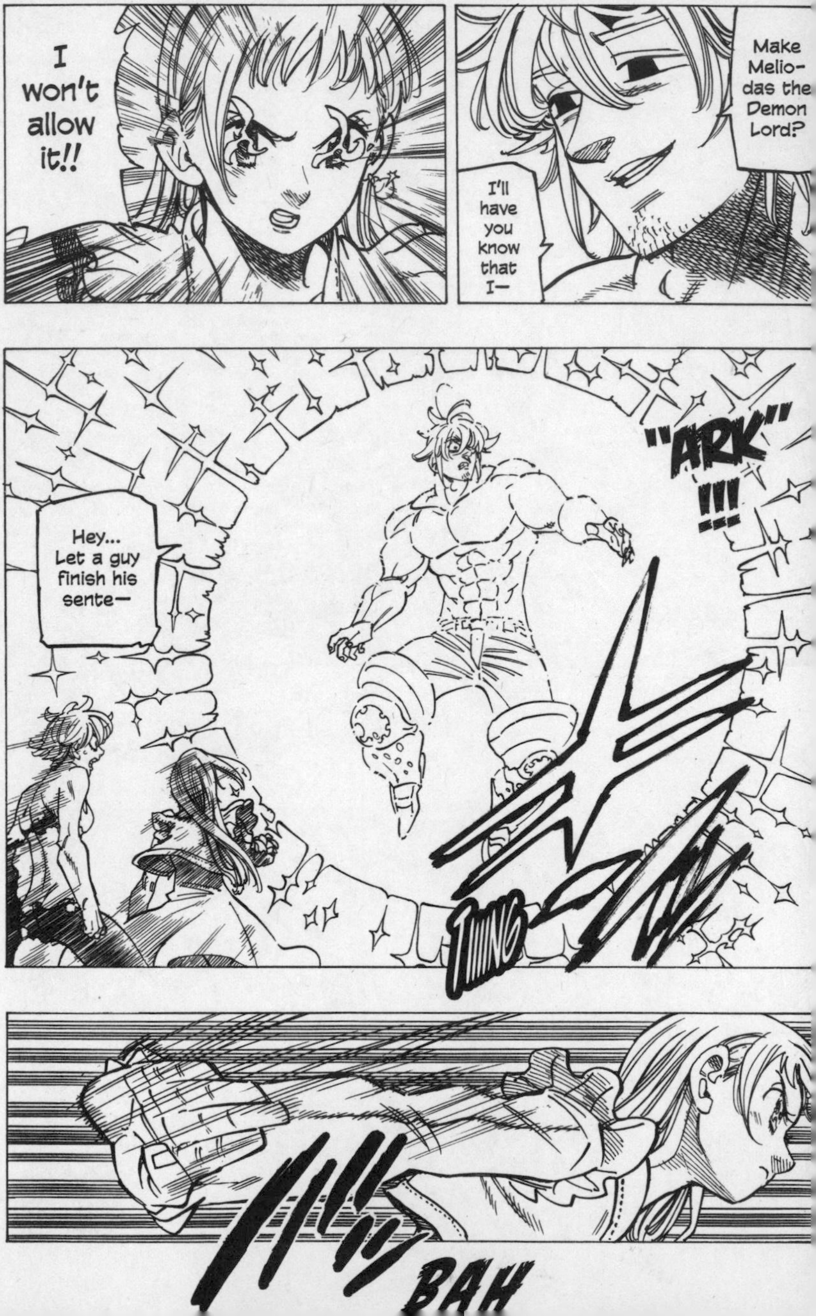
Make Melio-das the Demon Lord?
I'll have you know that I—
I won't allow it!!
"ARK"!!!
Hey... Let a guy finish his sente—
TING
BAH

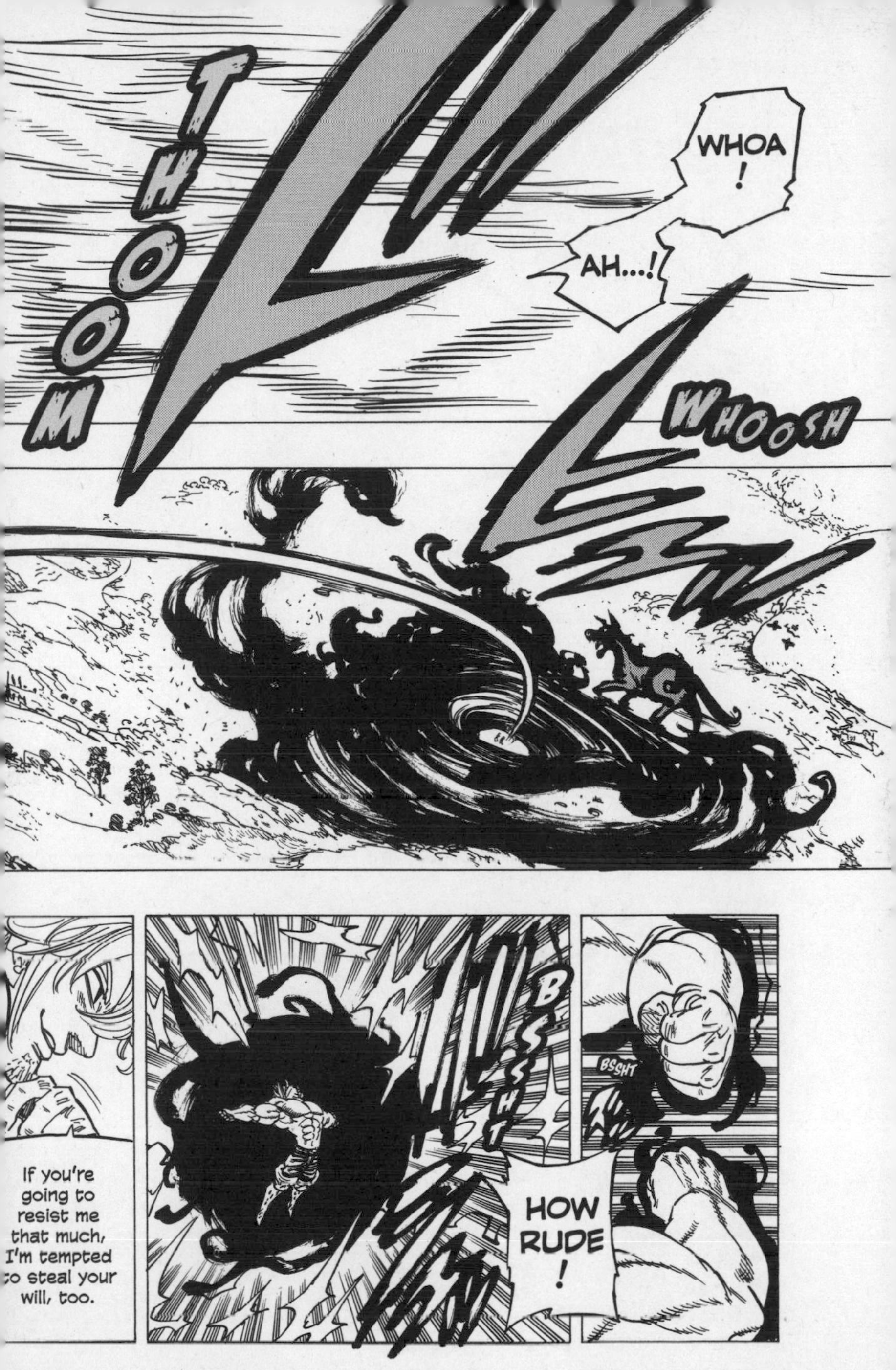
WHOA!
AH...!
THOOOM
WHOOSH
HOW RUDE!
BSSHT
BSSHT
If you're going to resist me that much, I'm tempted to steal your will, too.

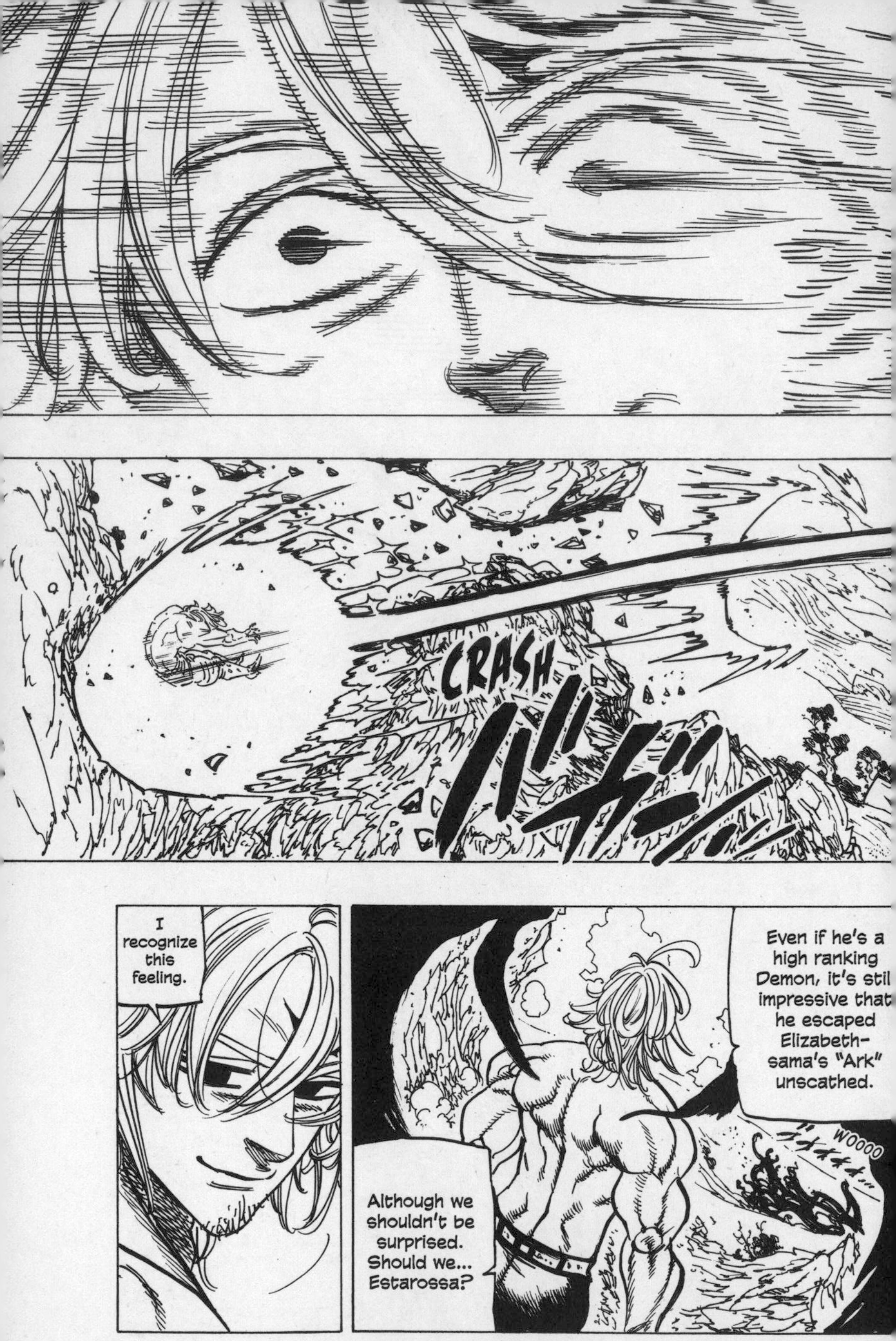
CRASH
Even if he's a high ranking Demon, it's stil impressive that he escaped Elizabeth-sama's "Ark" unscathed.
WOOOO
Although we shouldn't be surprised. Should we... Estarossa?
I recognize this feeling.

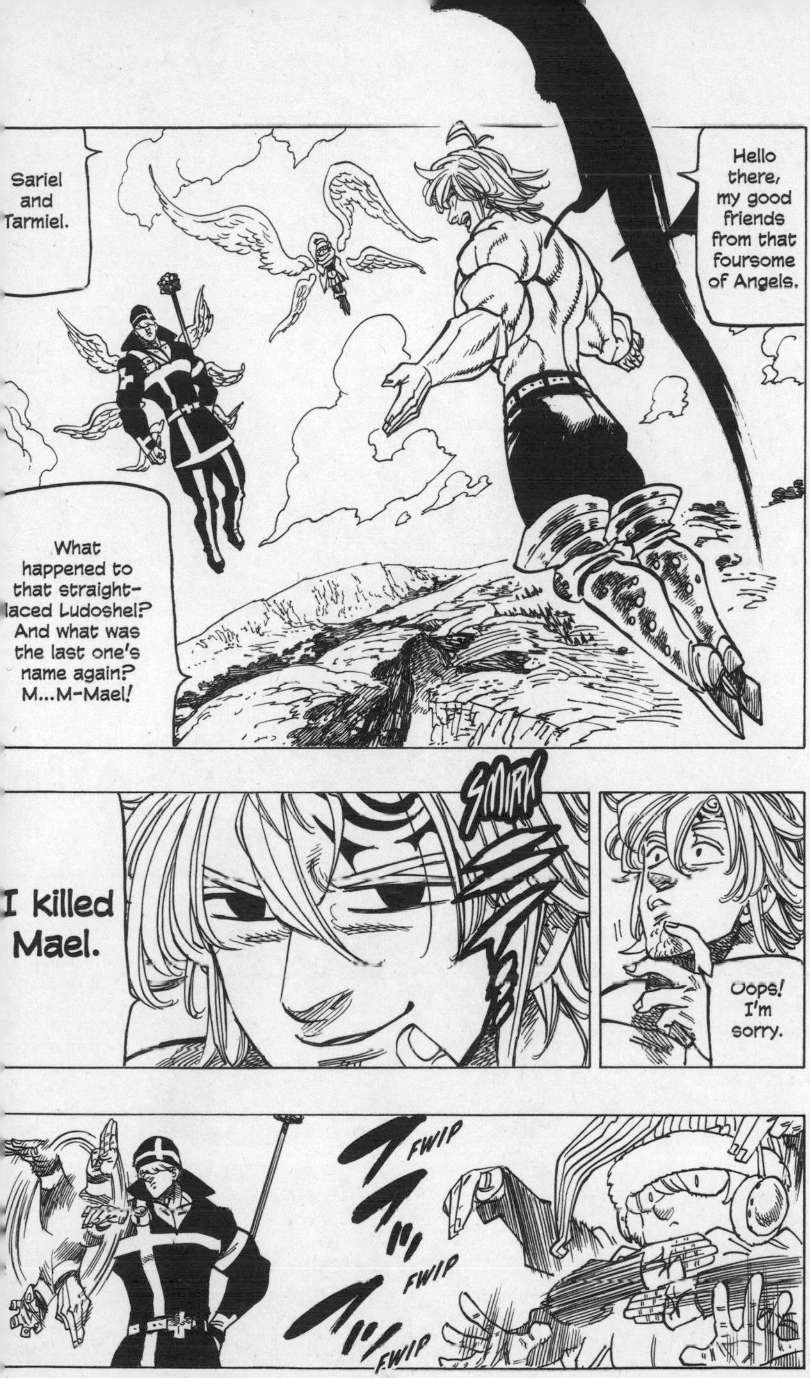

Hello there, my good friends from that foursome of Angels.
Sariel and Tarmiel.
What happened to that straight-laced Ludoshel? And what was the last one's name again? M...M-Mael!
Oops! I'm sorry.
SMIRK
I killed Mael.
FWIP
FWIP
FWIP

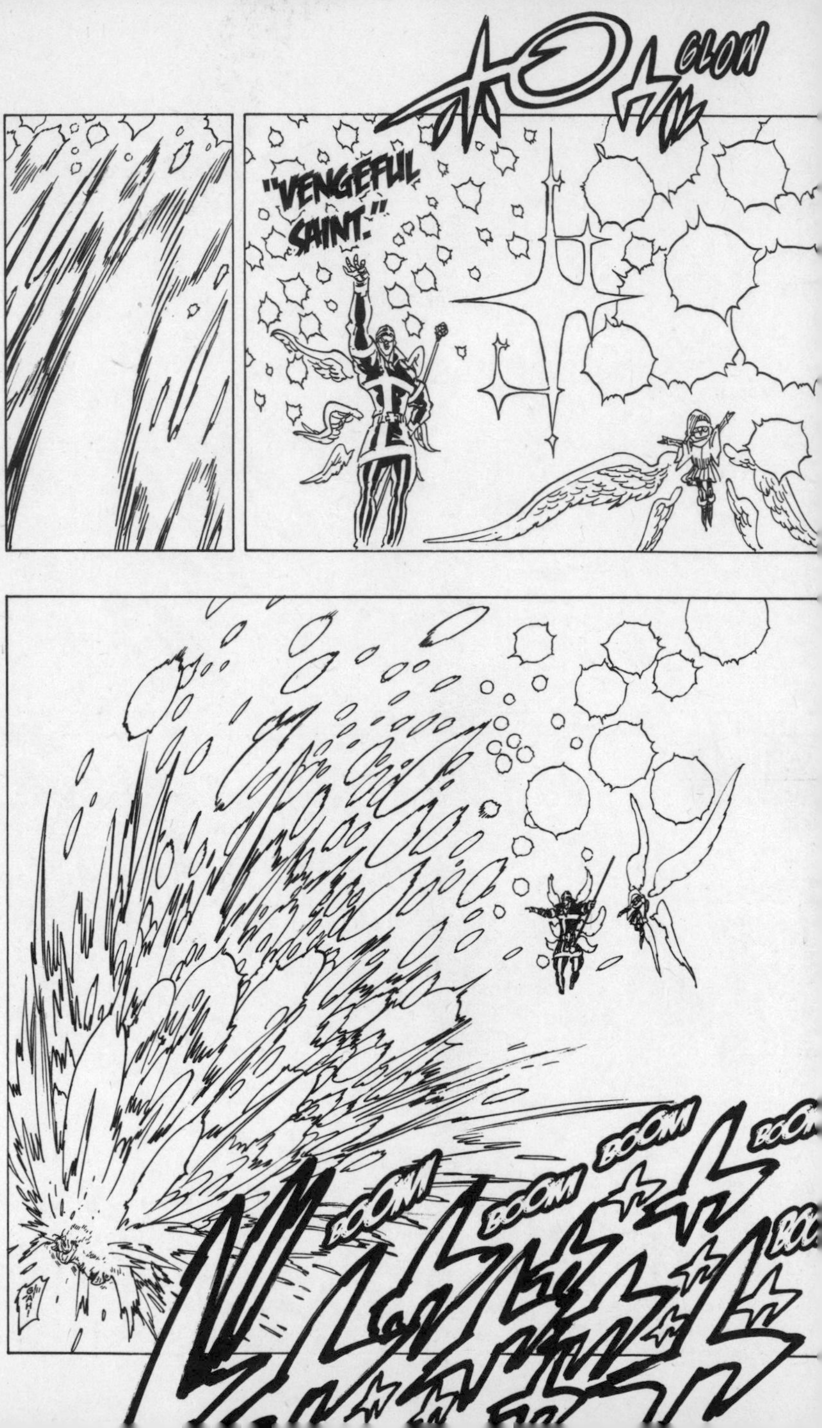
GLOW
"VENGEFUL SAINT."
BOOM
BOOM
BOOM
BOOM
BOOM
BOOM
GAH!

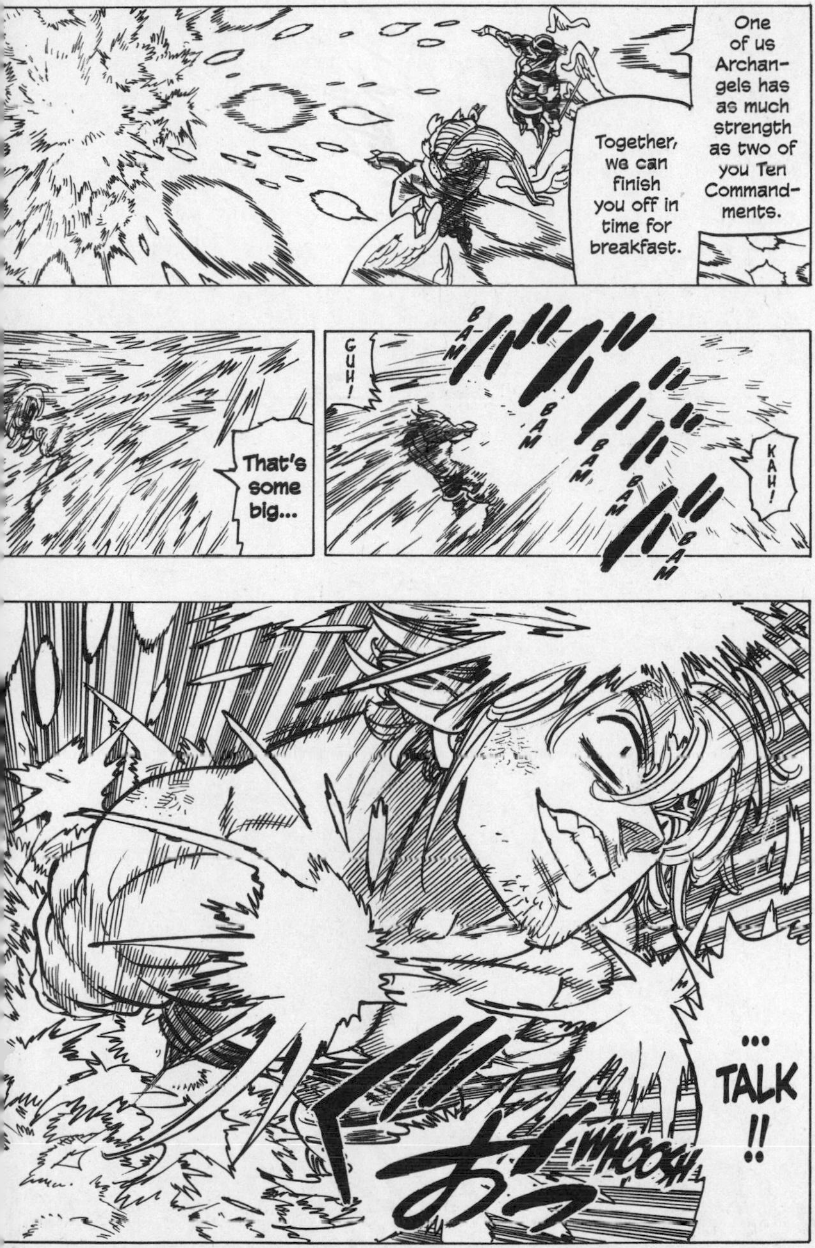
One of us Archangels has as much strength as two of you Ten Commandments.
Together, we can finish you off in time for breakfast.
KAH!
BAM BAM BAM BAM BAM BAM
GUH!
That's some big...
...TALK!!
WHOOSH

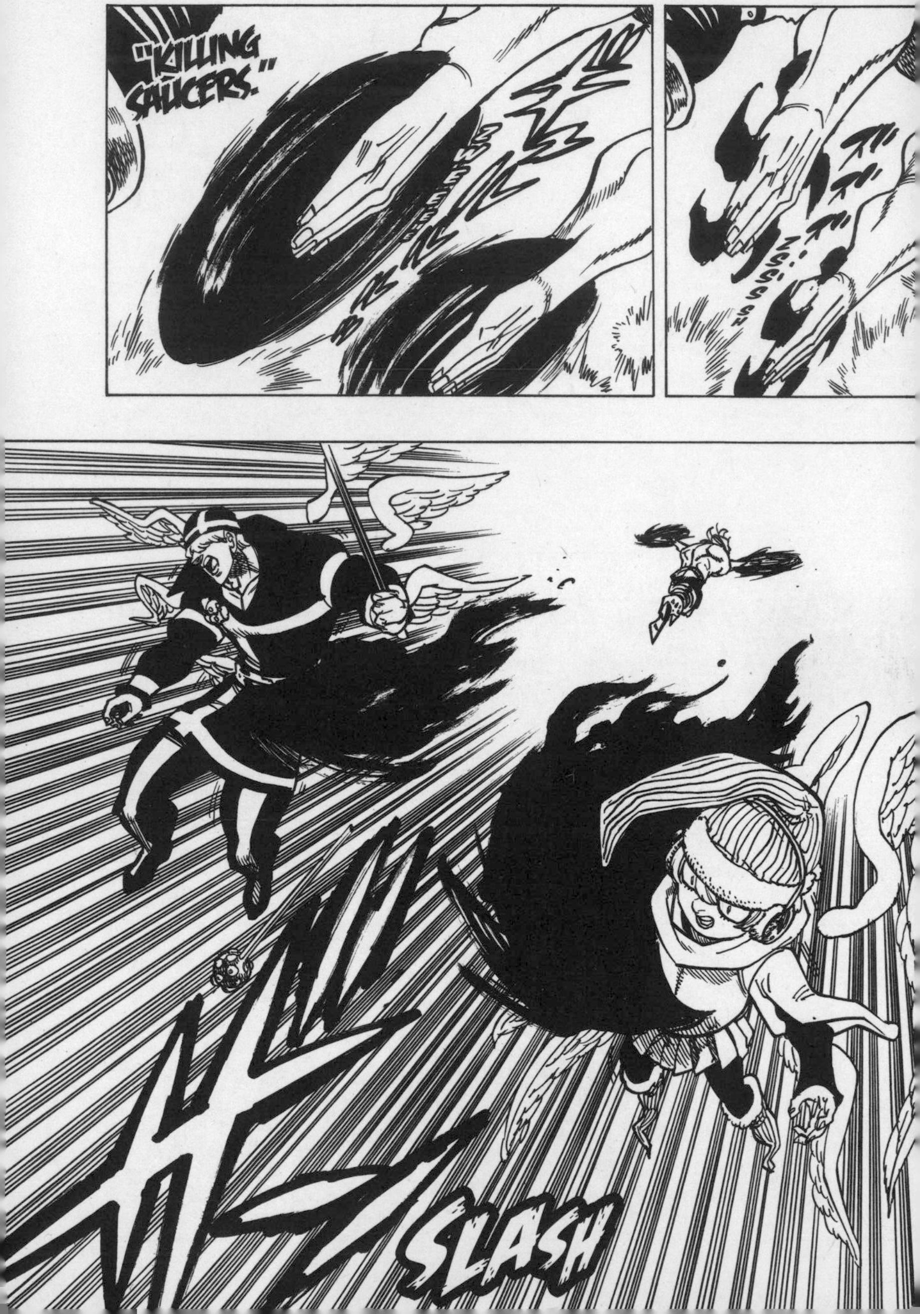
"KILLING SAUCERS."
SLASH

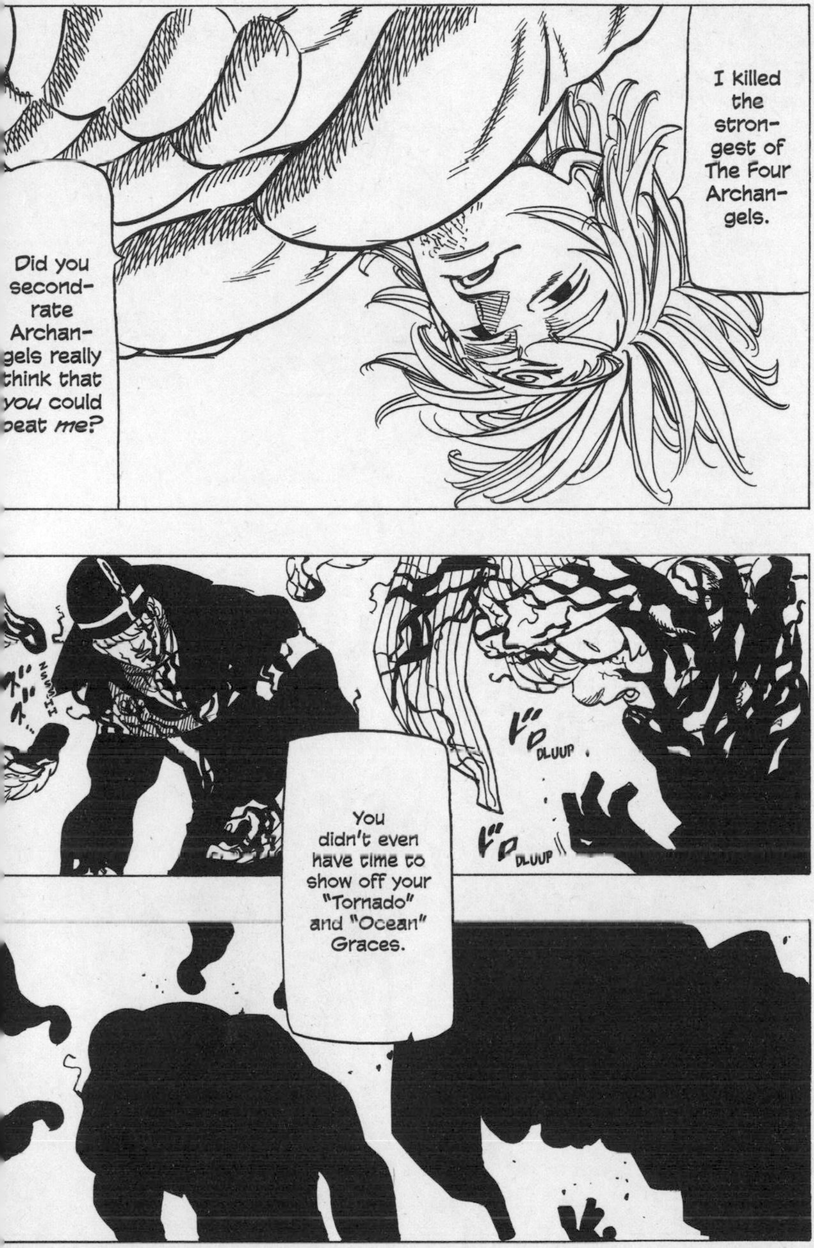
I killed the strongest of The Four Archangels.
Did you second-rate Archangels really think that *you* could beat *me*?
ドド DLUUP
ドド DLUUP
ズズ…
You didn't even have time to show off your "Tornado" and "Ocean" Graces.

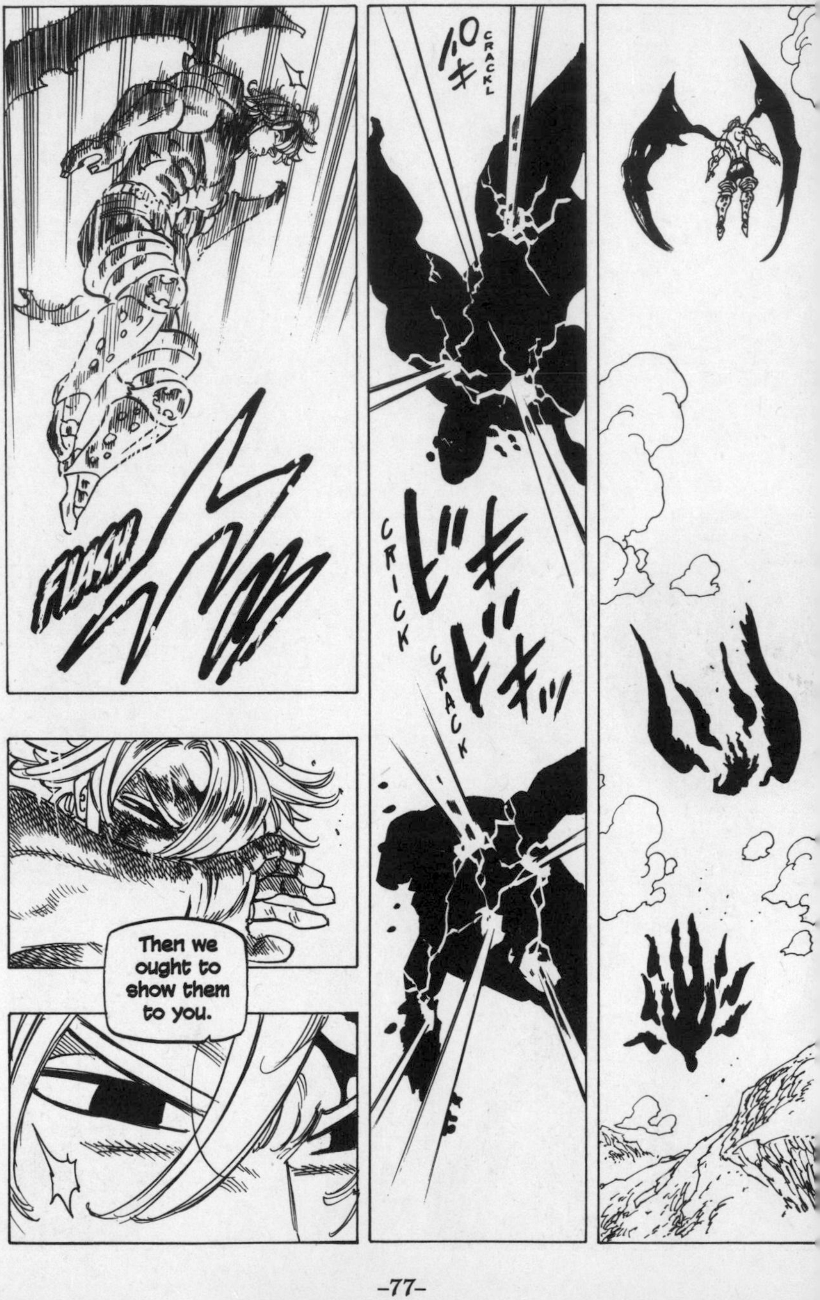
パキ
CRACKL
ビキビキッ
CRICK
CRACK
FLASH
Then we ought to show them to you.

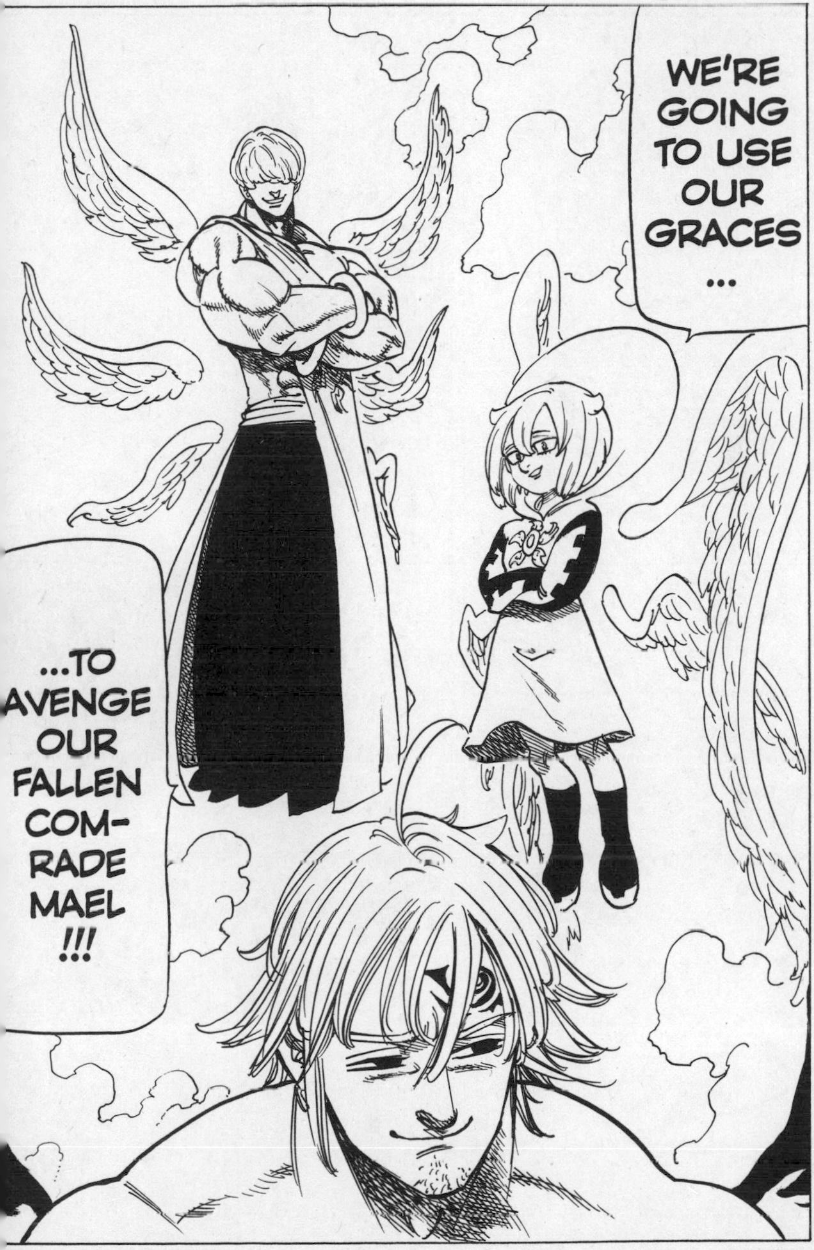
WE'RE GOING TO USE OUR GRACES ...
...TO AVENGE OUR FALLEN COM-RADE MAEL !!!

Chapter 263 - Splitting Darkness

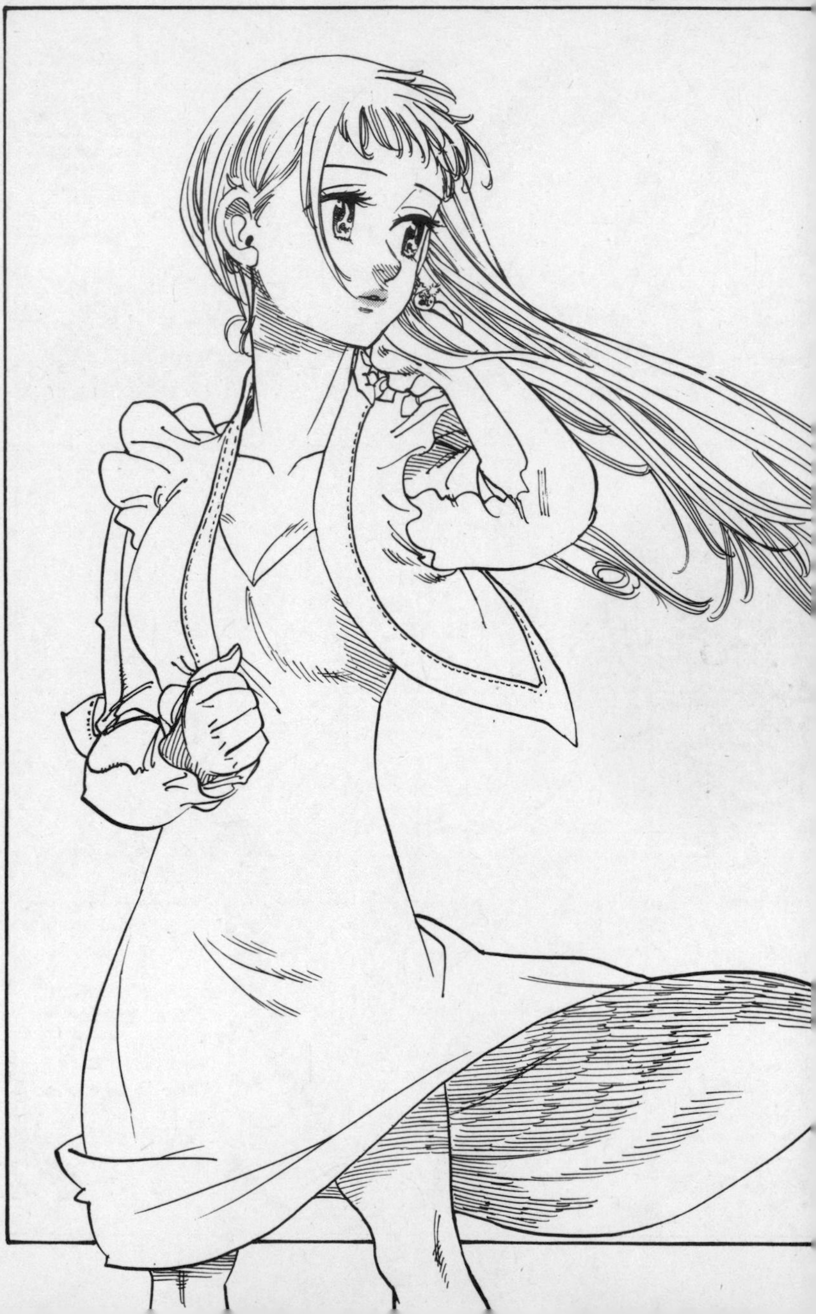

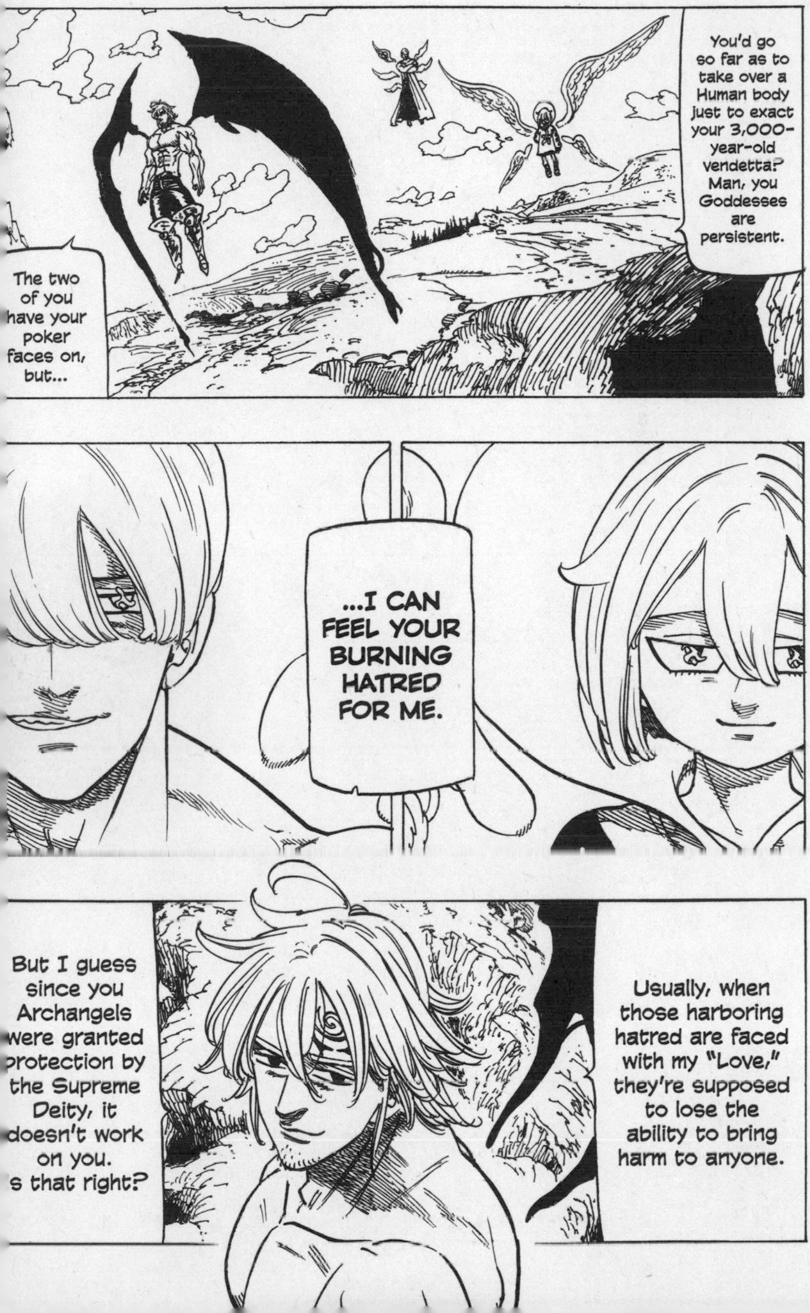
You'd go so far as to take over a Human body just to exact your 3,000-year-old vendetta? Man, you Goddesses are persistent.
The two of you have your poker faces on, but...
...I CAN FEEL YOUR BURNING HATRED FOR ME.
Usually, when those harboring hatred are faced with my "Love," they're supposed to lose the ability to bring harm to anyone.
But I guess since you Archangels were granted protection by the Supreme Deity, it doesn't work on you. 's that right?

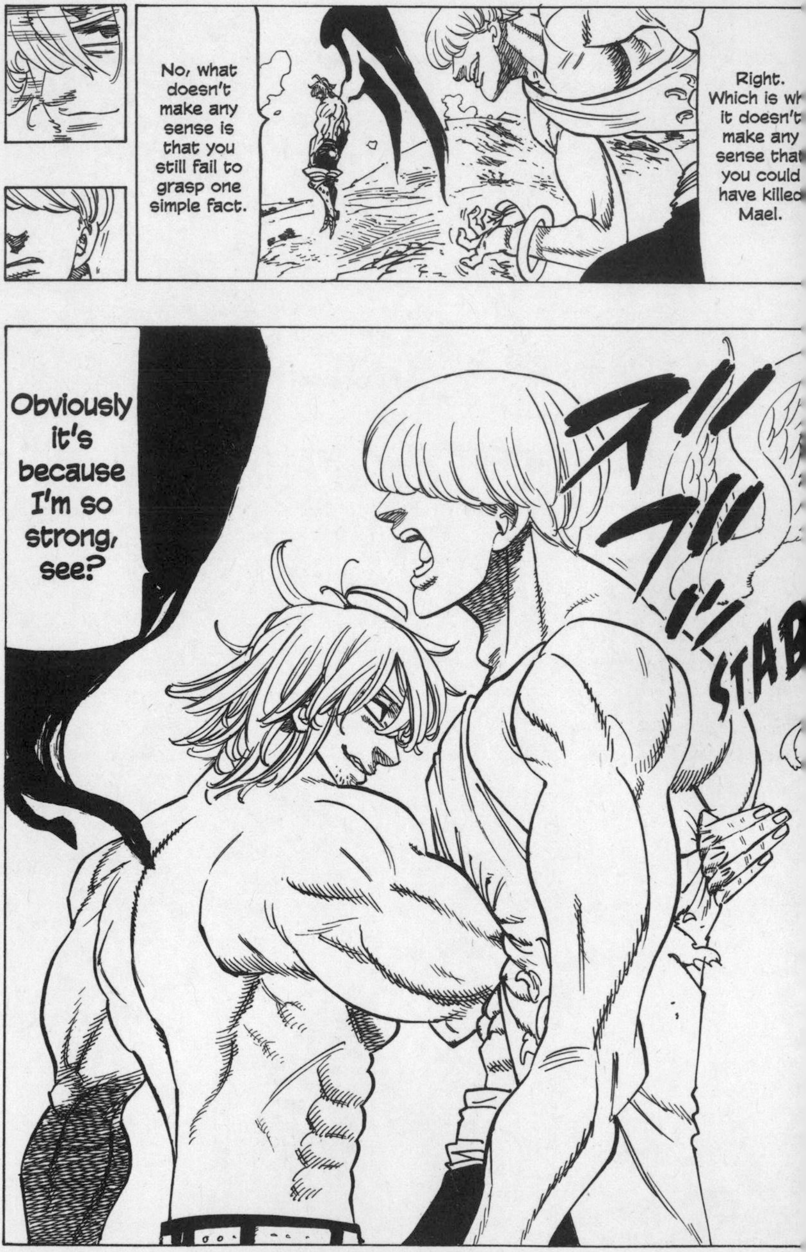
Right. Which is wh it doesn't make any sense tha you could have kille Mael.
No, what doesn't make any sense is that you still fail to grasp one simple fact.
Obviously it's because I'm so strong, see?
STAB

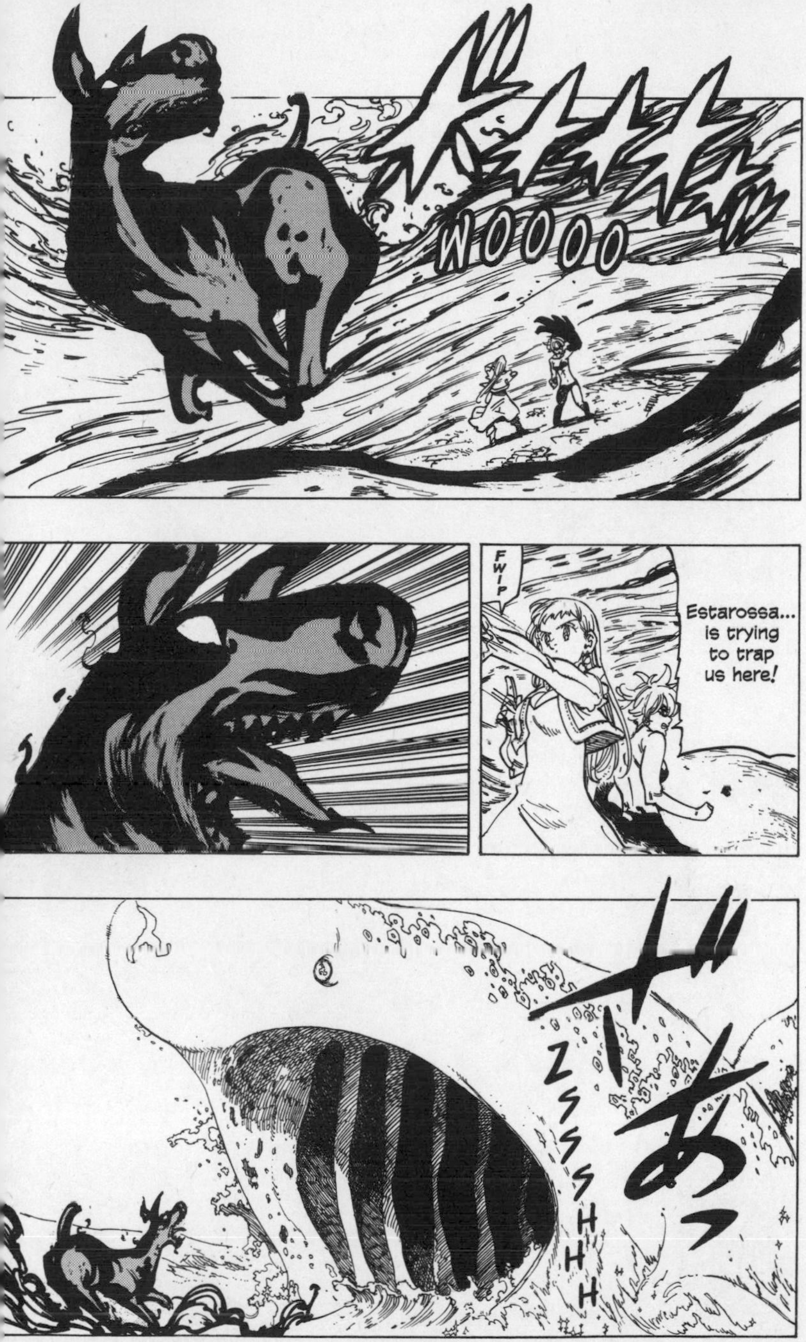
WOOOO
FWIP
Estarossa... is trying to trap us here!
ZSSSHHHH

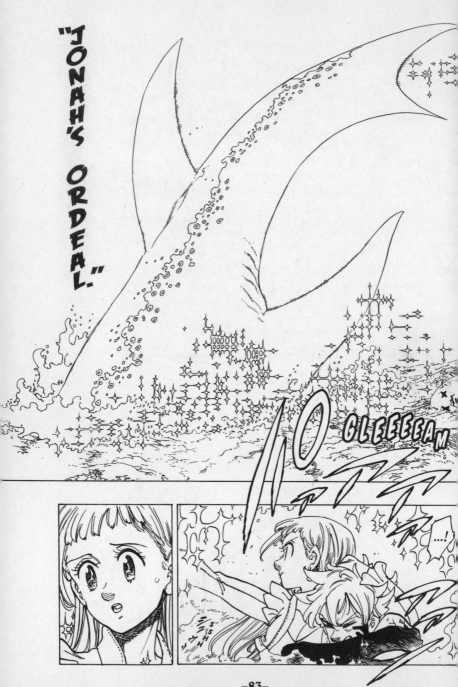

"JONAH'S ORDEAL."

GLEEEEAM

....!

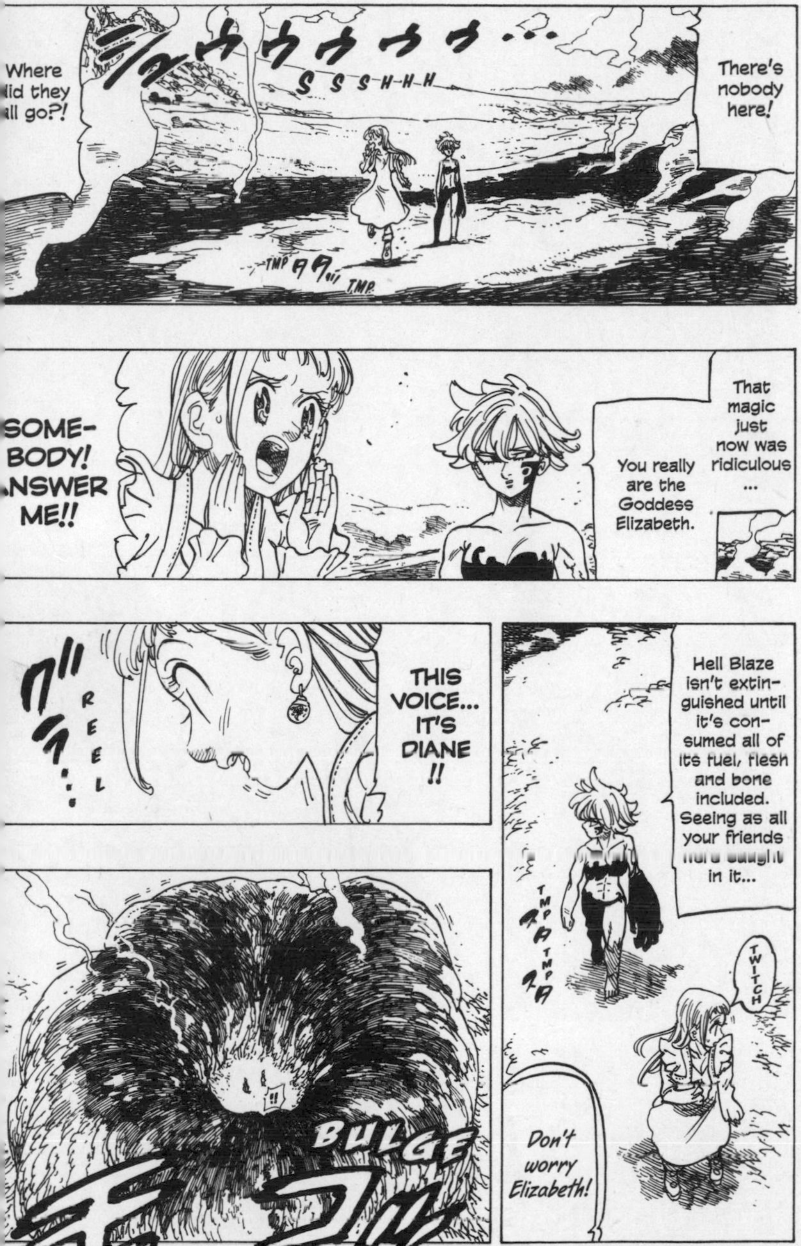
S S S-H-H-H
There's nobody here!
Where lid they ll go?!
TMP TMP
That magic just now was ridiculous...
You really are the Goddess Elizabeth.
SOME-BODY! NSWER ME!!
Hell Blaze isn't extin-guished until it's con-sumed all of its fuel, flesh and bone included. Seeing as all your friends were caught in it...
TMP TMP
TWITCH
Don't worry Elizabeth!
THIS VOICE... IT'S DIANE!!
REEL
BULGE

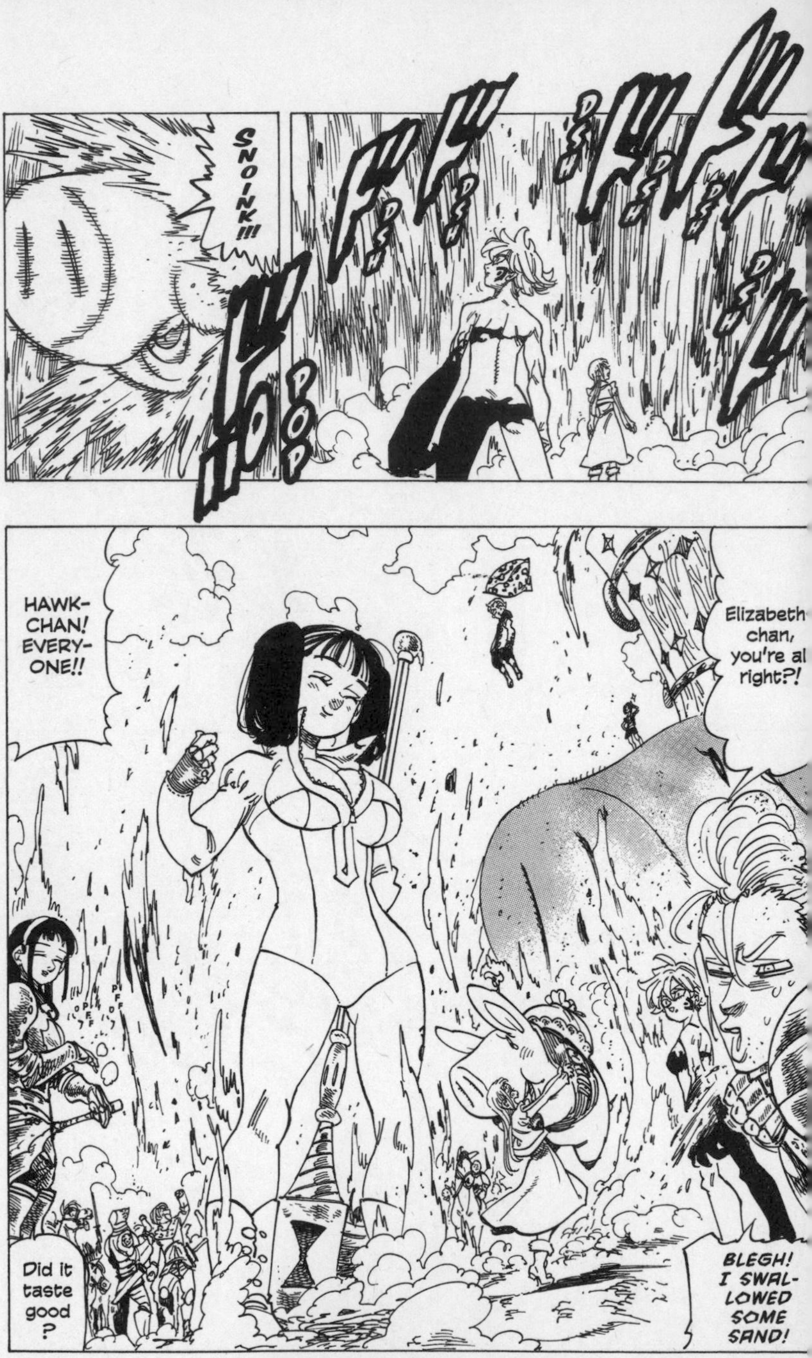
DSH
DSH
DSH
DSH
DSH
DSH
DSH
SNOINK!!!
POP
POP
Elizabeth chan, you're al right?!
HAWK-CHAN! EVERY-ONE!!
BLEGH! I SWAL-LOWED SOME SAND!
Did it taste good?

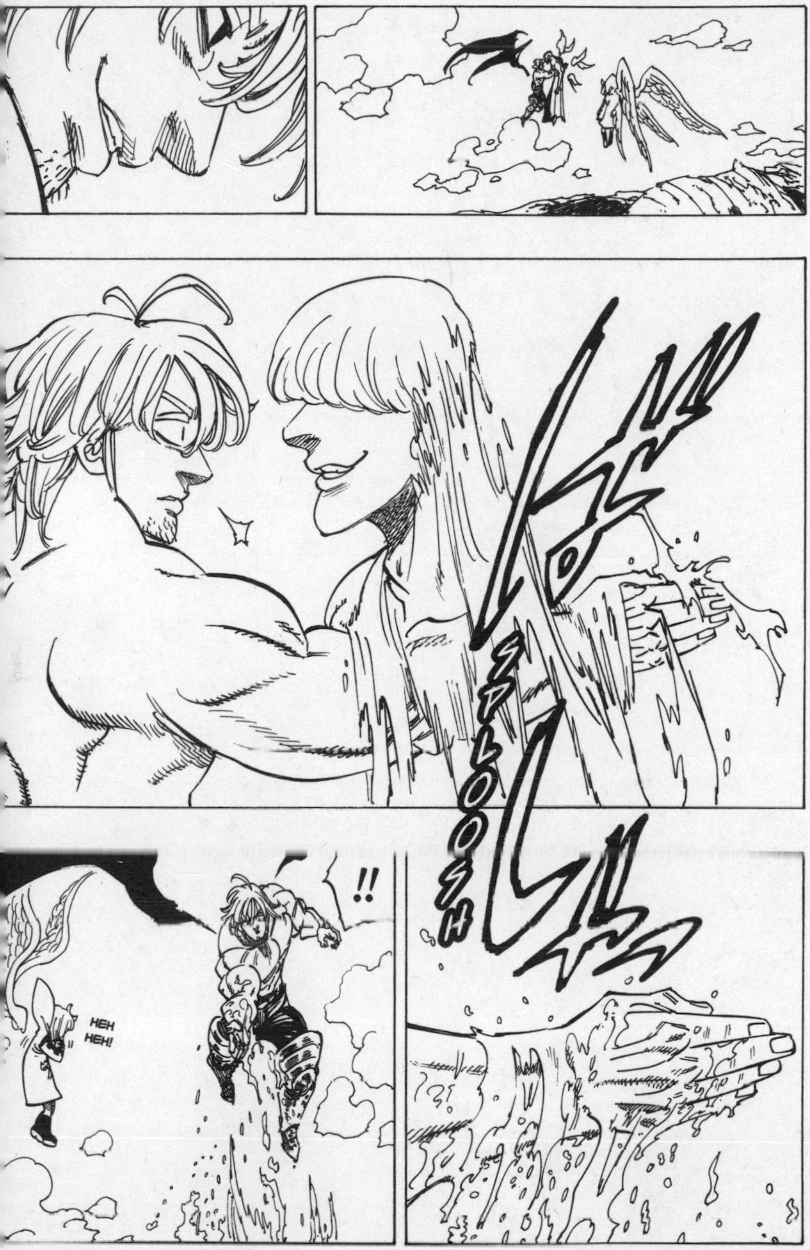
SPLOOOSH
!!
HEH HEH!

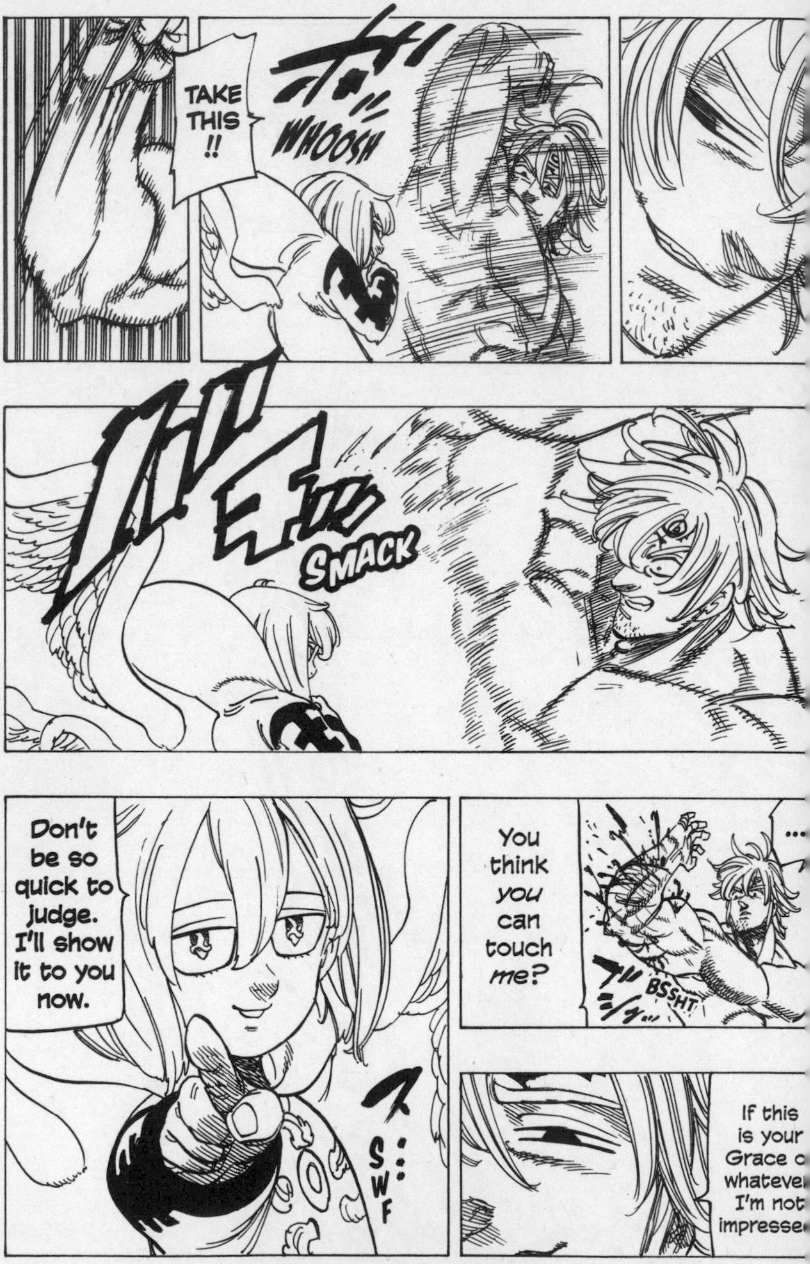
TAKE THIS !!
WHOOSH
SMACK
...
BSSHT
You think *you* can touch *me*?
If this is your Grace o whateve I'm not impresse
Don't be so quick to judge. I'll show it to you now.
SWF

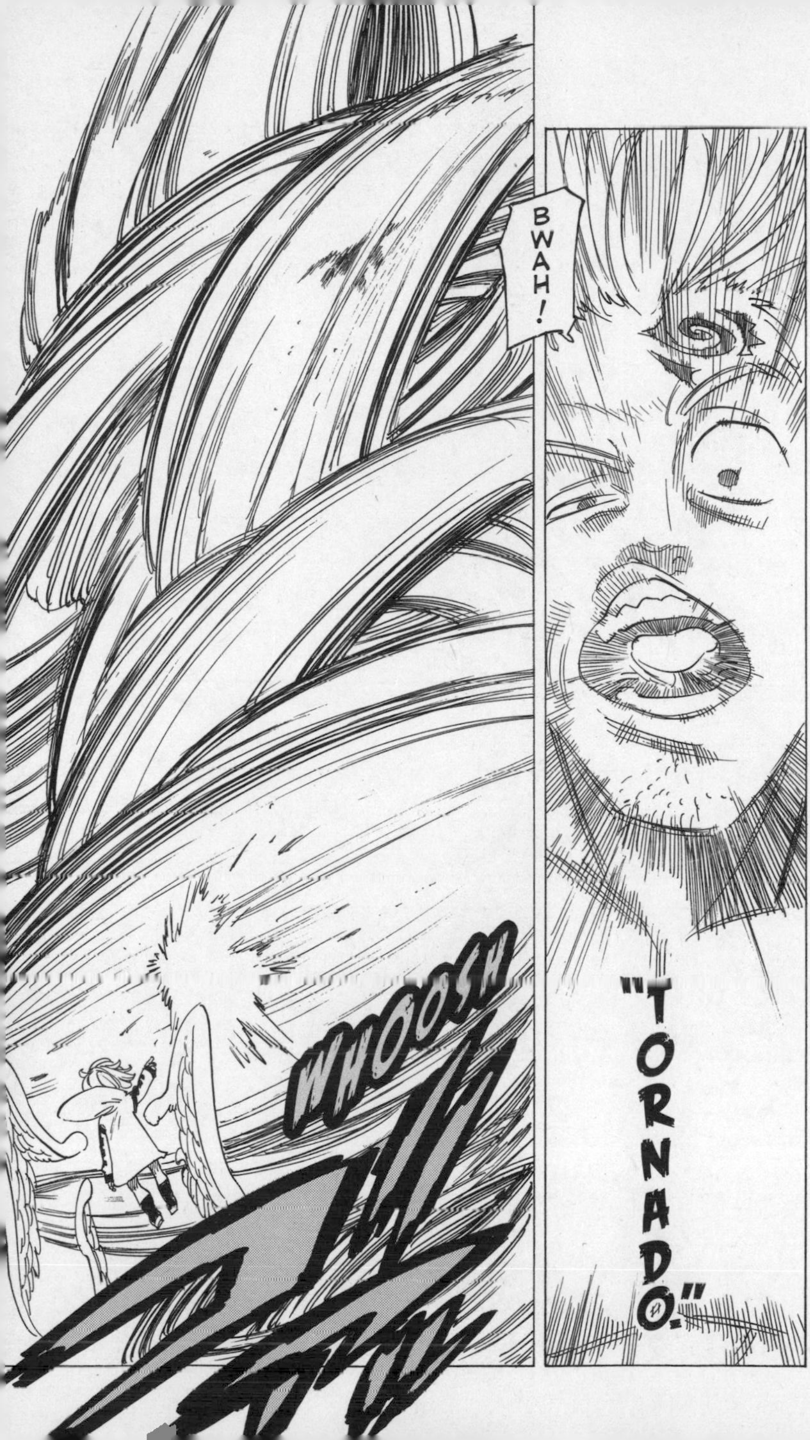
BWAH!
"TORNADO."
WHOOSH

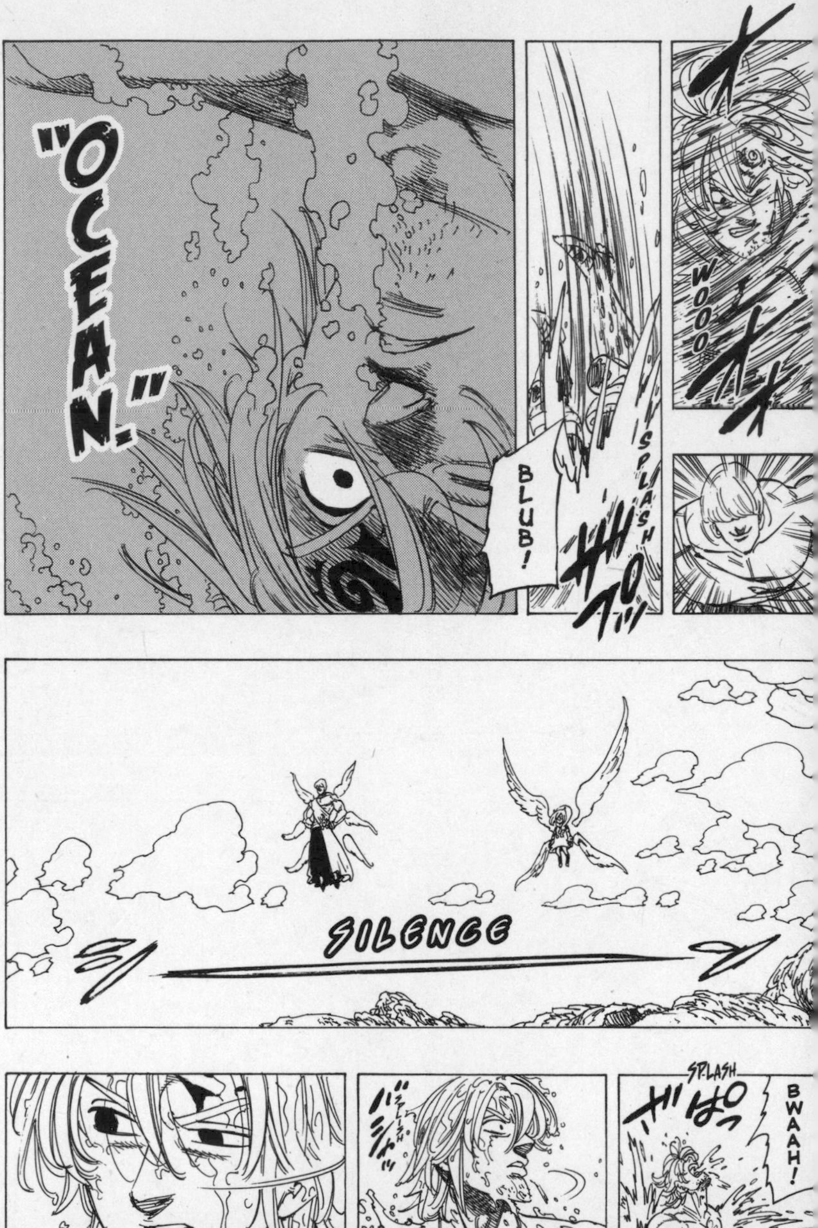
WOOO
SPLASH
BLUB!
"OCEAN."
SILENCE
SPLASH
BWAAH!

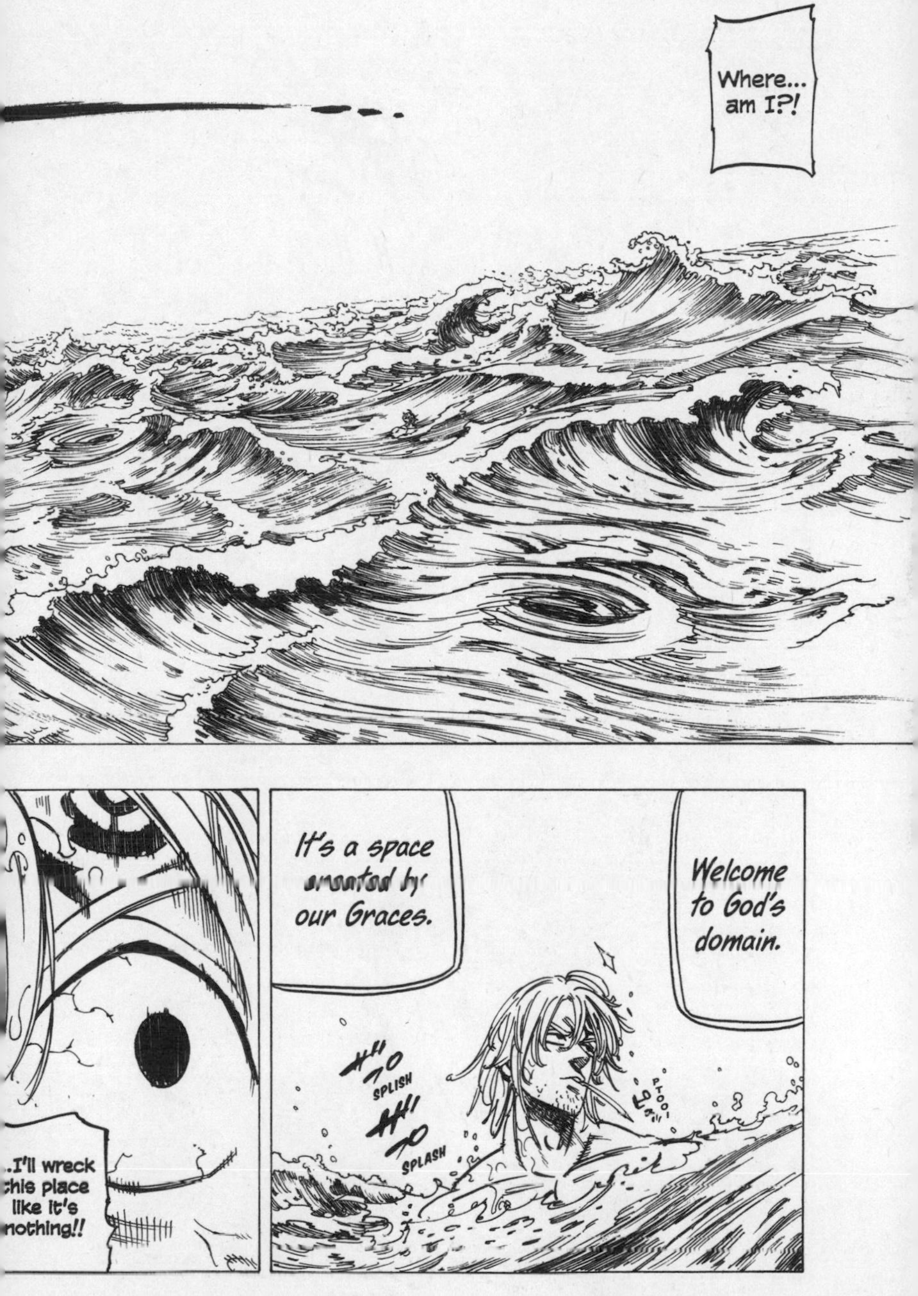
Where... am I?!
Welcome to God's domain.
It's a space created by our Graces.
PTOO!
SPLISH
SPLASH
...I'll wreck this place like it's nothing!!

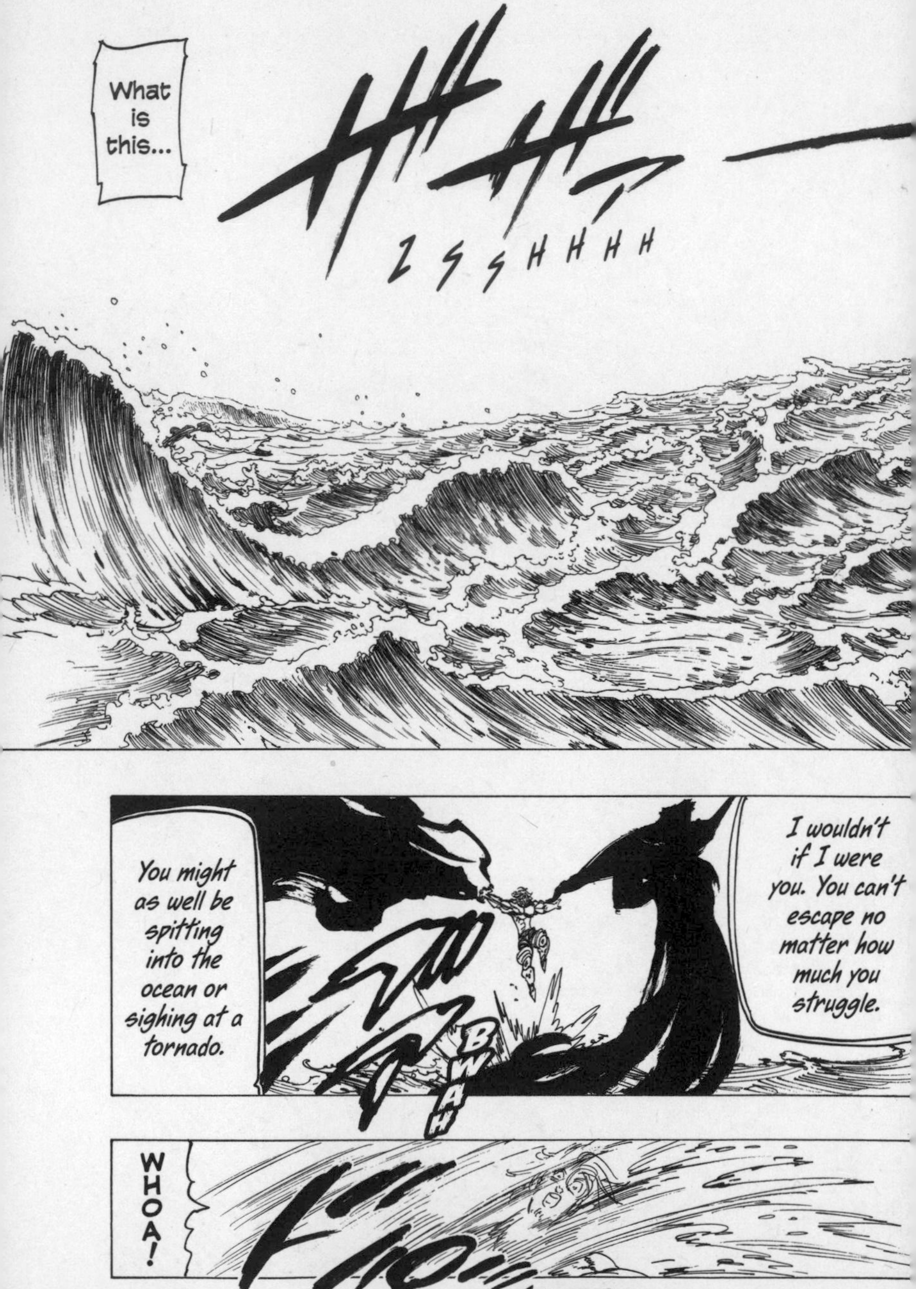
What is this...
ZSSHHHH
I wouldn't if I were you. You can't escape no matter how much you struggle.
You might as well be spitting into the ocean or sighing at a tornado.
BWAH
WHOA!
SPLOOSH

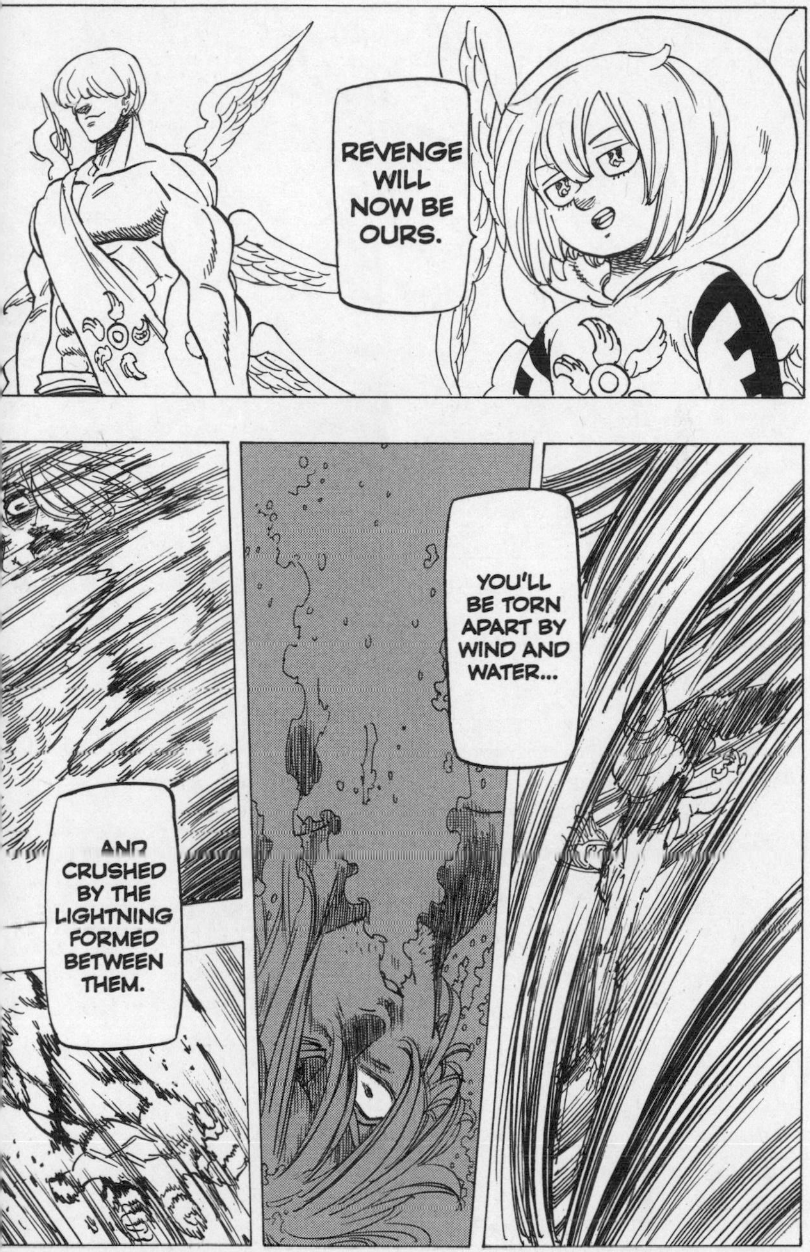
REVENGE WILL NOW BE OURS.
YOU'LL BE TORN APART BY WIND AND WATER...
AND CRUSHED BY THE LIGHTNING FORMED BETWEEN THEM.

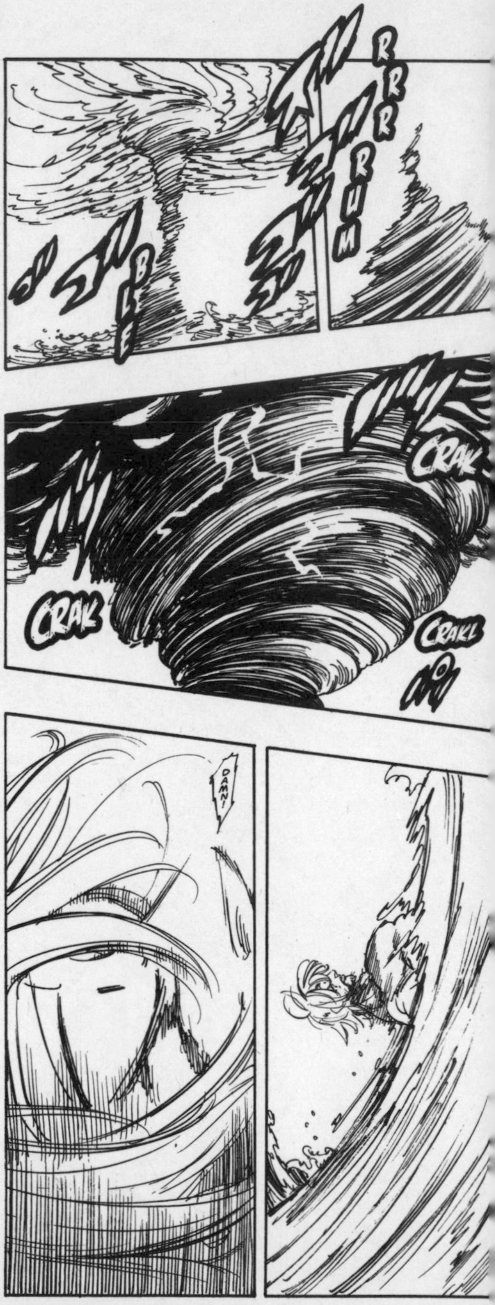
RRRRUM
BLE
CRAK
CRAKL
CRAK
DAMN!

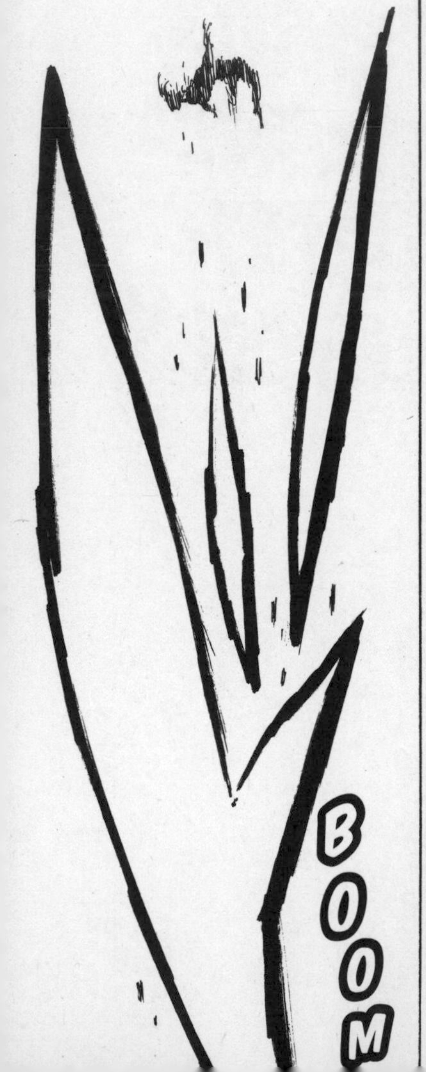
BOOM

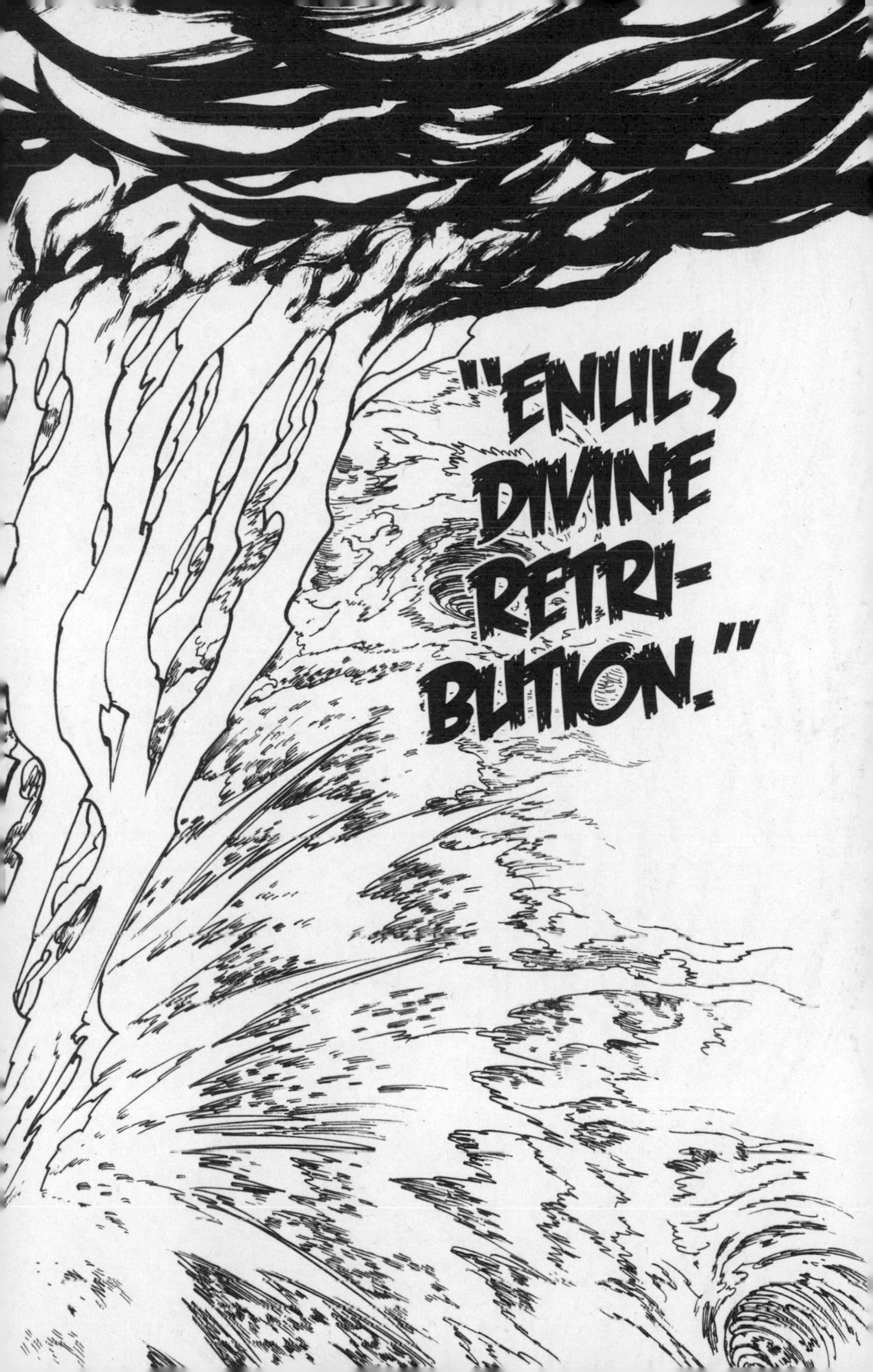
"ENLIL'S DIVINE RETRI-BUTION."

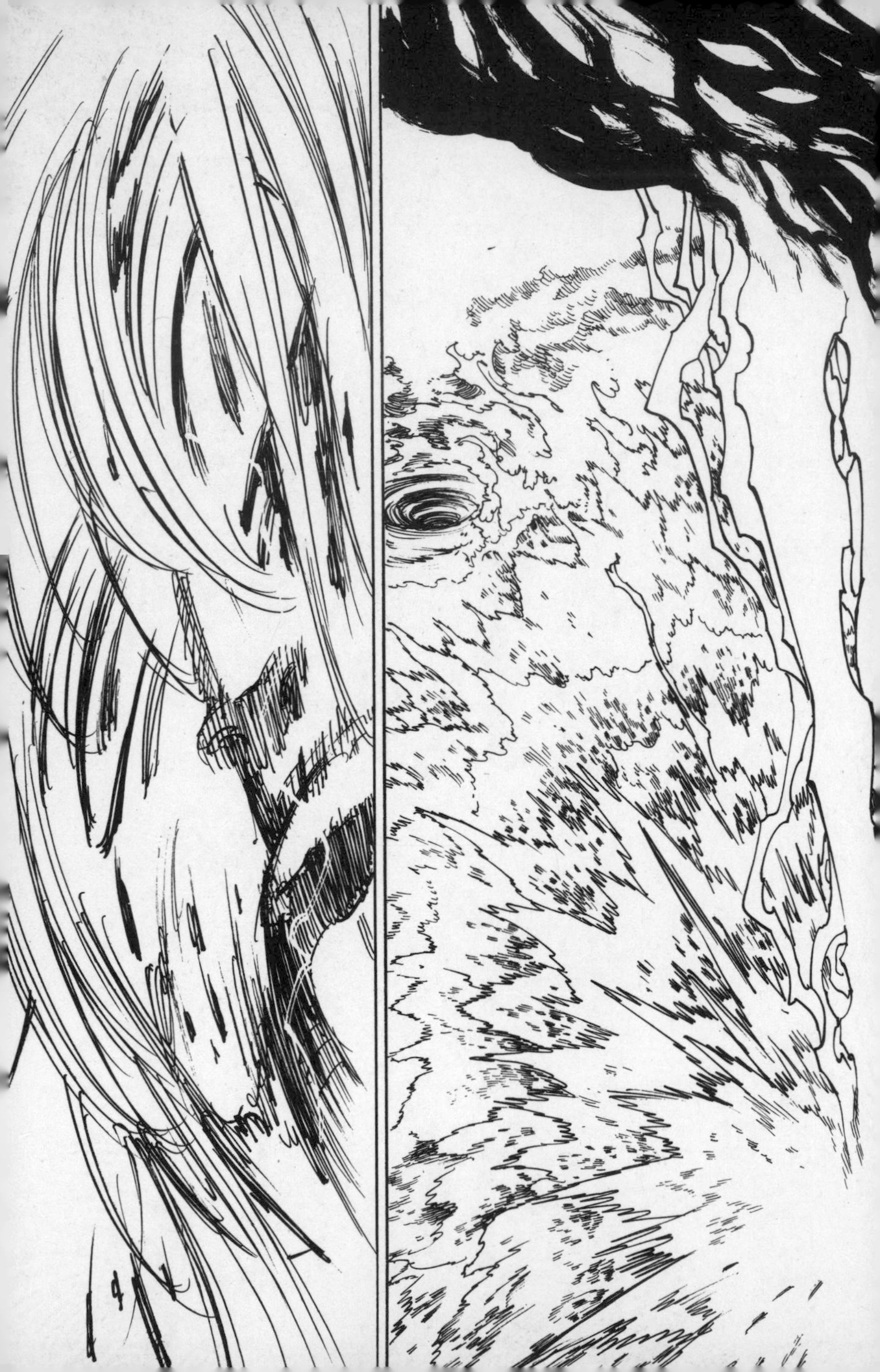

Rejected Clothing Designs ①

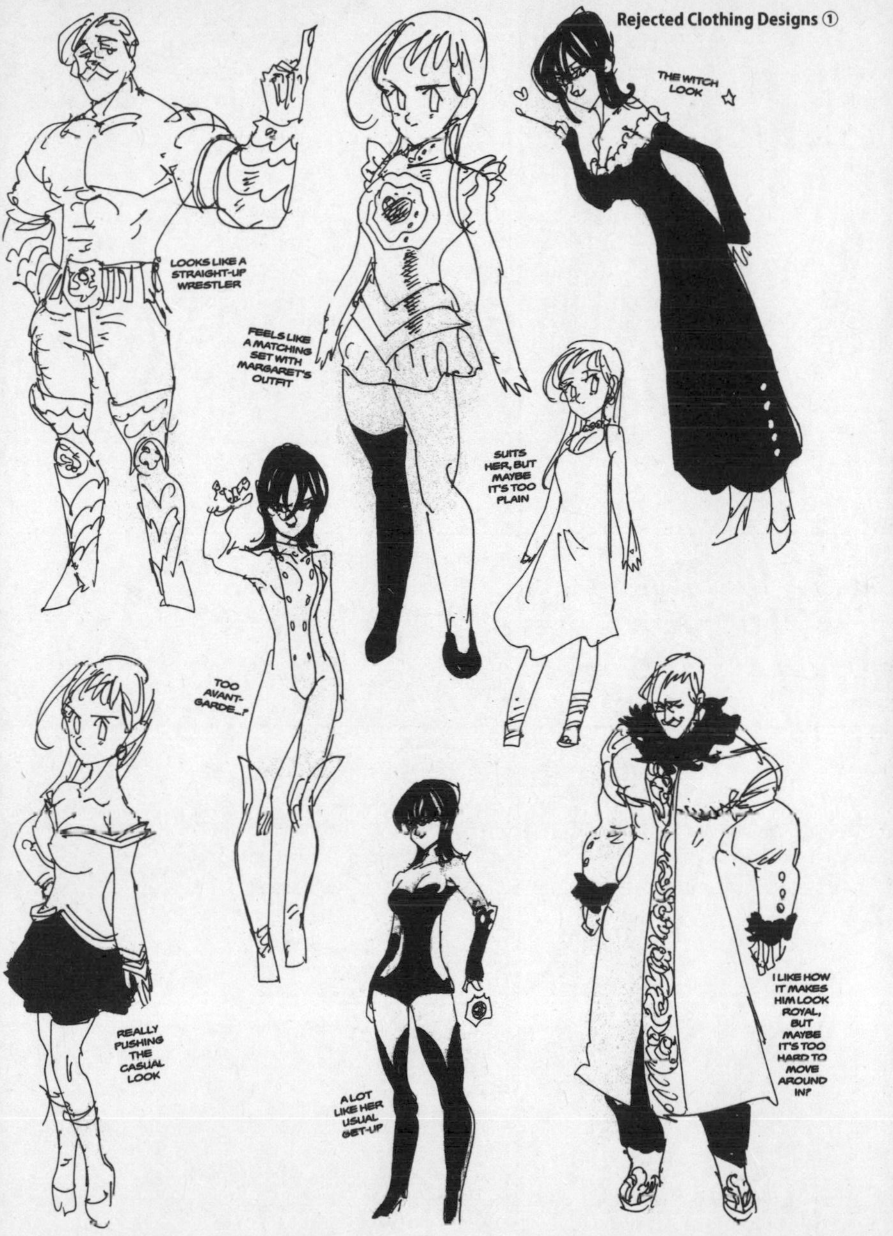
THE WITCH LOOK
LOOKS LIKE A STRAIGHT-UP WRESTLER
FEELS LIKE A MATCHING SET WITH MARGARET'S OUTFIT
SUITS HER, BUT MAYBE IT'S TOO PLAIN
TOO AVANT-GARDE...?
I LIKE HOW IT MAKES HIM LOOK ROYAL, BUT MAYBE IT'S TOO HARD TO MOVE AROUND IN?
REALLY PUSHING THE CASUAL LOOK
A LOT LIKE HER USUAL GET-UP

Chapter 264 - A Warped, Twisted, and Broken Man

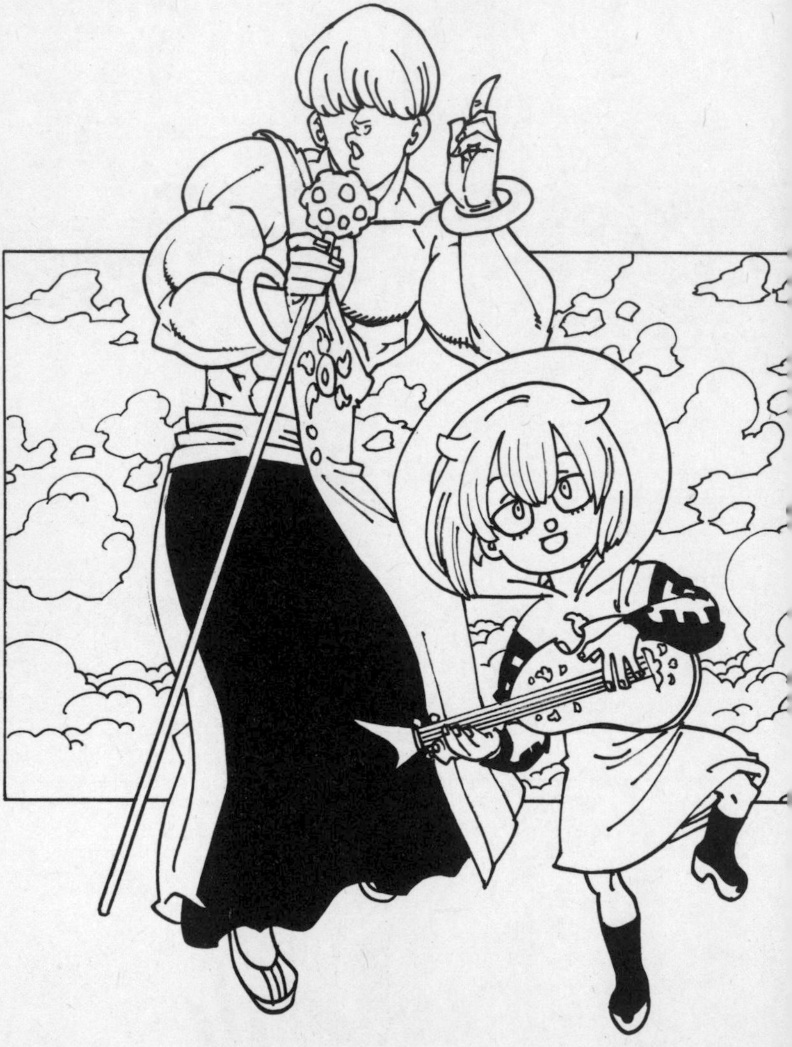

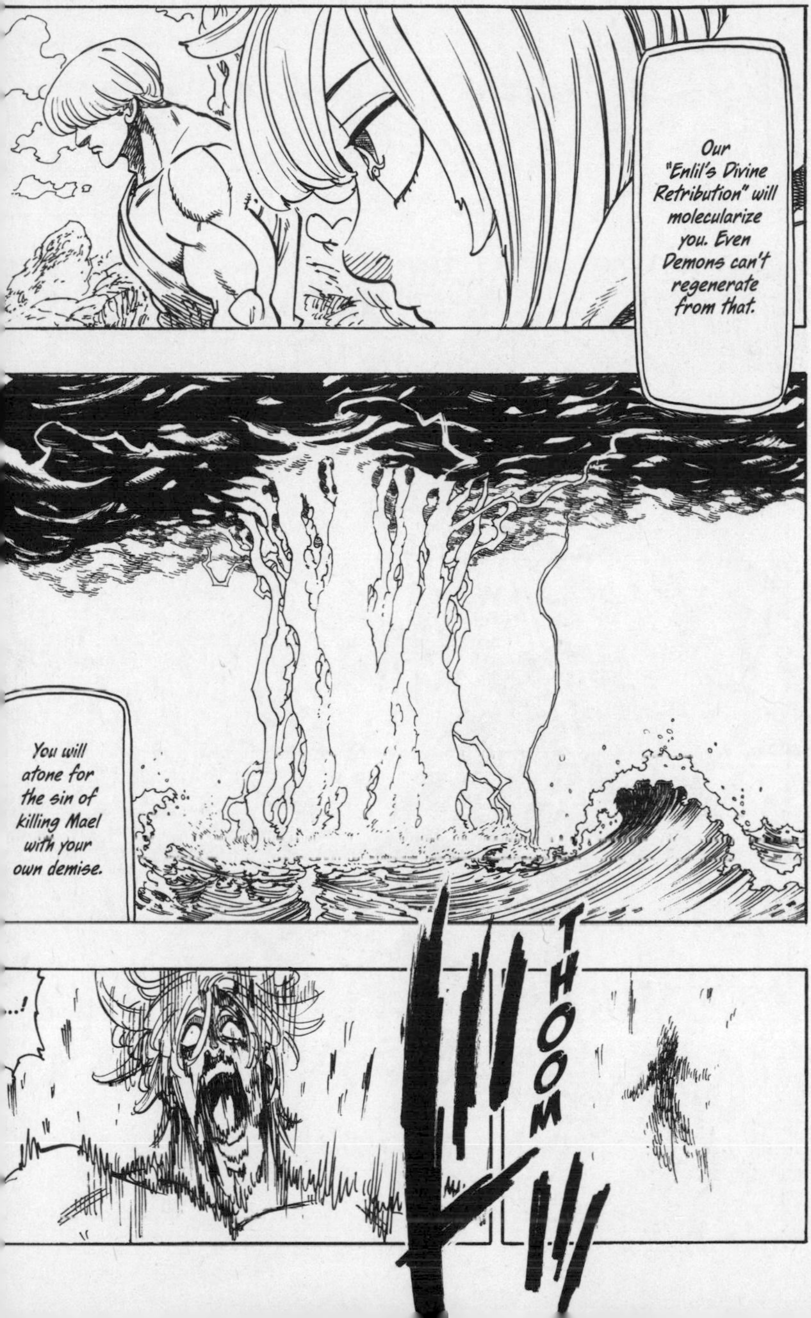
Our "Enlil's Divine Retribution" will molecularize you. Even Demons can't regenerate from that.
You will atone for the sin of killing Mael with your own demise.
THOOOM
...!

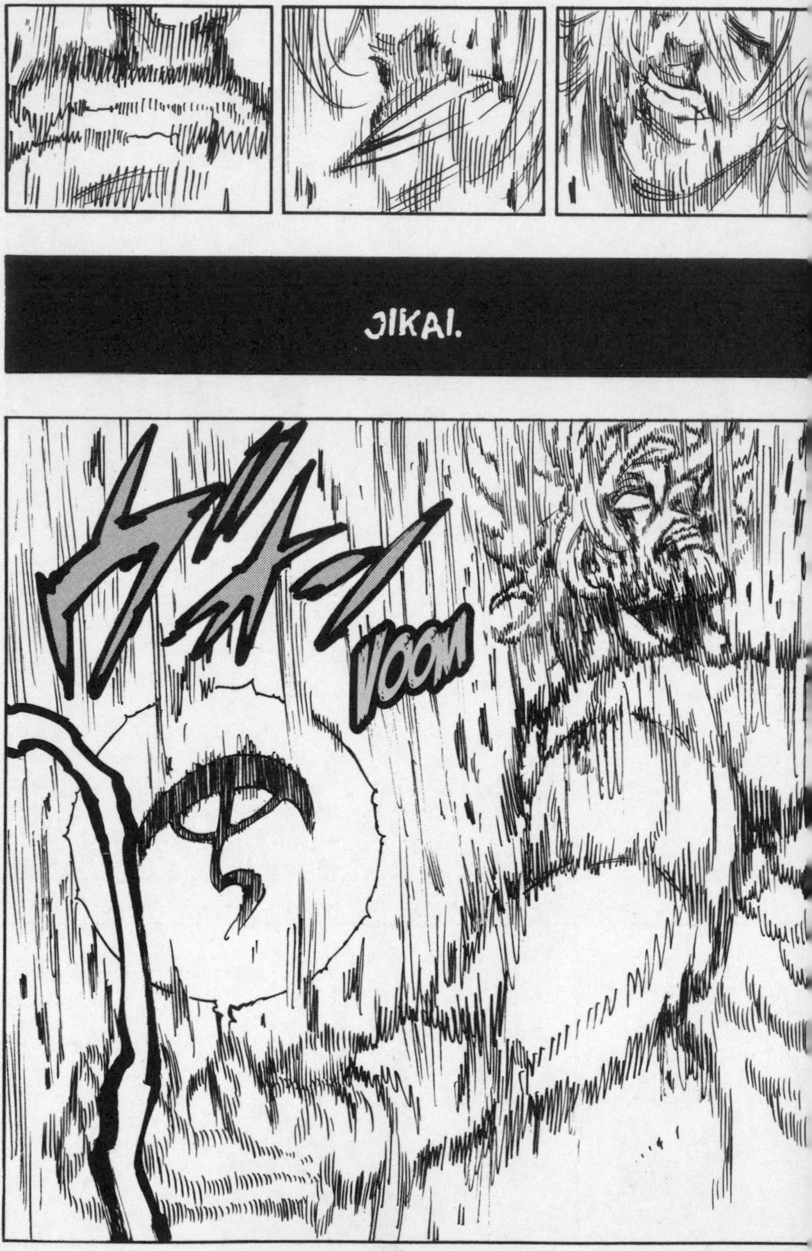
JIKAI.
VOOM

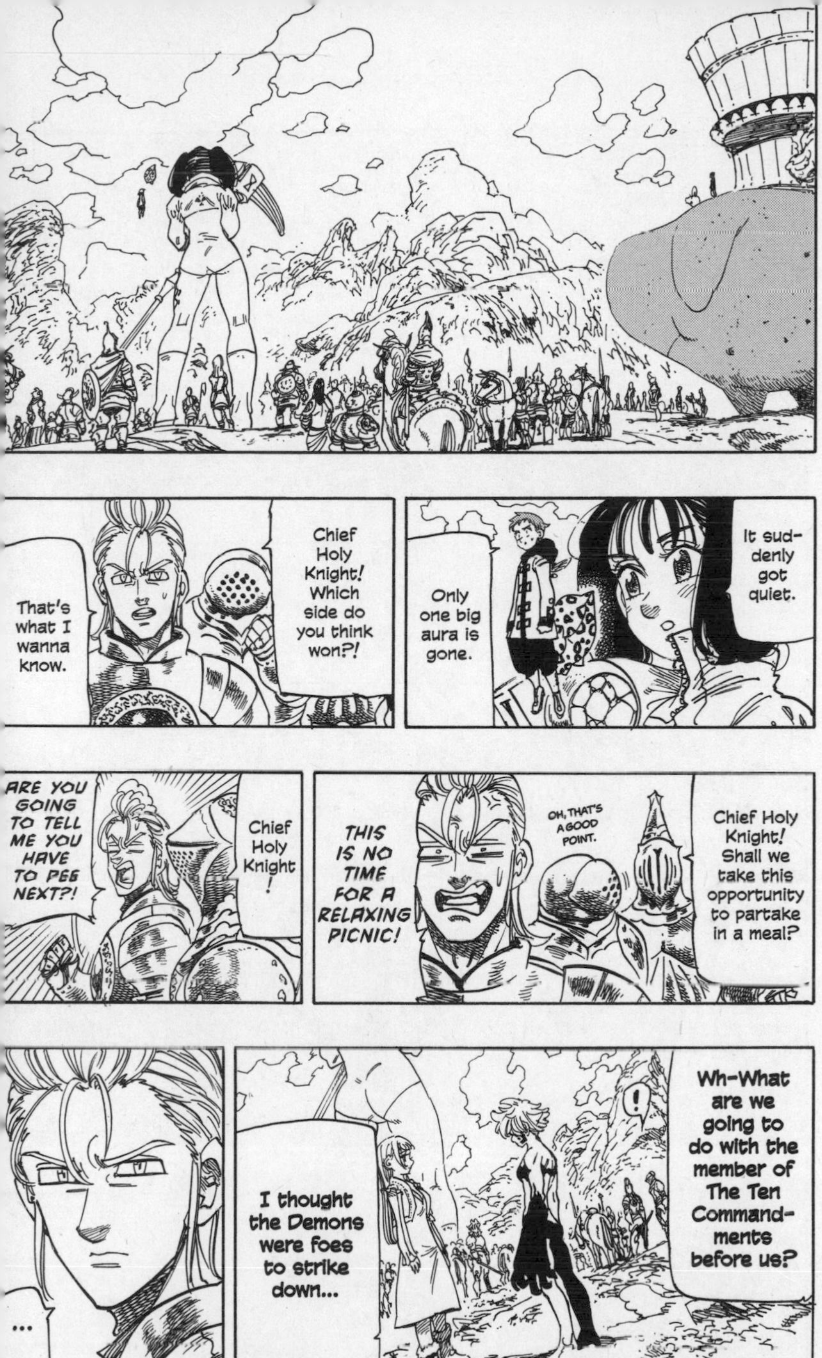

It suddenly got quiet.
Only one big aura is gone.
Chief Holy Knight! Which side do you think won?!
That's what I wanna know.
Chief Holy Knight! Shall we take this opportunity to partake in a meal?
OH, THAT'S A GOOD POINT.
THIS IS NO TIME FOR A RELAXING PICNIC!
Chief Holy Knight!
ARE YOU GOING TO TELL ME YOU HAVE TO PEE NEXT?!
Wh-What are we going to do with the member of The Ten Commandments before us?
!
I thought the Demons were foes to strike down...
...

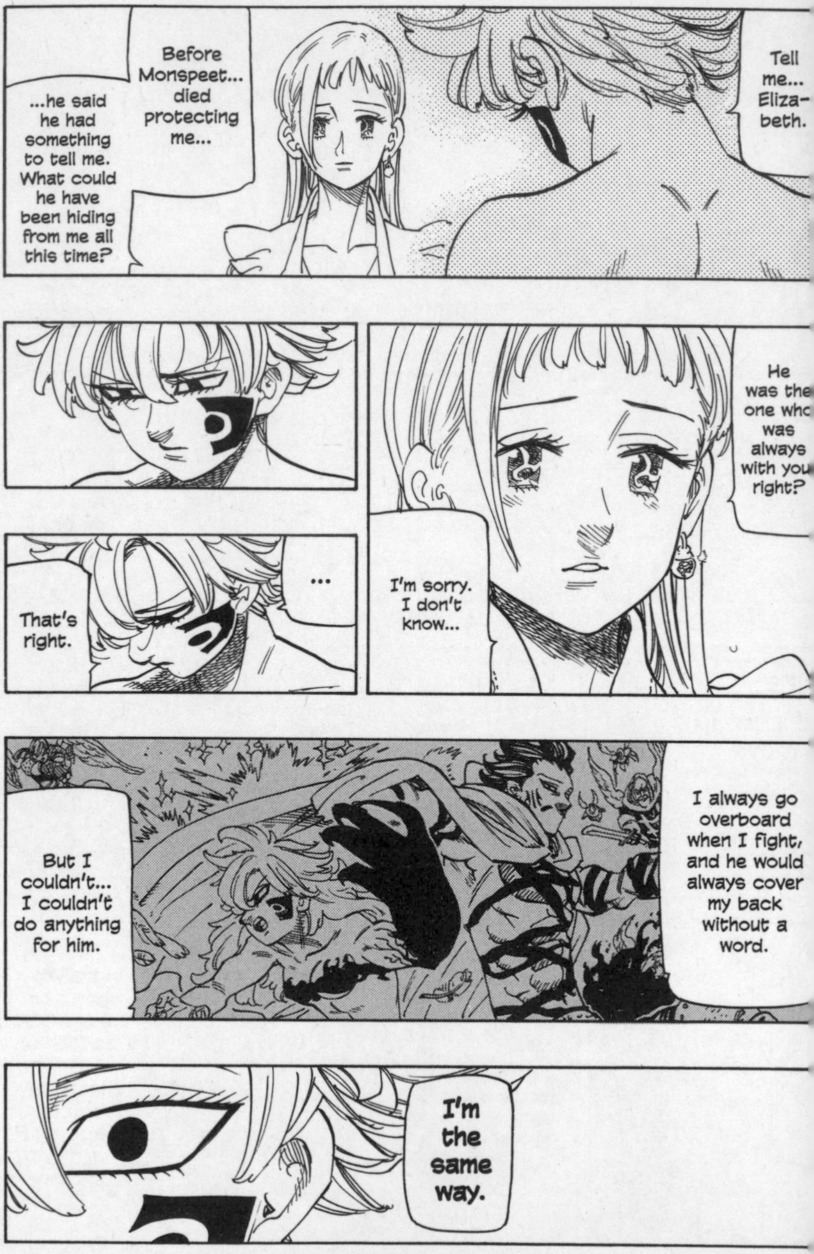
Tell me... Elizabeth.
Before Monspeet... died protecting me...
...he said he had something to tell me. What could he have been hiding from me all this time?
He was the one who was always with you right?
I'm sorry. I don't know...
...
That's right.
I always go overboard when I fight, and he would always cover my back without a word.
But I couldn't... I couldn't do anything for him.
I'm the same way.

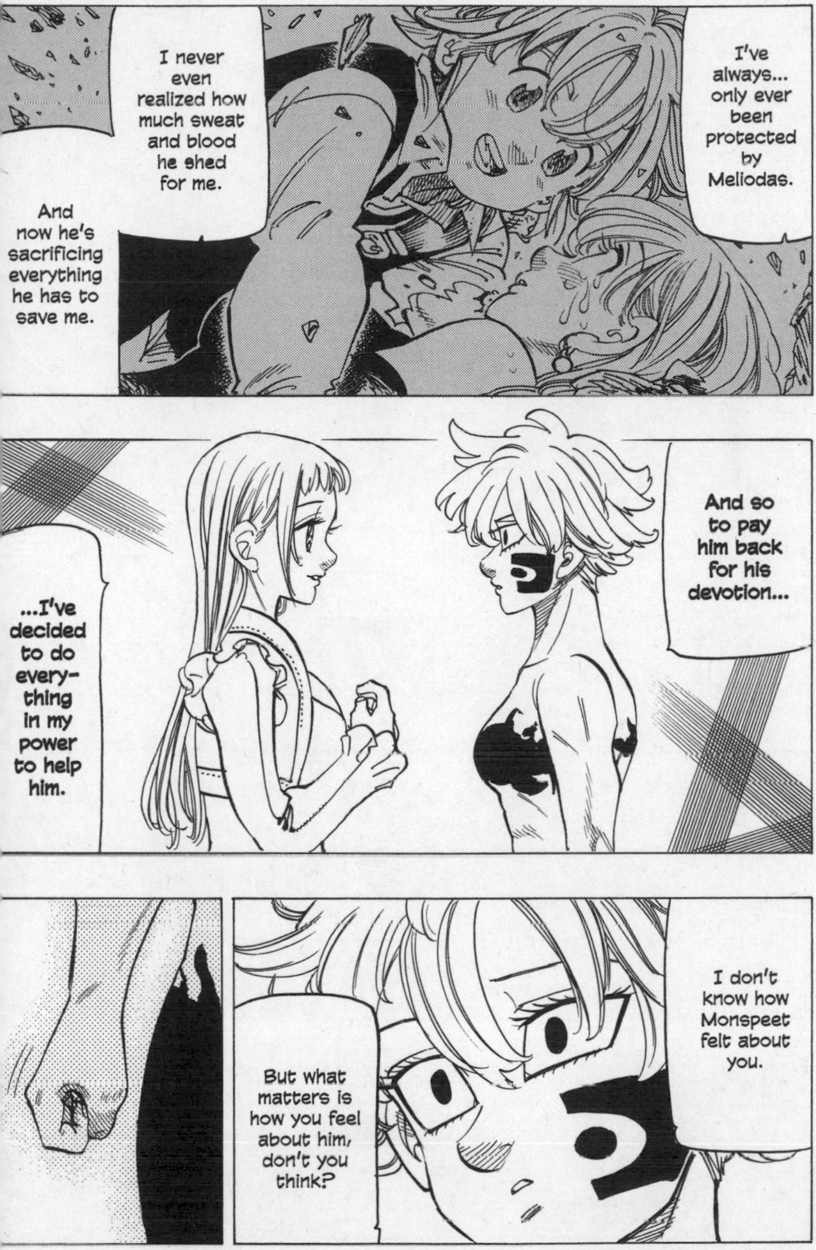
I've always... only ever been protected by Meliodas.
I never even realized how much sweat and blood he shed for me.
And now he's sacrificing everything he has to save me.
And so to pay him back for his devotion...
...I've decided to do every-thing in my power to help him.
I don't know how Monspeet felt about you.
But what matters is how you feel about him, don't you think?

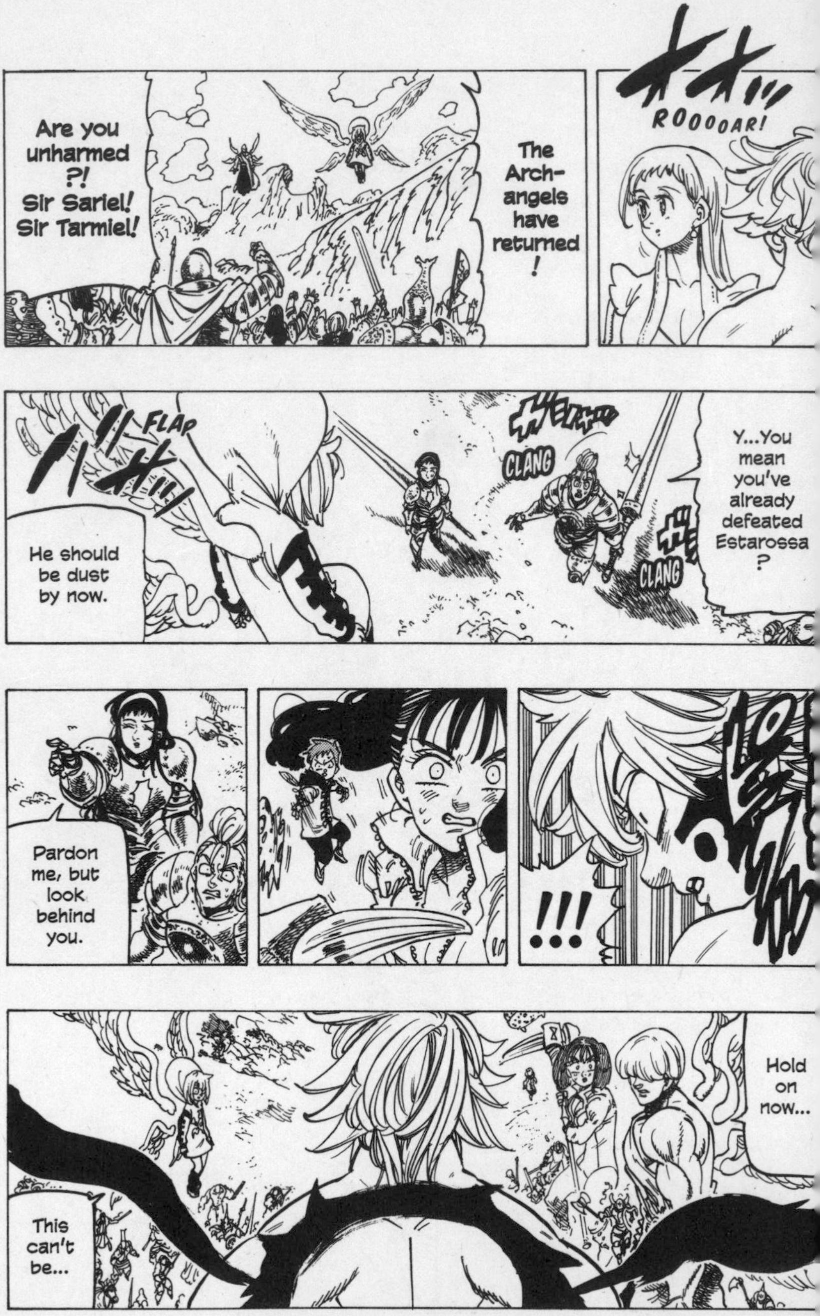
ROOOOAR!
The Arch-angels have returned!
Are you unharmed?! Sir Sariel! Sir Tarmiel!
Y...You mean you've already defeated Estarossa?
CLANG
CLANG
FLAP
He should be dust by now.
!!!
Pardon me, but look behind you.
Hold on now...
This can't be...

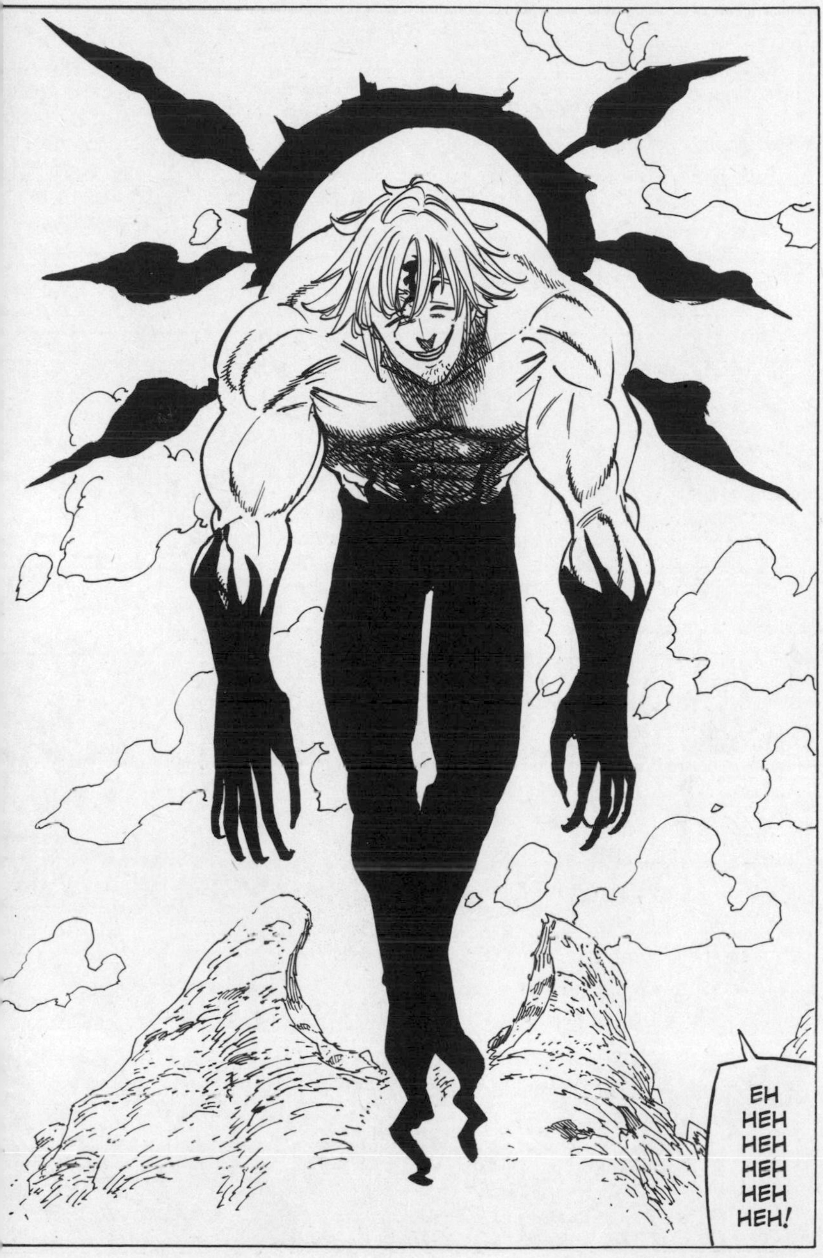
EH HEH HEH HEH HEH HEH!

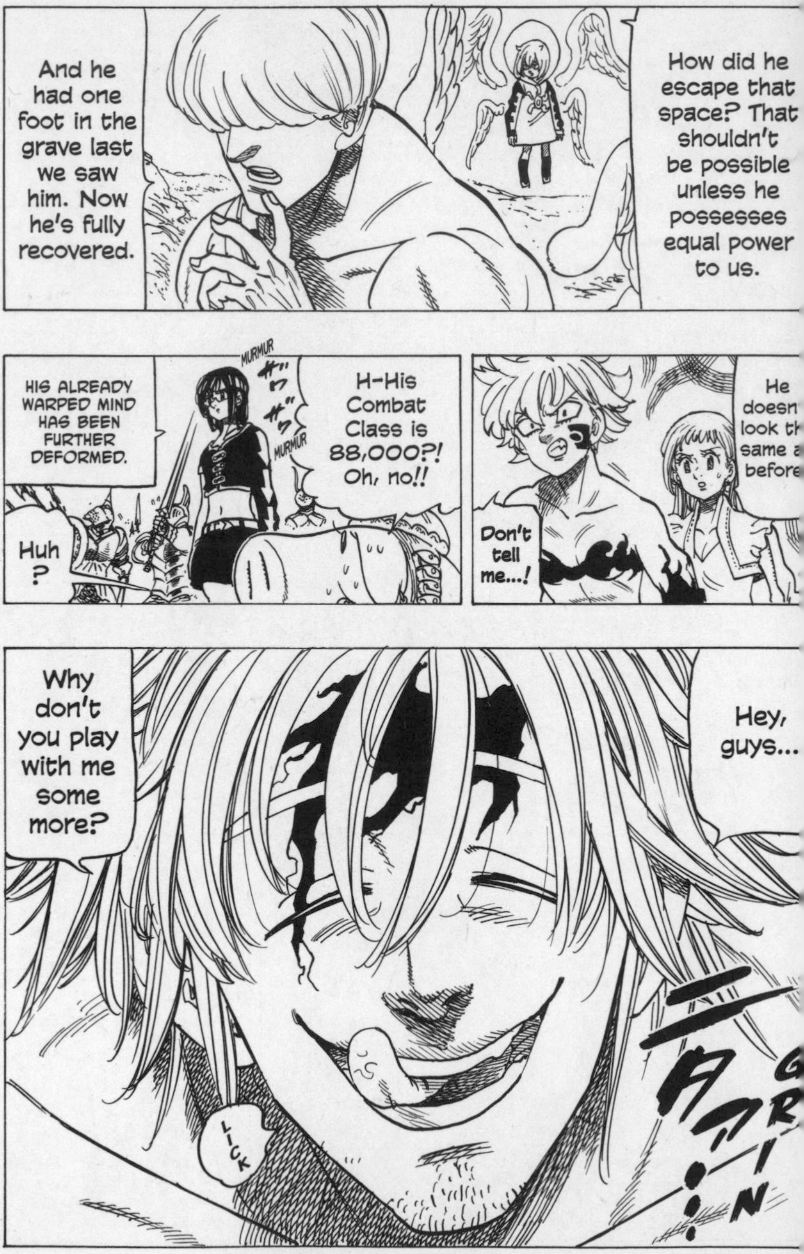
How did he escape that space? That shouldn't be possible unless he possesses equal power to us.
And he had one foot in the grave last we saw him. Now he's fully recovered.
He doesn look th same a before
Don't tell me...!
H-His Combat Class is 88,000?! Oh, no!!
MURMUR
MURMUR
HIS ALREADY WARPED MIND HAS BEEN FURTHER DEFORMED.
Huh?
Hey, guys...
Why don't you play with me some more?
GRIN
LICK

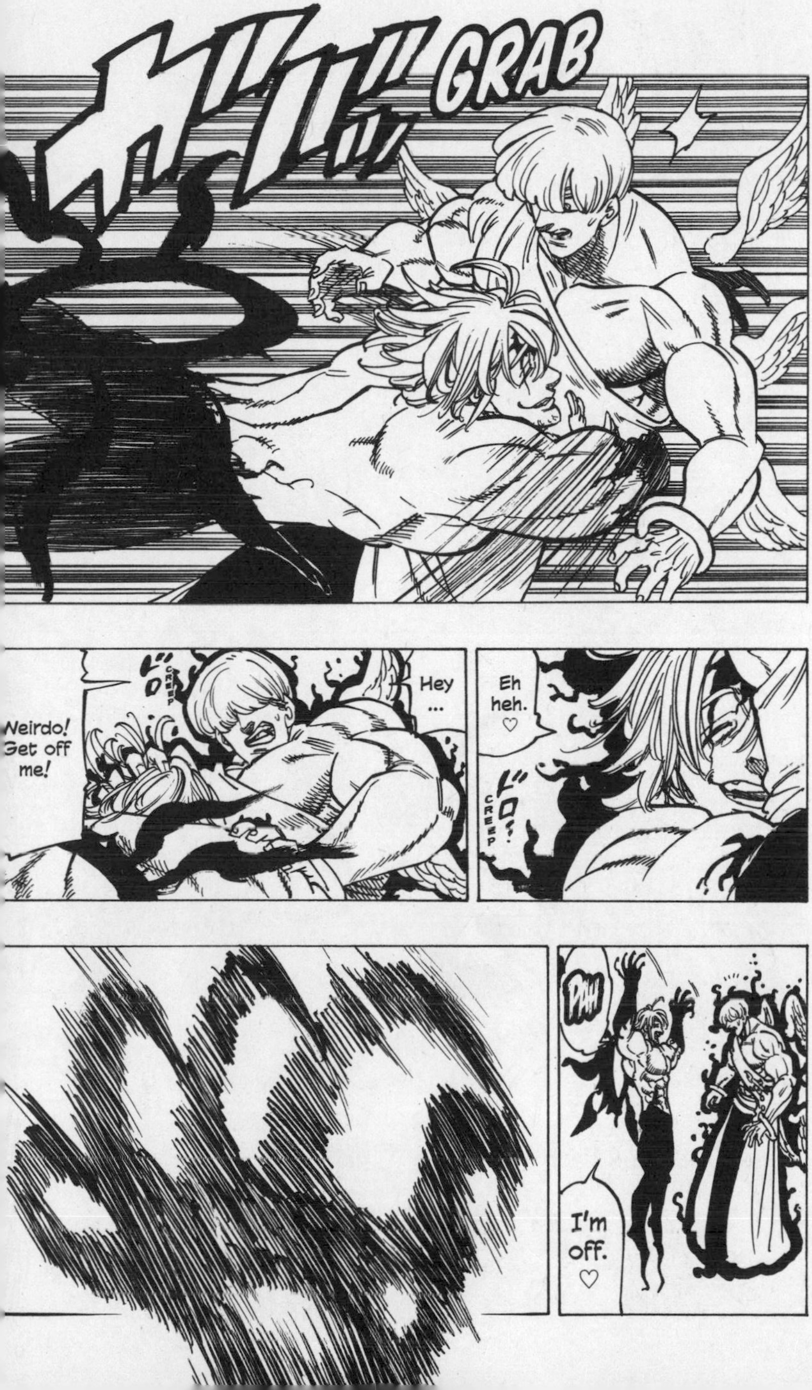
GRAB
Eh heh. ♡
CREEP
Hey ...
Weirdo! Get off me!
CREEP
DAH
I'm off. ♡

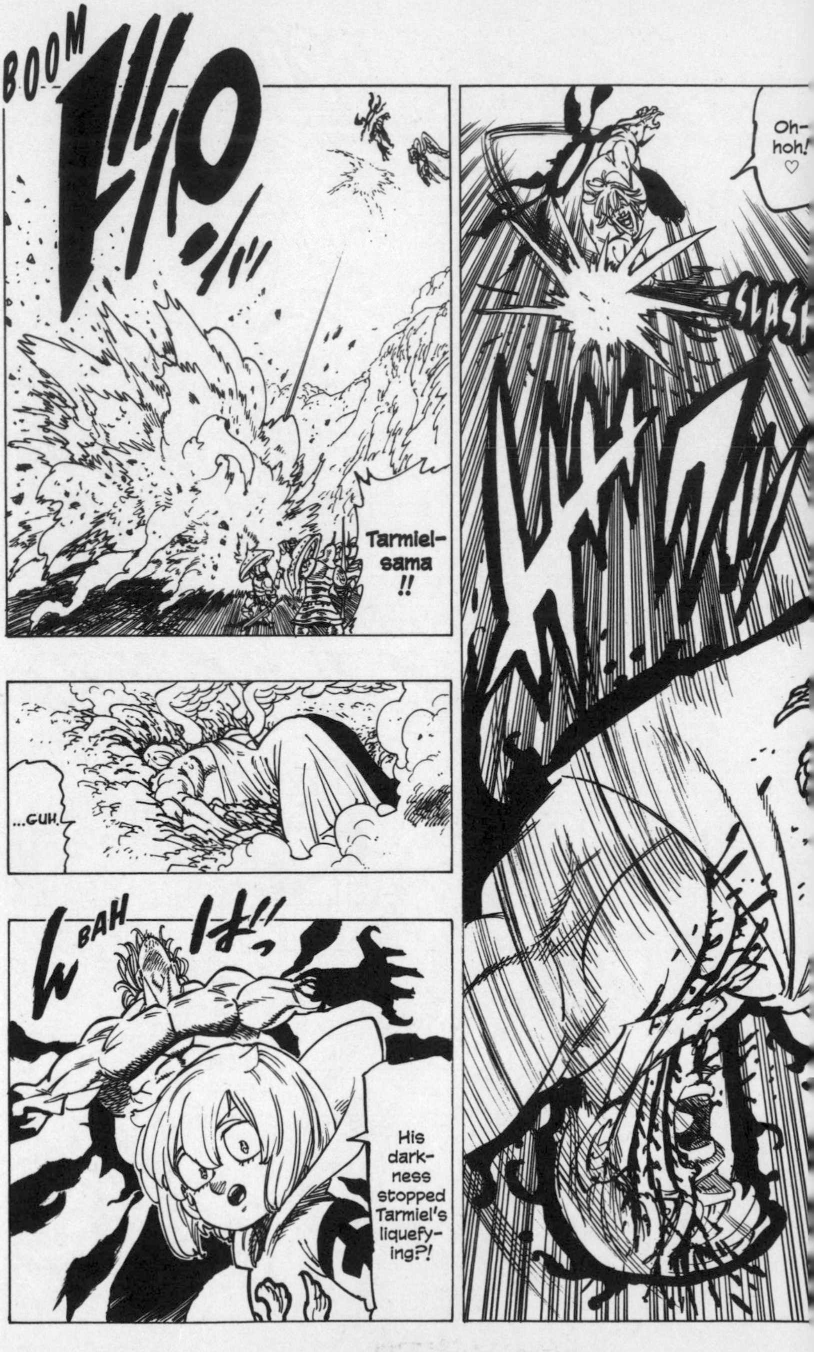
Oh-hoh! ♡
SLAS
BOOM
Tarmiel-sama!!
...GUH
BAH
His darkness stopped Tarmiel's liquefying?!

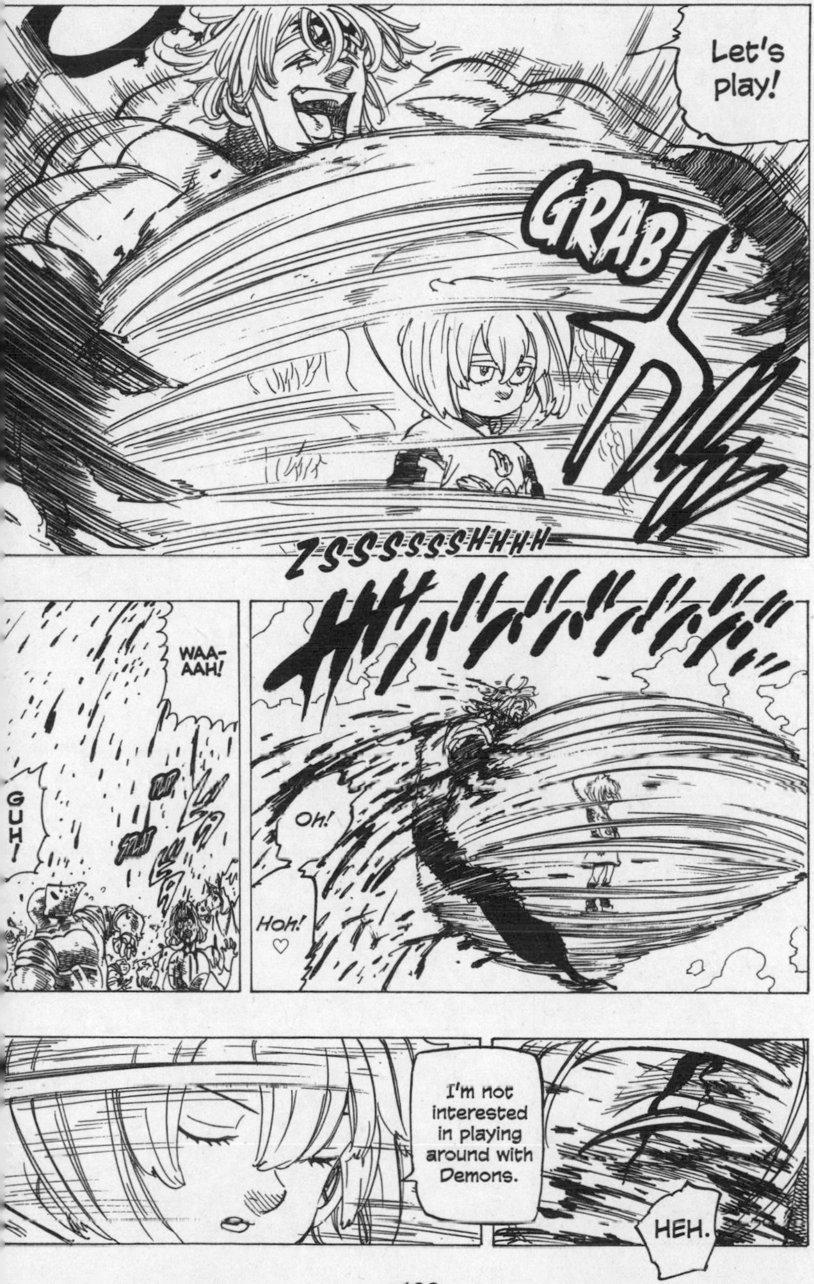
Let's play!
GRAB
ZSSSSSSHHHH
Oh!
Hoh! ♡
WAA-AAH!
GUH!
HEH.
I'm not interested in playing around with Demons.

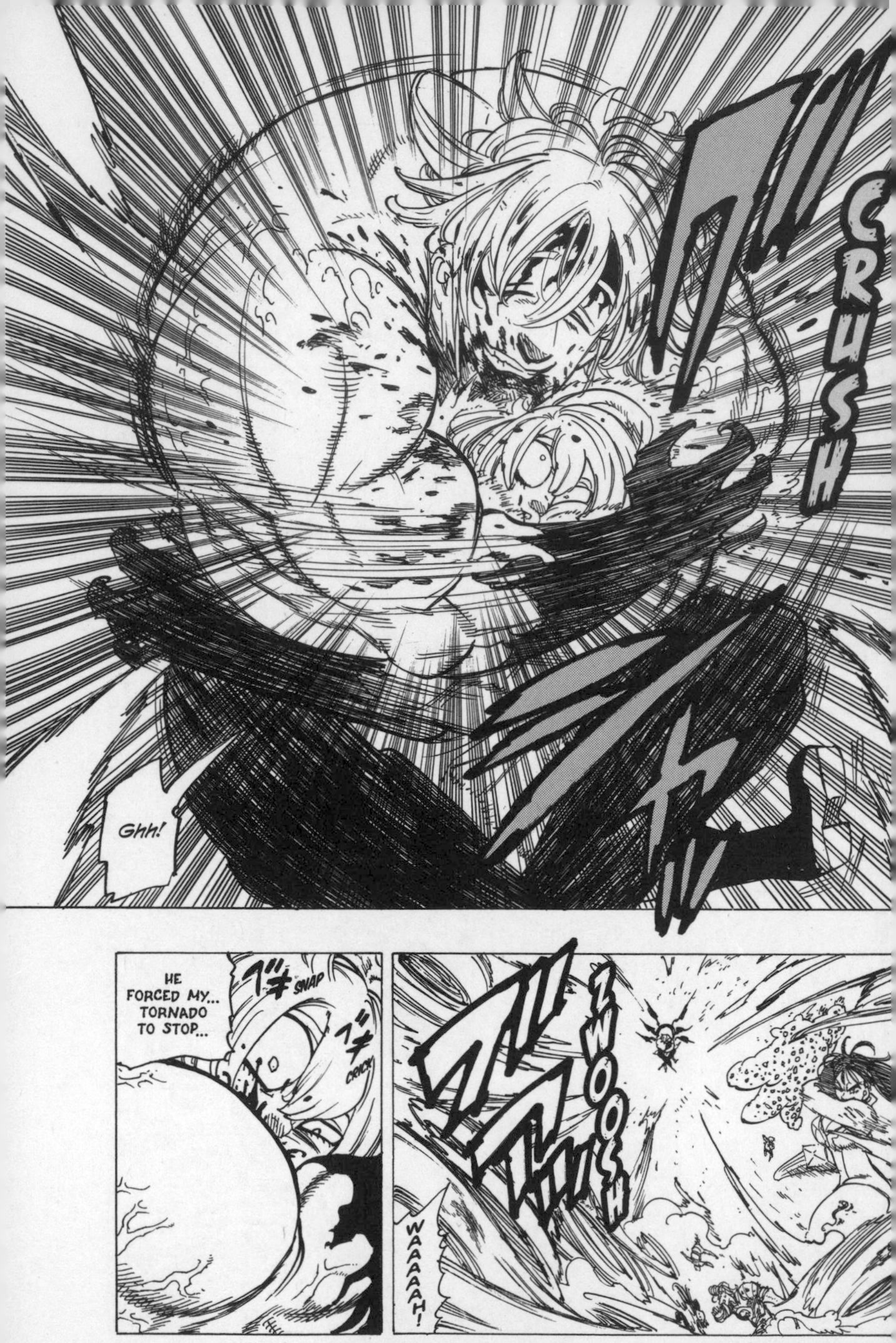
CRUSH
Ghh!
ZWOOSH
WAAAAAH!
HE FORCED MY... TORNADO TO STOP...
SNAP
CRICK

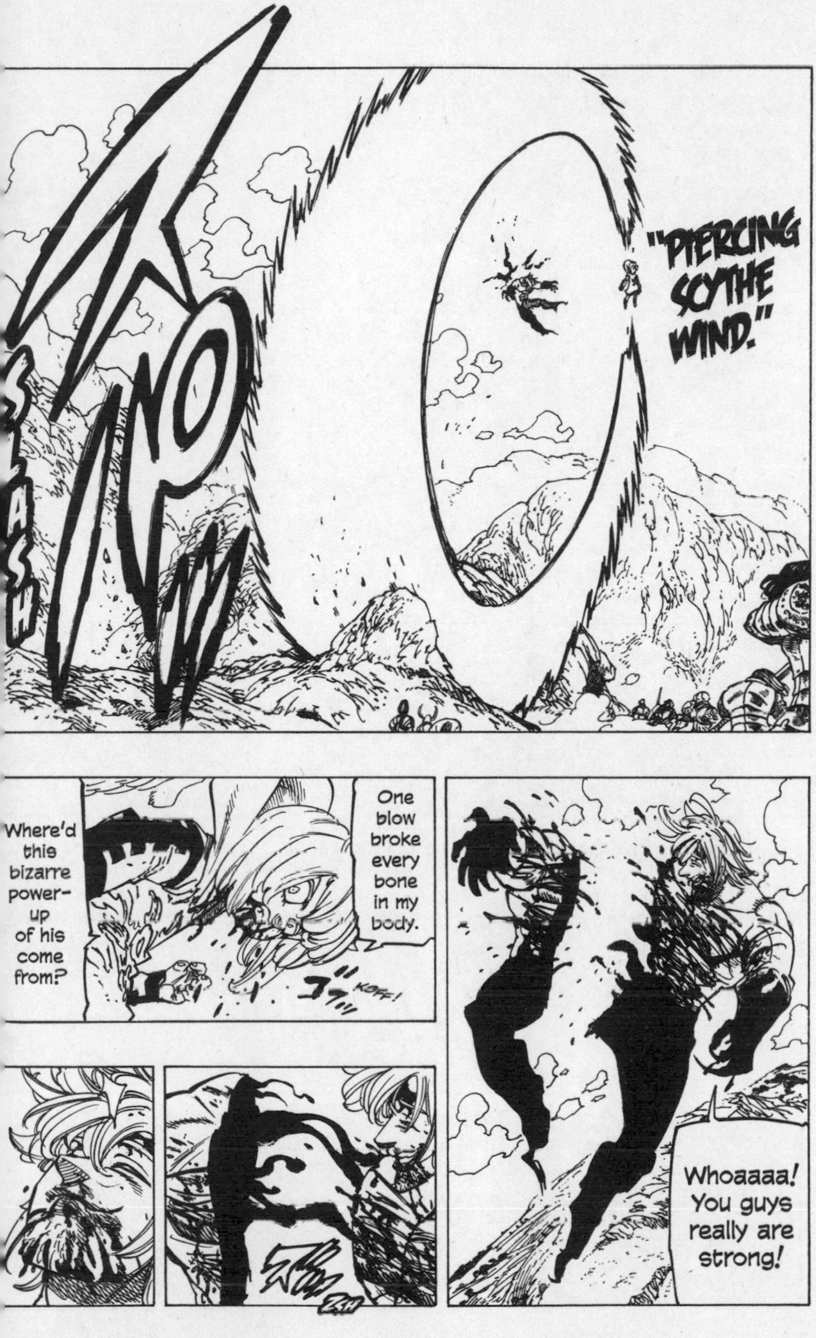
SLASH
"PIERCING SCYTHE WIND."
Whoaaaa! You guys really are strong!
One blow broke every bone in my body.
Where'd this bizarre power-up of his come from?
KOFF!

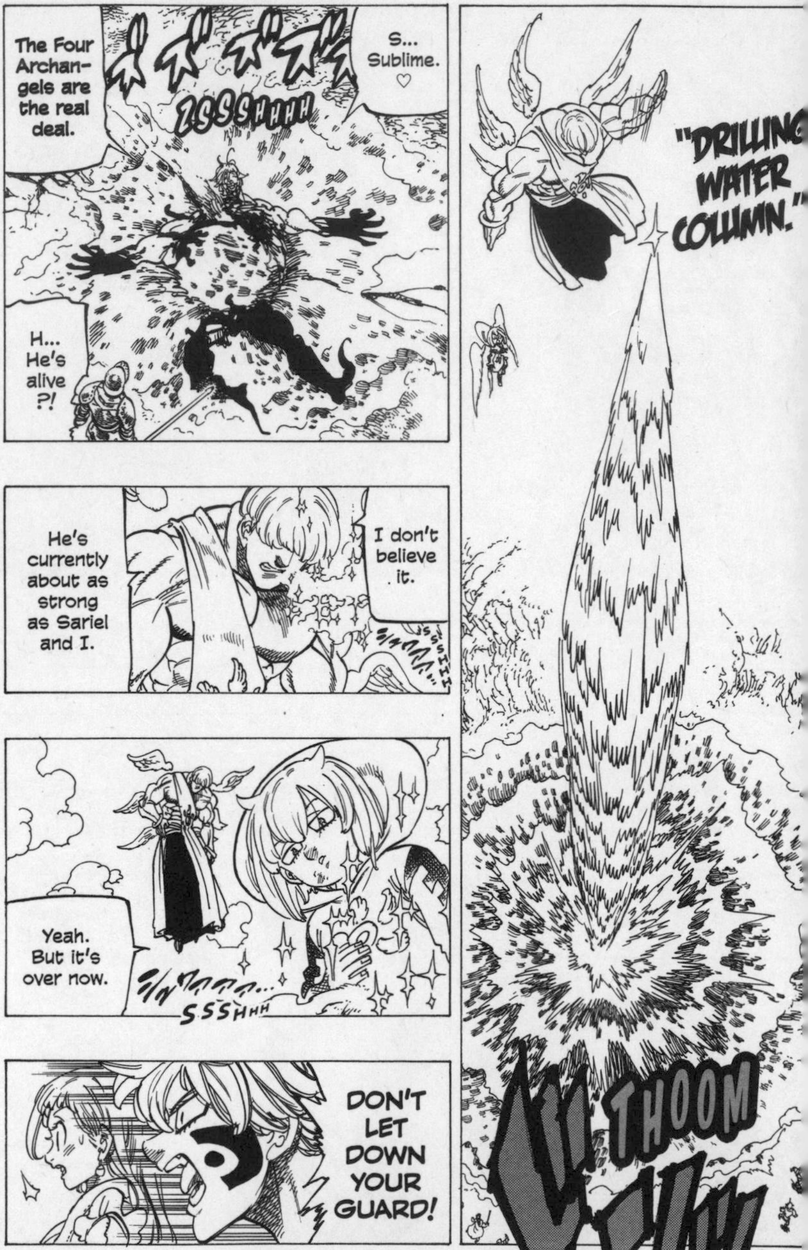
"DRILLING WATER COLUMN."
THOOM
S... Sublime. ♡
ZSSSHHHH
The Four Archangels are the real deal.
H... He's alive?!
I don't believe it.
SSHHH
He's currently about as strong as Sariel and I.
Yeah. But it's over now.
SSSHHH
DON'T LET DOWN YOUR GUARD!

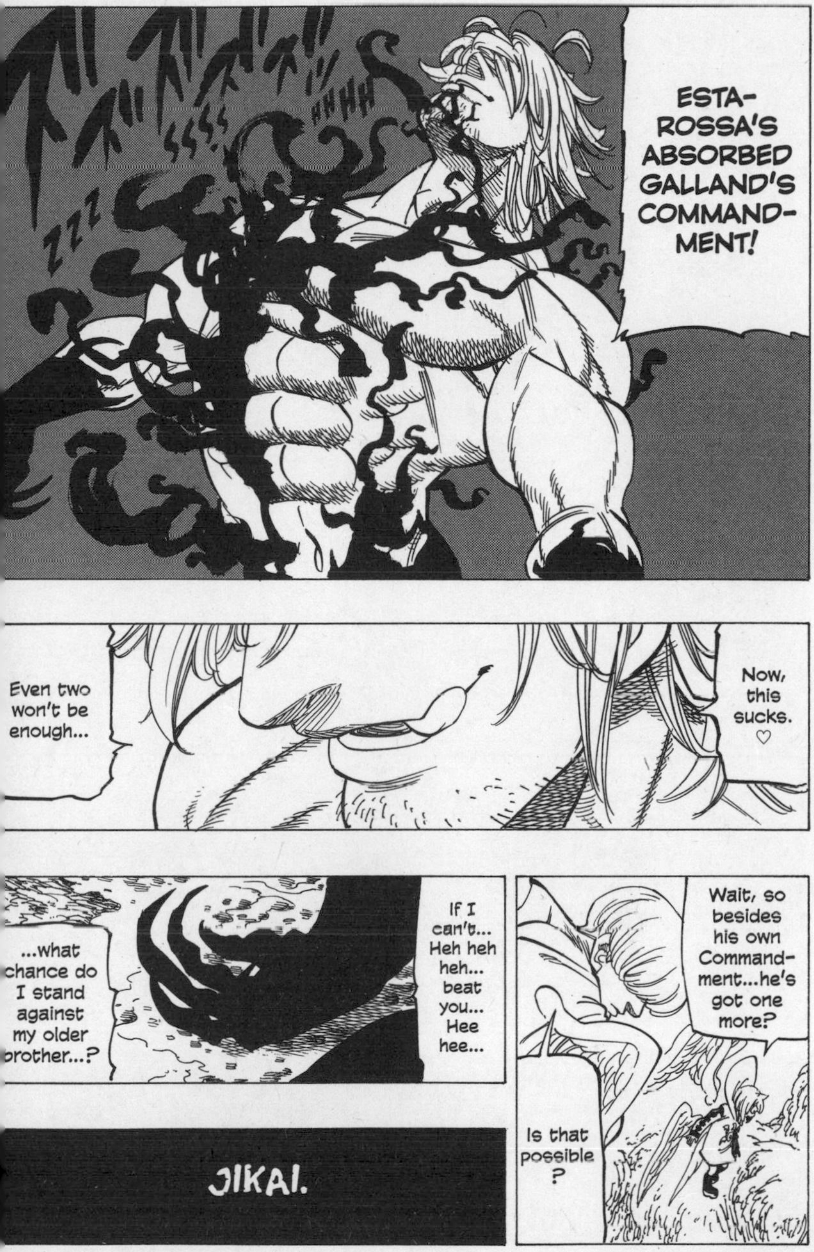
ESTA-ROSSA'S ABSORBED GALLAND'S COMMAND-MENT!
Now, this sucks. ♡
Even two won't be enough...
Wait, so besides his own Command-ment...he's got one more?
Is that possible?
If I can't... Heh heh heh... beat you... Hee hee...
...what chance do I stand against my older brother...?
JIKAI.

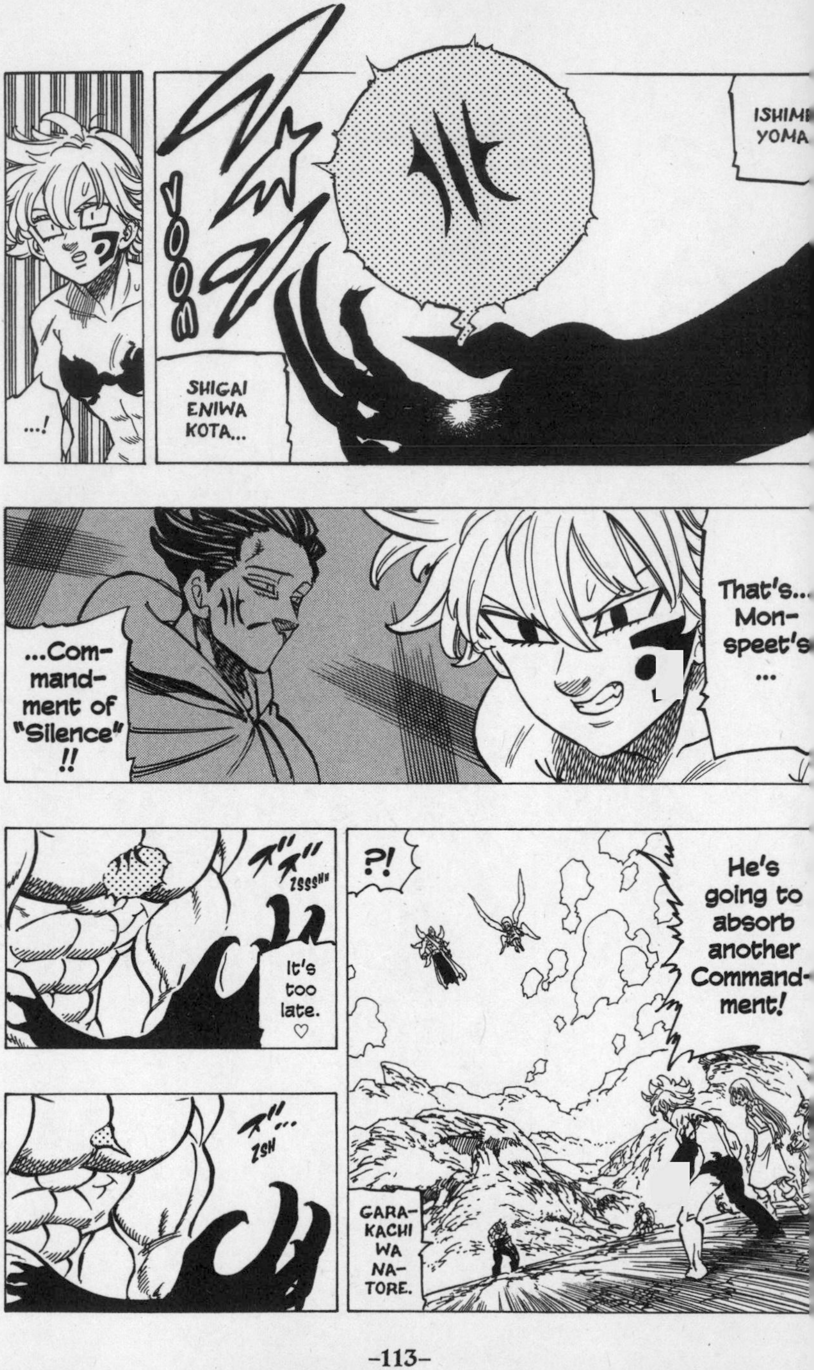
ISHIMI YOMA
VOOOM
SHIGAI ENIWA KOTA...
...!
That's... Monspeet's...
...Commandment of "Silence"!!
He's going to absorb another Commandment!
?!
GARAKACHI WA NATORE.
ZSSSHH
It's too late. ♡
ZSH

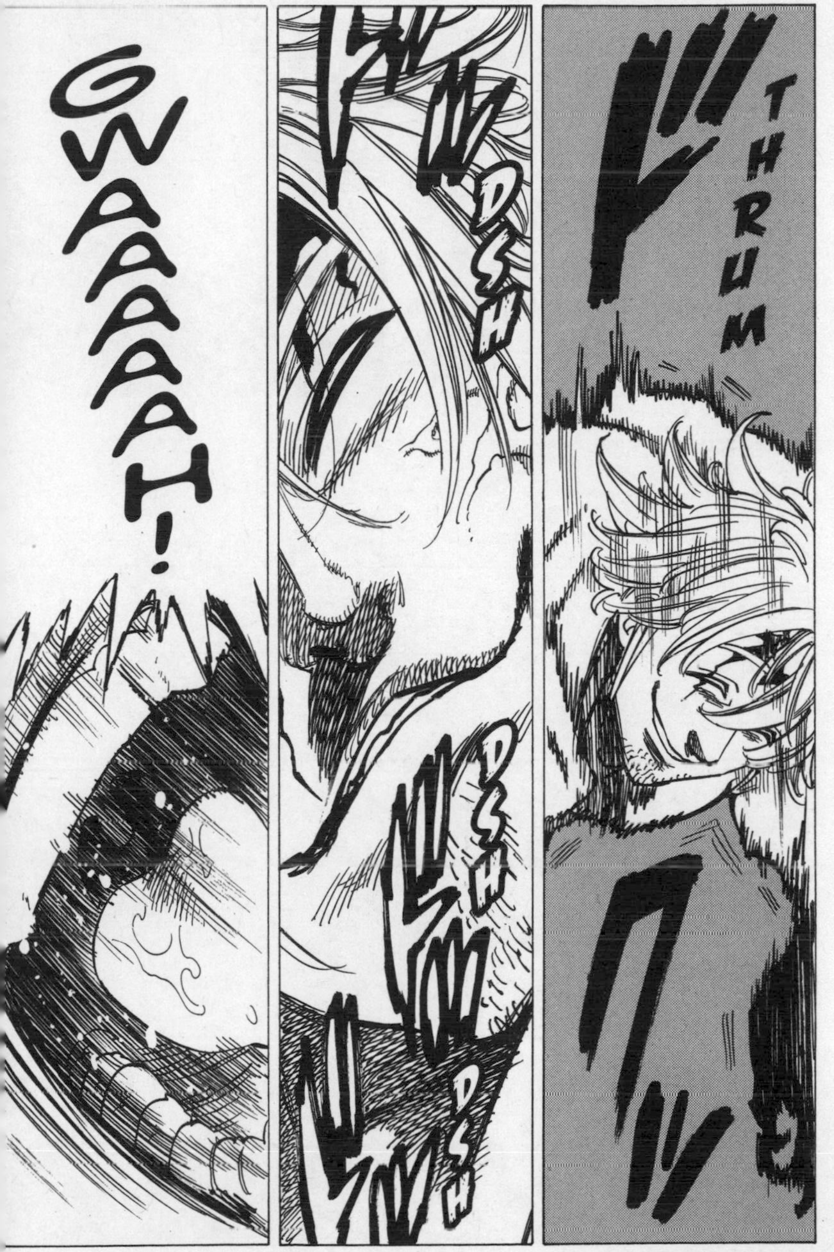
THRUM
DASH
DASH
DASH
GWAAAAAAH!

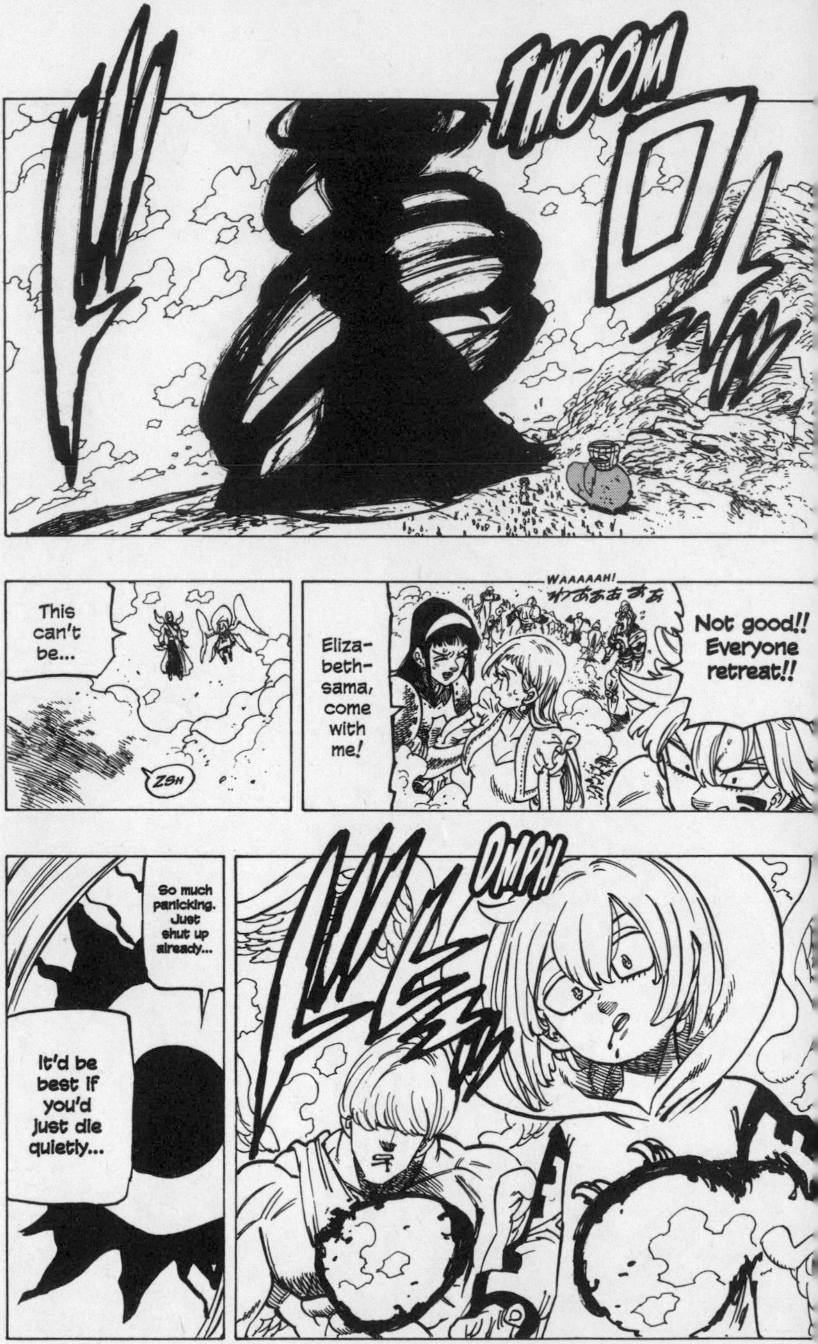
THOOM
WAAAAAH!
わあああ ああ
Not good!! Everyone retreat!!
Eliza-beth-sama, come with me!
This can't be...
ZSH
OMPH
So much panicking. Just shut up already...
It'd be best if you'd just die quietly...

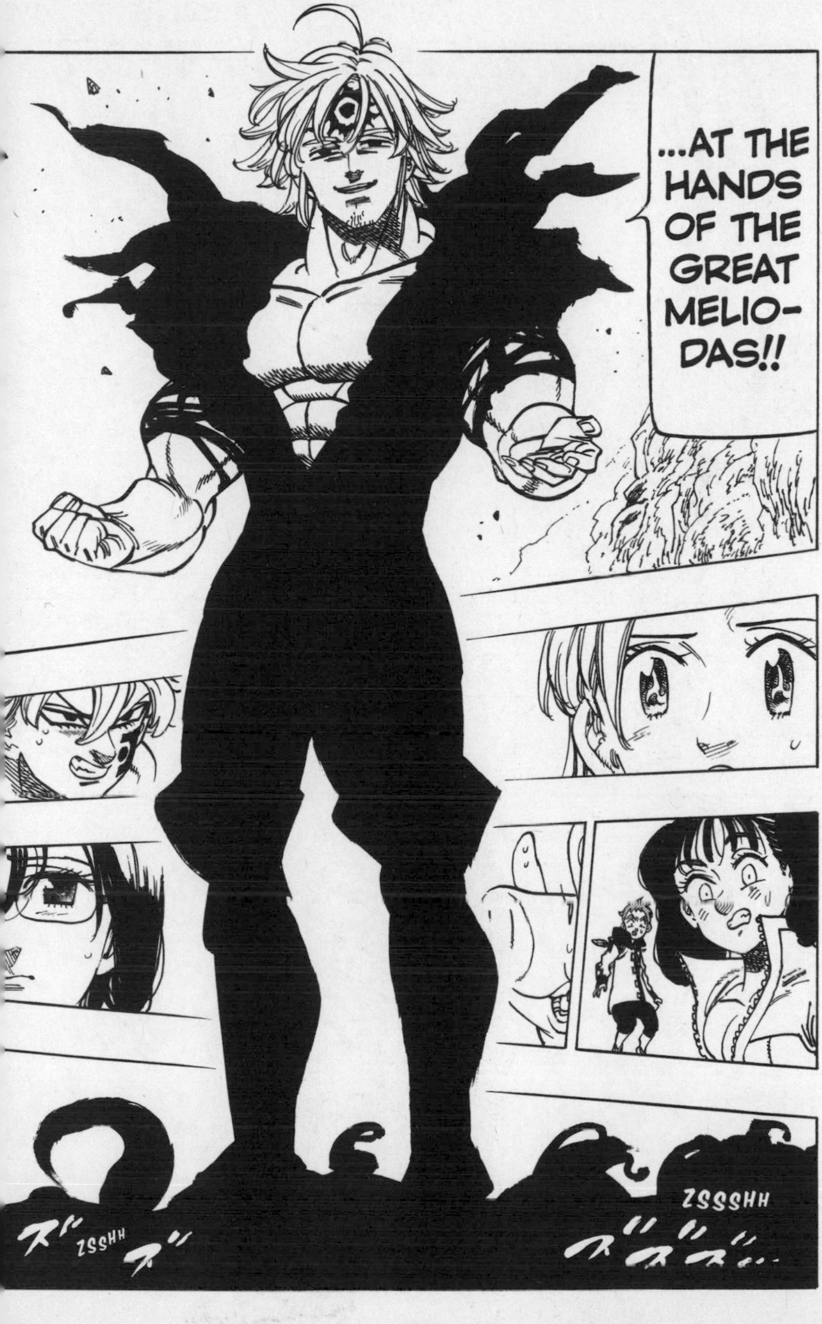
...AT THE HANDS OF THE GREAT MELIO-DAS!!
ZSSSHH
ZSSHH

Chapter 265 - Rampaging Love

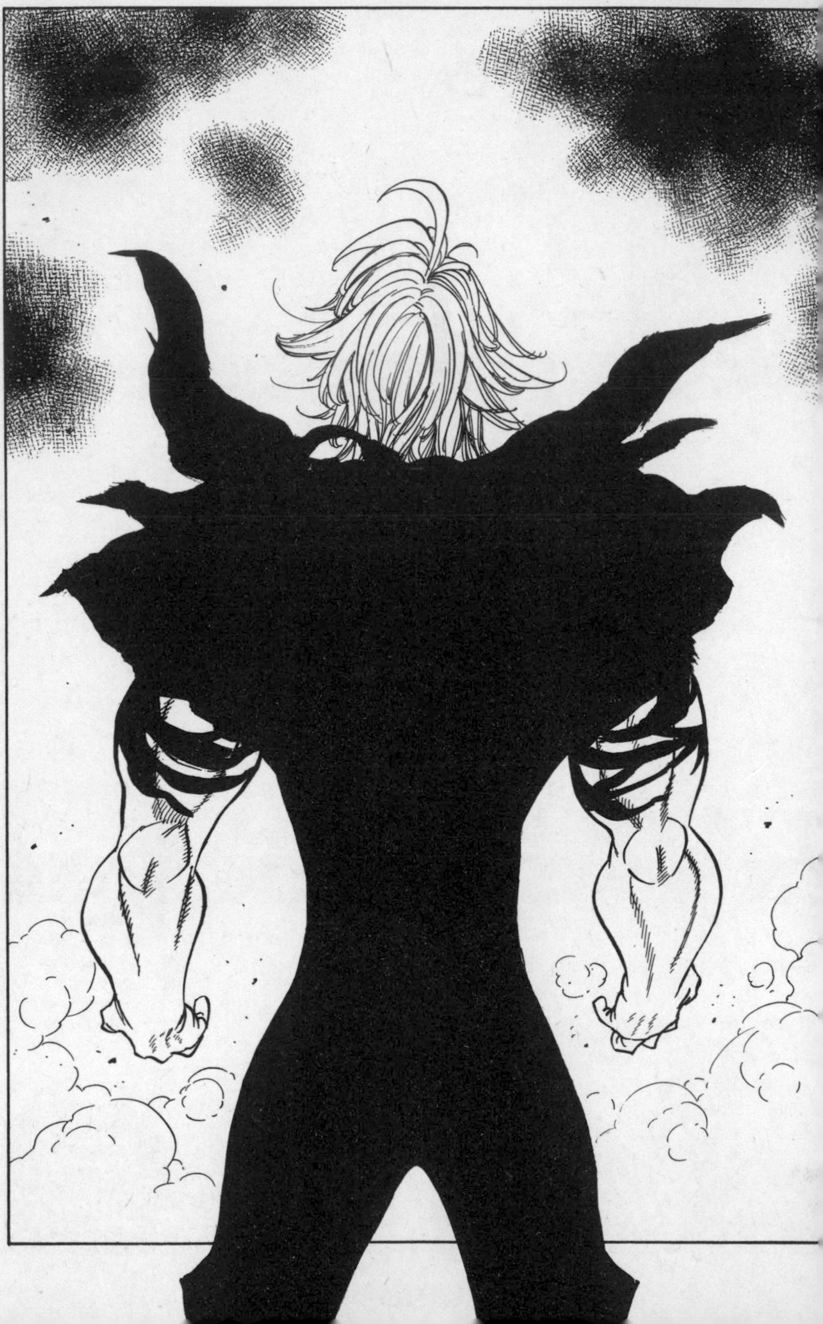

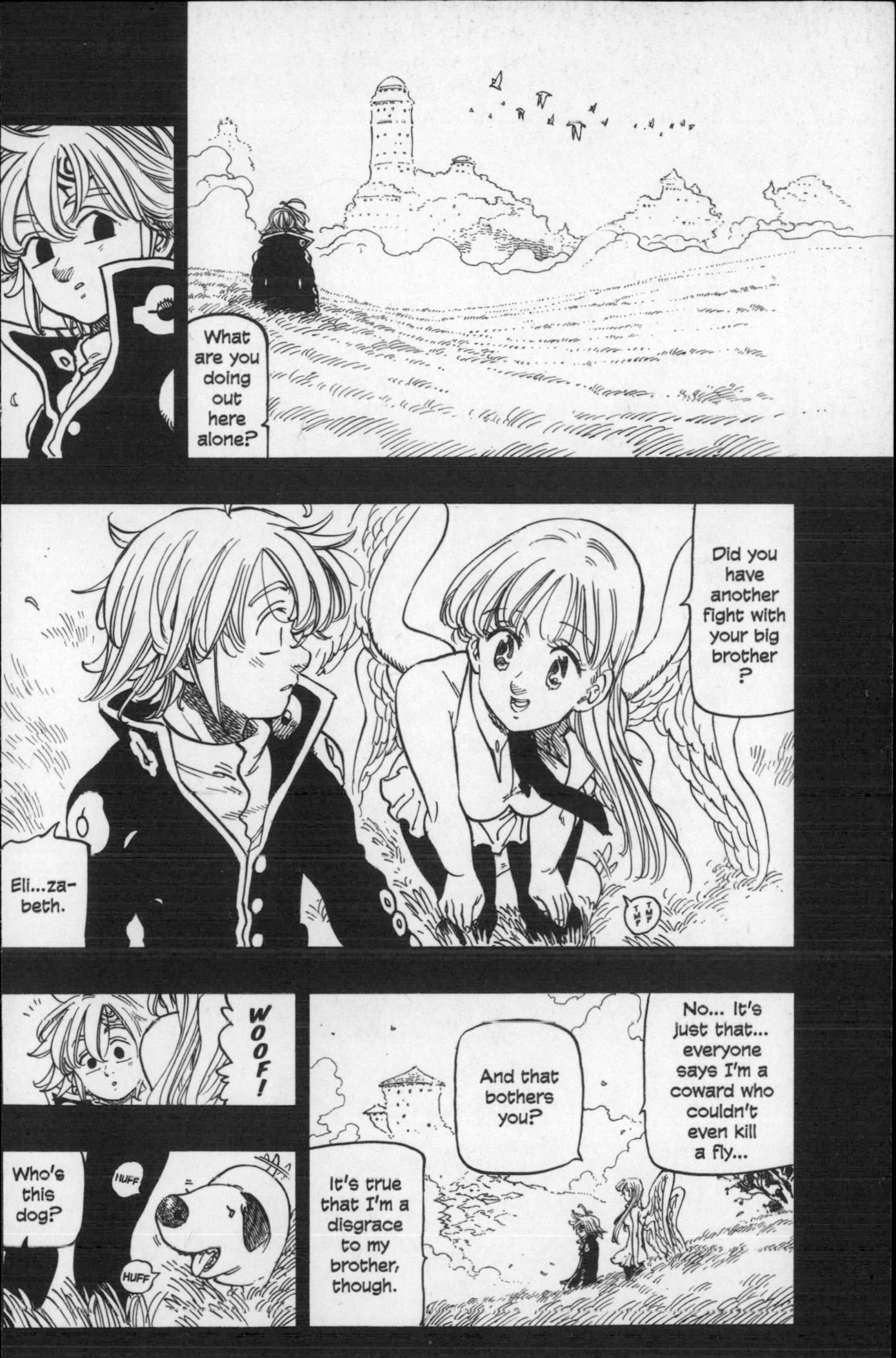
What are you doing out here alone?
Did you have another fight with your big brother?
Eli...za-beth.
TMP TMP
No... It's just that... everyone says I'm a coward who couldn't even kill a fly...
And that bothers you?
It's true that I'm a disgrace to my brother, though.
WOOF!
Who's this dog?
HUFF
HUFF

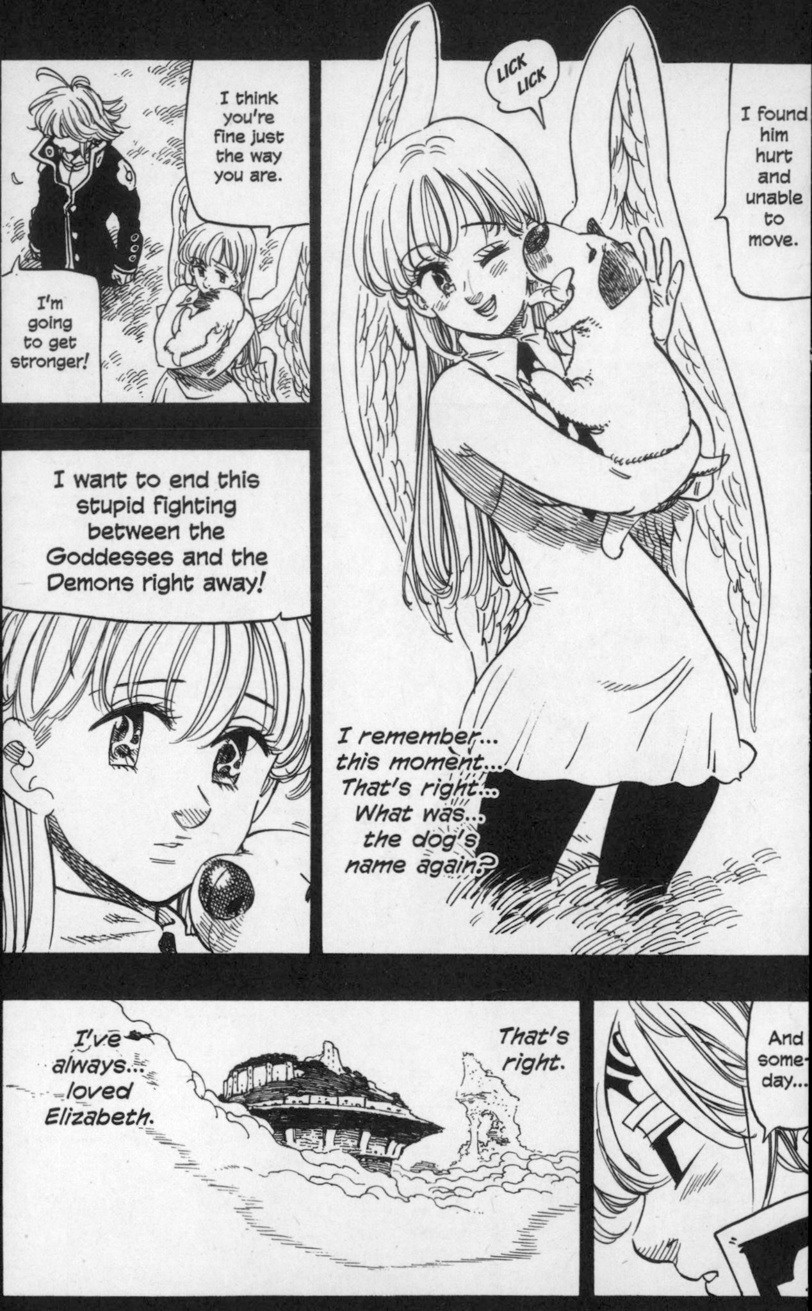
I found him hurt and unable to move.
LICK LICK
I remember... this moment... That's right... What was... the dog's name again?
I think you're fine just the way you are.
I'm going to get stronger!
I want to end this stupid fighting between the Goddesses and the Demons right away!
And someday...
That's right.
I've always... loved Elizabeth.

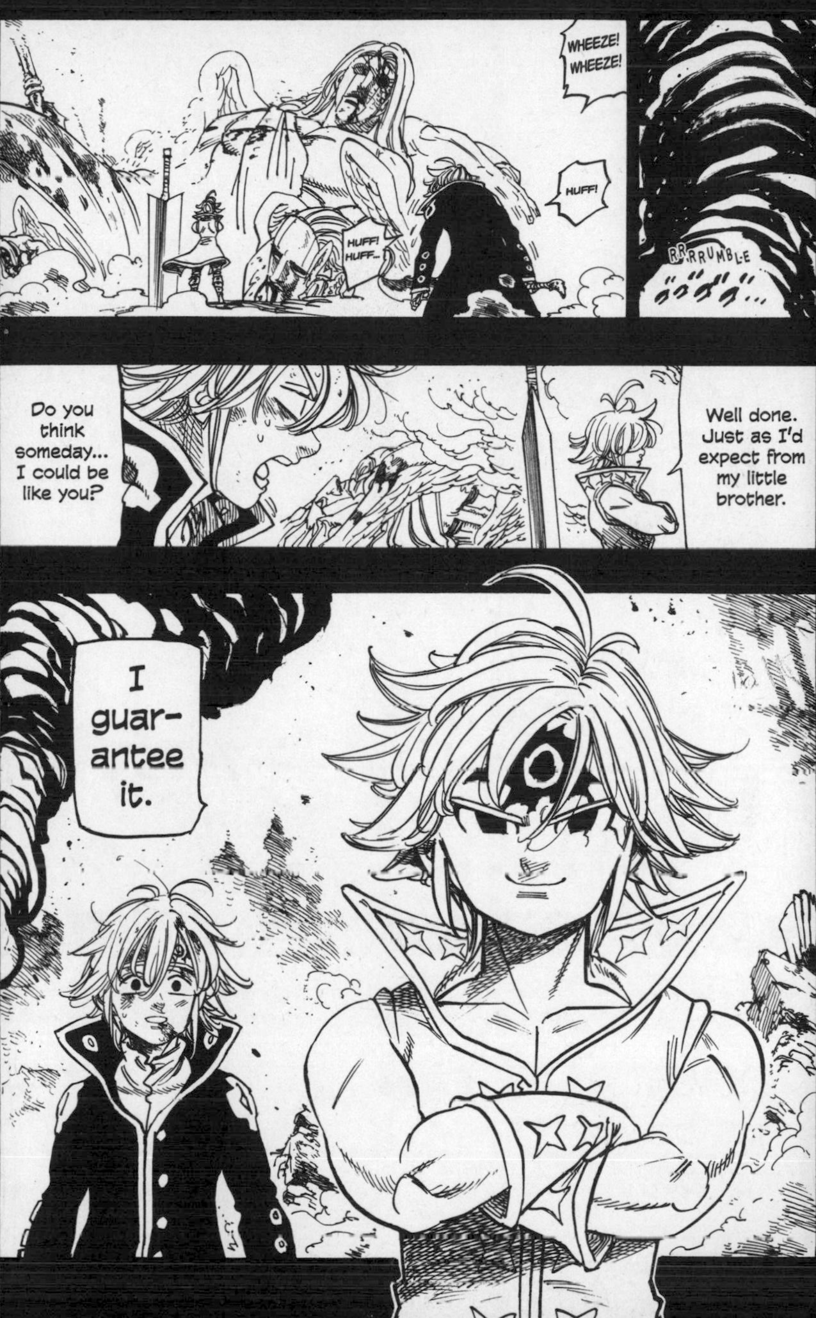
RRRRUMBLE
WHEEZE! WHEEZE!
HUFF!
HUFF! HUFF...
Well done. Just as I'd expect from my little brother.
Do you think someday... I could be like you?
I guar-antee it.

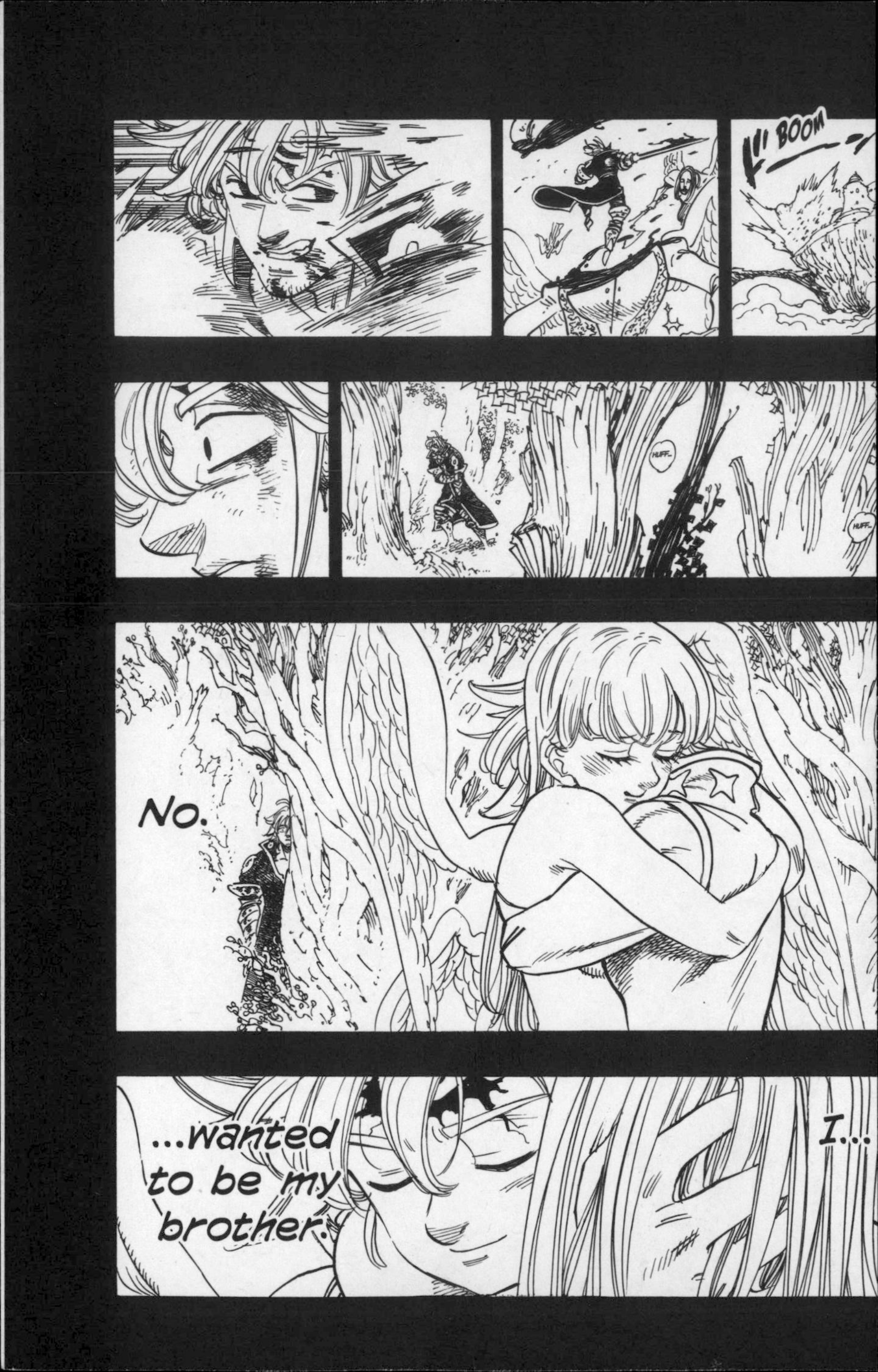
BOOM
HUFF...
HUFF...
No.
I...
...wanted to be my brother.

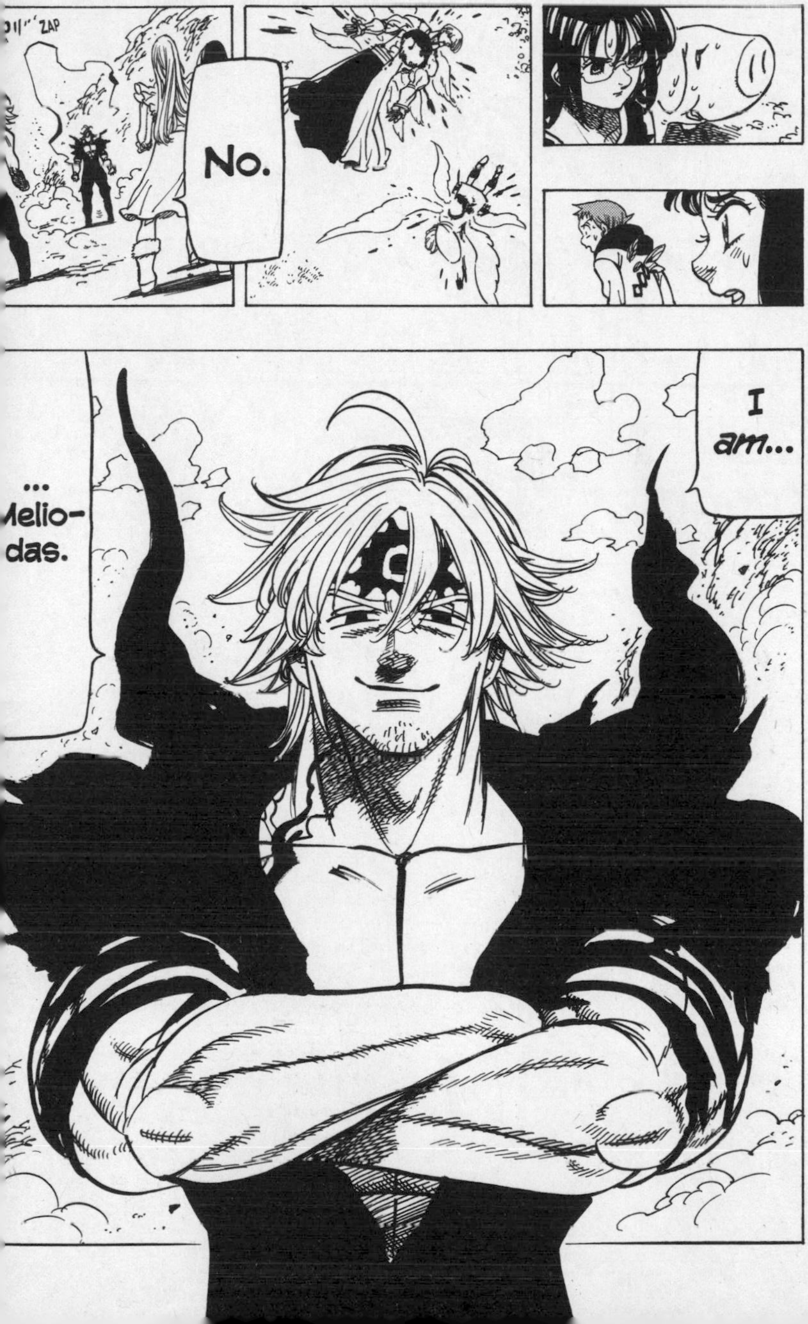
ZAP
No.
I am...
...
Melio-
das.

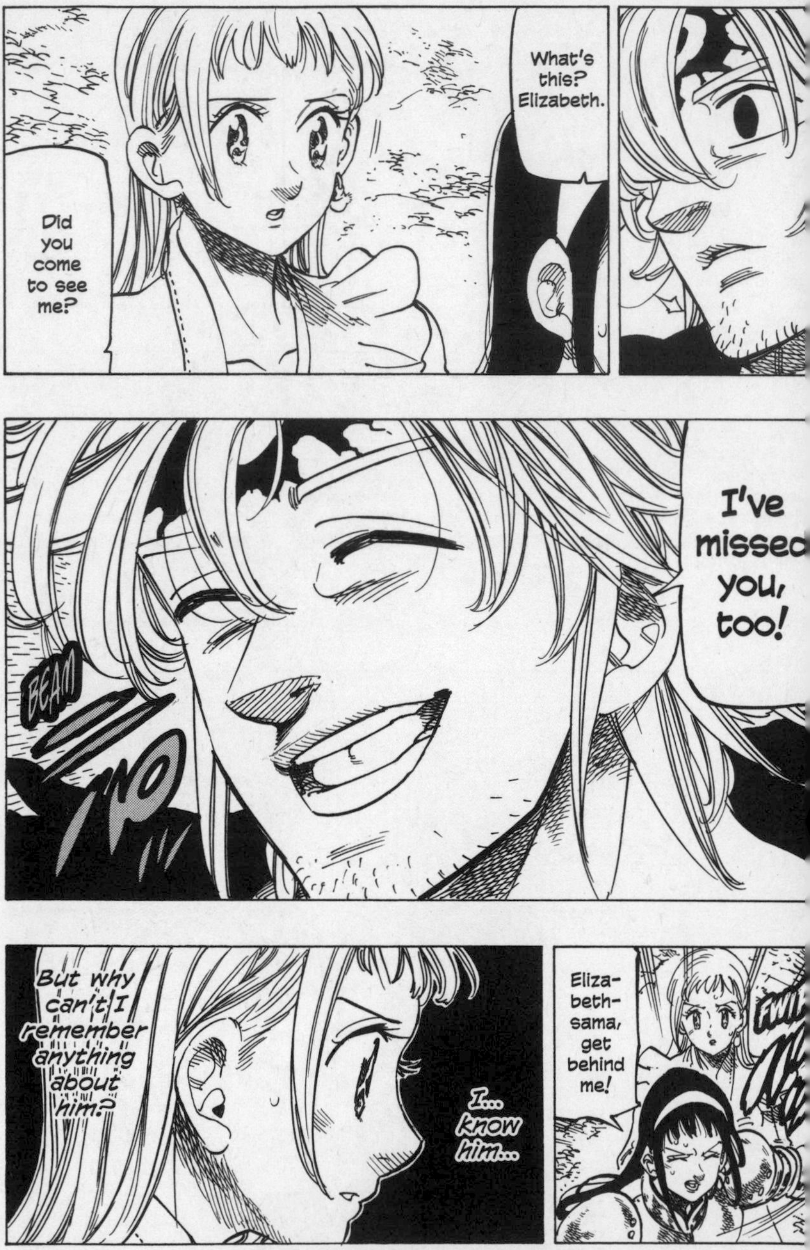
What's this? Elizabeth.
Did you come to see me?
I've missed you, too!
BEAM
Eliza-beth-sama, get behind me!
I... know him...
But why can't I remember anything about him?

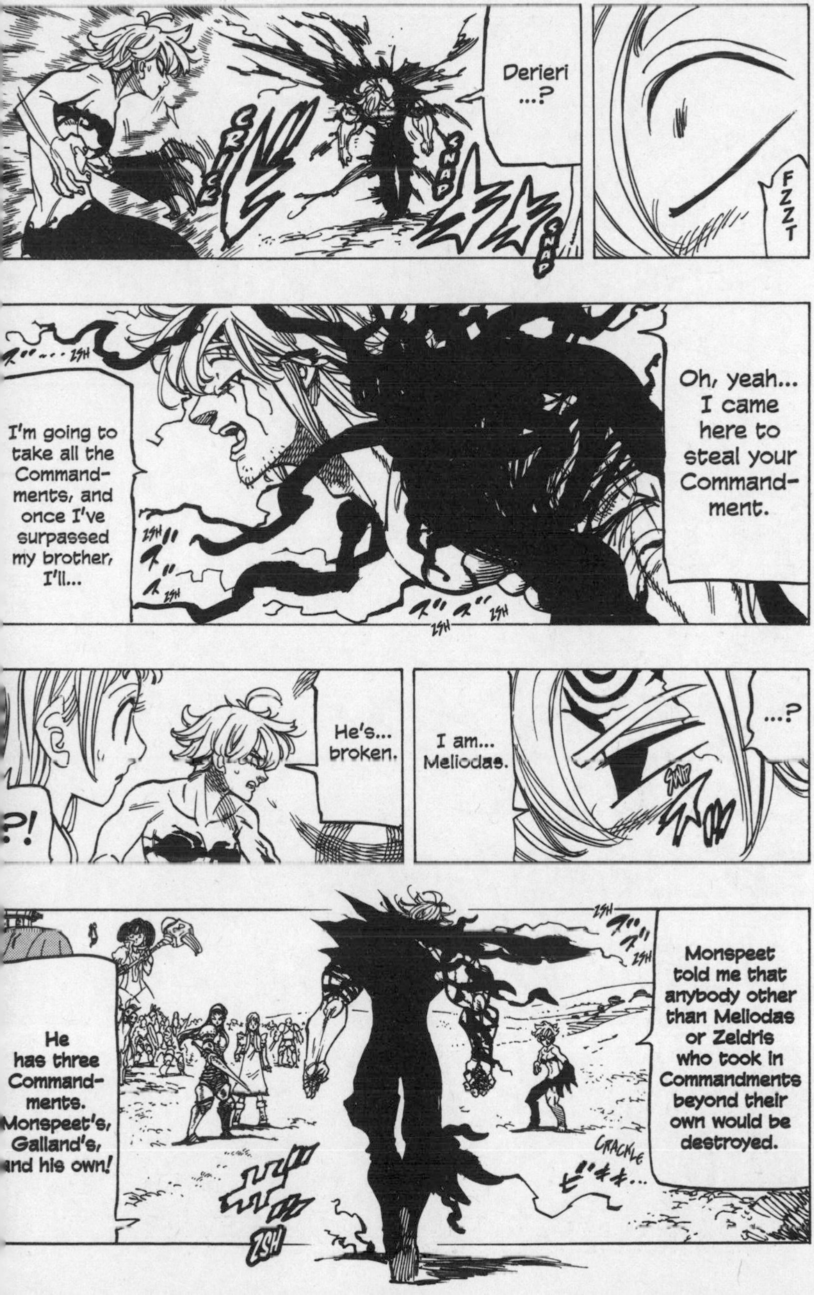
FZZT
Derieri ...?
SNAP
SNAP
CRICK
Oh, yeah... I came here to steal your Commandment.
ZSH
I'm going to take all the Commandments, and once I've surpassed my brother, I'll...
ZSH
ZSH
ZSH
...?
I am... Meliodas.
SNIP
He's... broken.
?!
Monspeet told me that anybody other than Meliodas or Zeldris who took in Commandments beyond their own would be destroyed.
ZSH
CRACKLE
He has three Commandments. Monspeet's, Galland's, and his own!
ZSH

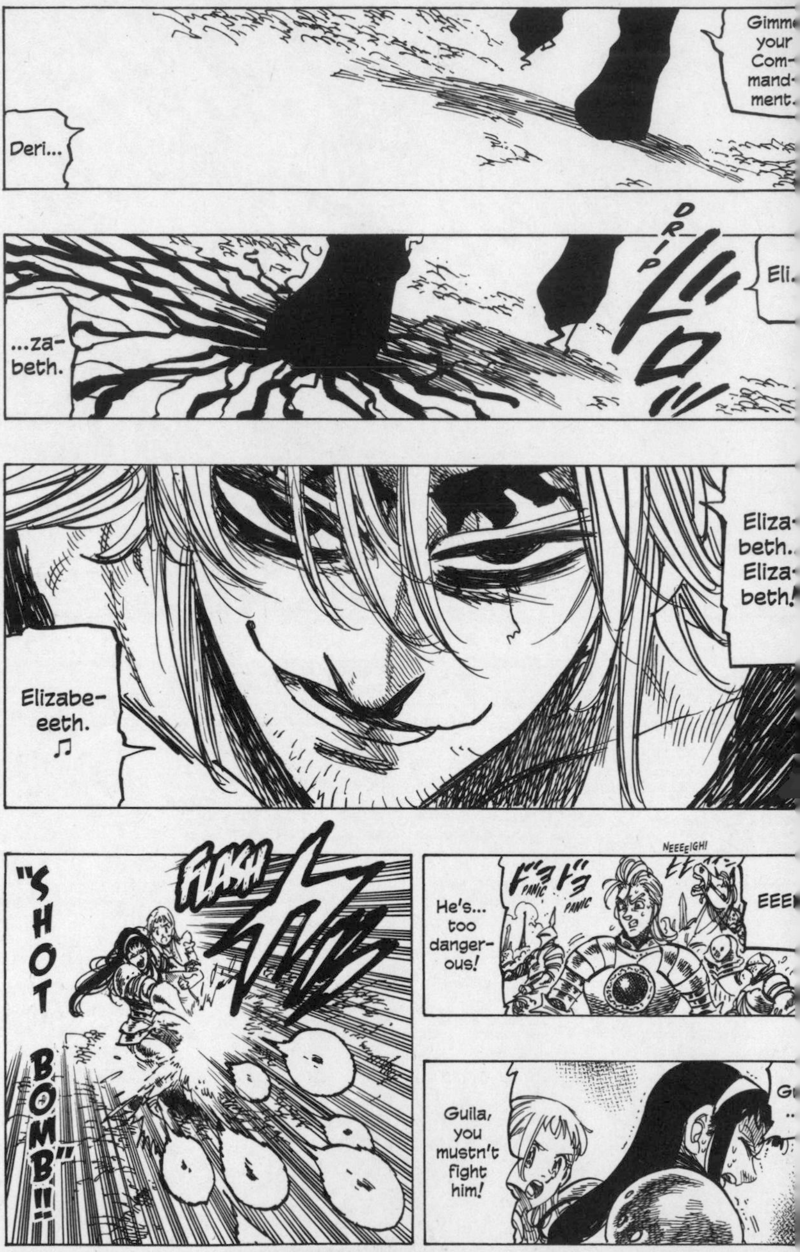

Gimm your Commandment.
Deri...
DRIP
Eli.
...zabeth.
Elizabeth... Elizabeth!
Elizabeeeth. ♫
NEEEEIGH!
EEE
PANIC
PANIC
He's... too dangerous!
Guila, you mustn't fight him!
FLASH
"SHOT BOMB"!!

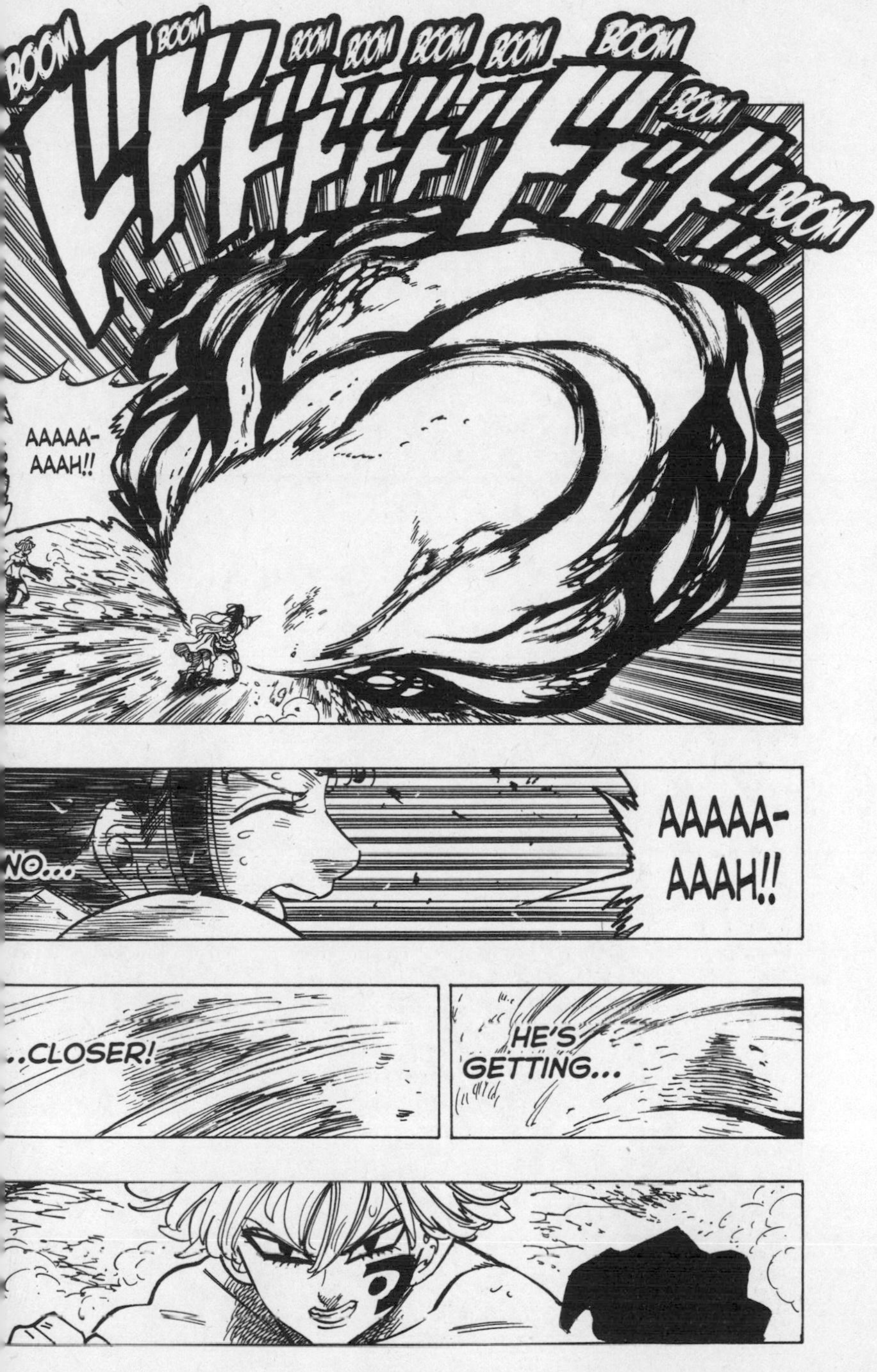
BOOM
BOOM
BOOM
BOOM
BOOM
BOOM
BOOM
BOOM
BOOM
AAAAA-AAAH!!
AAAAA-AAAH!!
NO...
HE'S GETTING...
...CLOSER!

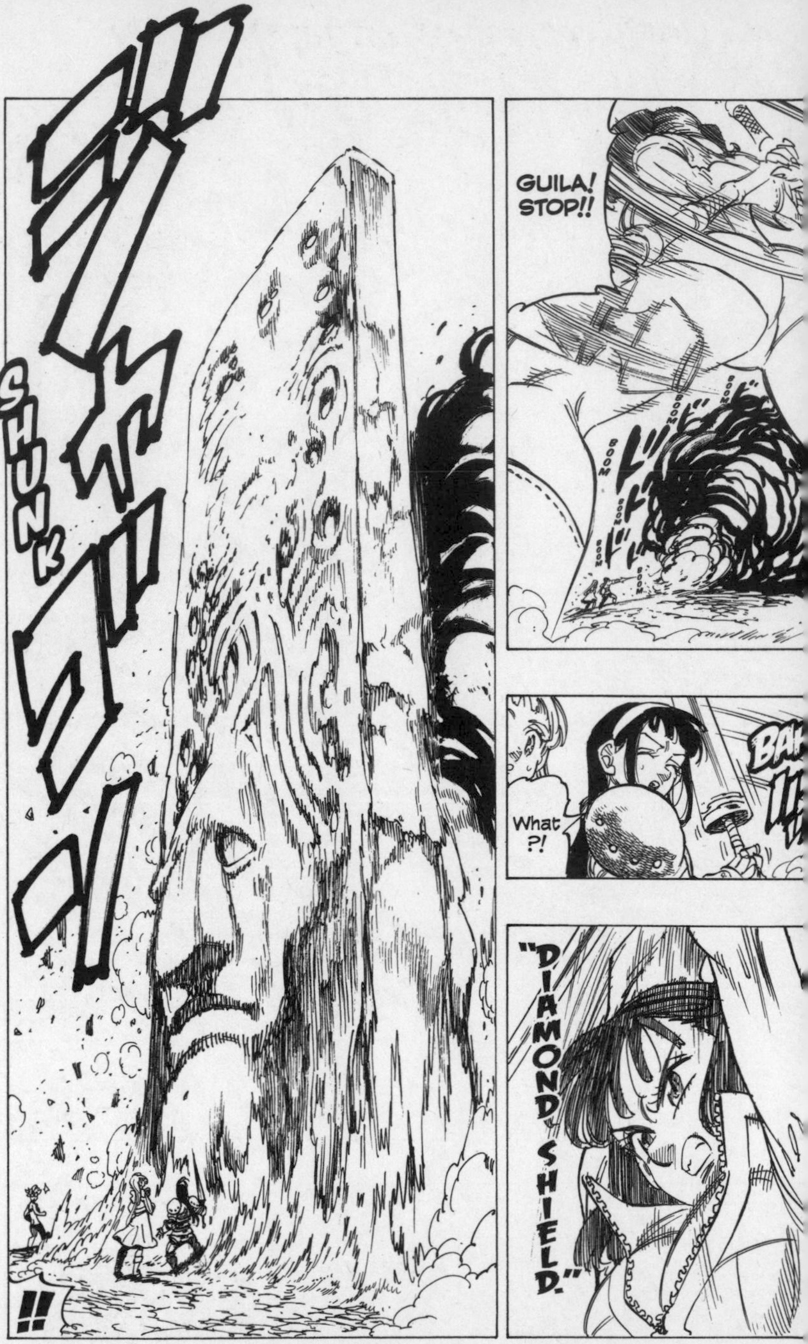
GUILA! STOP!!
BOOM BOOM BOOM BOOM BOOM BOOM
What ?!
"DIAMOND SHIELD."
SHUNK
!!

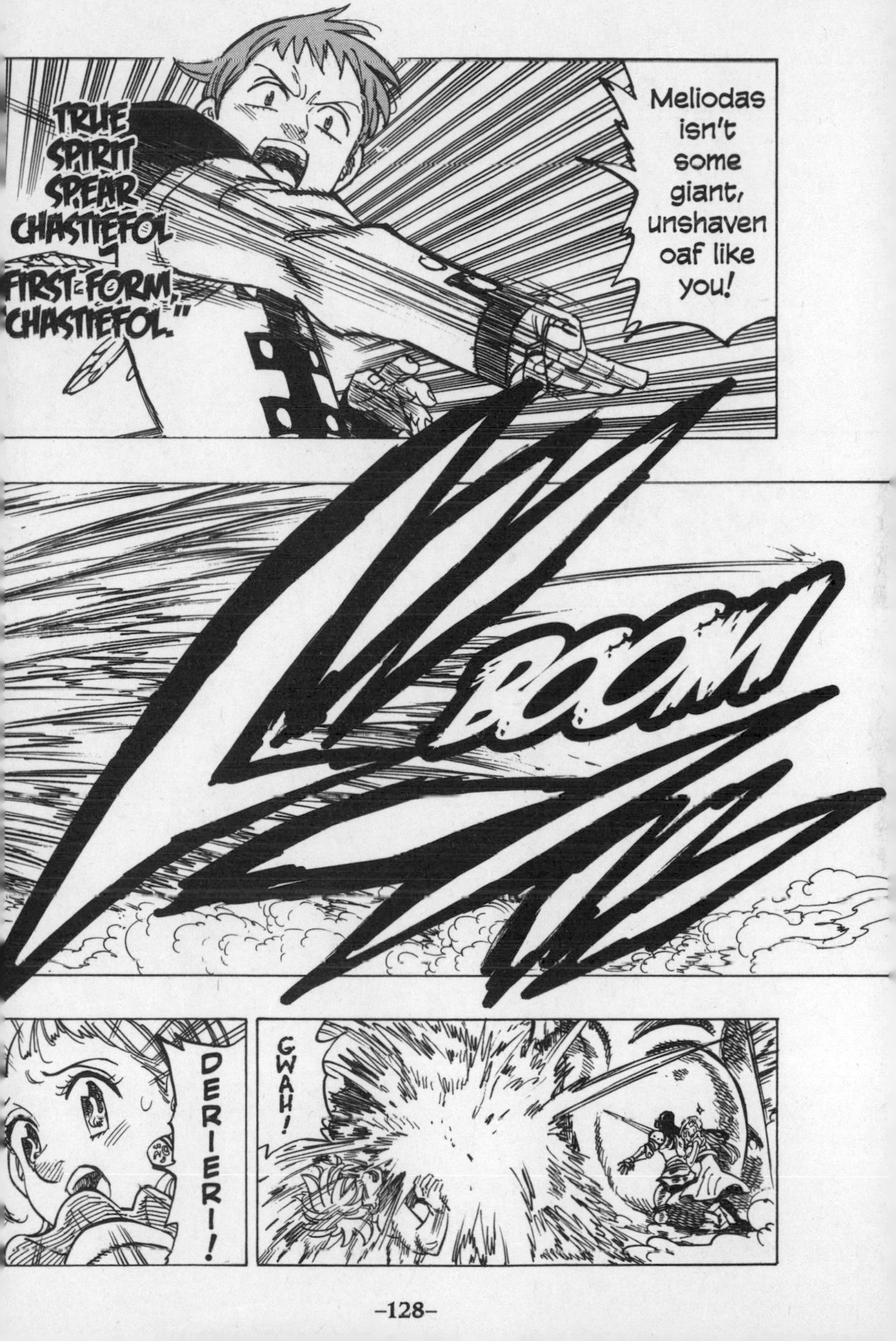
Meliodas isn't some giant, unshaven oaf like you!
TRUE SPIRIT SPEAR CHASTIEFOL
FIRST FORM, CHASTIEFOL."
BOOM
GWAH!
DERIERI!

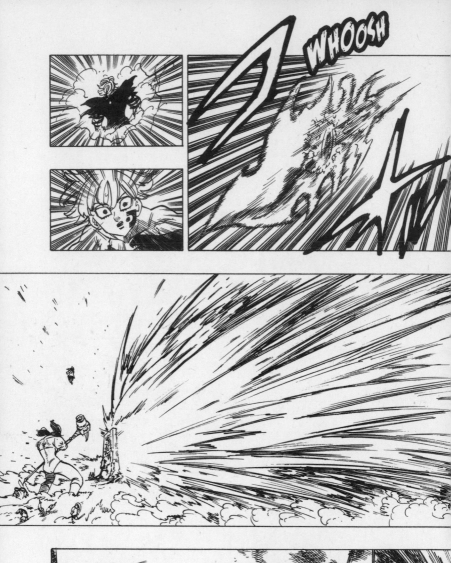

WHOOSH

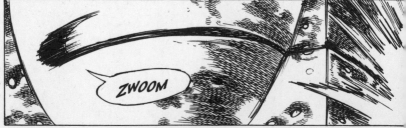

ZWOOM

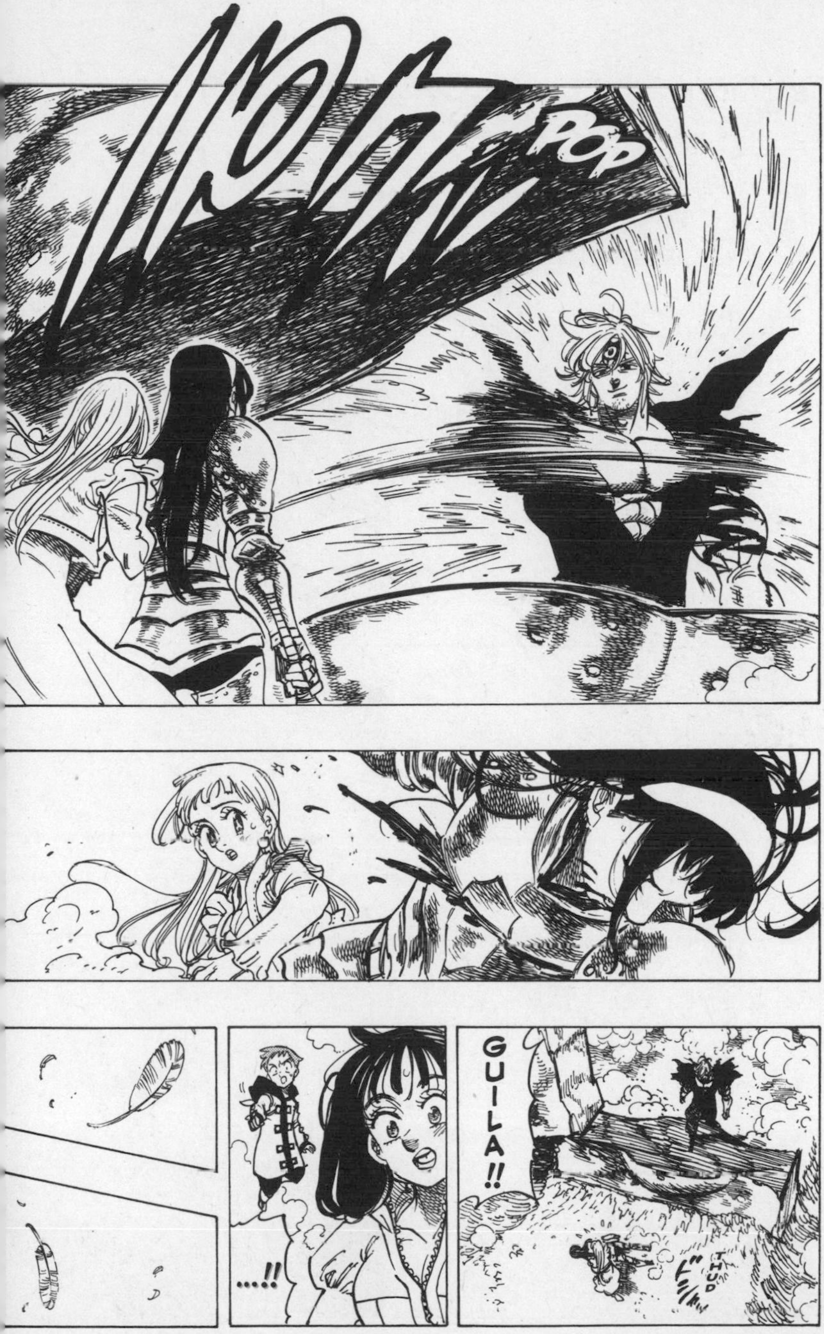
POP
GUILA!!
THUD
...!!

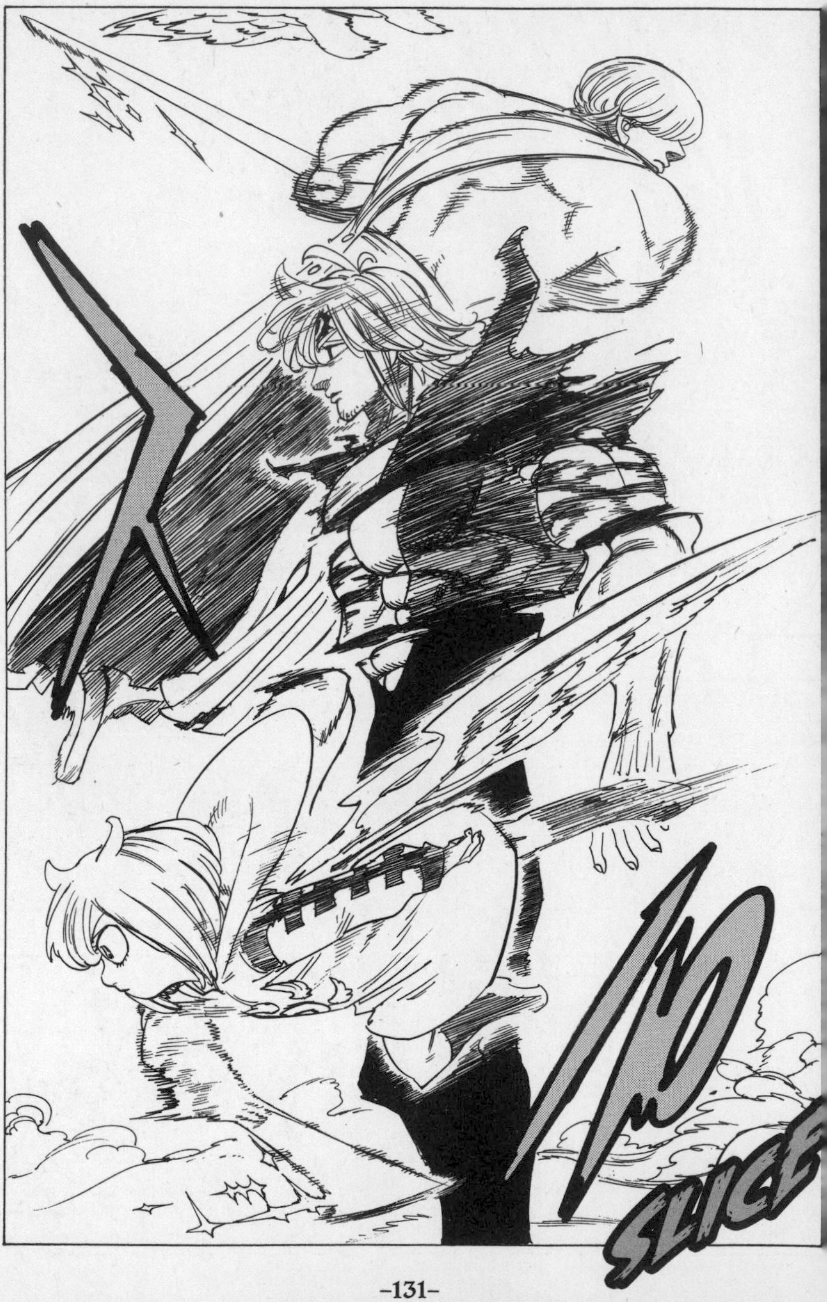
SLICE

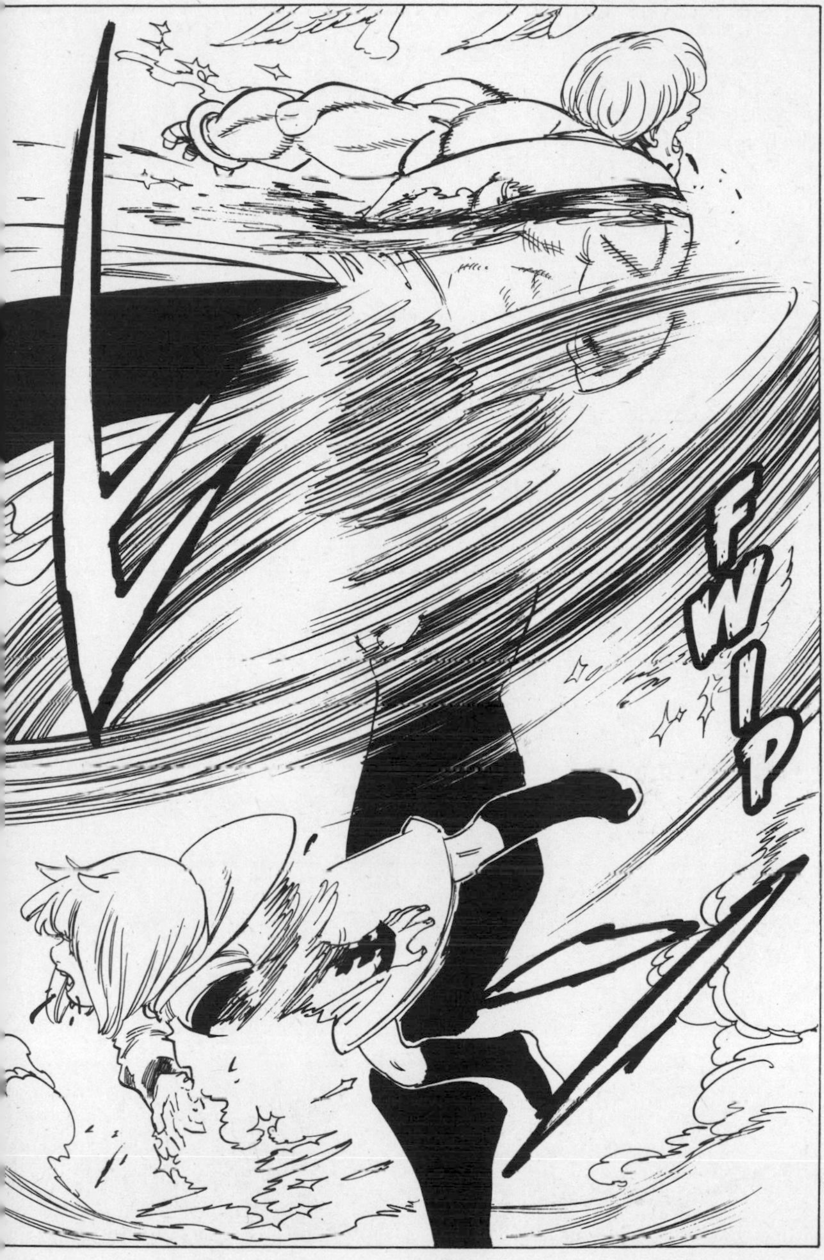
FWIP

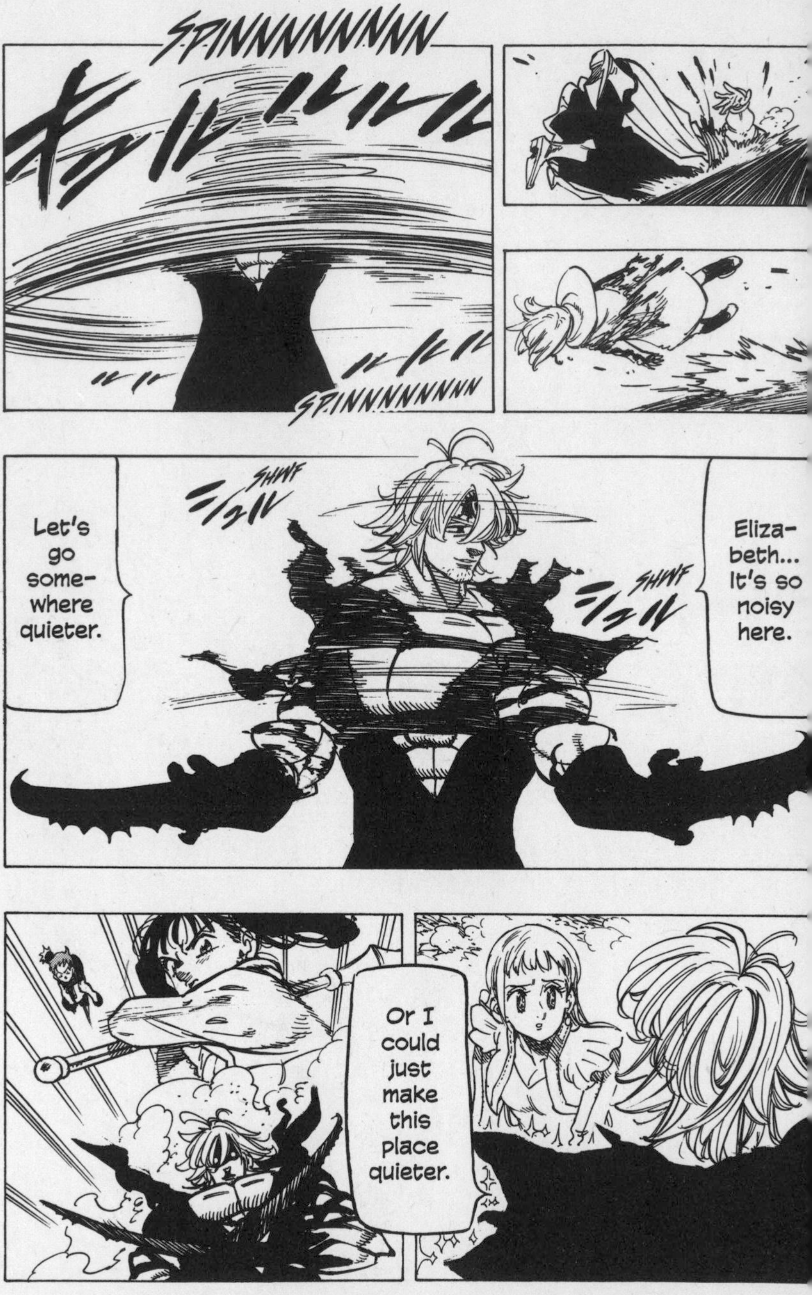
SPINNNNNNNNN
SPINNNNNNNNN
Eliza-beth... It's so noisy here.
SHWF
SHWF
Let's go some-where quieter.
Or I could just make this place quieter.

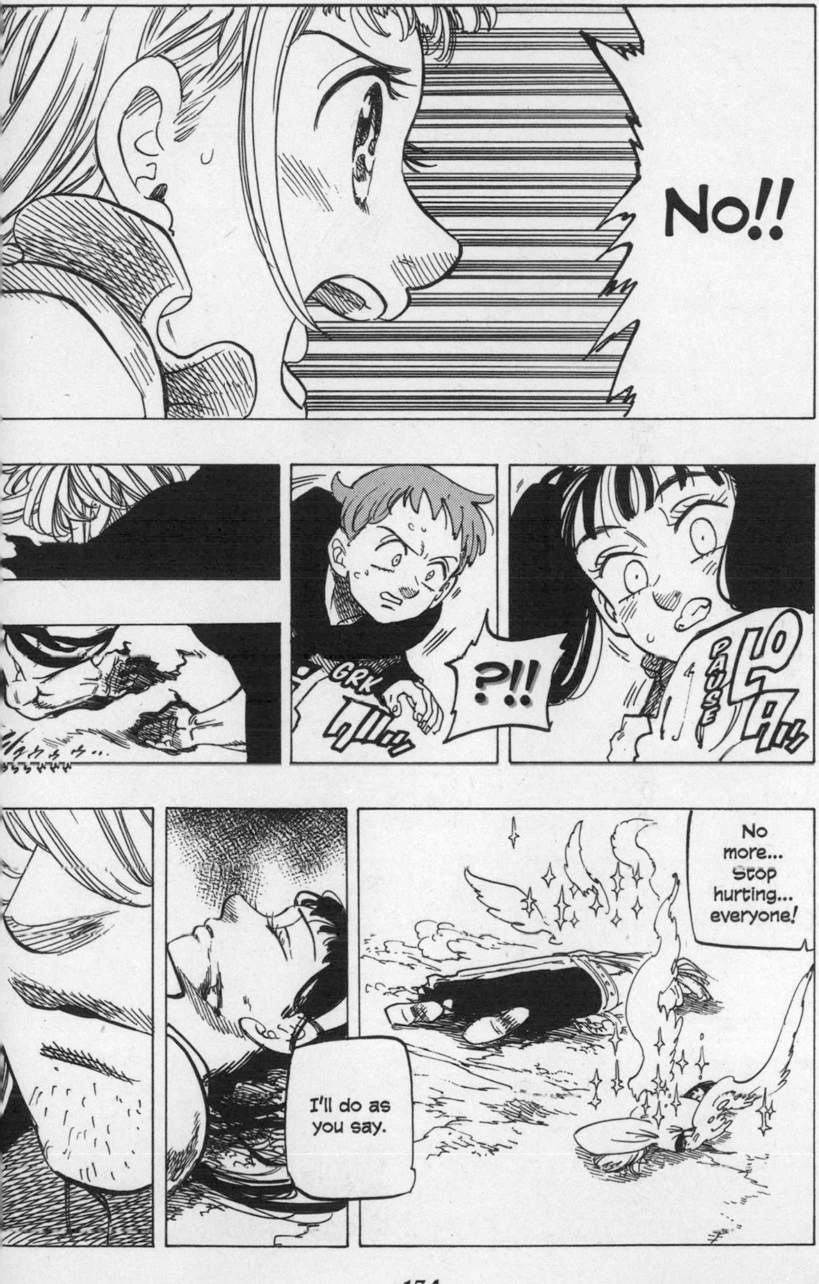
No!!
PAUSE
?!!
GRK
No more... Stop hurting... everyone!
I'll do as you say.

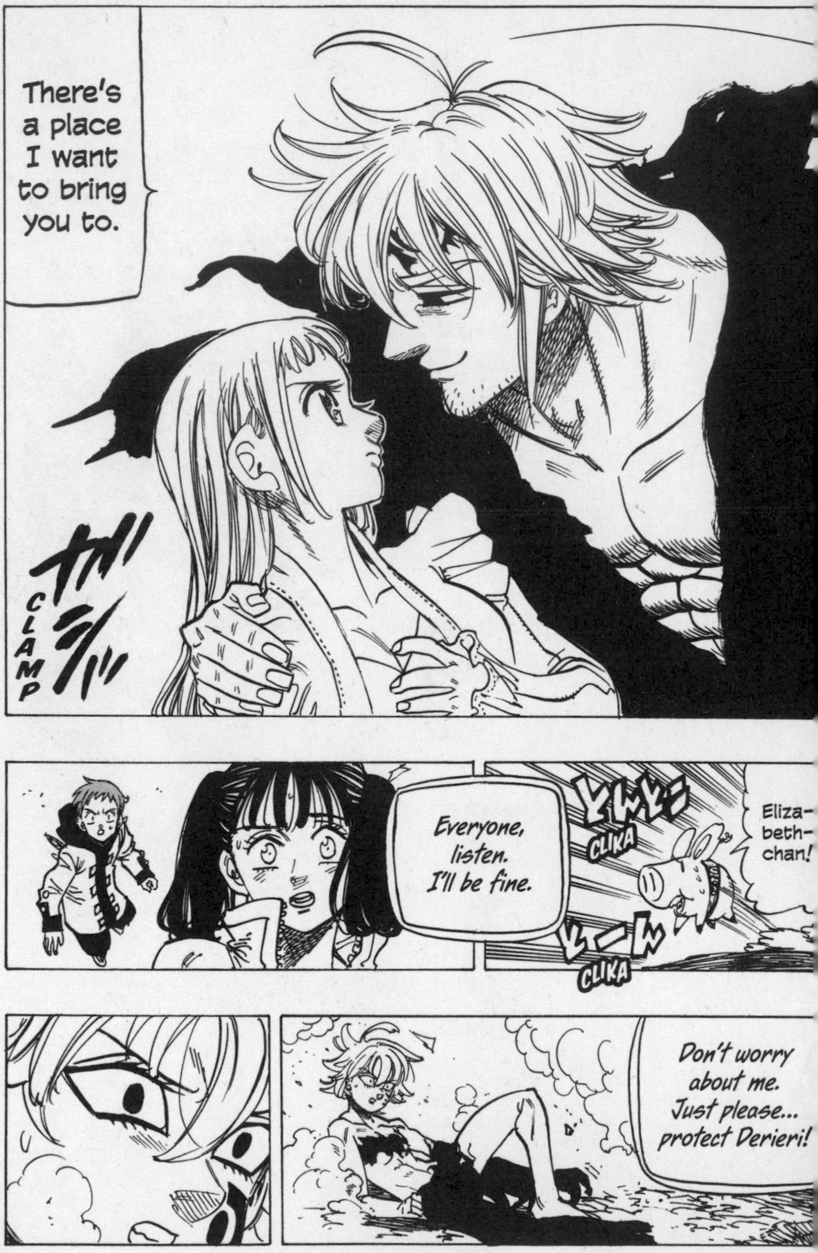
There's a place I want to bring you to.
CLAMP
Eliza-beth-chan!
CLIKA
CLIKA
Everyone, listen. I'll be fine.
Don't worry about me. Just please... protect Derieri!

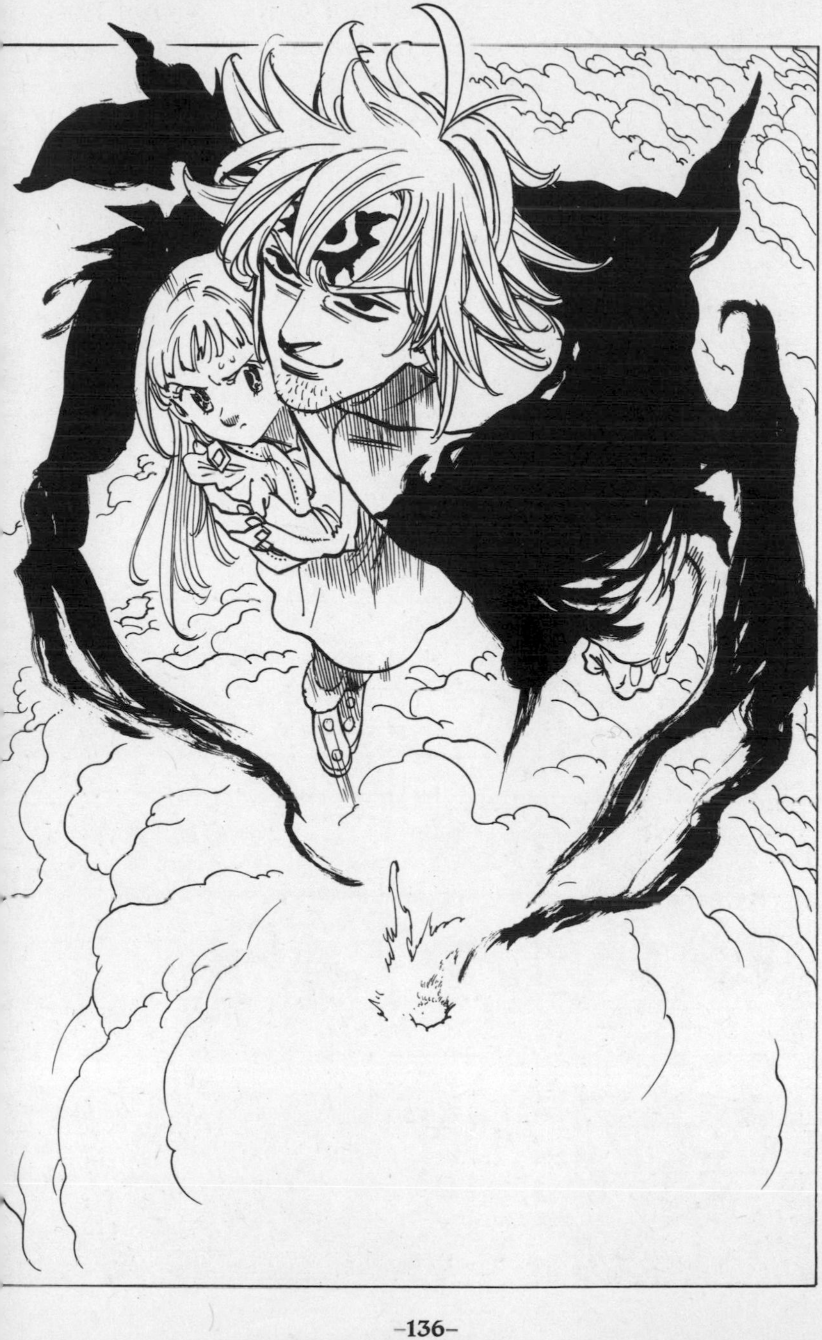

Bonus Story - Sweet Dreams

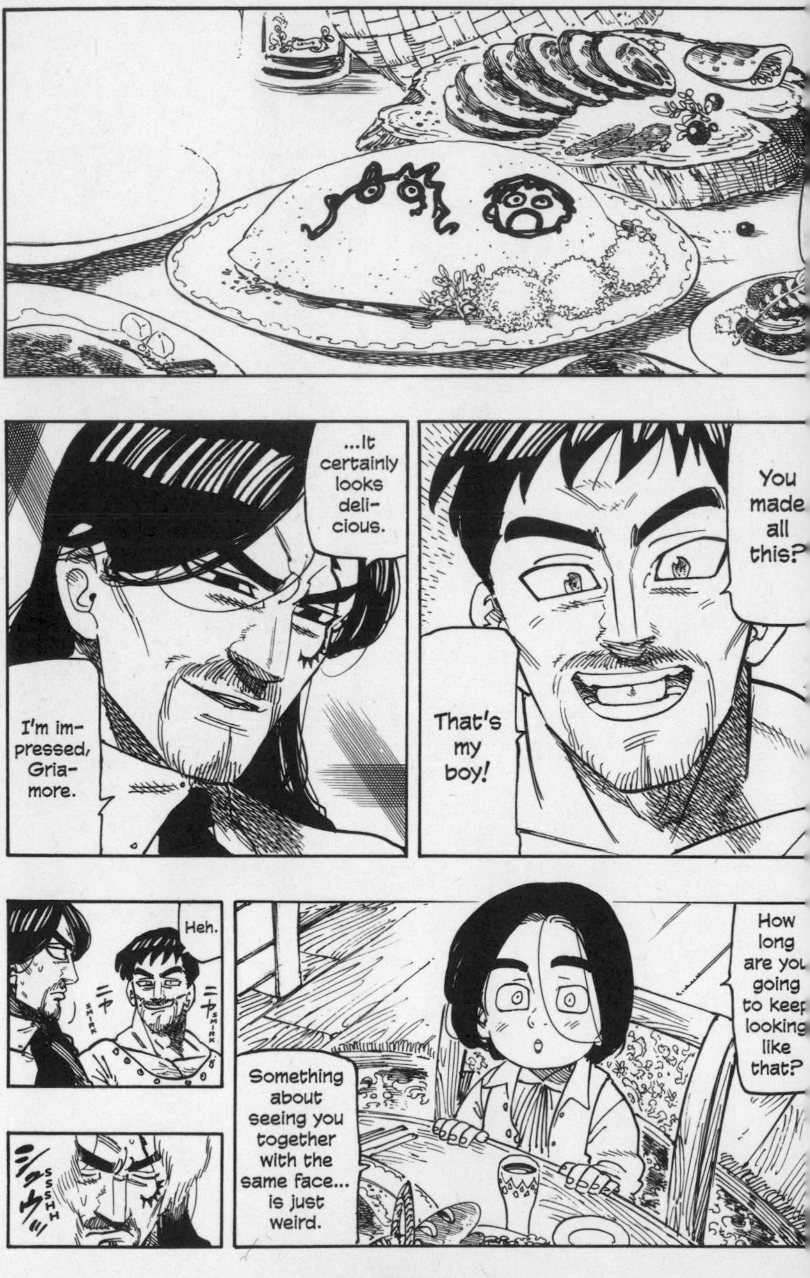
You made all this?
That's my boy!
...It certainly looks delicious.
I'm impressed, Griamore.
How long are you going to keep looking like that?
Something about seeing you together with the same face... is just weird.
Heh.
ニヤ SMIRK
ニヤ SMIRK
SSSHH

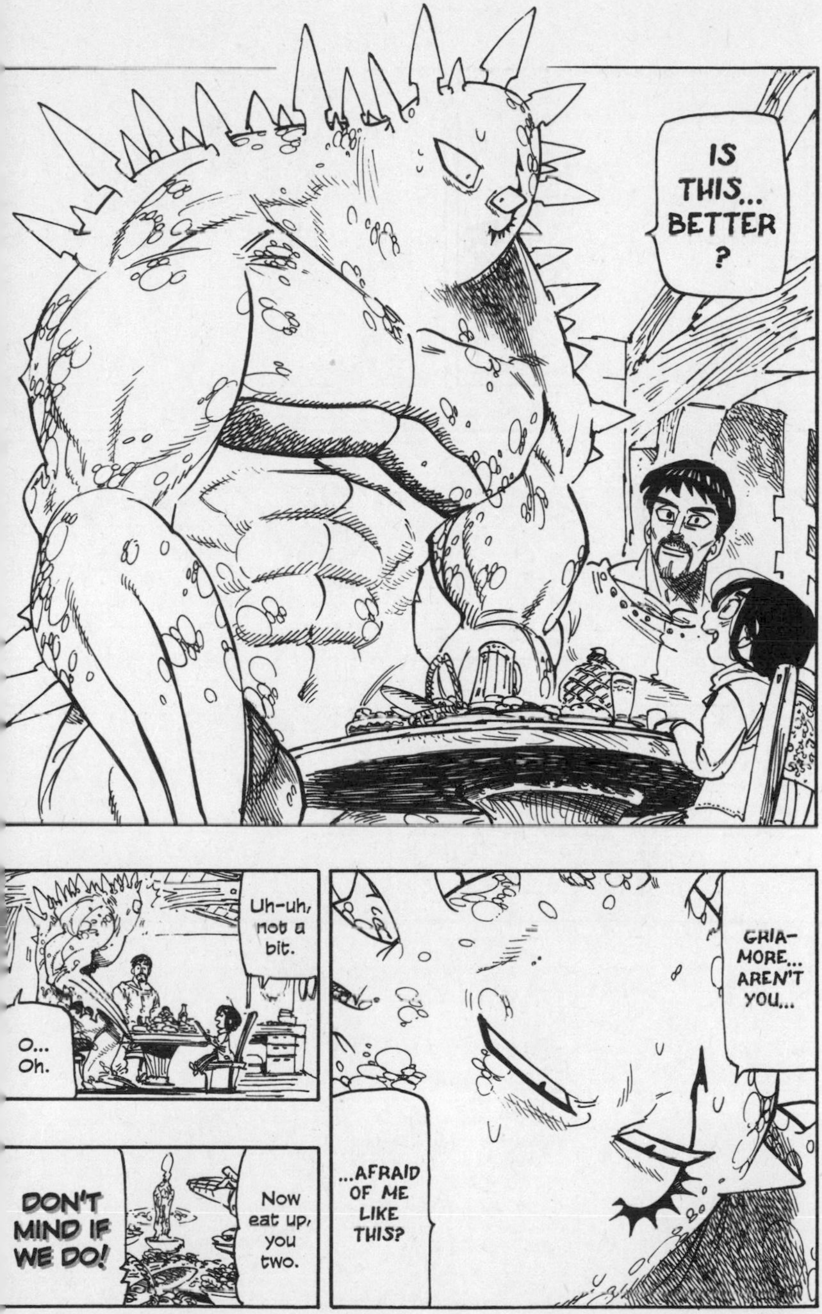
IS THIS... BETTER ?
GRIA-MORE... AREN'T YOU...
...AFRAID OF ME LIKE THIS?
Uh-uh, not a bit.
O... Oh.
Now eat up, you two.
DON'T MIND IF WE DO!

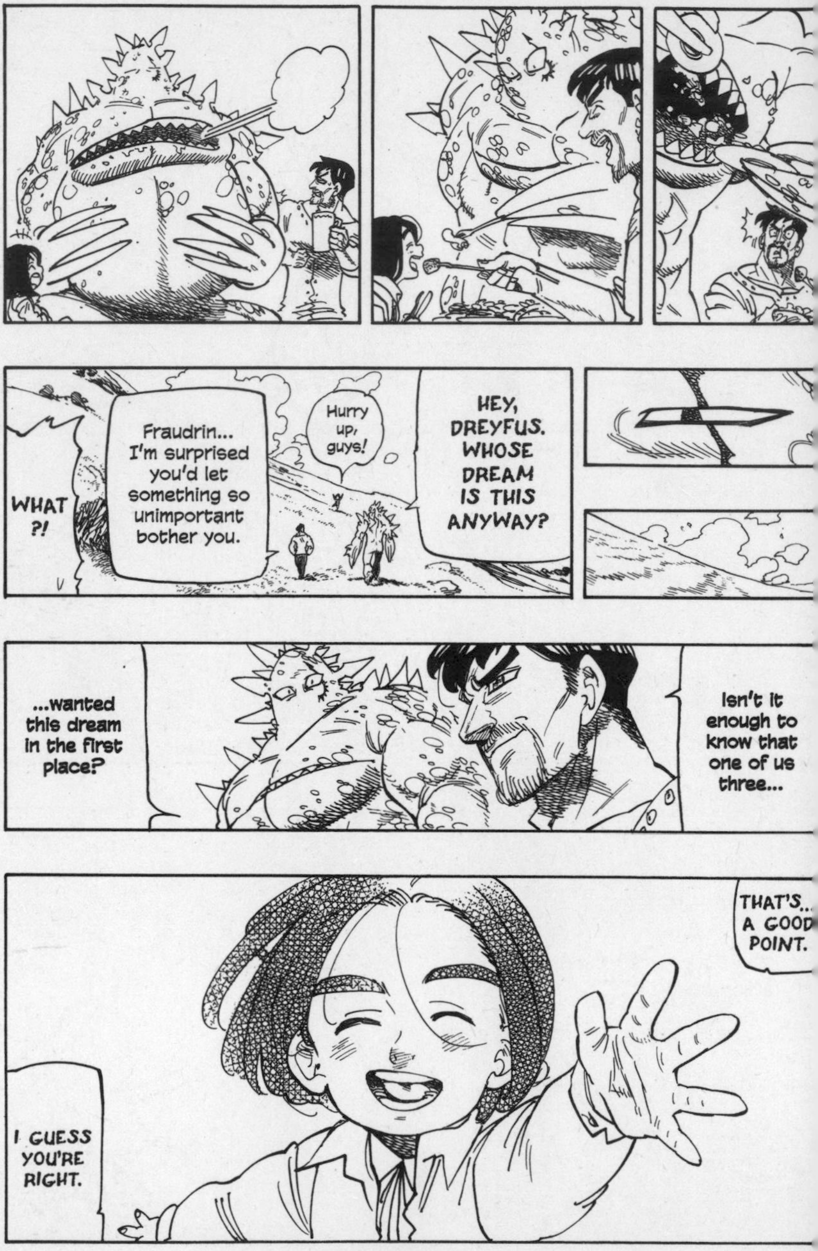
HEY, DREYFUS. WHOSE DREAM IS THIS ANYWAY?
Hurry up, guys!
Fraudrin... I'm surprised you'd let something so unimportant bother you.
WHAT ?!
Isn't it enough to know that one of us three...
...wanted this dream in the first place?
THAT'S... A GOOD POINT.
I GUESS YOU'RE RIGHT.

The End

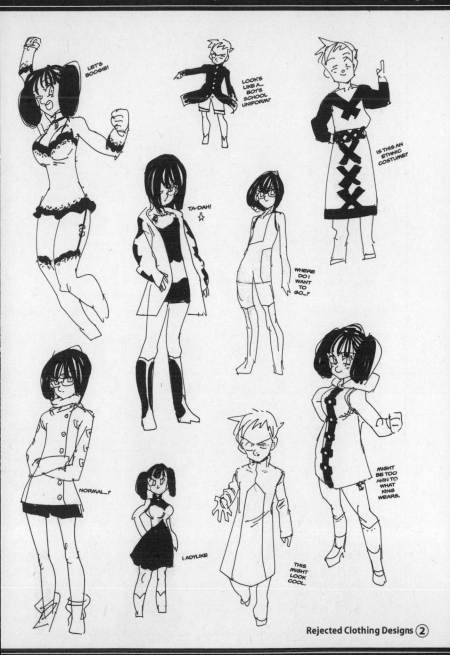

LET'S BOOGIE!

LOOKS LIKE A... BOY'S SCHOOL UNIFORM?

IS THIS AN ETHNIC COSTUME?

TA-DAH! ☆

WHERE DO I WANT TO GO...?

NORMAL...?

LADYLIKE

THIS MIGHT LOOK COOL.

MIGHT BE TOO AKIN TO WHAT KING WEARS.

Rejected Clothing Designs ②

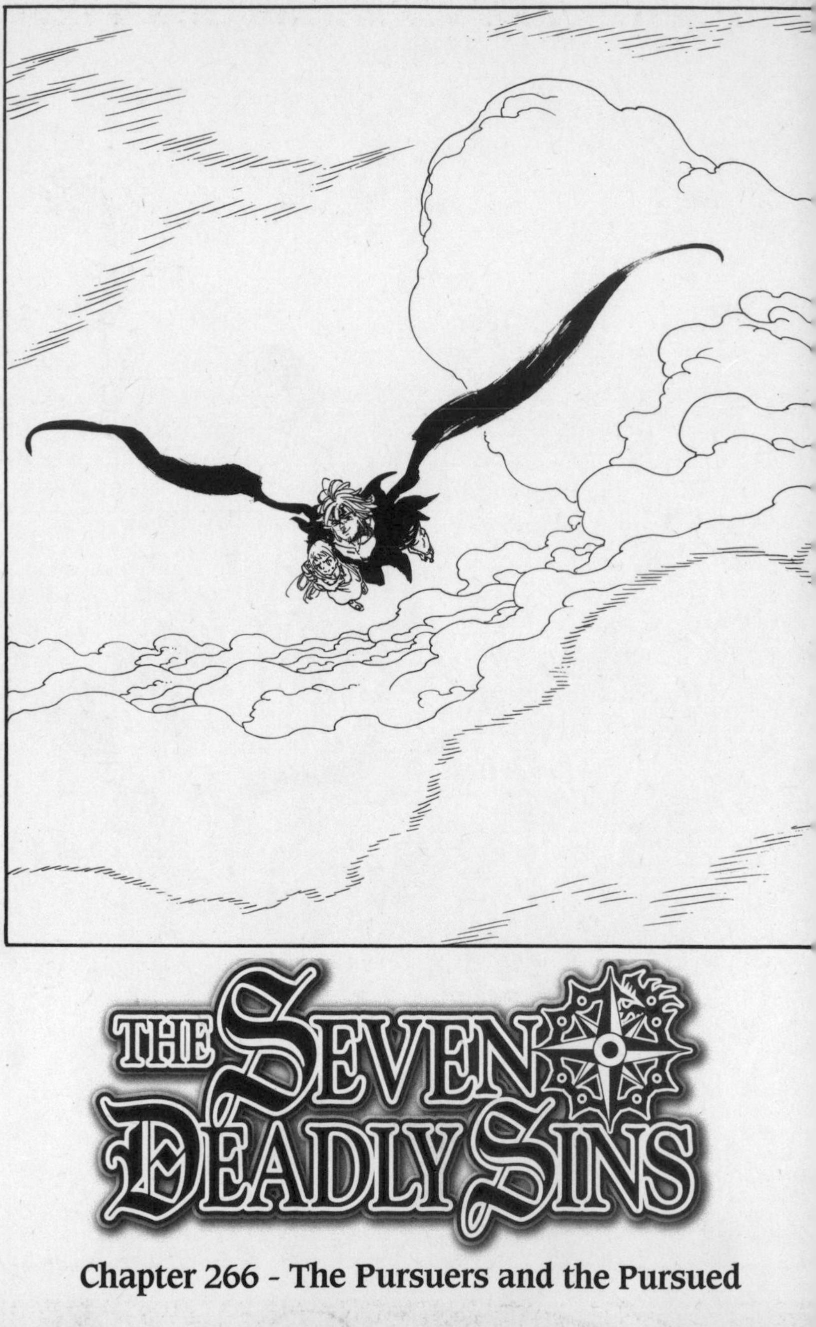

THE SEVEN DEADLY SINS

Chapter 266 - The Pursuers and the Pursued

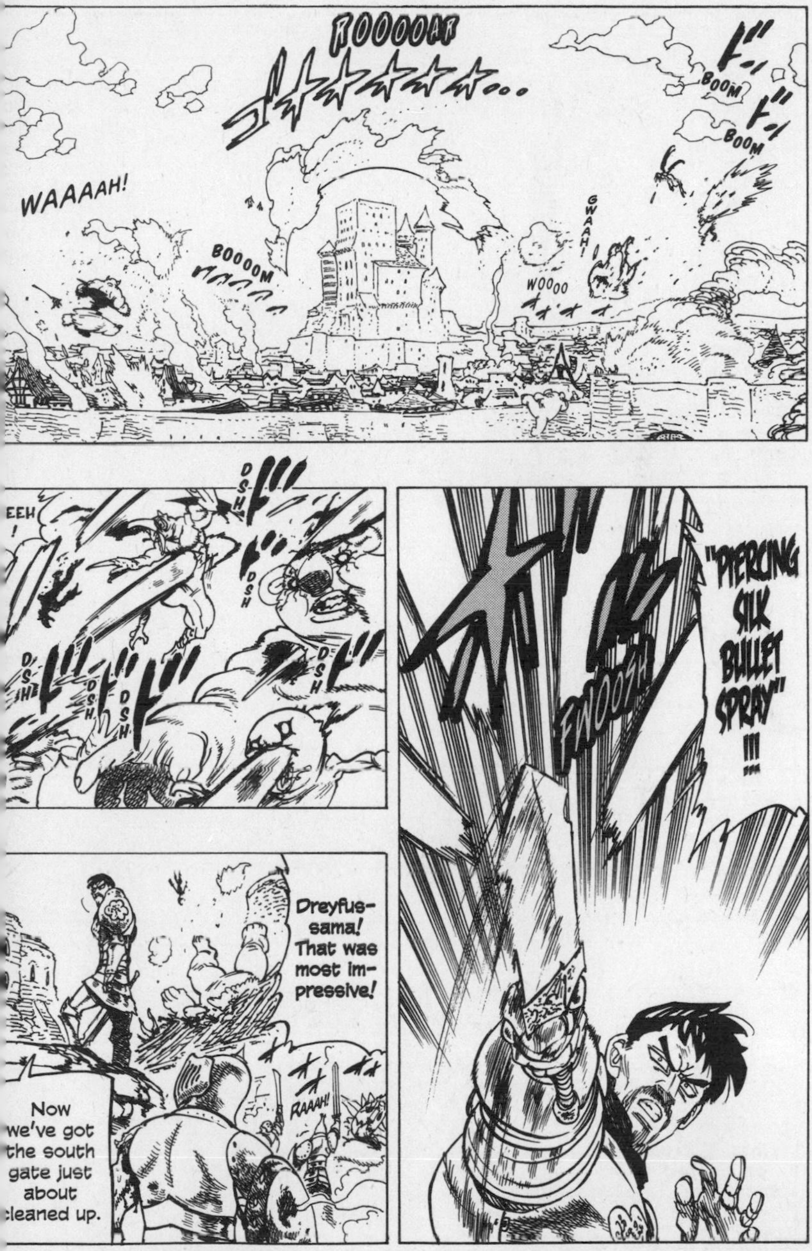

ROOOOAR
BOOM
BOOM
WAAAAH!
GWAAH!
BOOOOM
WOOO
EEH!
DSH
DSH
DSH
DSH
DSH
DSH
"PIERCING SILK BULLET SPRAY"!!!
FWOOSH
Dreyfus-sama! That was most impressive!
RAAAH!
Now we've got the south gate just about cleaned up.

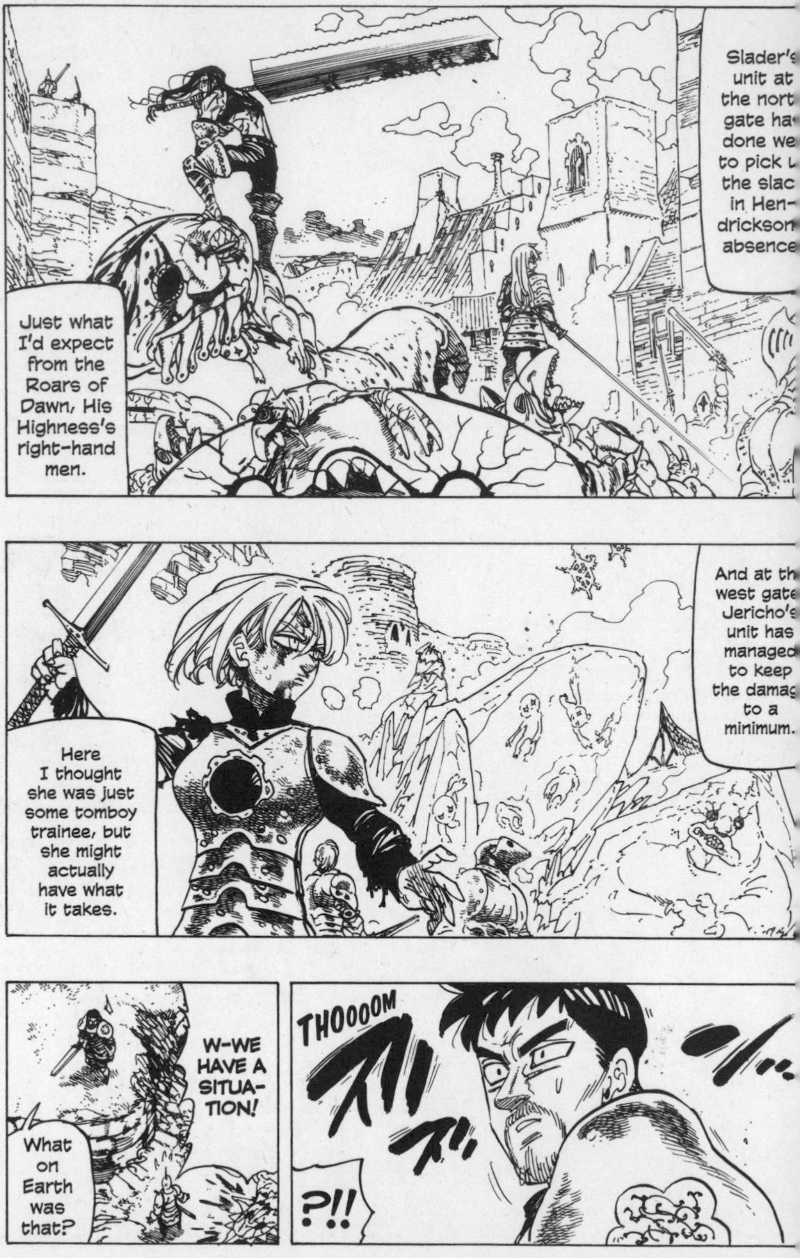
Slader's unit at the nort gate ha done we to pick u the slac in Hen-drickson absence
Just what I'd expect from the Roars of Dawn, His Highness's right-hand men.
And at th west gate Jericho's unit has manage to keep the damag to a minimum.
Here I thought she was just some tomboy trainee, but she might actually have what it takes.
THOOOOM
?!!
W-WE HAVE A SITUA-TION!
What on Earth was that?

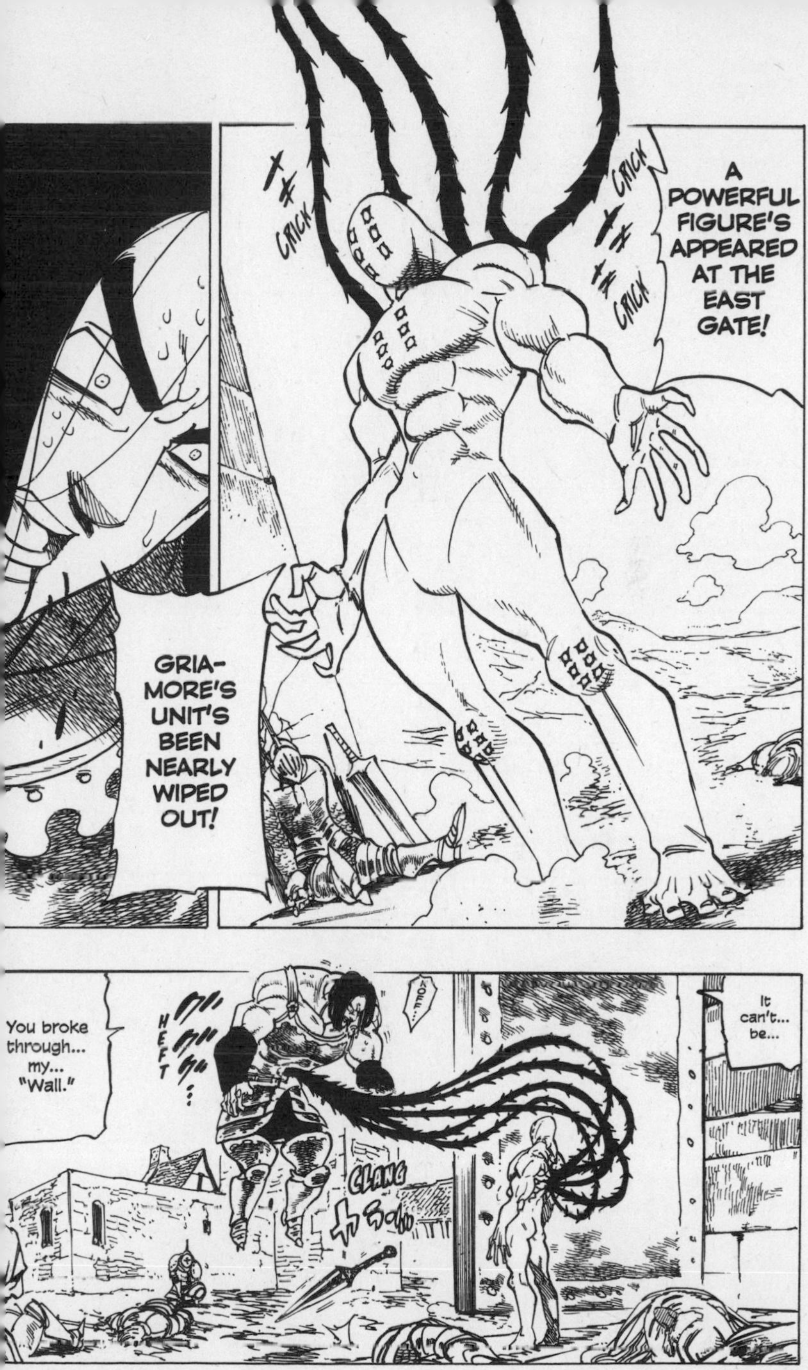
CRICK
CRICK
CRICK
A POWERFUL FIGURE'S APPEARED AT THE EAST GATE!
GRIA-MORE'S UNIT'S BEEN NEARLY WIPED OUT!
It can't... be...
OOF...
CLANG
HEFT
You broke through... my... "Wall."

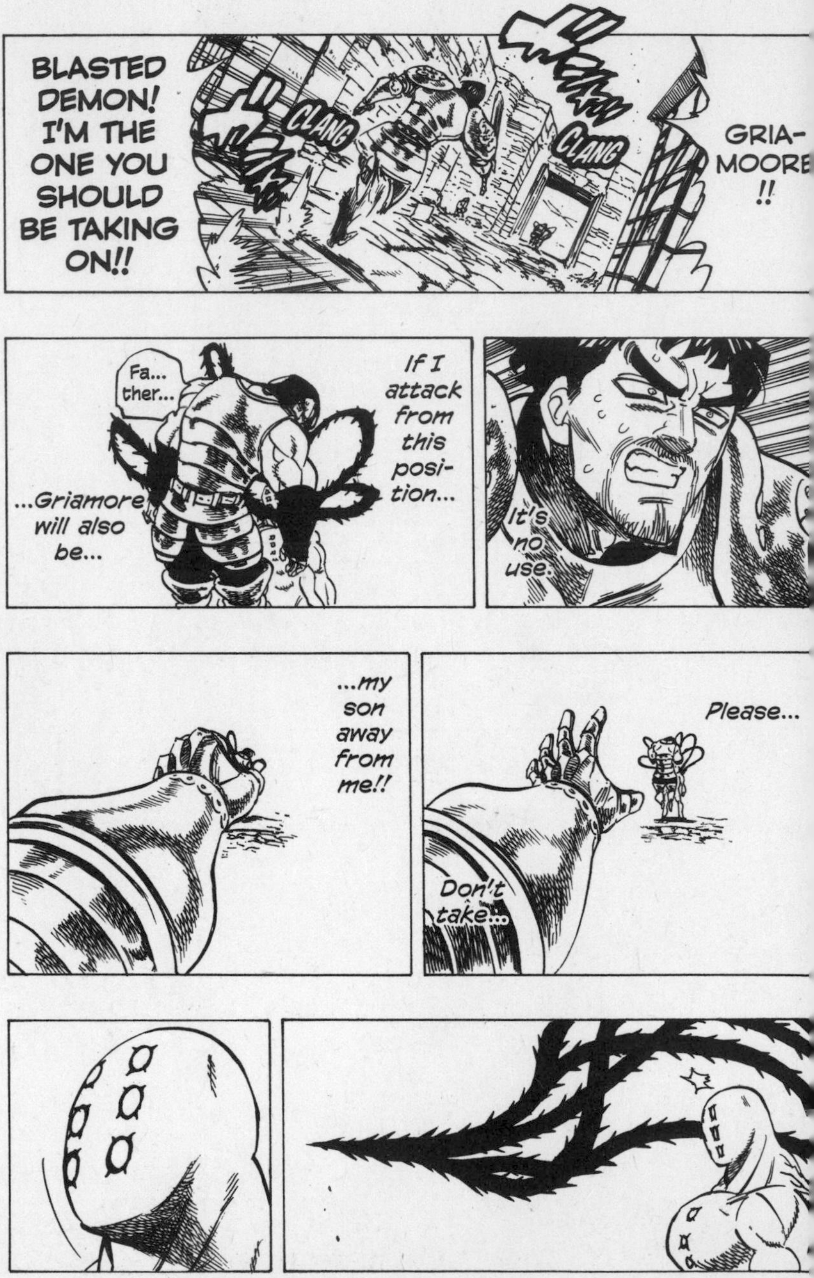
GRIA-MOORE!!
CLANG
CLANG
BLASTED DEMON! I'M THE ONE YOU SHOULD BE TAKING ON!!
It's no use.
If I attack from this position...
Fa... ther...
...Griamore will also be...
Please...
Don't take...
...my son away from me!!

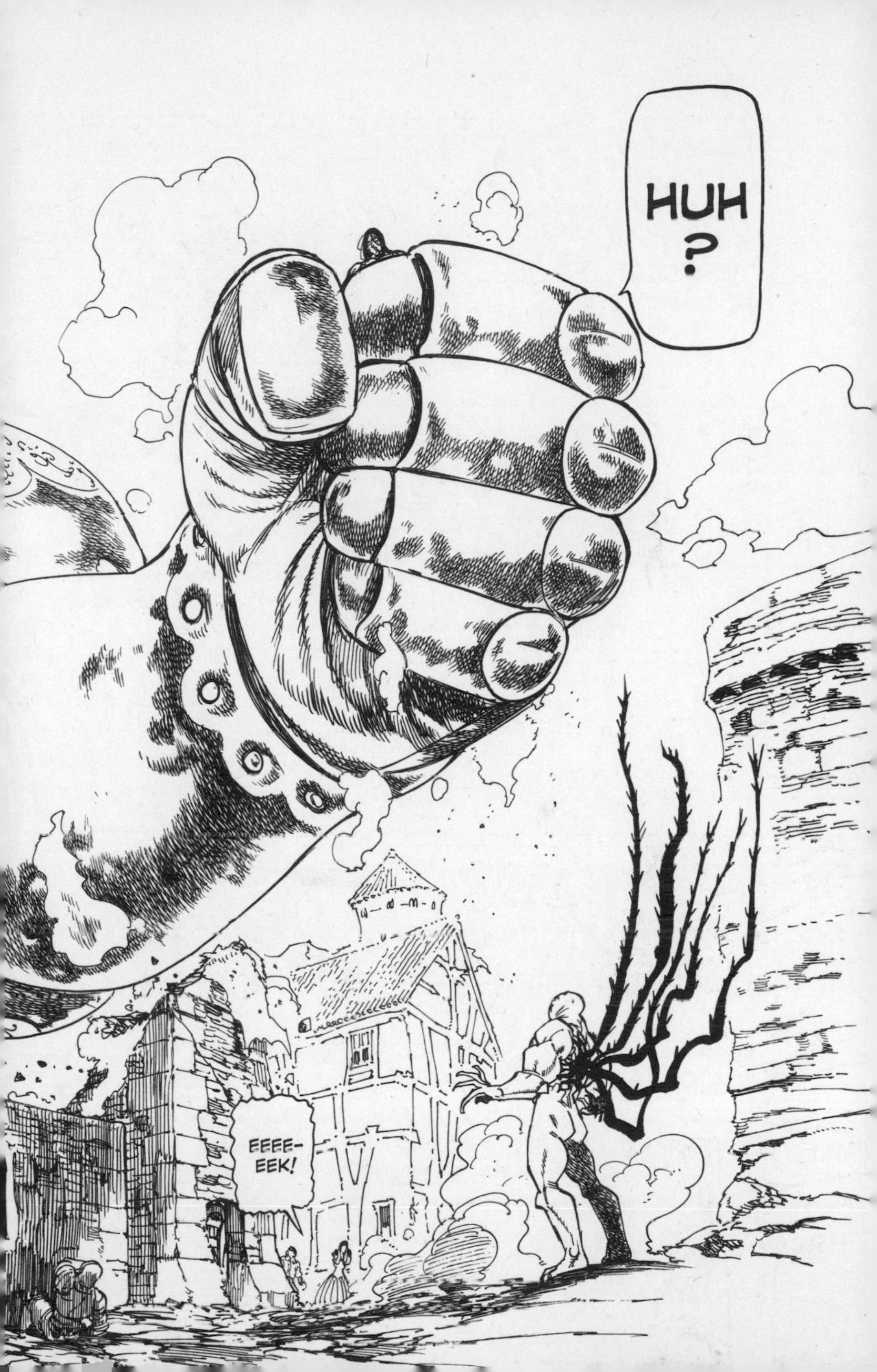
HUH?
EEEE-EEK!

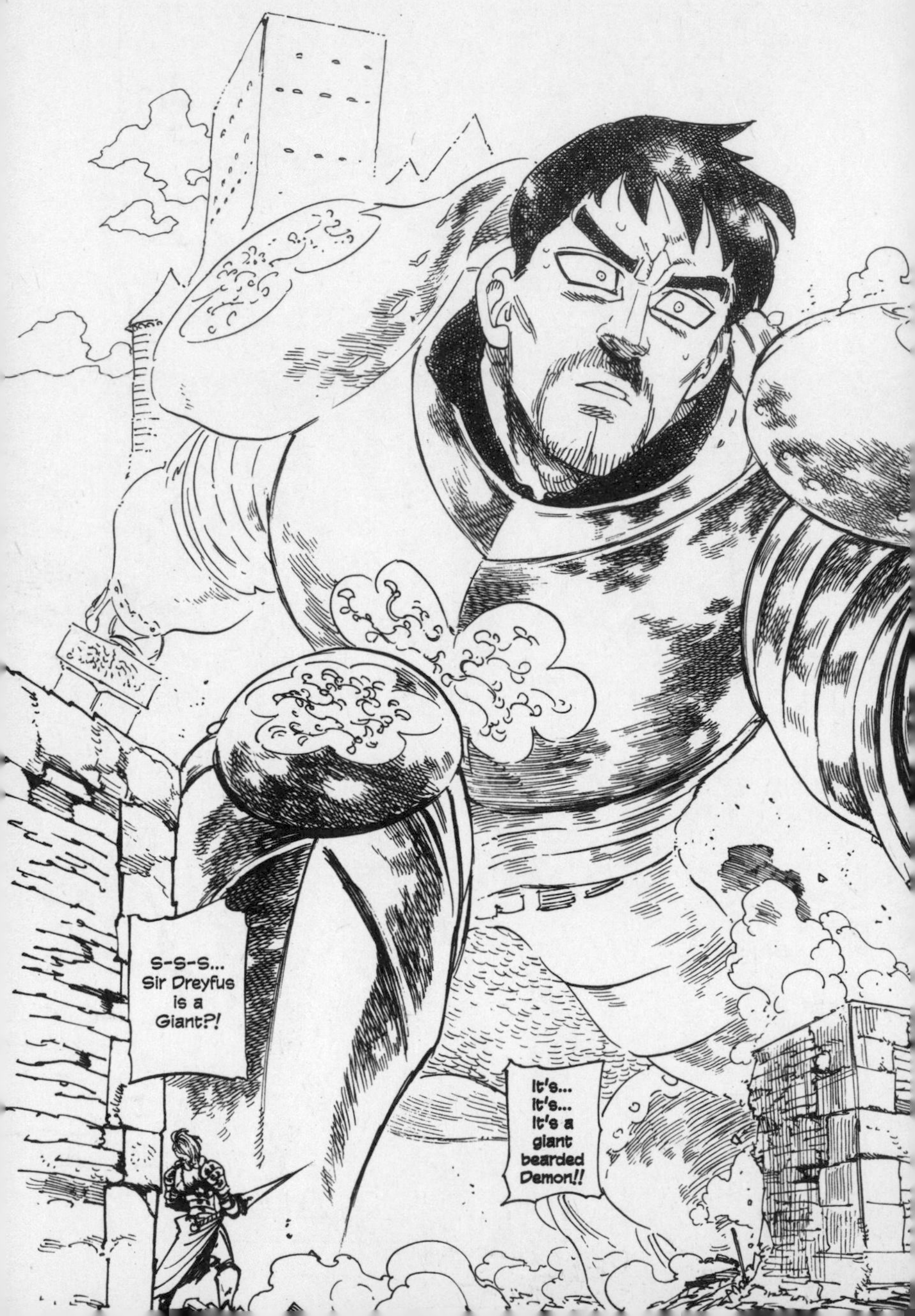
It's... it's... It's a giant bearded Demon!!
S-S-S... Sir Dreyfus is a Giant?!

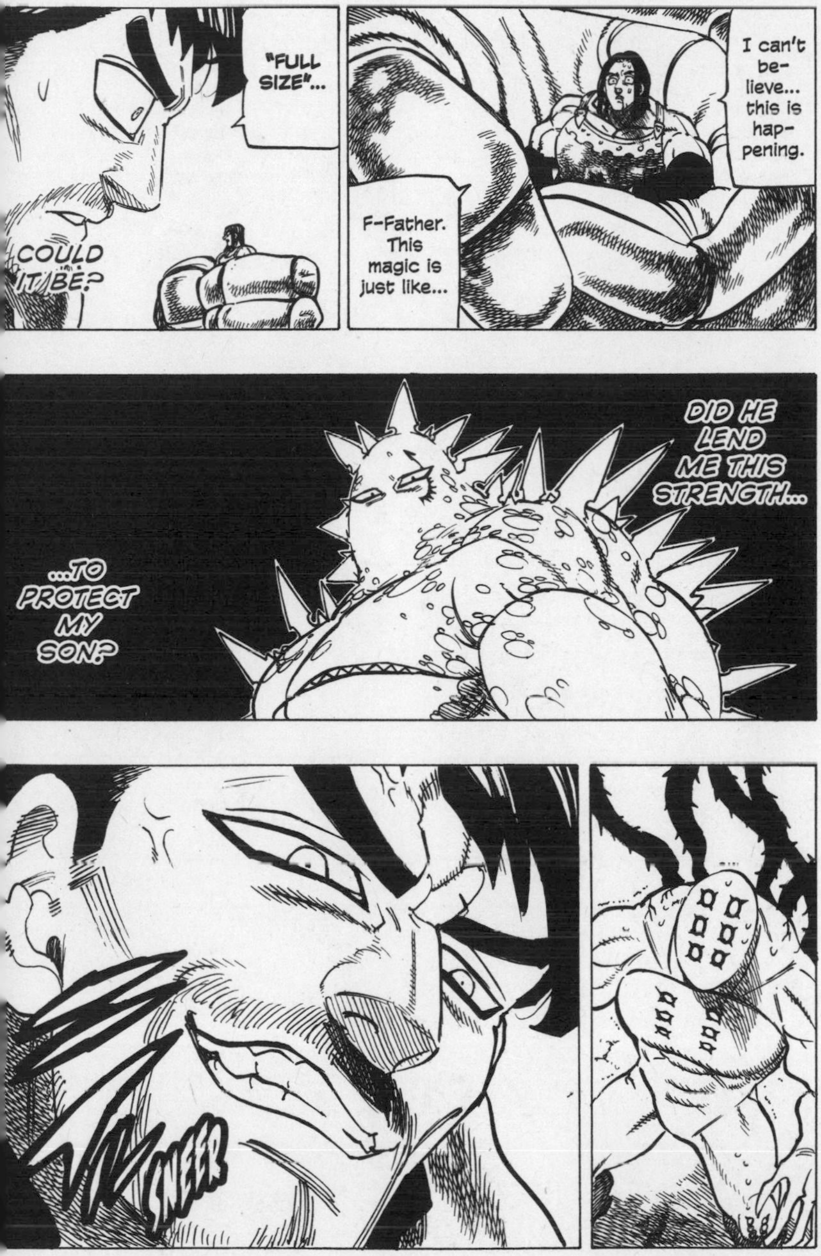
I can't be-lieve... this is hap-pening.
F-Father. This magic is just like...
"FULL SIZE"...
COULD IT BE?
DID HE LEND ME THIS STRENGTH...
...TO PROTECT MY SON?
SNEER

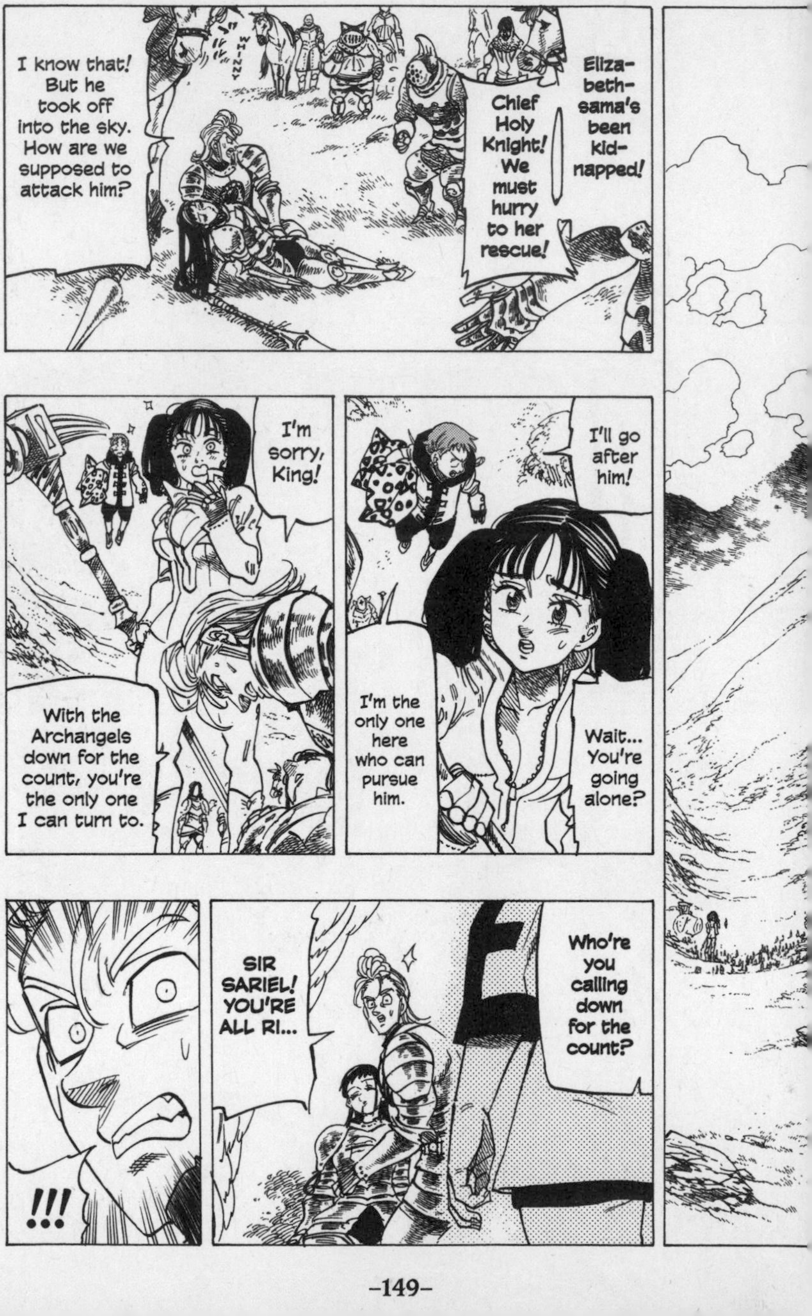
Eliza-beth-sama's been kid-napped!
Chief Holy Knight! We must hurry to her rescue!
WHINNY
I know that! But he took off into the sky. How are we supposed to attack him?
I'll go after him!
Wait... You're going alone?
I'm the only one here who can pursue him.
I'm sorry, King!
With the Archangels down for the count, you're the only one I can turn to.
Who're you calling down for the count?
SIR SARIEL! YOU'RE ALL RI...
!!!

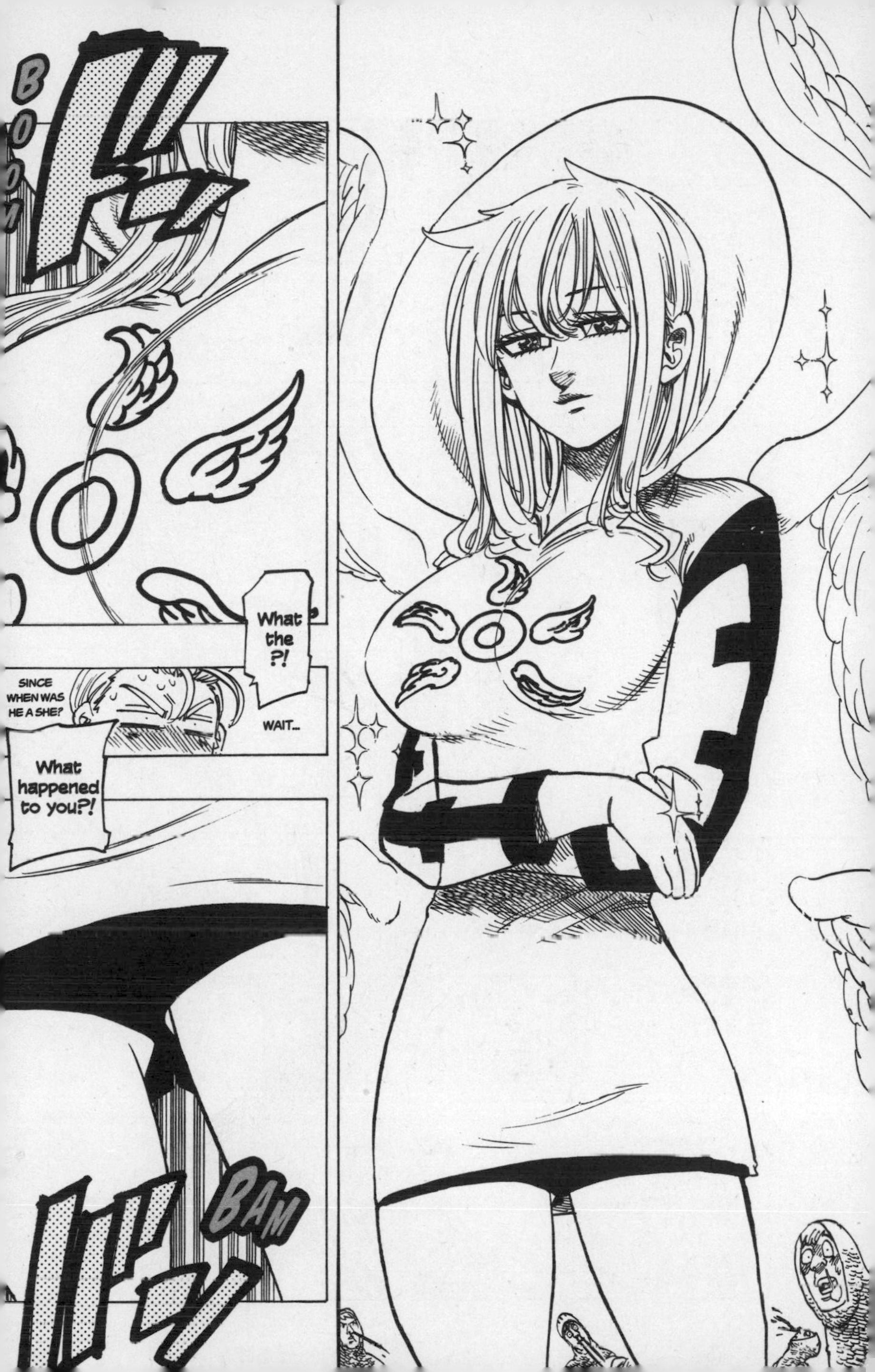
BOOM
What the ?!
WAIT...
SINCE WHEN WAS HE A SHE?
What happened to you?!
BAM

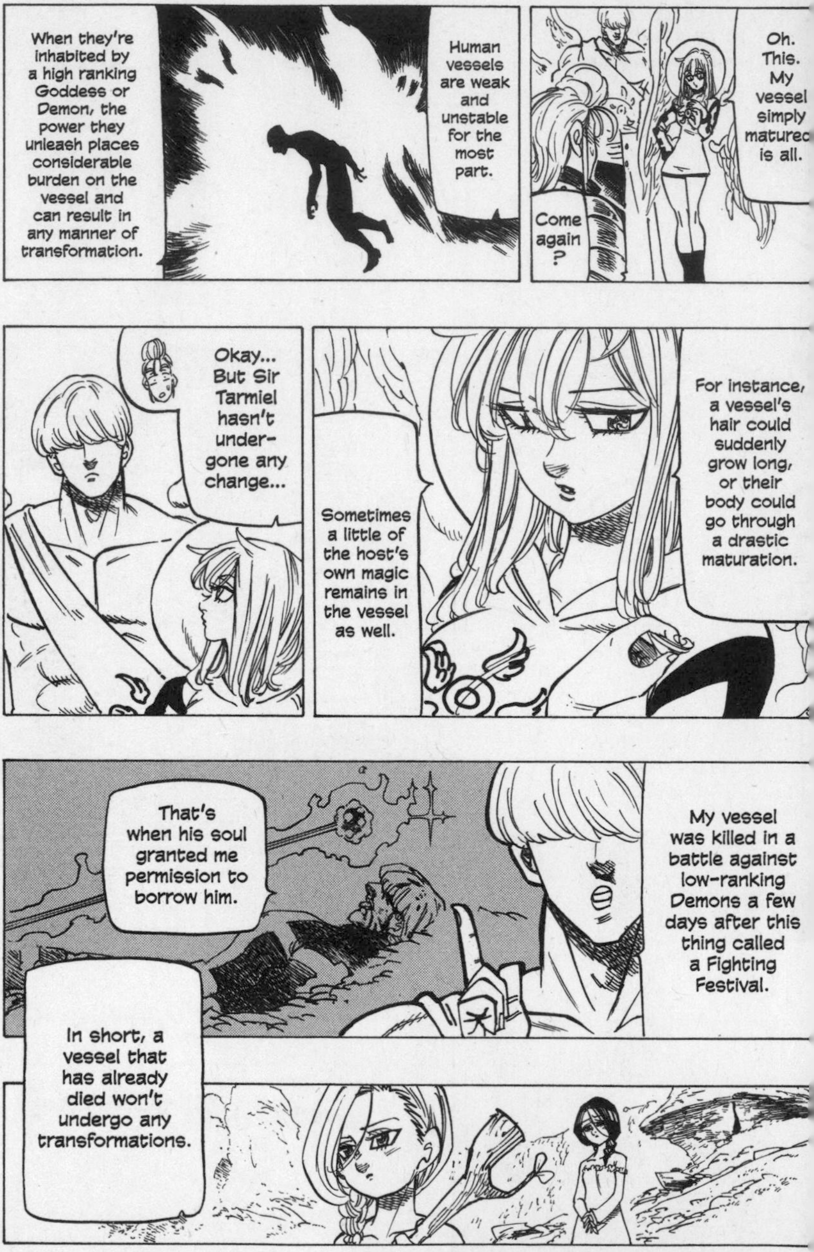

Oh. This. My vessel simply matured is all.
Come again?
Human vessels are weak and unstable for the most part.
When they're inhabited by a high ranking Goddess or Demon, the power they unleash places considerable burden on the vessel and can result in any manner of transformation.
For instance, a vessel's hair could suddenly grow long, or their body could go through a drastic maturation.
Sometimes a little of the host's own magic remains in the vessel as well.
Okay... But Sir Tarmiel hasn't under-gone any change...
My vessel was killed in a battle against low-ranking Demons a few days after this thing called a Fighting Festival.
That's when his soul granted me permission to borrow him.
In short, a vessel that has already died won't undergo any transformations.

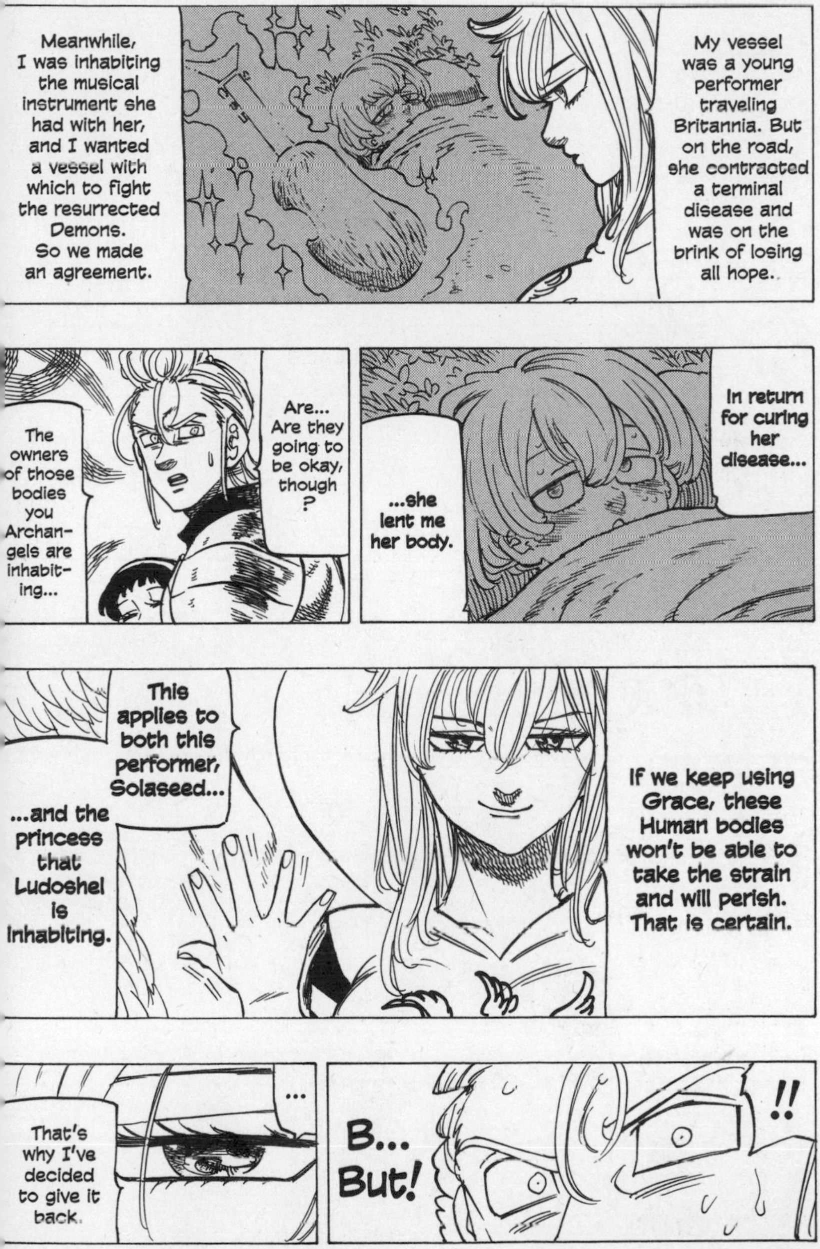
My vessel was a young performer traveling Britannia. But on the road, she contracted a terminal disease and was on the brink of losing all hope.
Meanwhile, I was inhabiting the musical instrument she had with her, and I wanted a vessel with which to fight the resurrected Demons. So we made an agreement.
In return for curing her disease...
...she lent me her body.
Are... Are they going to be okay, though?
The owners of those bodies you Archangels are inhabiting...
If we keep using Grace, these Human bodies won't be able to take the strain and will perish. That is certain.
This applies to both this performer, Solaseed...
...and the princess that Ludoshel is inhabiting.
!!
B... But!
...
That's why I've decided to give it back.

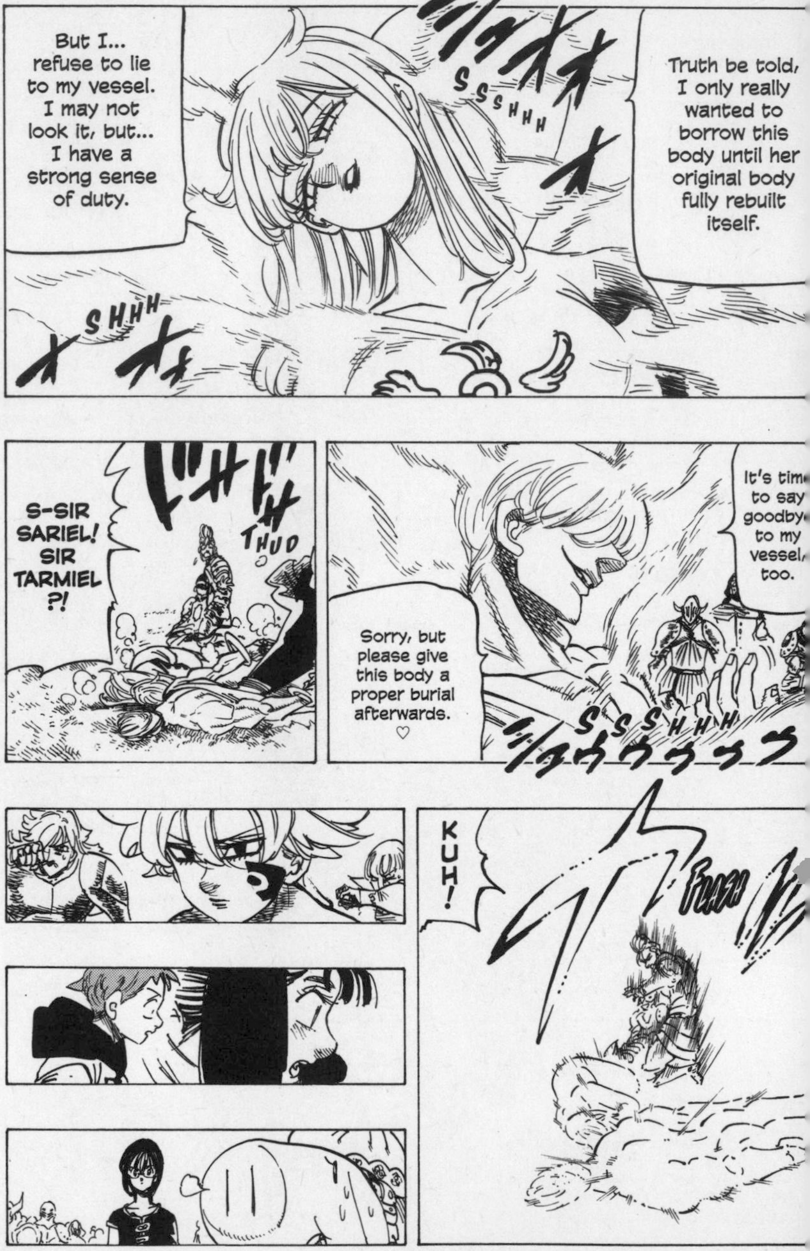
Truth be told, I only really wanted to borrow this body until her original body fully rebuilt itself.
SSSHHH
But I... refuse to lie to my vessel. I may not look it, but... I have a strong sense of duty.
SHHH
It's tim to say goodby to my vessel, too.
Sorry, but please give this body a proper burial afterwards. ♡
SSSHHHH
THUD
S-SIR SARIEL! SIR TARMIEL?!
KUH!

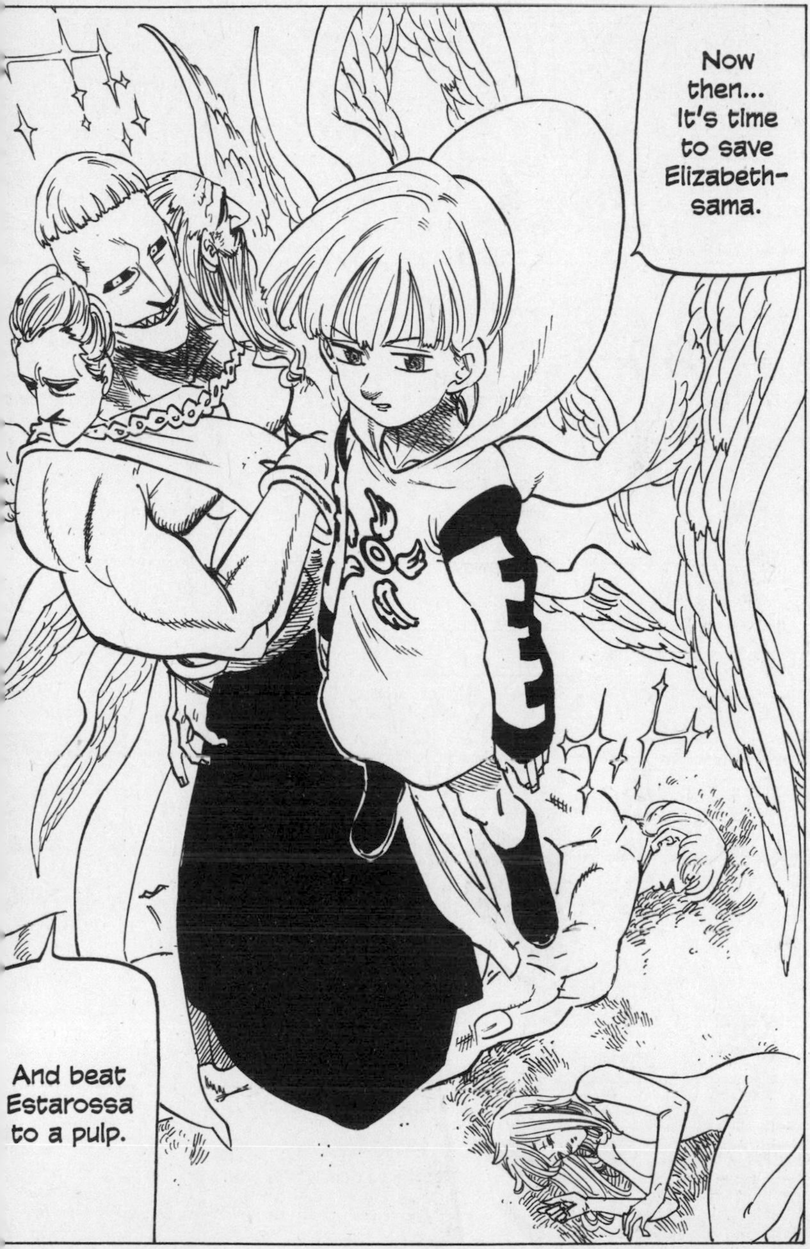
Now then... It's time to save Elizabeth-sama.
And beat Estarossa to a pulp.

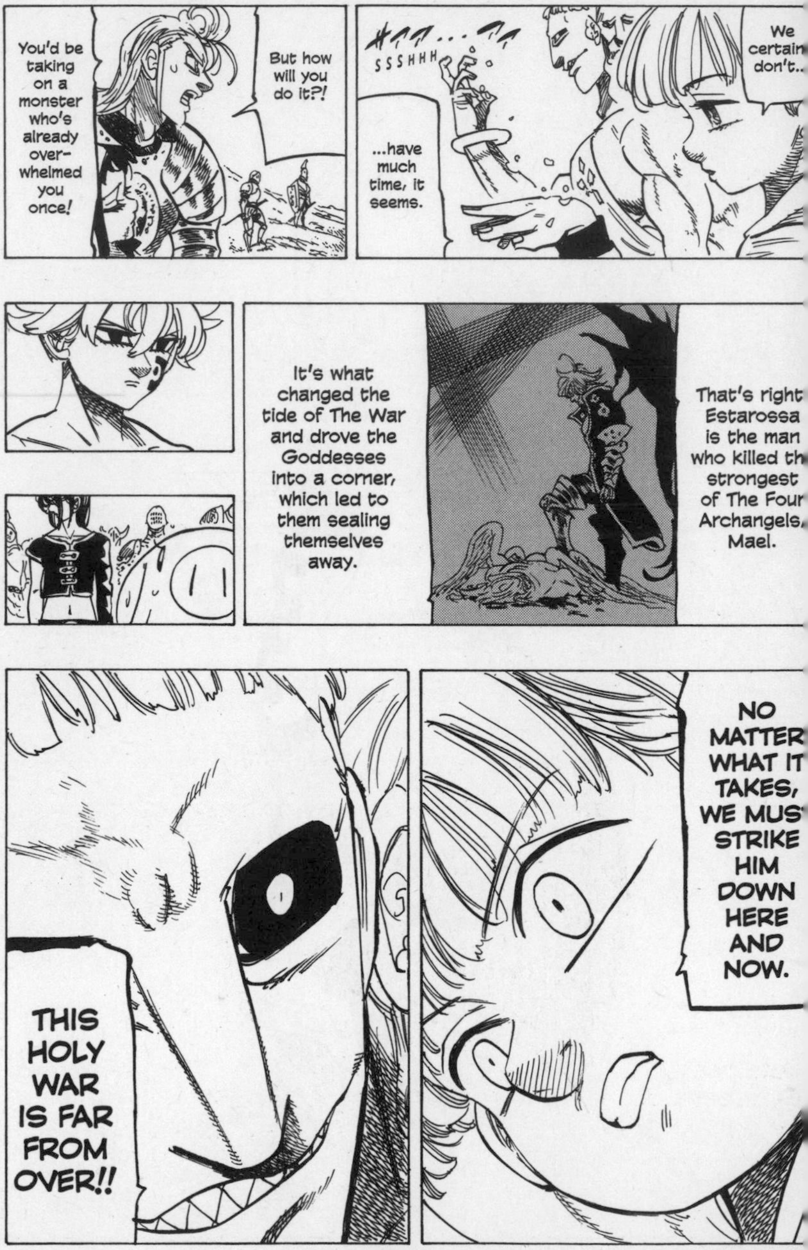
We certain don't..
SSSHHH
...have much time, it seems.
But how will you do it?!
You'd be taking on a monster who's already over-whelmed you once!
That's right Estarossa is the man who killed th strongest of The Four Archangels, Mael.
It's what changed the tide of The War and drove the Goddesses into a corner, which led to them sealing themselves away.
NO MATTER WHAT IT TAKES, WE MUS STRIKE HIM DOWN HERE AND NOW.
THIS HOLY WAR IS FAR FROM OVER!!

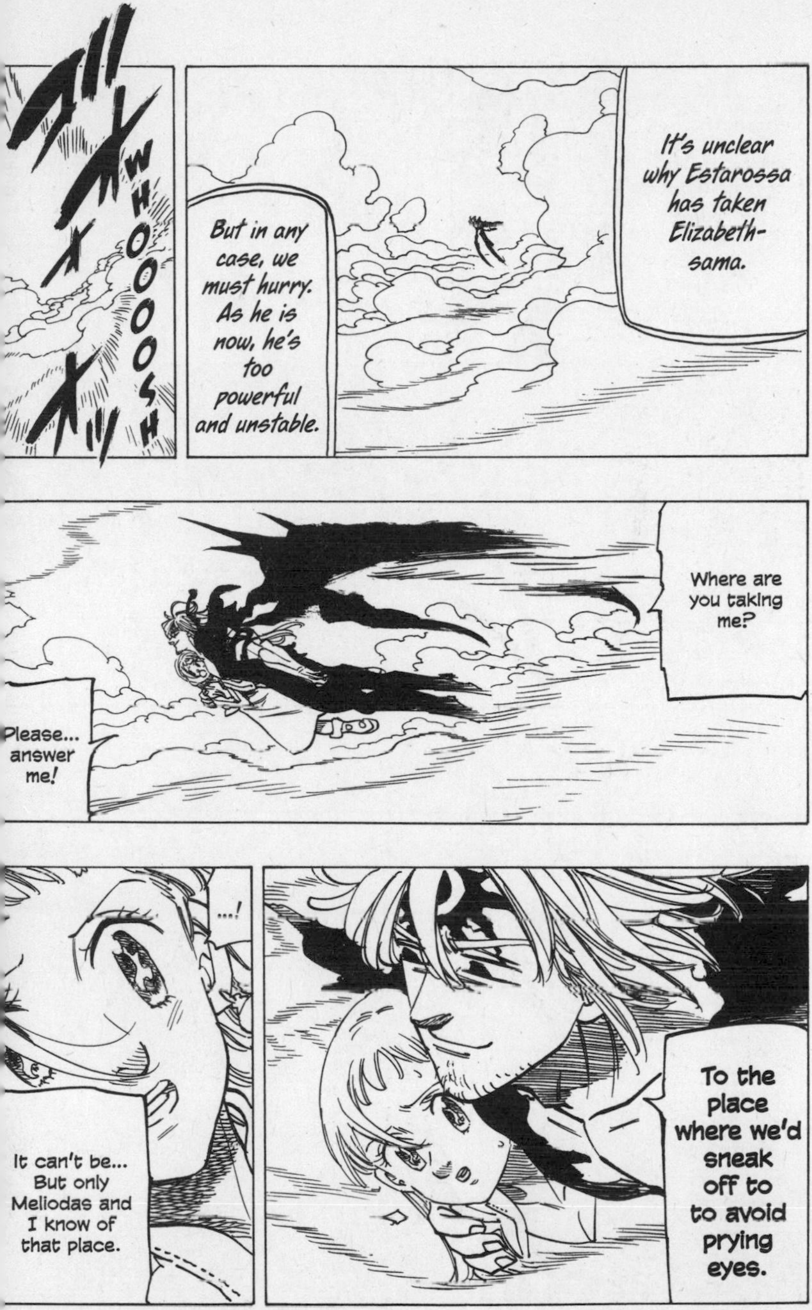
It's unclear why Estarossa has taken Elizabeth-sama.
But in any case, we must hurry. As he is now, he's too powerful and unstable.
WHOOOOSH
Where are you taking me?
Please... answer me!
To the place where we'd sneak off to to avoid prying eyes.
...!
It can't be... But only Meliodas and I know of that place.

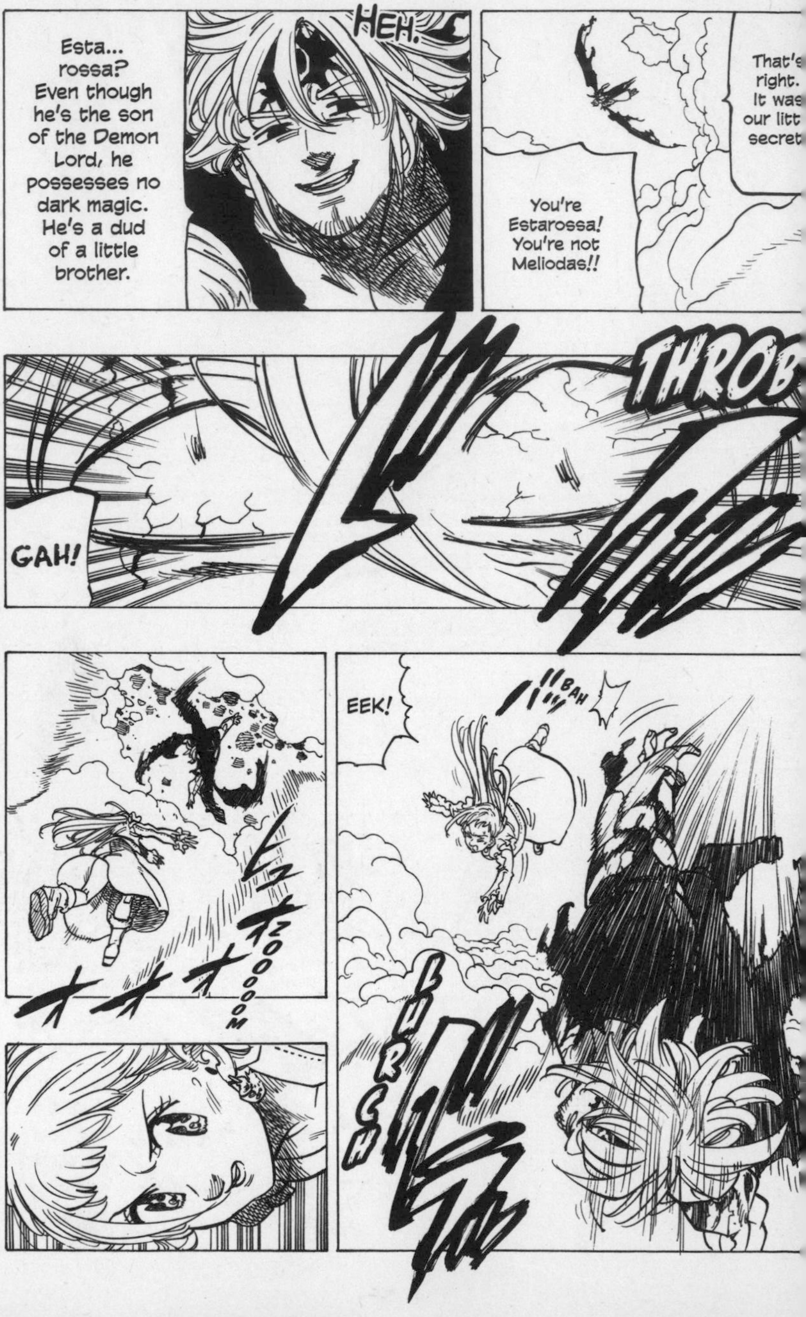
That's right. It was our litt secret
You're Estarossa! You're not Meliodas!!
HEH.
Esta... rossa? Even though he's the son of the Demon Lord, he possesses no dark magic. He's a dud of a little brother.
THROB
GAH!
BAH
EEK!
BURCH
ZOOOOOOM

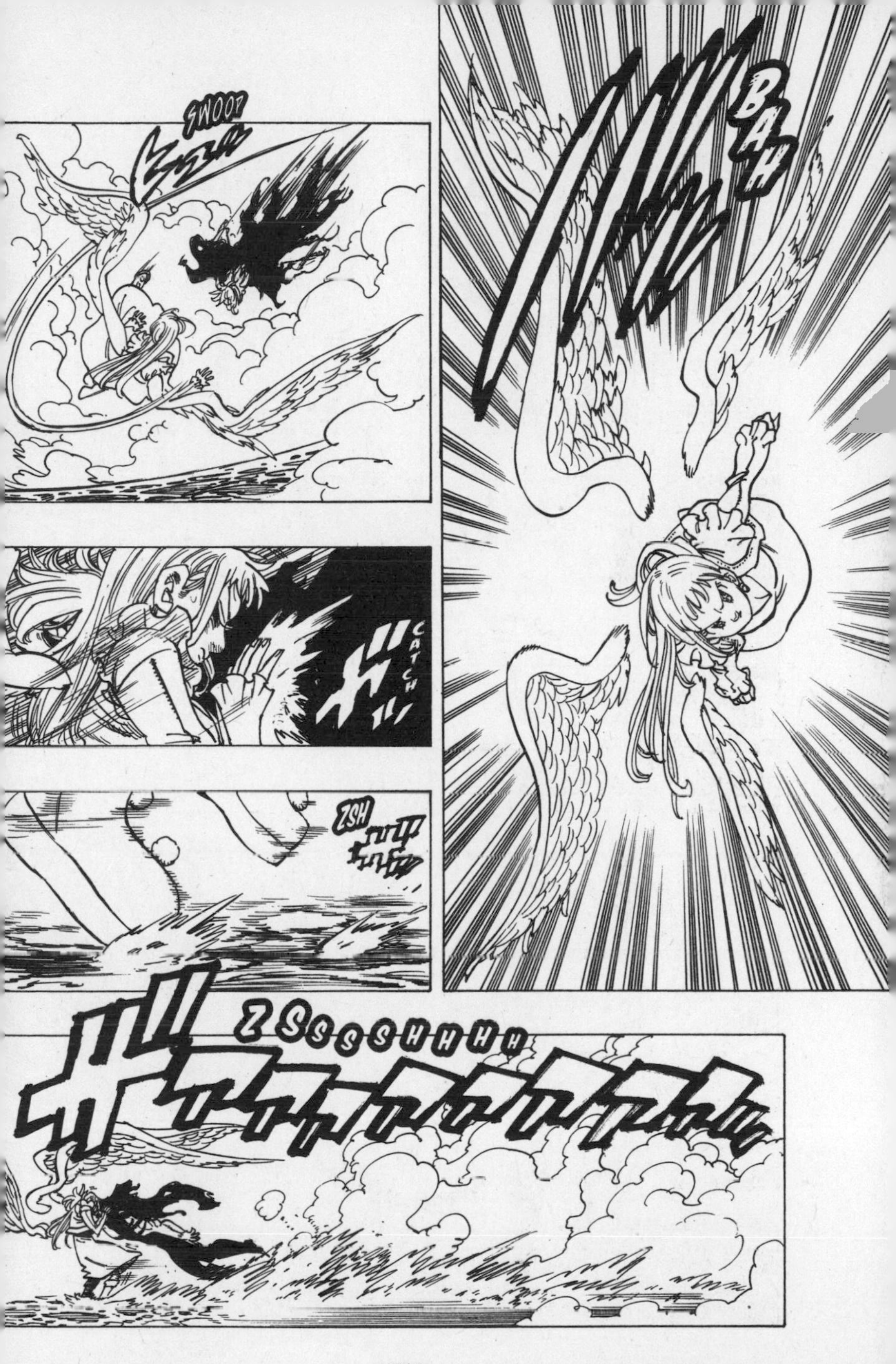
BAH
SWOOP
CATCH
ZSH
ZSSSSHHHH

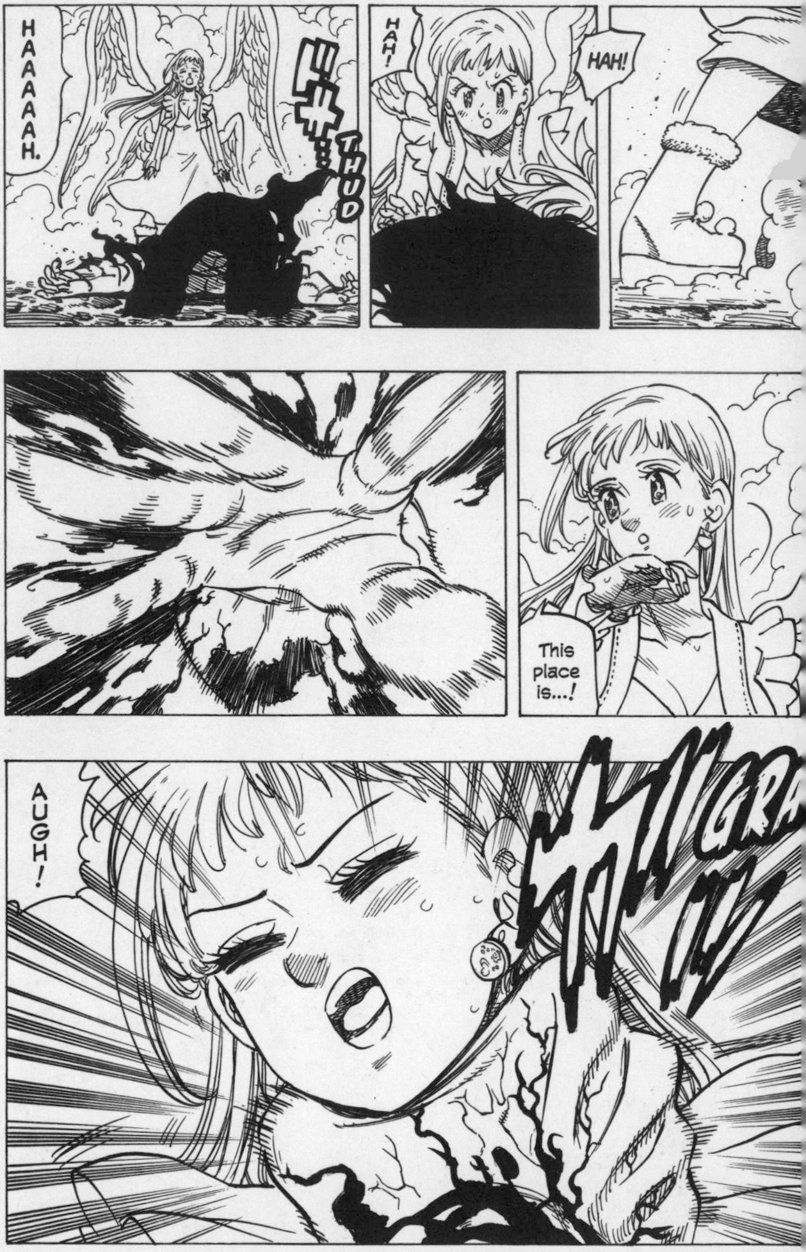
HAH!
HAH!
HAAAAAAH.
THUD
This place is...!
AUGH!

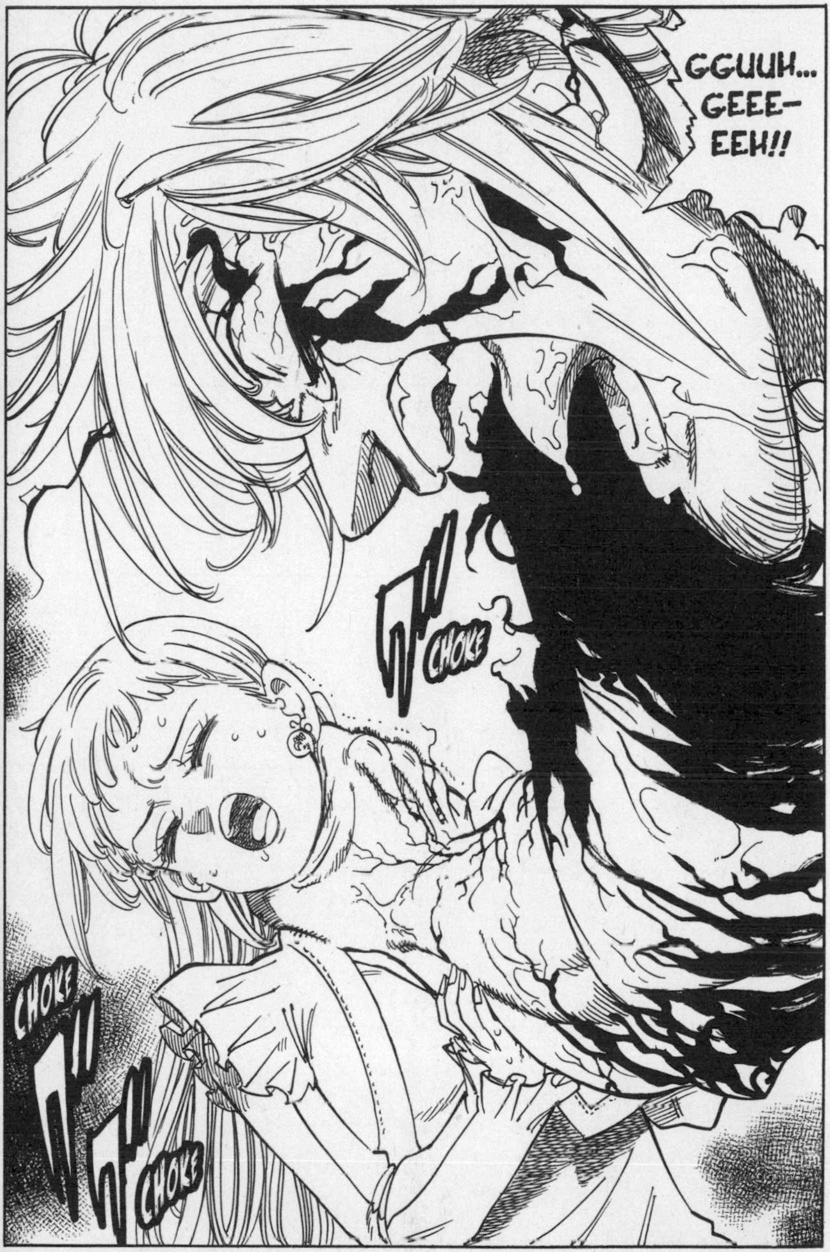
GGUUH... GEEE-EEH!!
CHOKE
CHOKE
CHOKE

To Be Continued in Volume 33...

Side Story - Fight!! Captain of the Knighthood of Scraps Disposal

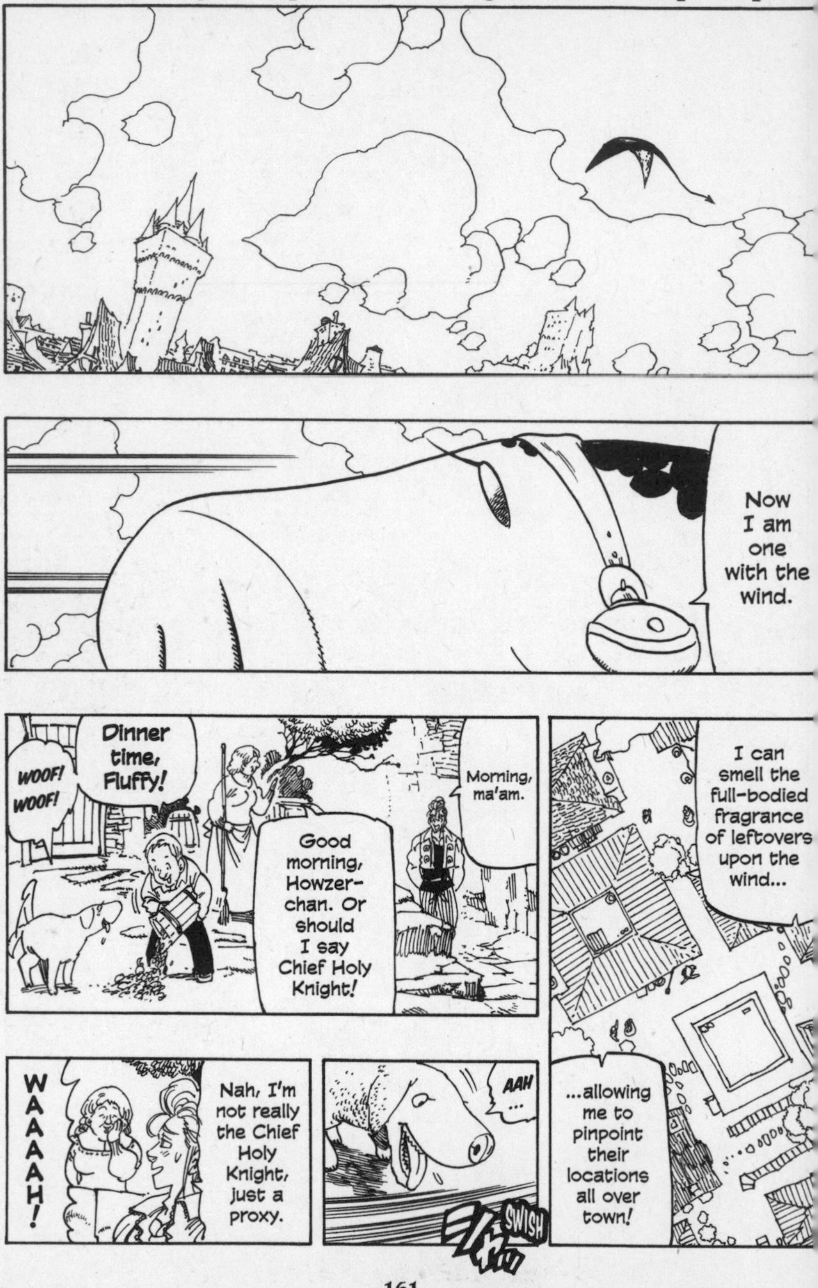
Now I am one with the wind.
I can smell the full-bodied fragrance of leftovers upon the wind...
...allowing me to pinpoint their locations all over town!
Morning, ma'am.
Good morning, Howzer-chan. Or should I say Chief Holy Knight!
Dinner time, Fluffy!
WOOF! WOOF!
AAH...
SWISH
Nah, I'm not really the Chief Holy Knight, just a proxy.
WAAAAAH!

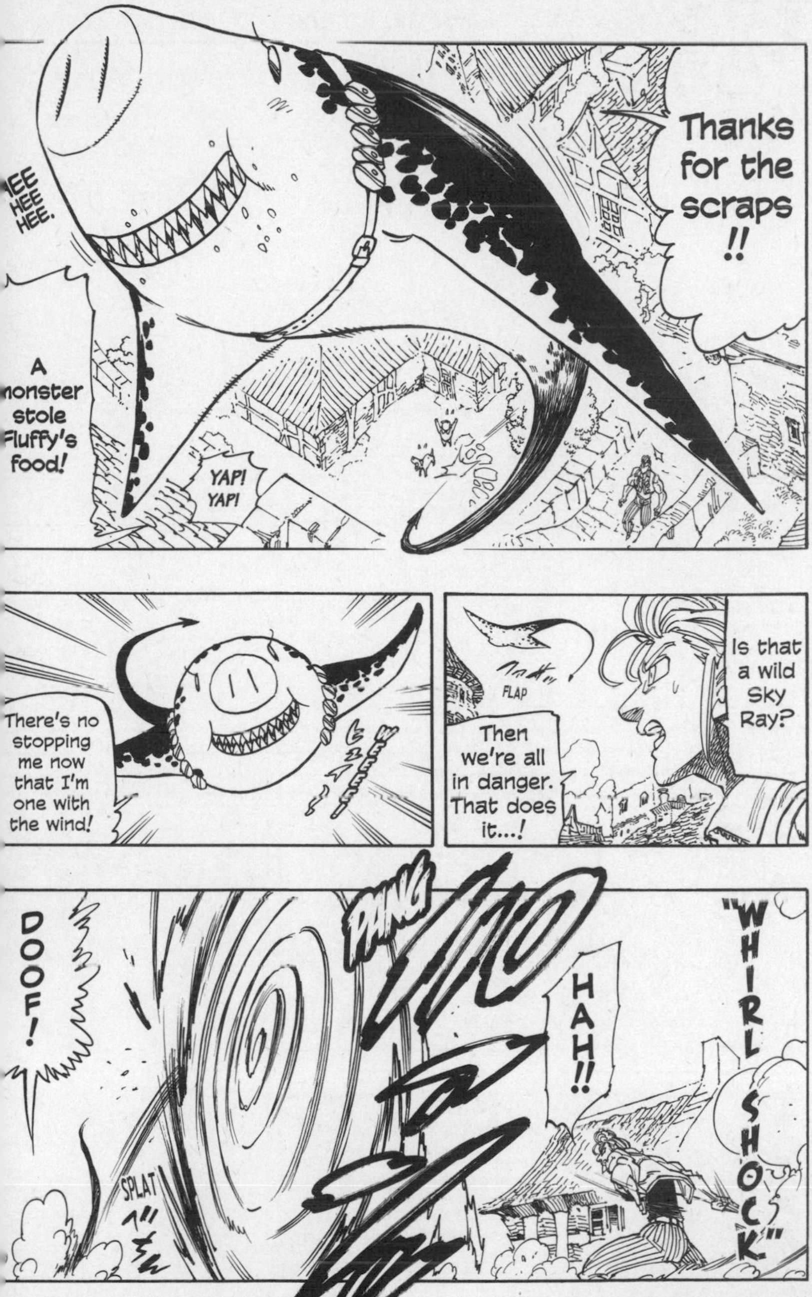
Thanks for the scraps!!
HEE HEE HEE.
A monster stole Fluffy's food!
YAP! YAP!
Is that a wild Sky Ray?
FLAP
Then we're all in danger. That does it...!
There's no stopping me now that I'm one with the wind!
"WHIRL SHOCK"
HAH!!
PING
DOOF!
SPLAT

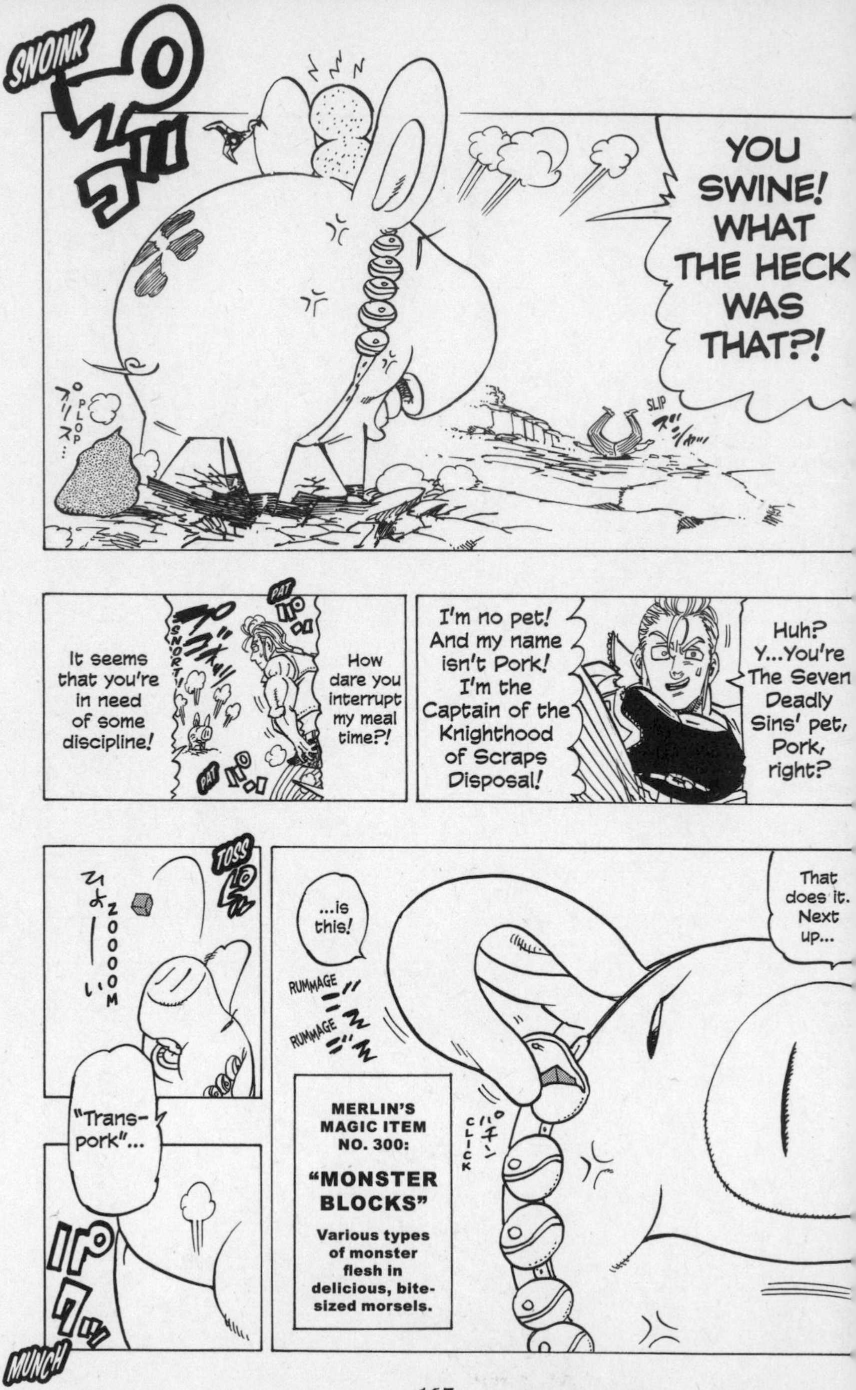
SNOINK
YOU SWINE! WHAT THE HECK WAS THAT?!
PLOP
SLIP
Huh? Y...You're The Seven Deadly Sins' pet, Pork, right?
I'm no pet! And my name isn't Pork! I'm the Captain of the Knighthood of Scraps Disposal!
How dare you interrupt my meal time?!
PAT
SNORT
It seems that you're in need of some discipline!
PAT
That does it. Next up...
...is this!
RUMMAGE
RUMMAGE
CLICK
MERLIN'S MAGIC ITEM NO. 300:
"MONSTER BLOCKS"
Various types of monster flesh in delicious, bite-sized morsels.
TOSS
ZOOOOOM
"Trans-pork"...
MUNCH

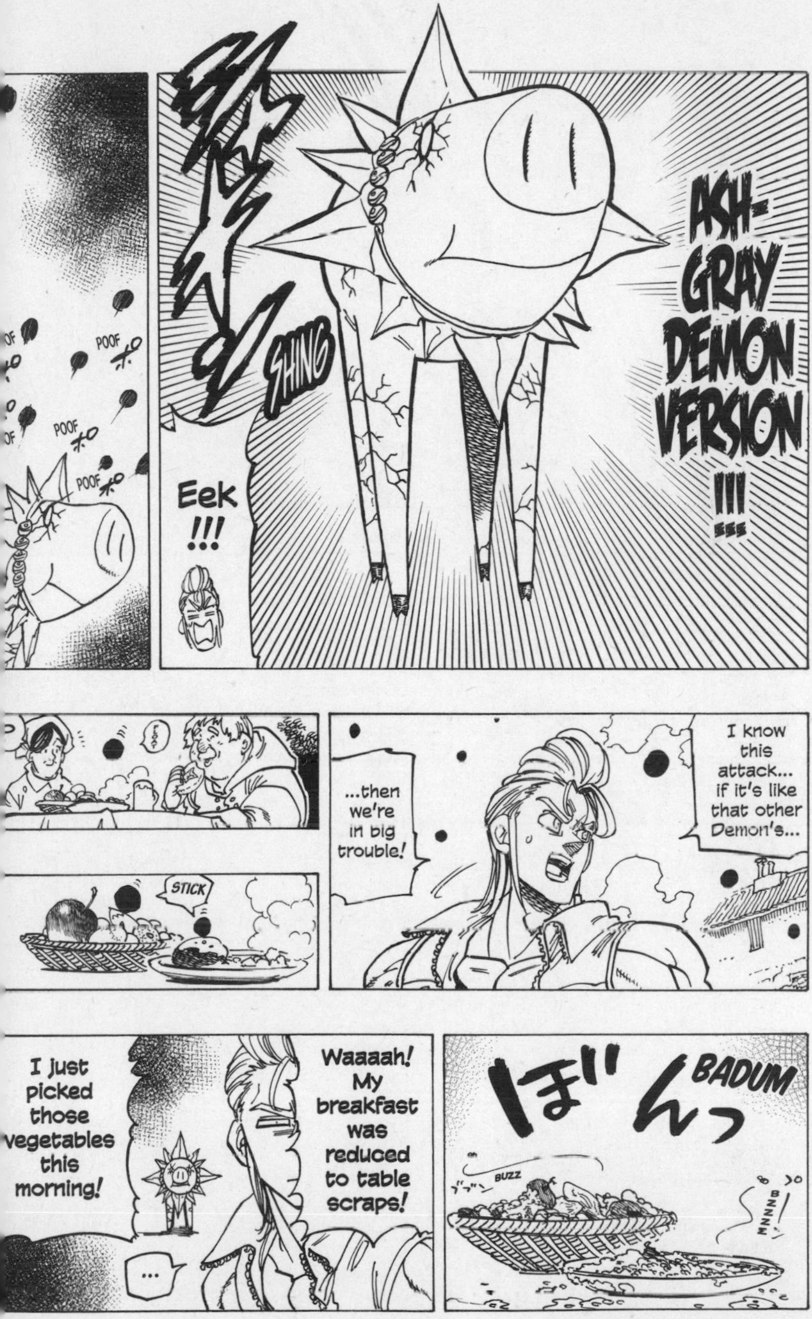

ASH-GRAY DEMON VERSION!!!
SHING
Eek!!!
POOF
POOF
POOF
POOF
I know this attack... if it's like that other Demon's...
...then we're in big trouble!
STICK
ぼんっ
BADUM
ブブーン
BUZZ
Waaaah! My breakfast was reduced to table scraps!
I just picked those vegetables this morning!
...

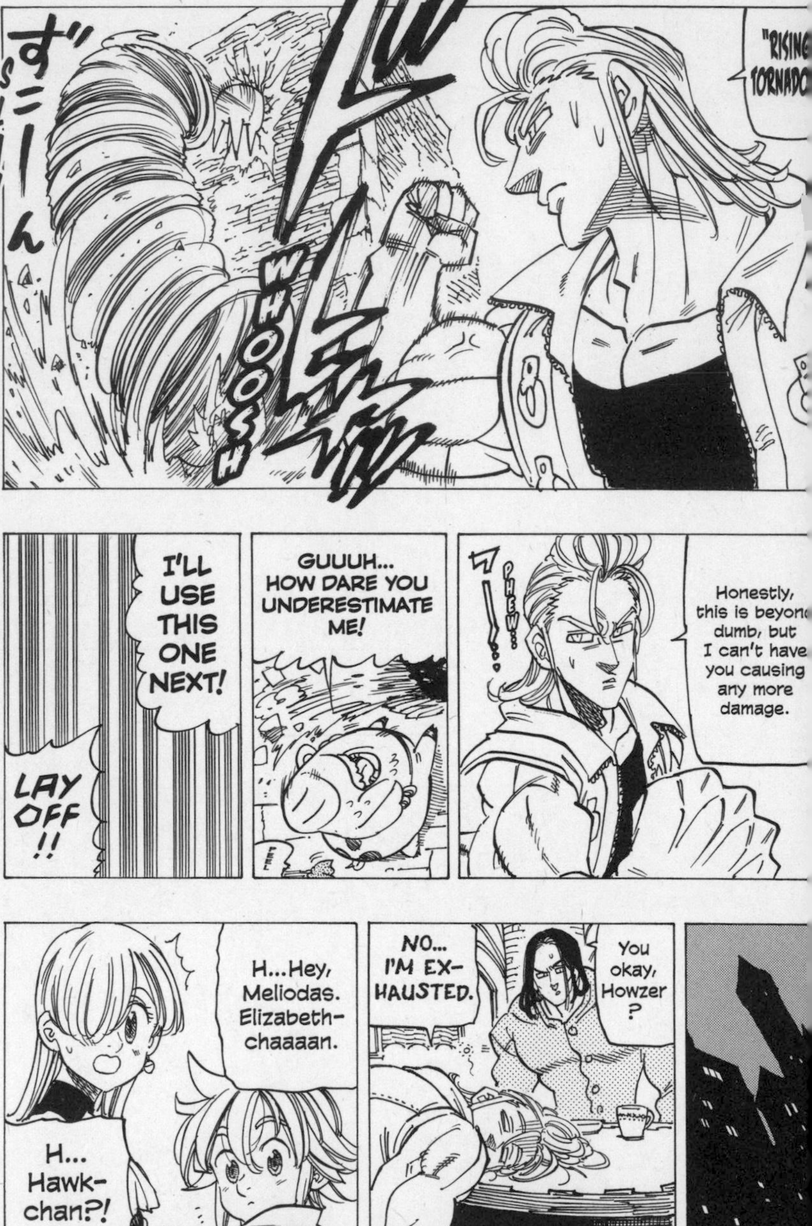
"RISING TORNADO
WHOOOSH
ずーん
SLAM
PHEW!!
Honestly, this is beyon dumb, but I can't have you causing any more damage.
GUUUH... HOW DARE YOU UNDERESTIMATE ME!
FEL
I'LL USE THIS ONE NEXT!
LAY OFF!!
You okay, Howzer?
NO... I'M EX-HAUSTED.
H...Hey, Meliodas. Elizabeth-chaaaan.
H... Hawk-chan?!

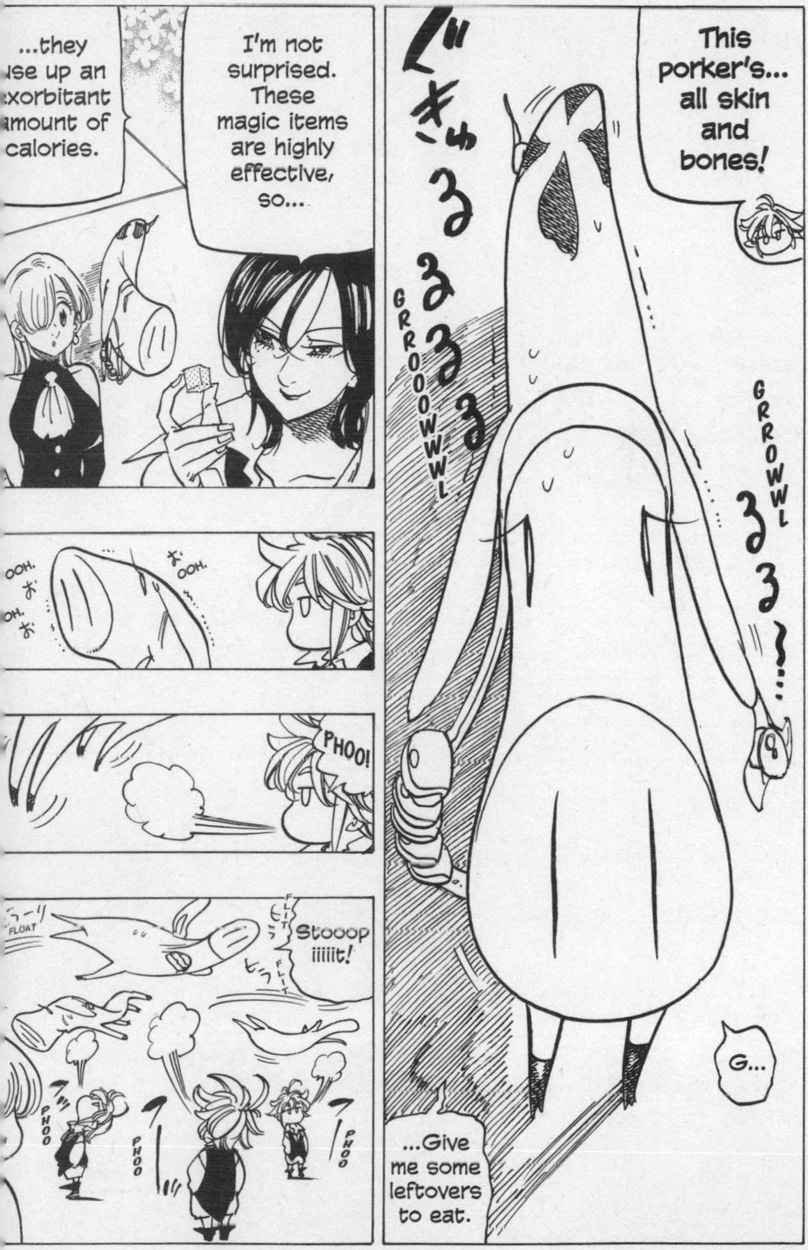
This porker's... all skin and bones!
ぐぎゅるるるる
GRROOOWWWL
GRROWWL
るる~...
G...
...Give me some leftovers to eat.
I'm not surprised. These magic items are highly effective, so...
...they use up an exorbitant amount of calories.
OOH.
OOH.
OOH.
PHOO!
FLOAT
FLIT
Stooop iiiiit!
PHOO
PHOO
PHOO

THE END

Side Story - In Search of Panties

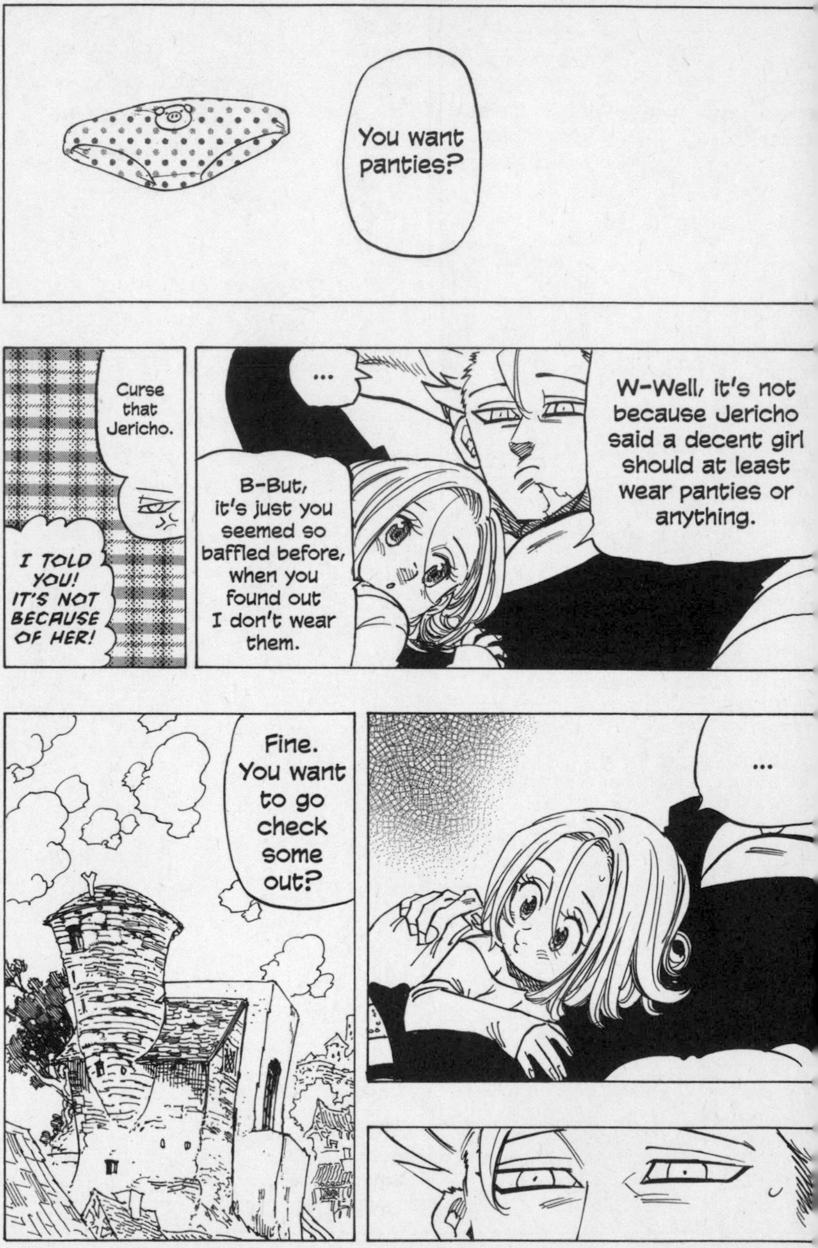
You want panties?
W-Well, it's not because Jericho said a decent girl should at least wear panties or anything.
...
B-But, it's just you seemed so baffled before, when you found out I don't wear them.
Curse that Jericho.
I TOLD YOU! IT'S NOT BECAUSE OF HER!
...
Fine. You want to go check some out?

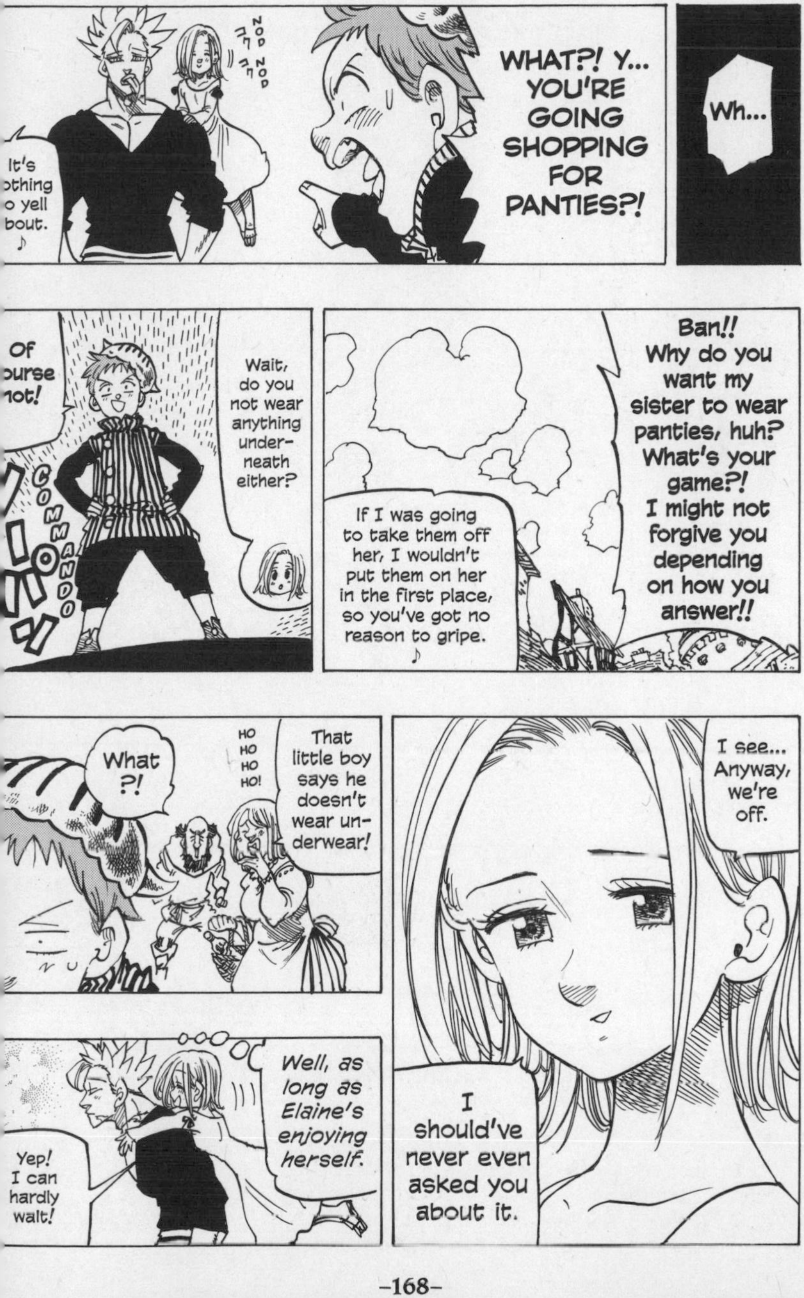
Wh...
WHAT?! Y... YOU'RE GOING SHOPPING FOR PANTIES?!
NOD NOD
It's othing o yell bout. ♪
Ban!! Why do you want my sister to wear panties, huh? What's your game?! I might not forgive you depending on how you answer!!
If I was going to take them off her, I wouldn't put them on her in the first place, so you've got no reason to gripe. ♪
Wait, do you not wear anything underneath either?
Of ourse not!
COMMANDO
I see... Anyway, we're off.
I should've never even asked you about it.
That little boy says he doesn't wear underwear!
HO HO HO HO!
What?!
Well, as long as Elaine's enjoying herself.
Yep! I can hardly wait!

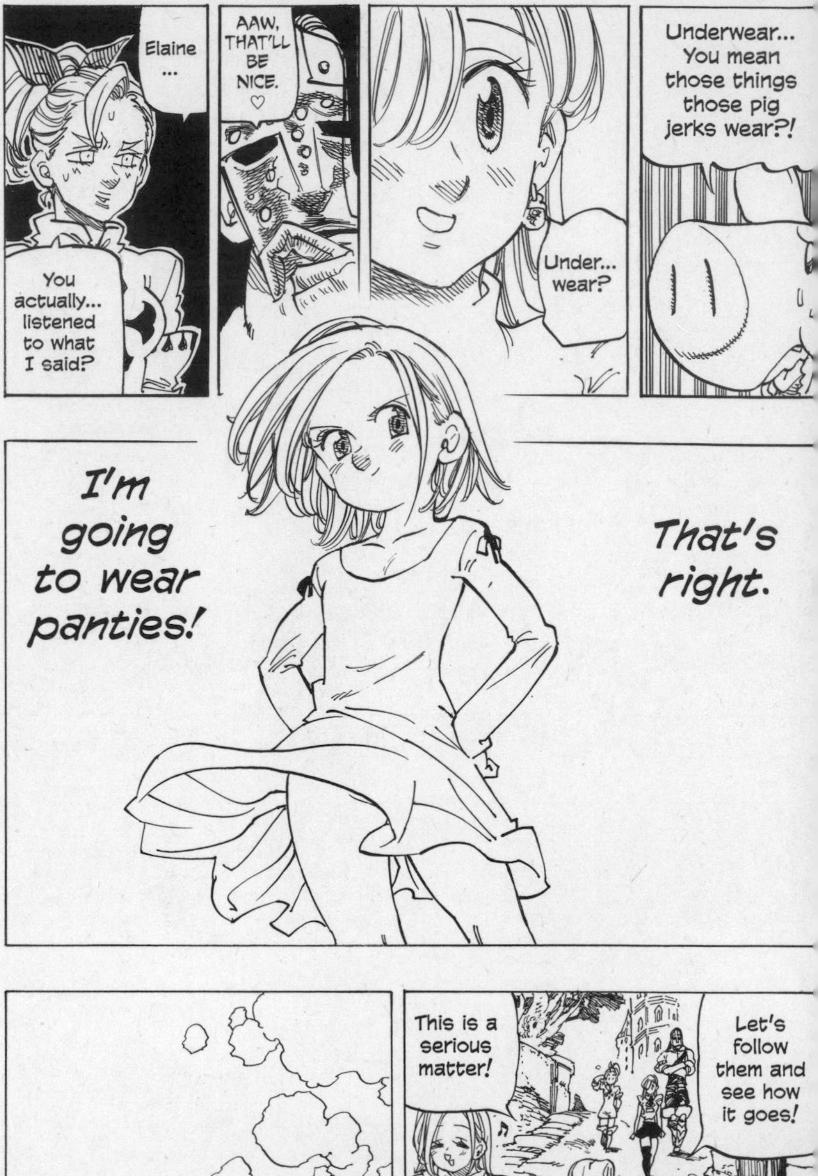

Underwear... You mean those things those pig jerks wear?!
Under... wear?
AAW, THAT'LL BE NICE. ♡
Elaine ...
You actually... listened to what I said?
That's right.
I'm going to wear panties!
Let's follow them and see how it goes!
This is a serious matter!

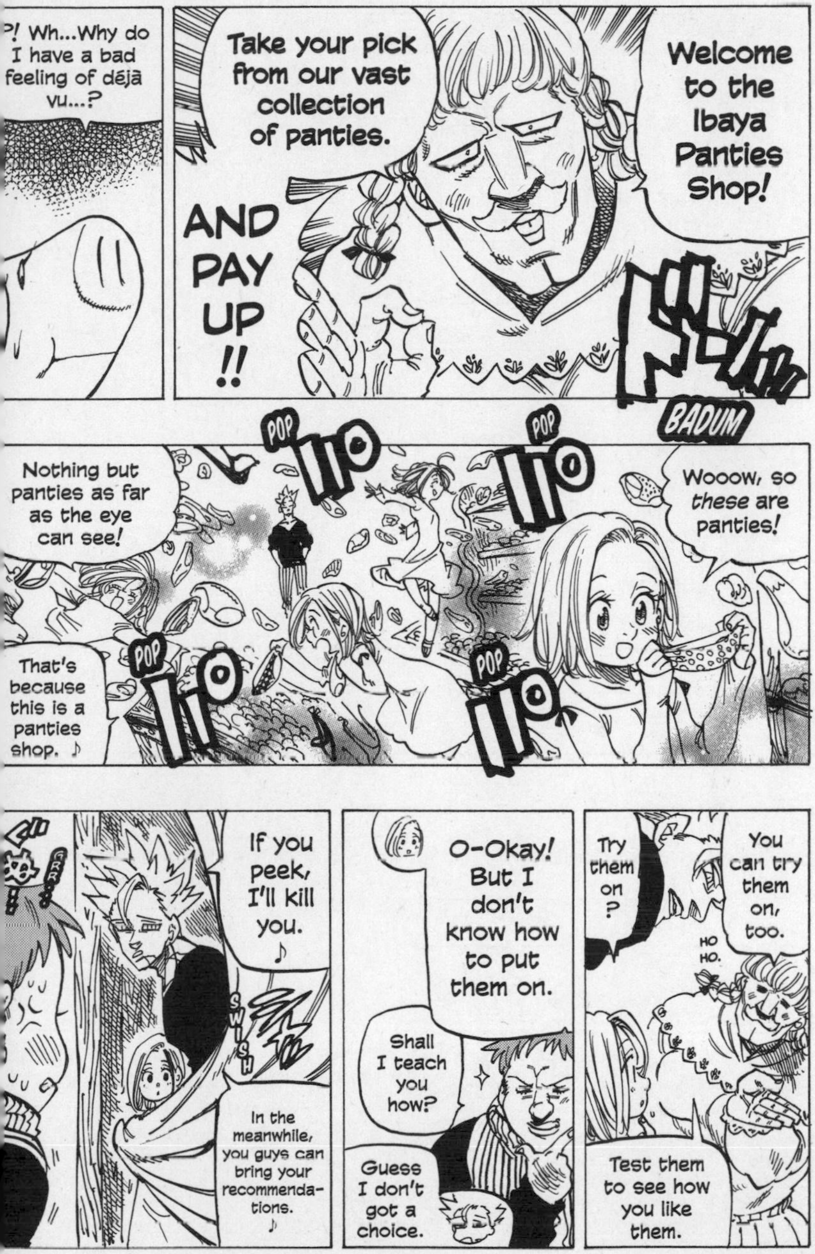
Welcome to the Ibaya Panties Shop!
Take your pick from our vast collection of panties.
AND PAY UP !!
BADUM
?! Wh...Why do I have a bad feeling of déjà vu...?
Wooow, so these are panties!
POP
POP
Nothing but panties as far as the eye can see!
POP
POP
That's because this is a panties shop. ♪
You can try them on, too.
HO HO.
Try them on?
Test them to see how you like them.
O-Okay! But I don't know how to put them on.
Shall I teach you how?
Guess I don't got a choice.
If you peek, I'll kill you. ♪
SWISH
GRR
In the meanwhile, you guys can bring your recommendations. ♪

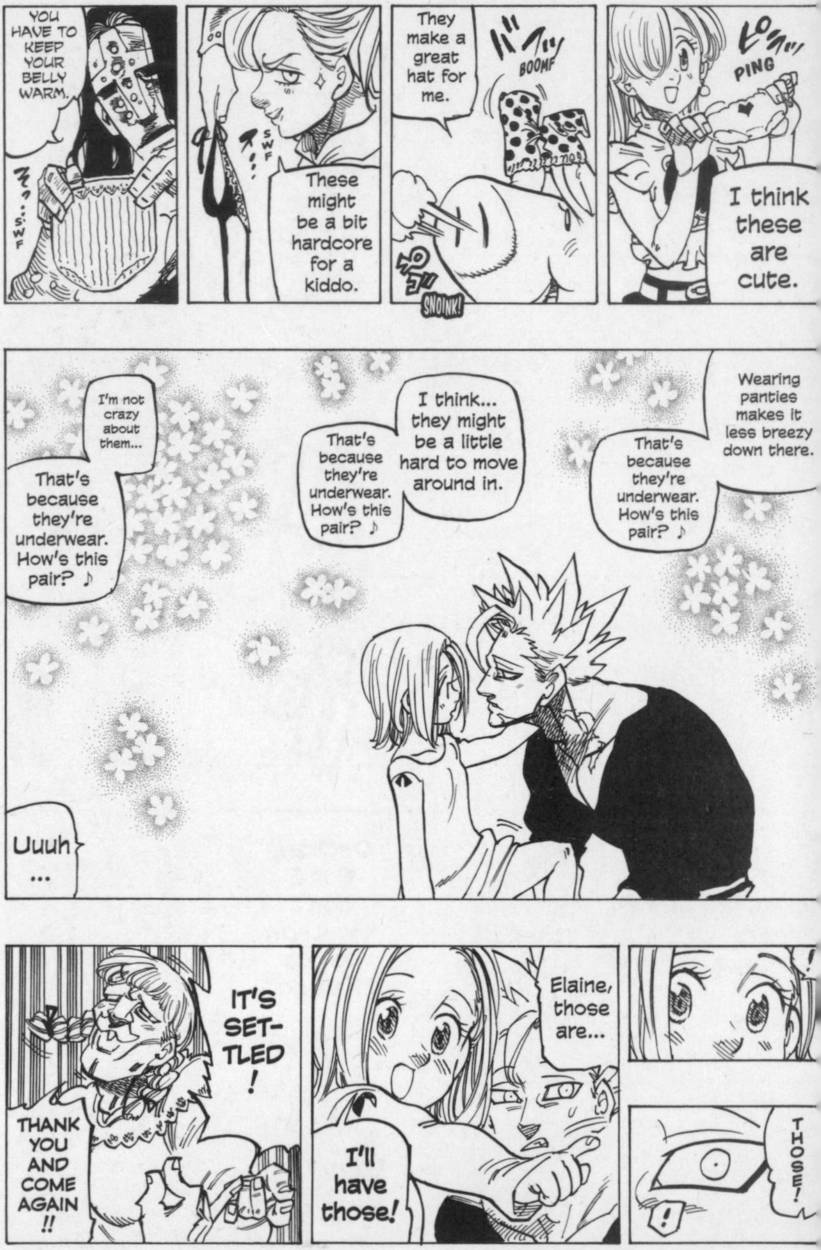
PING
I think these are cute.
They make a great hat for me.
BOOMF
SNOINK!
These might be a bit hardcore for a kiddo.
SWF
YOU HAVE TO KEEP YOUR BELLY WARM.
SWF
Wearing panties makes it less breezy down there.
That's because they're underwear. How's this pair? ♪
I think... they might be a little hard to move around in.
That's because they're underwear. How's this pair? ♪
I'm not crazy about them...
That's because they're underwear. How's this pair? ♪
Uuuh...
THOSE!
!
Elaine, those are...
I'll have those!
IT'S SET-TLED!
THANK YOU AND COME AGAIN!!

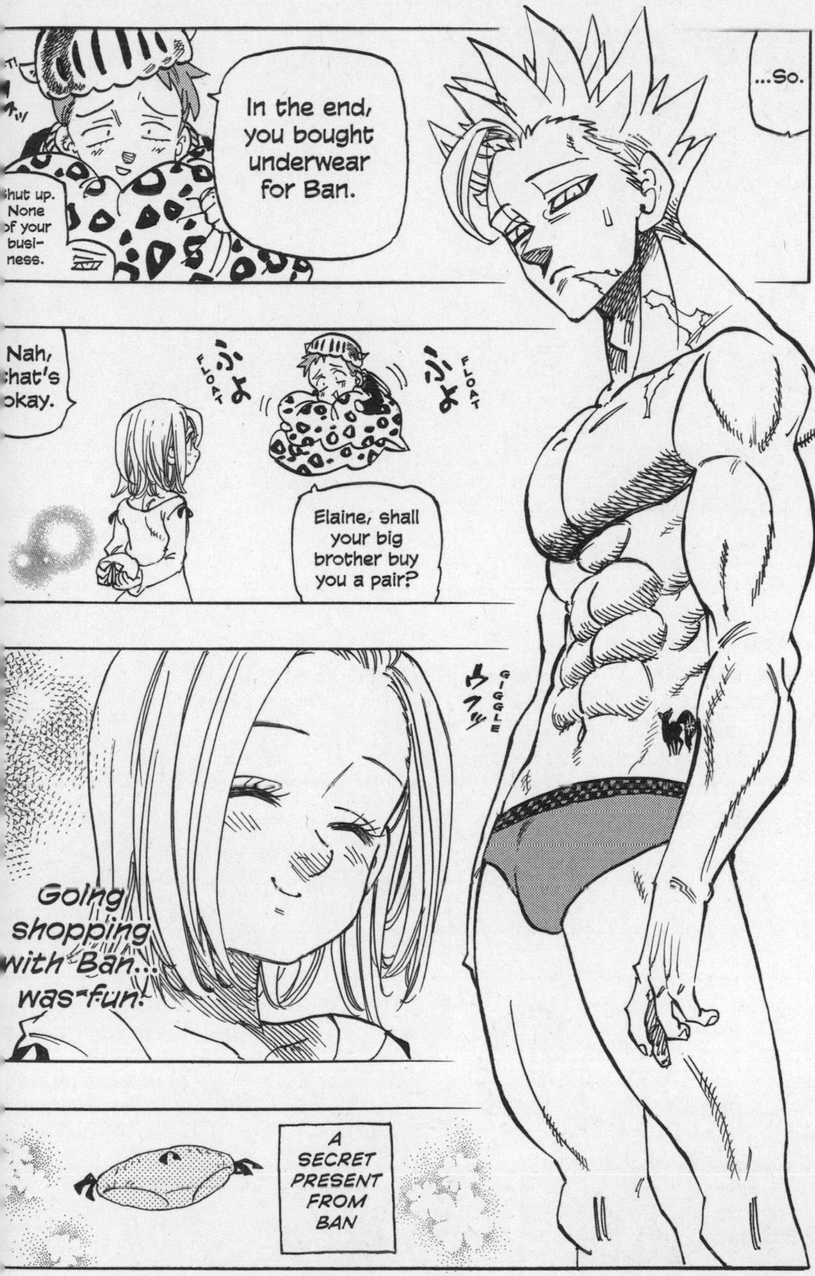
...So.
In the end, you bought underwear for Ban.
Shut up. None of your busi-ness.
ふよ FLOAT
ふよ FLOAT
Elaine, shall your big brother buy you a pair?
Nah, that's okay.
ウフッ GIGGLE
Going shopping with Ban... was fun.
A SECRET PRESENT FROM BAN

THE END

Side Story - On the Subject of Reopening Boar Ha

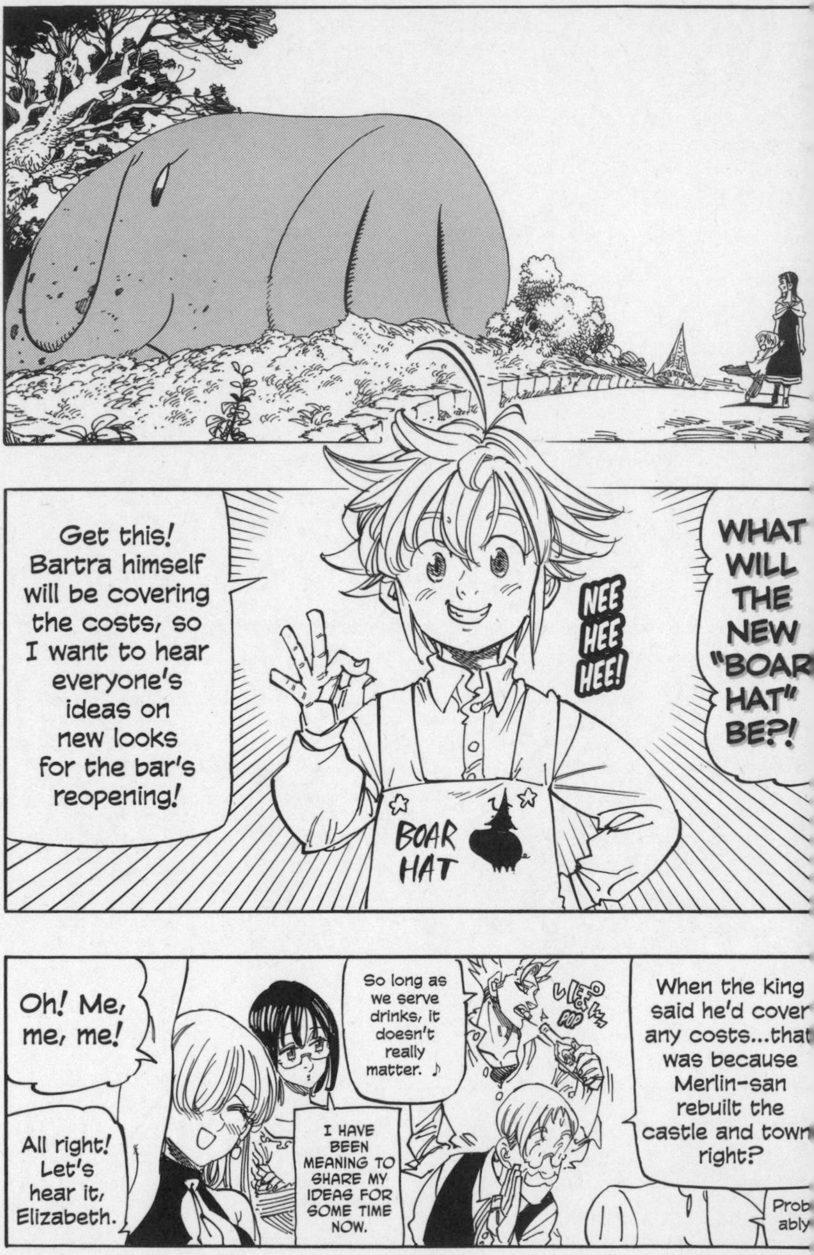
WHAT WILL THE NEW "BOAR HAT" BE?!
NEE HEE HEE!
BOAR HAT
Get this! Bartra himself will be covering the costs, so I want to hear everyone's ideas on new looks for the bar's reopening!
When the king said he'd cover any costs...that was because Merlin-san rebuilt the castle and town, right?
Prob ably
POP
So long as we serve drinks, it doesn't really matter. ♪
I HAVE BEEN MEANING TO SHARE MY IDEAS FOR SOME TIME NOW.
Oh! Me, me, me!
All right! Let's hear it, Elizabeth.

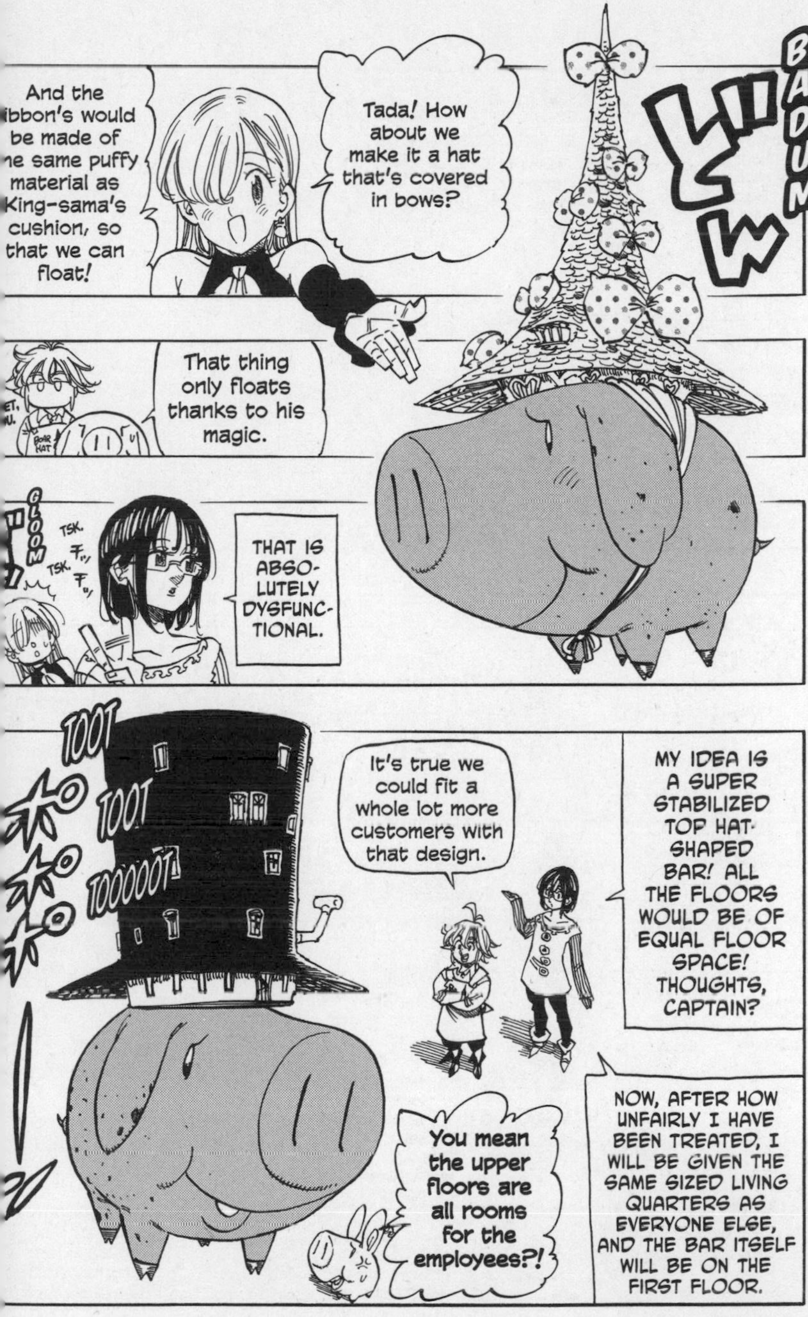
BADUM
Tada! How about we make it a hat that's covered in bows?
And the ibbon's would be made of ne same puffy material as King-sama's cushion, so that we can float!
That thing only floats thanks to his magic.
GLOOM
TSK. TSK.
THAT IS ABSOLUTELY DYSFUNCTIONAL.
MY IDEA IS A SUPER STABILIZED TOP HAT-SHAPED BAR! ALL THE FLOORS WOULD BE OF EQUAL FLOOR SPACE! THOUGHTS, CAPTAIN?
It's true we could fit a whole lot more customers with that design.
NOW, AFTER HOW UNFAIRLY I HAVE BEEN TREATED, I WILL BE GIVEN THE SAME SIZED LIVING QUARTERS AS EVERYONE ELSE, AND THE BAR ITSELF WILL BE ON THE FIRST FLOOR.
You mean the upper floors are all rooms for the employees?!
TOOT
TOOT
TOOOOOT

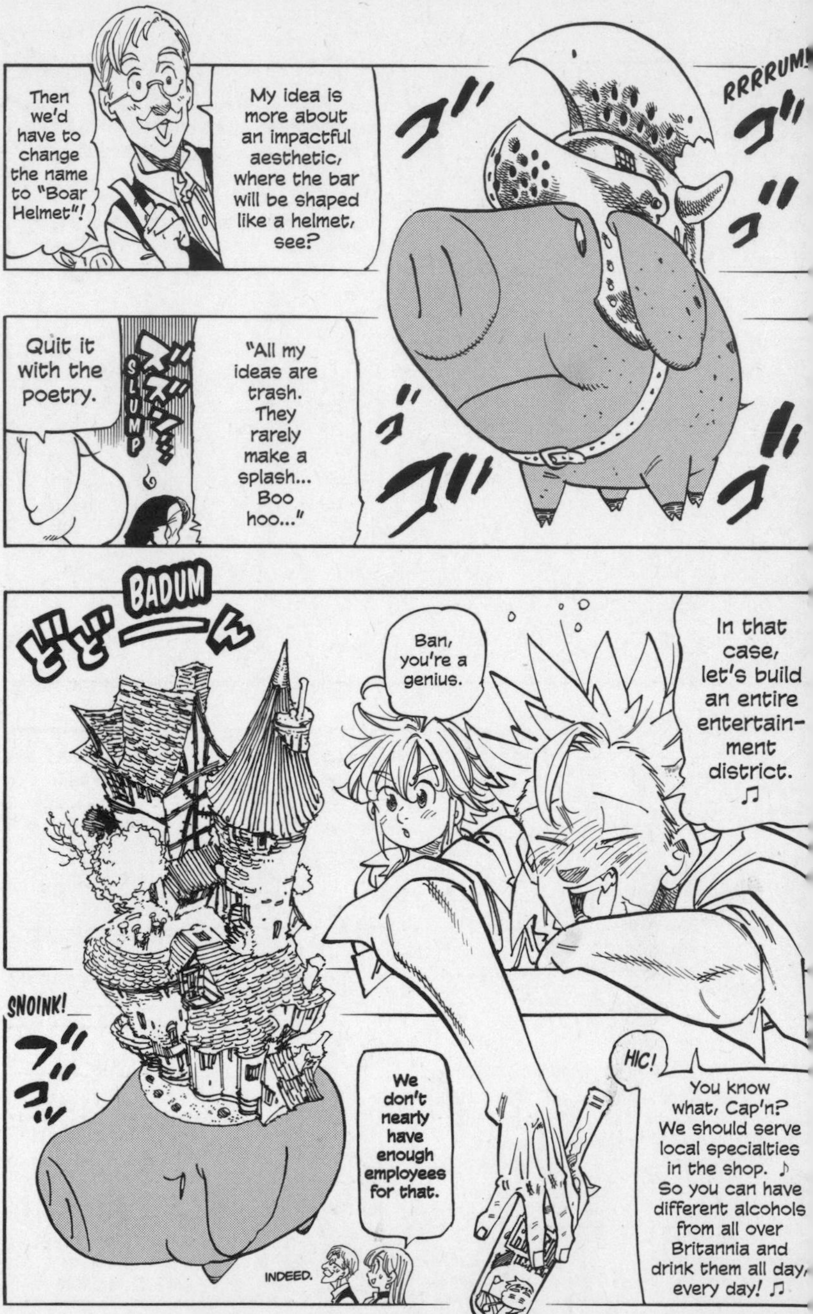
RRRRUM!
My idea is more about an impactful aesthetic, where the bar will be shaped like a helmet, see?
Then we'd have to change the name to "Boar Helmet"!
"All my ideas are trash. They rarely make a splash... Boo hoo..."
SLUMP
Quit it with the poetry.
In that case, let's build an entire entertainment district. ♫
Ban, you're a genius.
BADUM
HIC!
You know what, Cap'n? We should serve local specialties in the shop. ♪ So you can have different alcohols from all over Britannia and drink them all day, every day! ♫
We don't nearly have enough employees for that.
INDEED.
SNOINK!

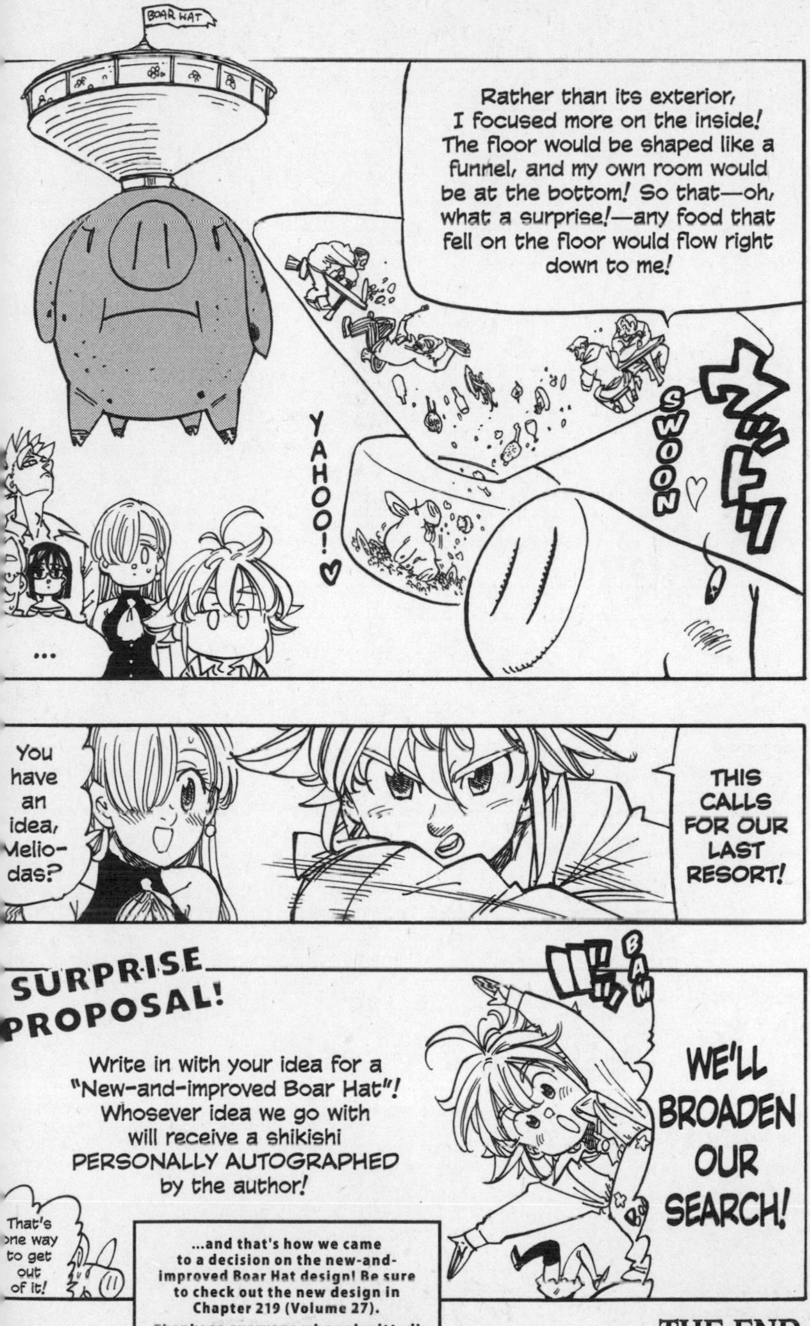
BOAR HAT
Rather than its exterior, I focused more on the inside! The floor would be shaped like a funnel, and my own room would be at the bottom! So that—oh, what a surprise!—any food that fell on the floor would flow right down to me!
SWOON ♡
YAHOO! ♥
...
THIS CALLS FOR OUR LAST RESORT!
You have an idea, Melio-das?
BAM
WE'LL BROADEN OUR SEARCH!
SURPRISE PROPOSAL!
Write in with your idea for a "New-and-improved Boar Hat"! Whosever idea we go with will receive a shikishi PERSONALLY AUTOGRAPHED by the author!
...and that's how we came to a decision on the new-and-improved Boar Hat design! Be sure to check out the new design in Chapter 219 (Volume 27).
Thanks to everyone who submitted!
That's one way to get out of it!

THE END

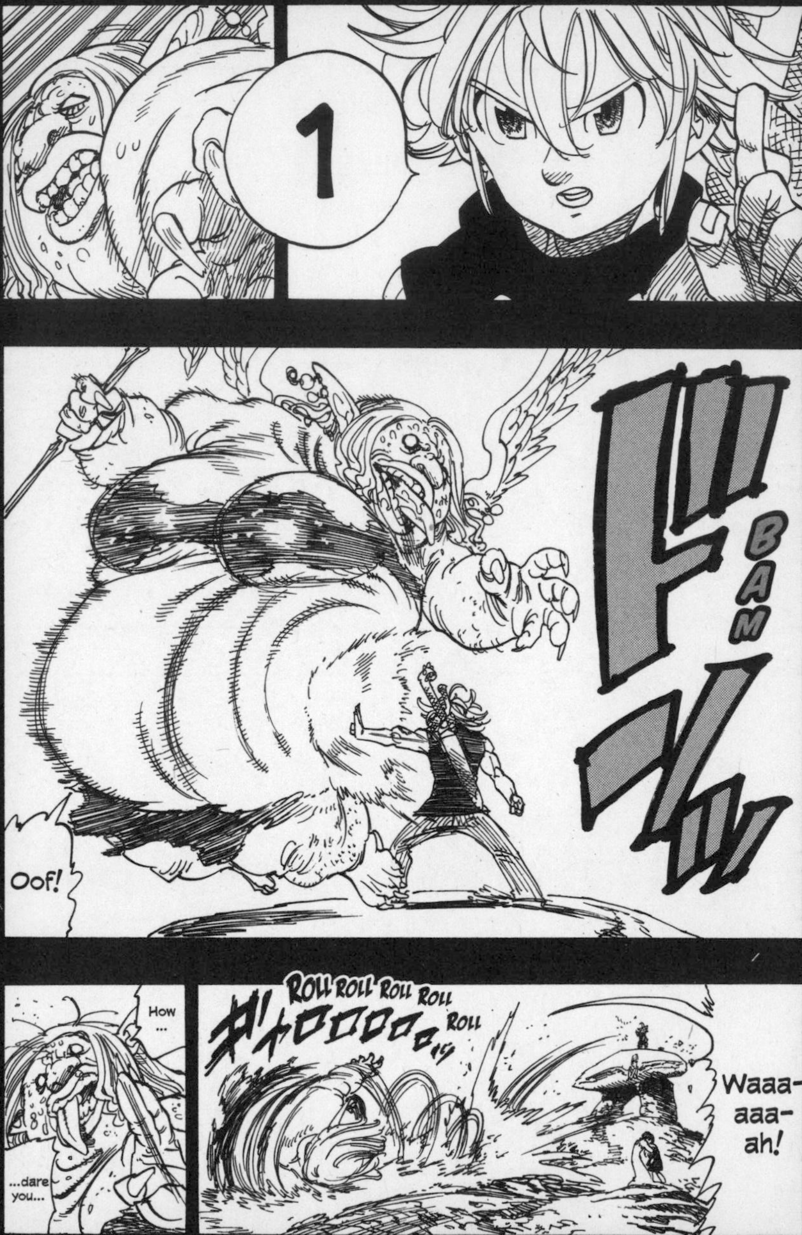
1
ドン
BAM
Oof!
ROLL ROLL ROLL ROLL
ROLL
Waaa-aaa-ah!
How ...
...dare you...

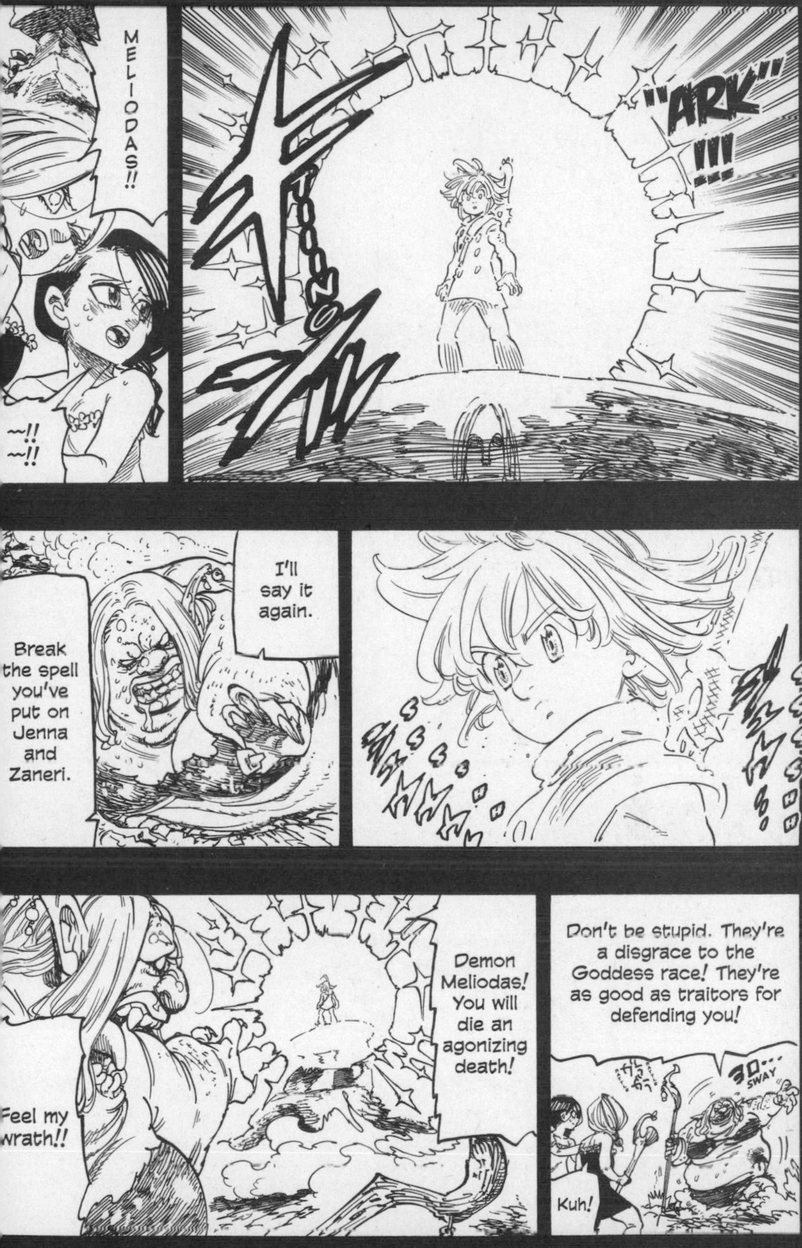
"ARK"!!!
MELIODAS!!
~!!
~!!
I'll say it again.
Break the spell you've put on Jenna and Zaneri.
Don't be stupid. They're a disgrace to the Goddess race! They're as good as traitors for defending you!
SWAY
Kuh!
Demon Meliodas! You will die an agonizing death!
Feel my wrath!!

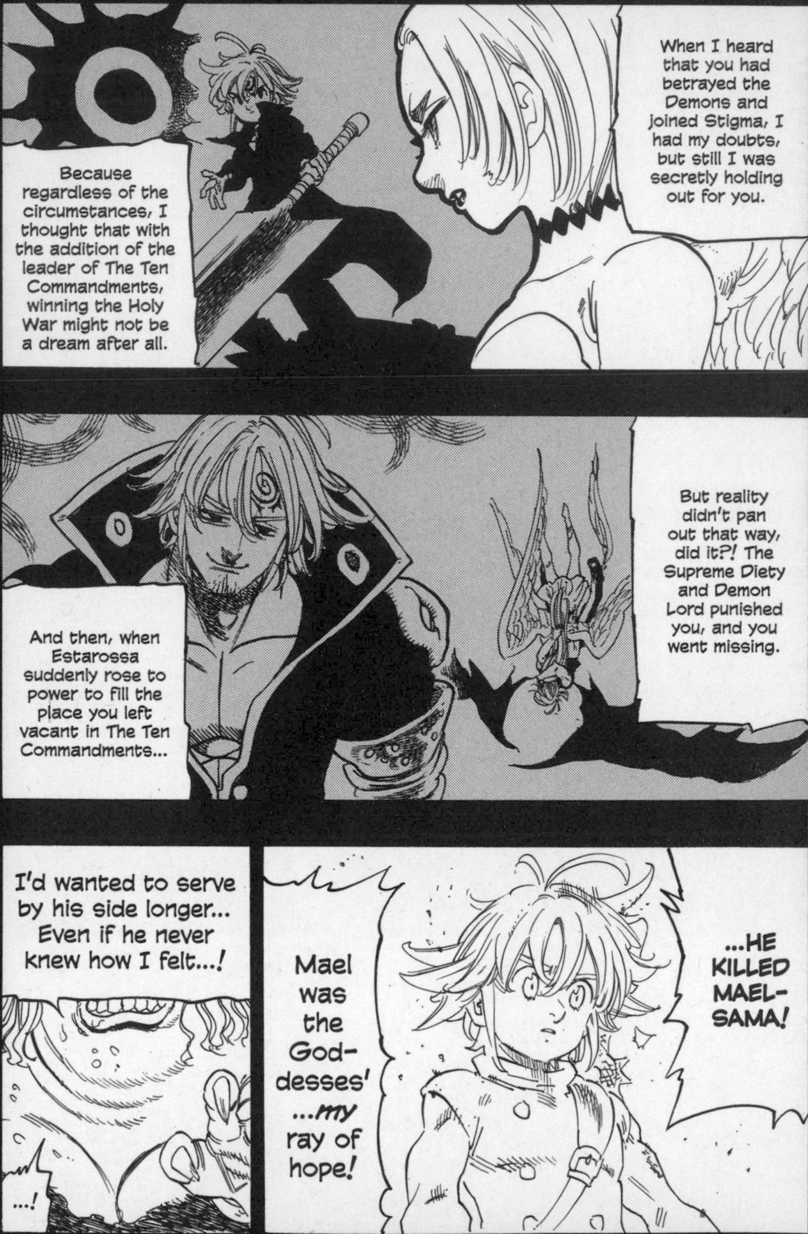
When I heard that you had betrayed the Demons and joined Stigma, I had my doubts, but still I was secretly holding out for you.
Because regardless of the circumstances, I thought that with the addition of the leader of The Ten Commandments, winning the Holy War might not be a dream after all.
But reality didn't pan out that way, did it?! The Supreme Diety and Demon Lord punished you, and you went missing.
And then, when Estarossa suddenly rose to power to fill the place you left vacant in The Ten Commandments...
...HE KILLED MAEL-SAMA!
Mael was the God-desses' ...*my* ray of hope!
I'd wanted to serve by his side longer... Even if he never knew how I felt...!
...!

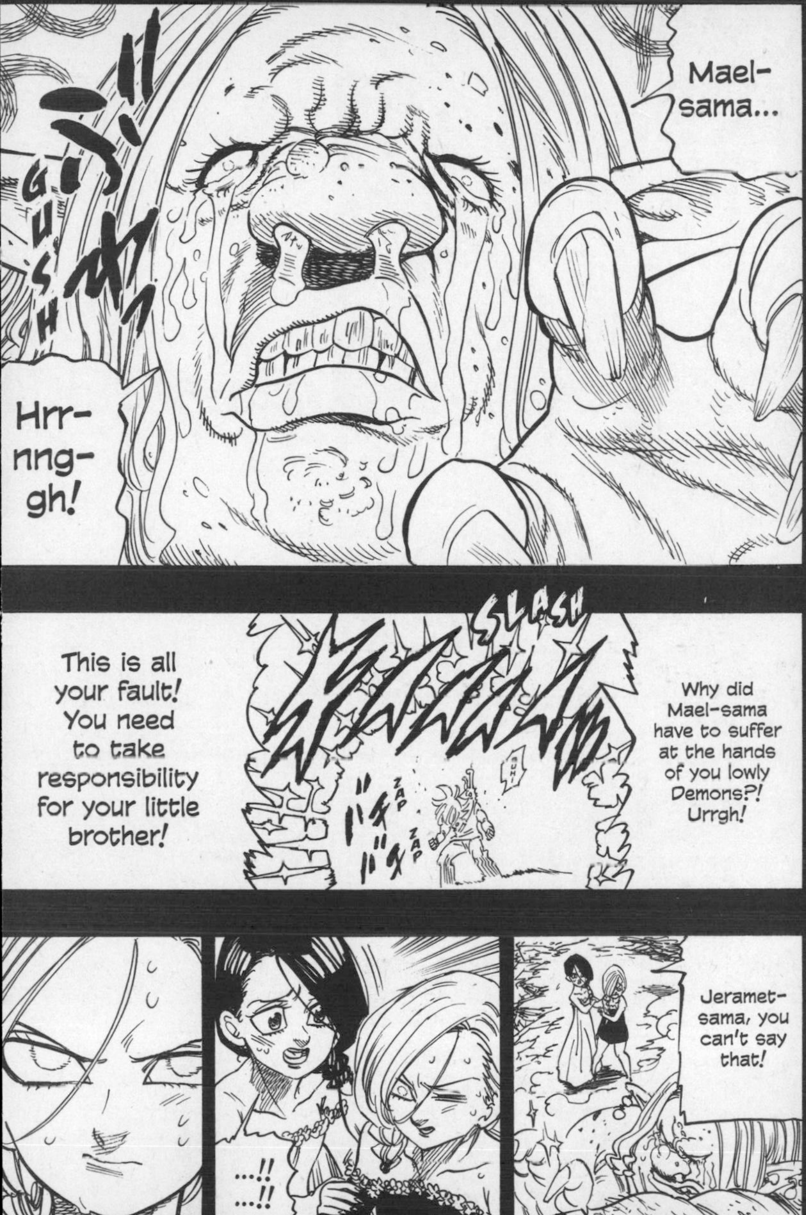
Mael-sama...
GUSH
Hrrr-nng-gh!
Why did Mael-sama have to suffer at the hands of you lowly Demons?! Urrgh!
SLASH
ZAP
ZAP
This is all your fault! You need to take responsibility for your little brother!
Jeramet-sama, you can't say that!
...!!
...!!

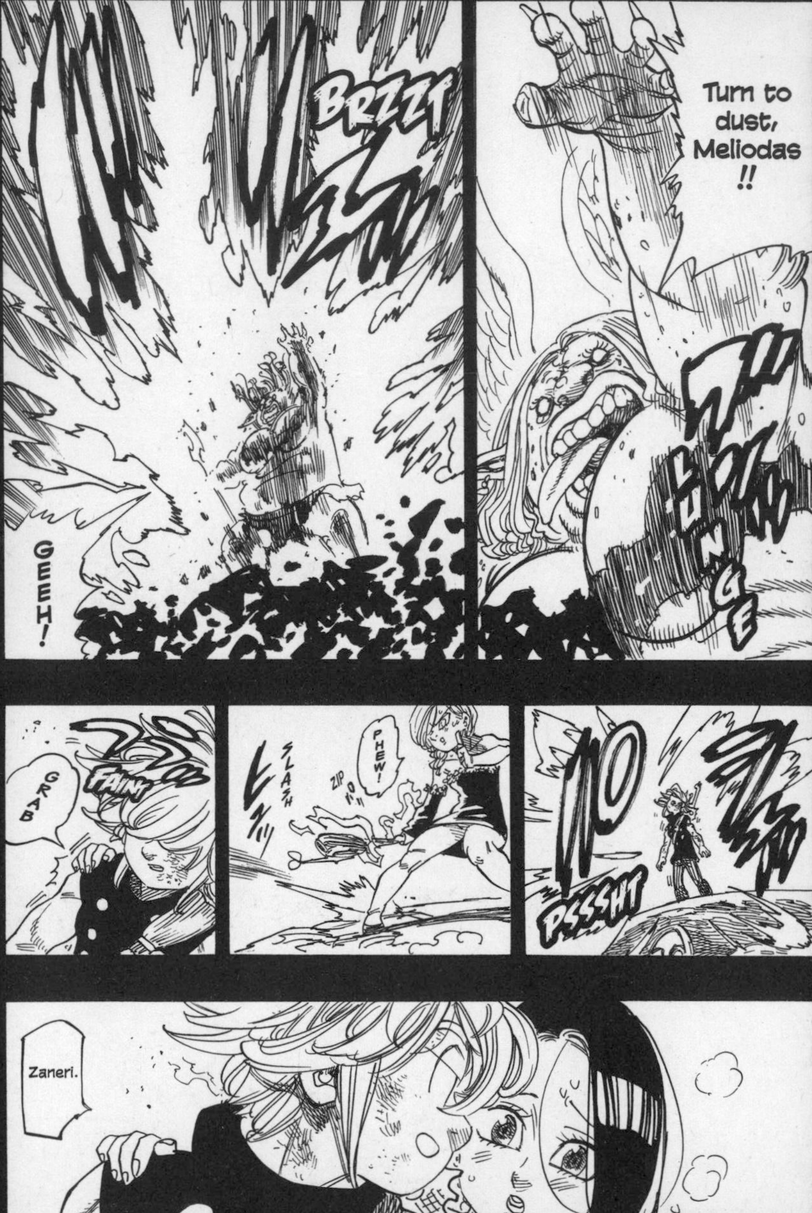
Turn to dust, Meliodas !!
LUNGE
BRZZT
GEEH!
PSSSHT
PHEW!
SLASH
ZIP
FAINT
GRAB
Zaneri.

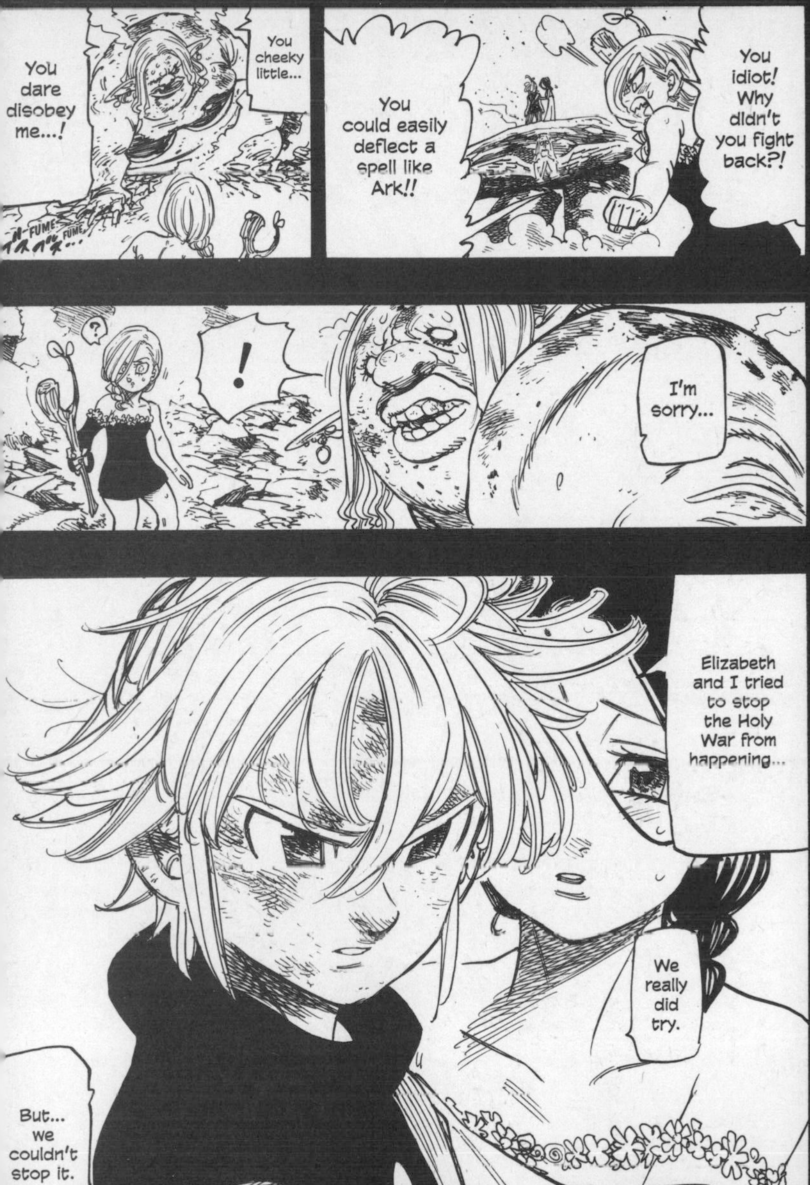

You idiot! Why didn't you fight back?!
You could easily deflect a spell like Ark!!
You cheeky little...
You dare disobey me...!
FUME FUME FUME...
I'm sorry...
!
?
Elizabeth and I tried to stop the Holy War from happening...
We really did try.
But... we couldn't stop it.

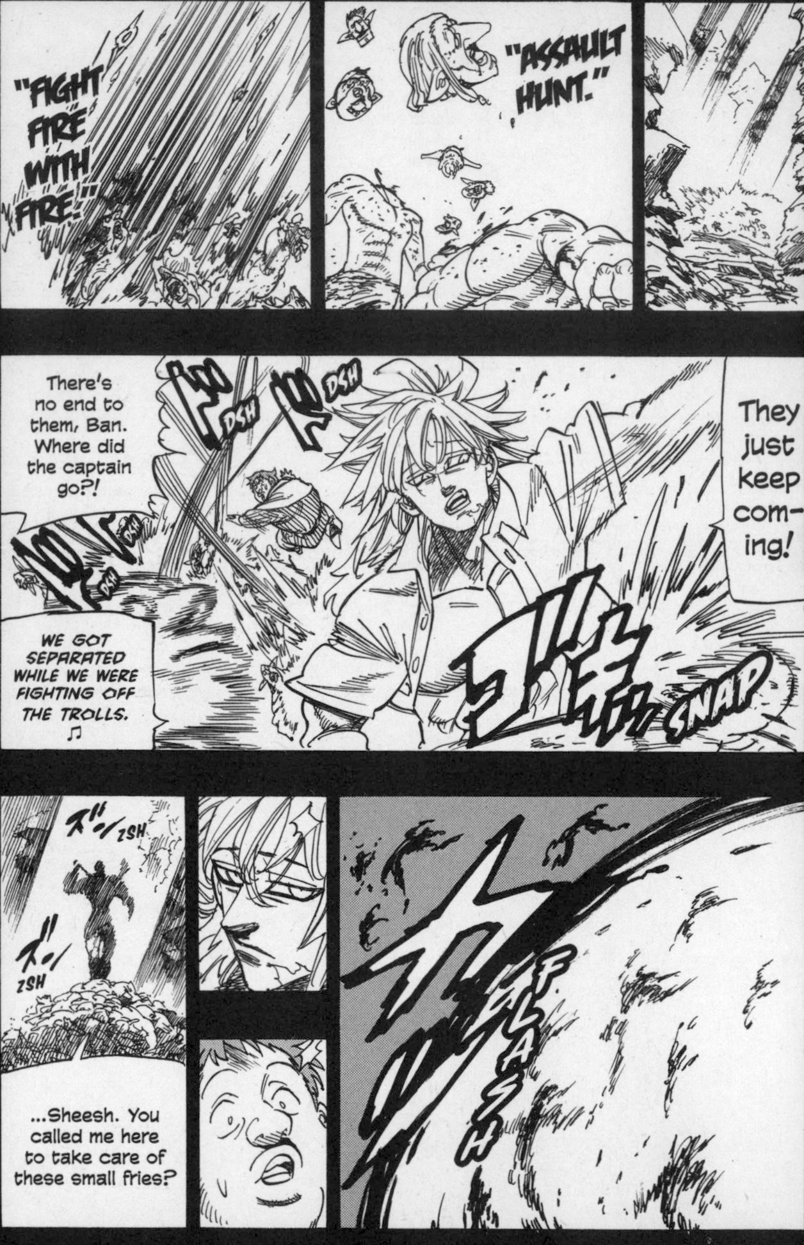
"ASSAULT HUNT."
"FIGHT FIRE WITH FIRE!!"
They just keep coming!
DSH
DSH
There's no end to them, Ban. Where did the captain go?!
DSH
DSH
WE GOT SEPARATED WHILE WE WERE FIGHTING OFF THE TROLLS. ♫
SNAP
FLASH
ZSH
ZSH
...Sheesh. You called me here to take care of these small fries?

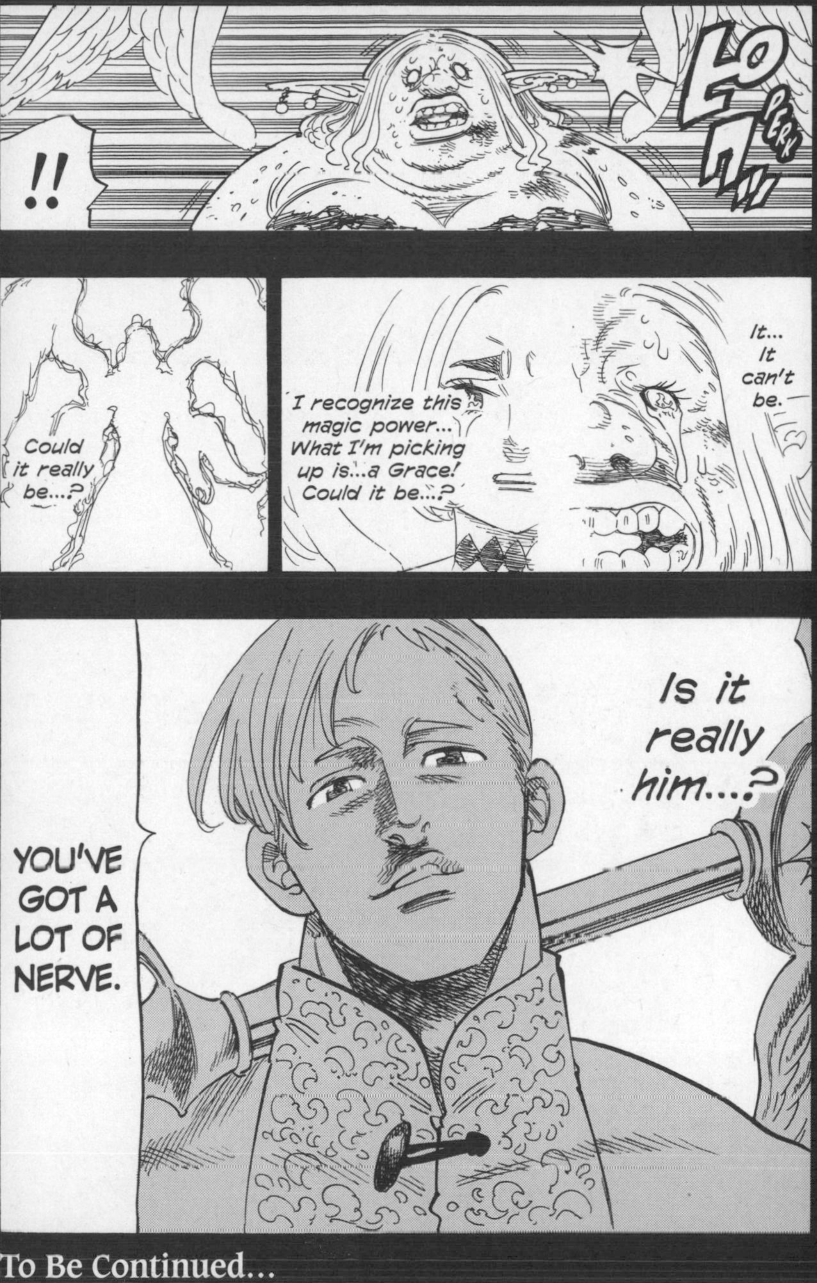
PERK
!!
It... It can't be.
I recognize this magic power... What I'm picking up is...a Grace! Could it be...?
Could it really be...?
Is it really him...?
YOU'VE GOT A LOT OF NERVE.

To Be Continued...

"THE SEVEN DEADLY SINS" ILLUSTRATION CORNER

"THE DRAWING KNIGHTHOOD" SPACE

Be sure to include your name and address on your postcard!

M = H = E = D = B = K = G = Mer = Esc = El = J =

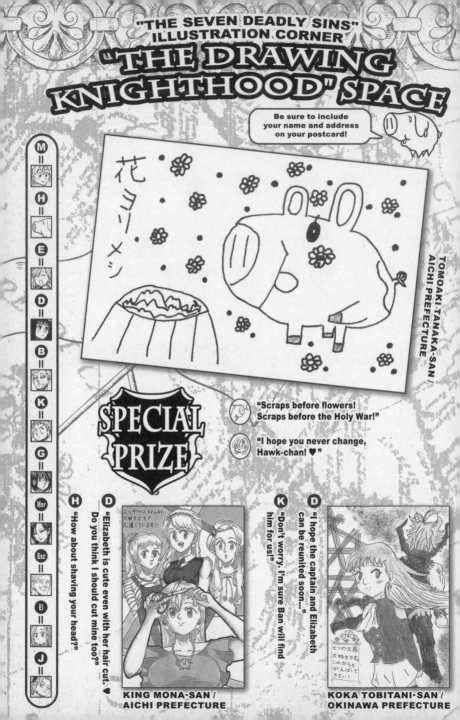

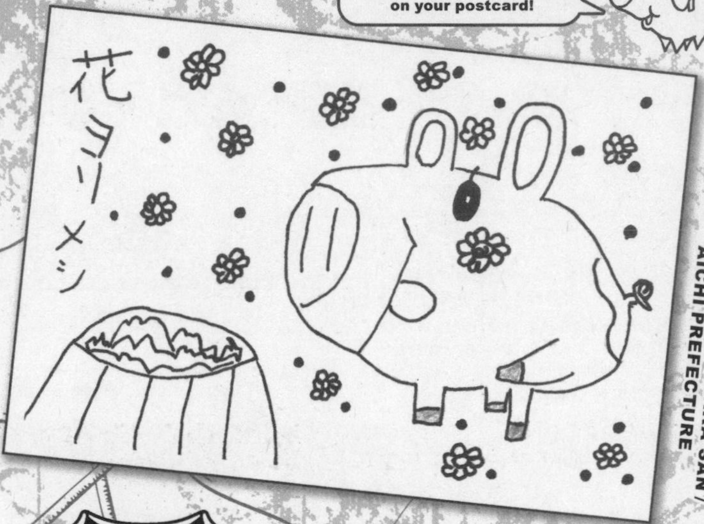
花ヨリメシ

TOMOAKI TANAKA-SAN / AICHI PREFECTURE

SPECIAL PRIZE

"Scraps before flowers! Scraps before the Holy War!"

"I hope you never change, Hawk-chan! ♥"

H "How about shaving your head?"

D "Elizabeth is cute even with her hair cut. Do you think I should cut mine too? ♥"

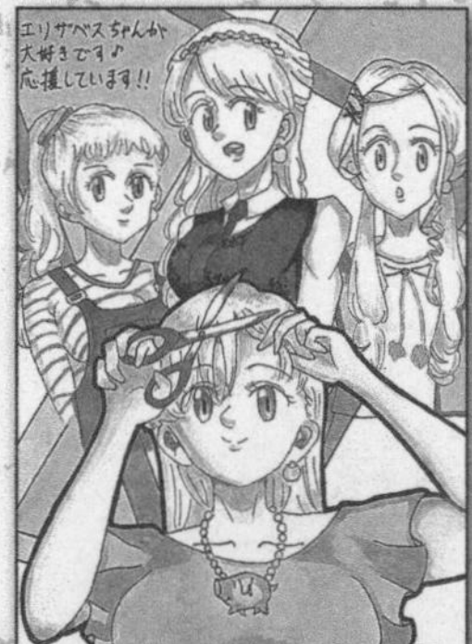
エリザベスちゃんが
大好きです♪
応援しています!!

KING MONA-SAN / AICHI PREFECTURE

K "Don't worry. I'm sure Ban will find him for us!"

D "I hope the captain and Elizabeth can be reunited soon..."

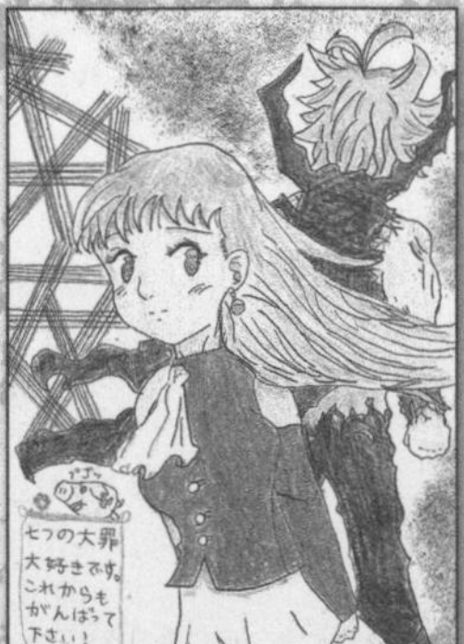
七つの大罪
大好きです。
これからも
がんばって
下さい!

KOKA TOBITANI-SAN / OKINAWA PREFECTURE

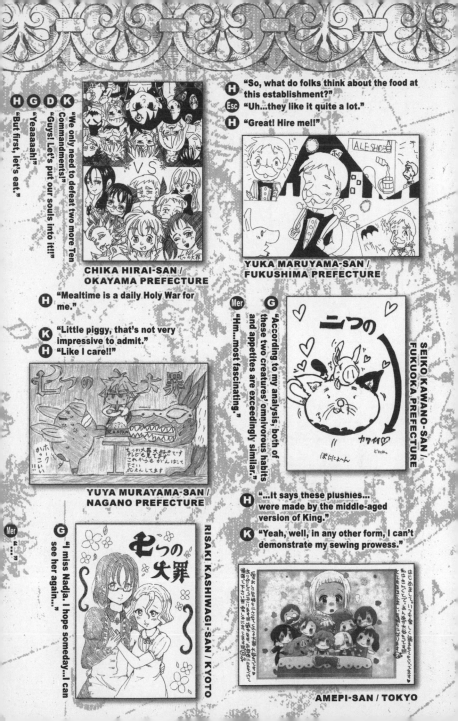

H "So, what do folks think about the food at this establishment?"

Esc "Uh...they like it quite a lot."

H "Great! Hire me!!"

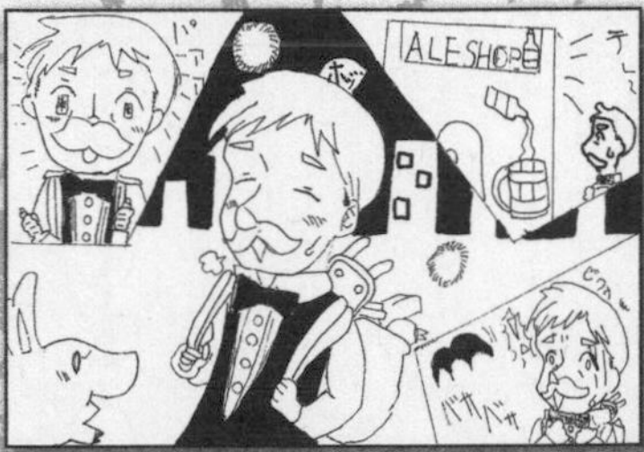
ALE SHOP

YUKA MARUYAMA-SAN / FUKUSHIMA PREFECTURE

K "We only need to defeat two more Ten Commandments!"

D "Guys! Let's put our souls into it!!"

G "Yeaaaaah!"

H "But first, let's eat."

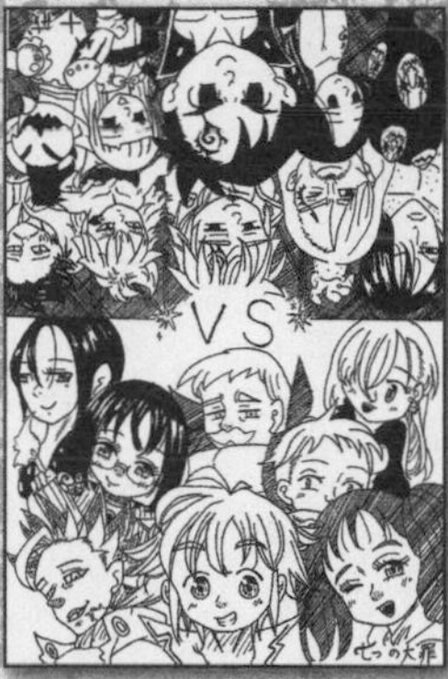
VS

CHIKA HIRAI-SAN / OKAYAMA PREFECTURE

H "Mealtime is a daily Holy War for me."

K "Little piggy, that's not very impressive to admit."

H "Like I care!!"

G "According to my analysis, both of these two creatures' omnivorous habits and appetites are exceedingly similar."

Mer "Hm...most fascinating."

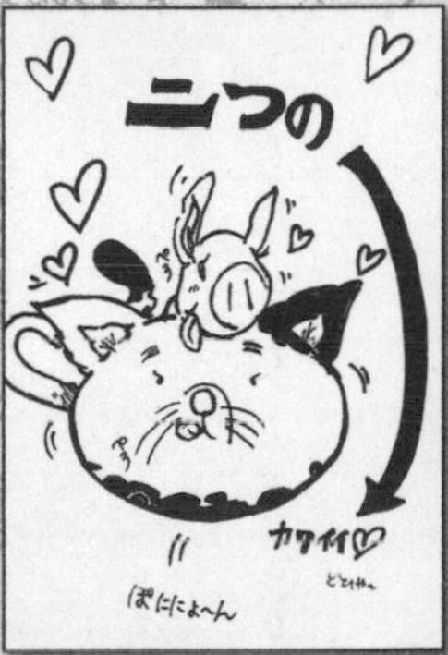
二つの
カワイイ♡
ぽににょ〜ん

SEIKO KAWANO-SAN / FUKUOKA PREFECTURE

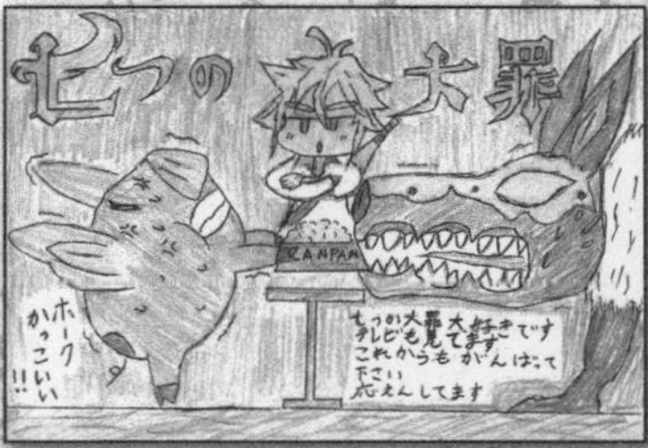
七つの大罪

YUYA MURAYAMA-SAN / NAGANO PREFECTURE

H "...It says these plushies... were made by the middle-aged version of King."

K "Yeah, well, in any other form, I can't demonstrate my sewing prowess."

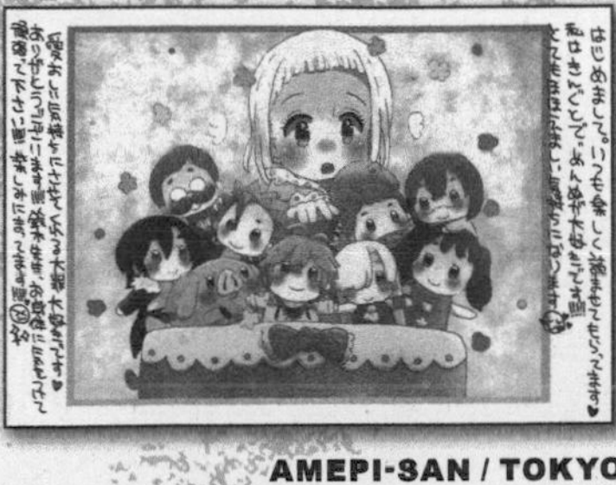

AMEPI-SAN / TOKYO

G "I miss Nadja. I hope someday...I can see her again..."

Mer "..."

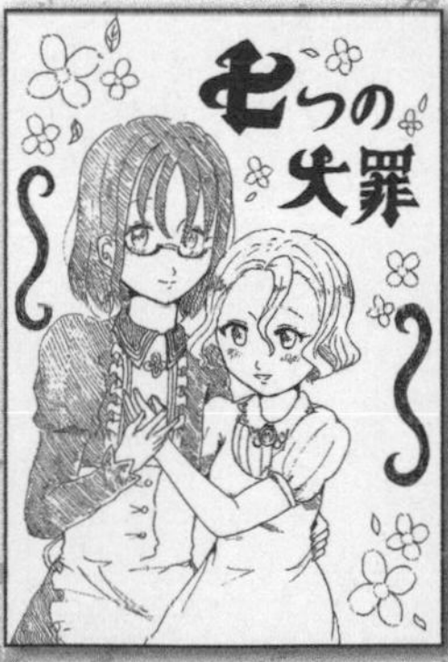
七つの大罪

RISAKI KASHIWAGI-SAN / KYOTO

HYOGO PREFECTURE

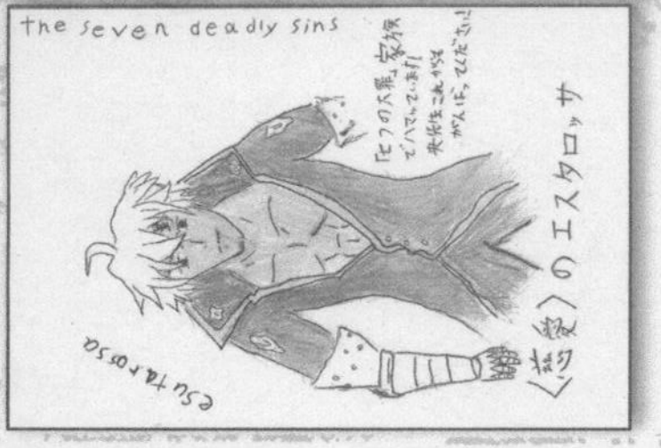
the seven deadly sins
esutarossa
〈慈愛〉のエスタロッサ

E "Something about him...feels familiar somehow... Something deep inside my mind is getting stuck on this guy. What could it be?"

SHIGA PREFECTURE

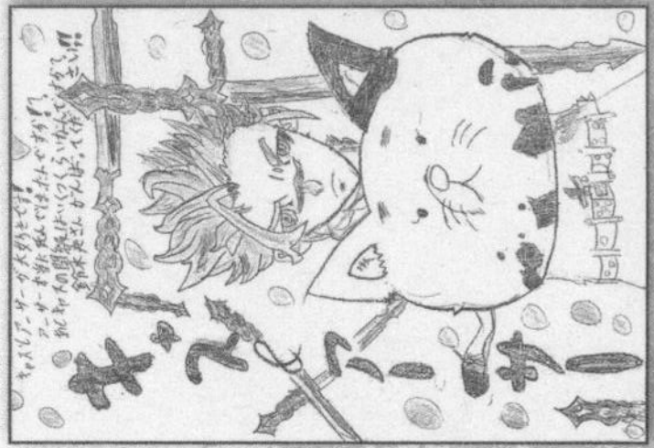

Mer "I swear I will avenge Arthur... And I shall instill such fear and destruction that I have no more regrets."

IBARAKI PREFECTURE

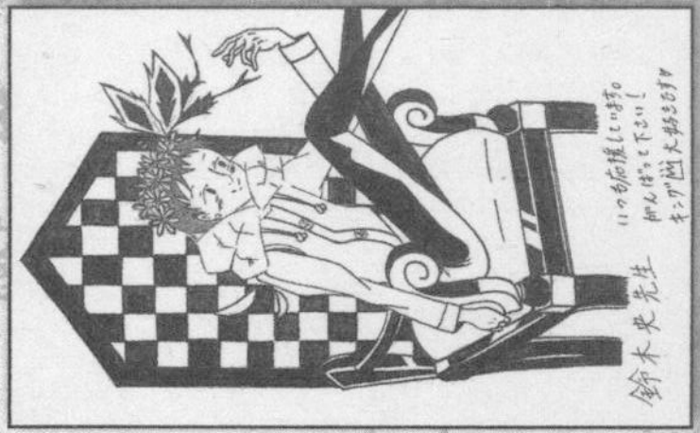
鈴木央先生

D "Seeing him like this, King does have a rather royal air about him."

K "A-Aww... (blush) Y-You really think so? (blush)"

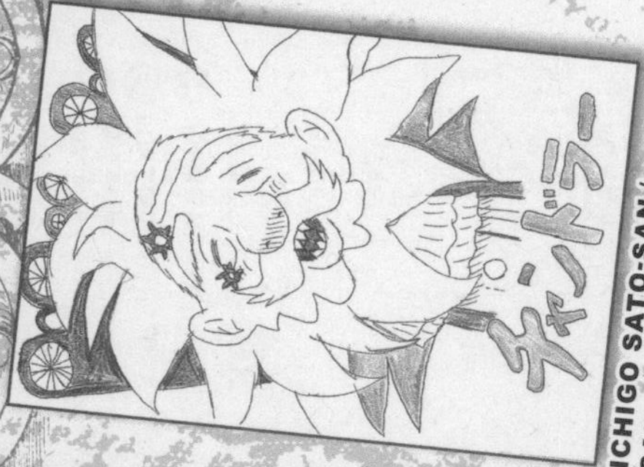
チャンドラー

ICHIGO SATO-SAN / SAITAMA PREFECTURE

D "...I don't like this old geezer."

H "Aw, come on. All he did was dote on Meliodas too much."

K "That's also scary."

SAKURA ☆-SAN / FUKUOKA PREFECTURE

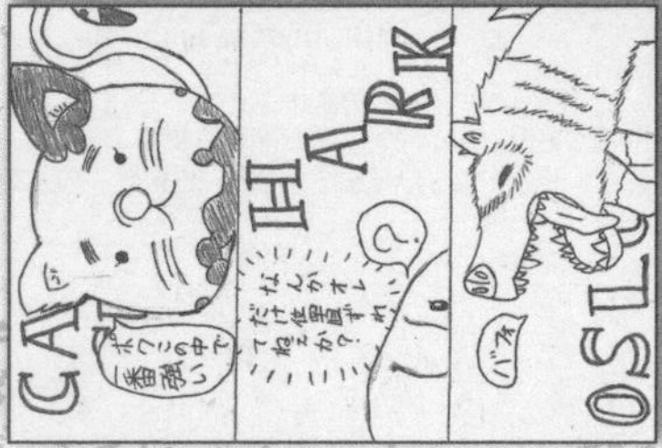
CA
ボクこの中で一番強い
HARK
?
OSL

H "The day will come when we must battle for who is the number one mascot of the series!"

Oslo "Woof?"

Cath "Cath!"

HIROSAWA KOKONO-SAN / OSAKA

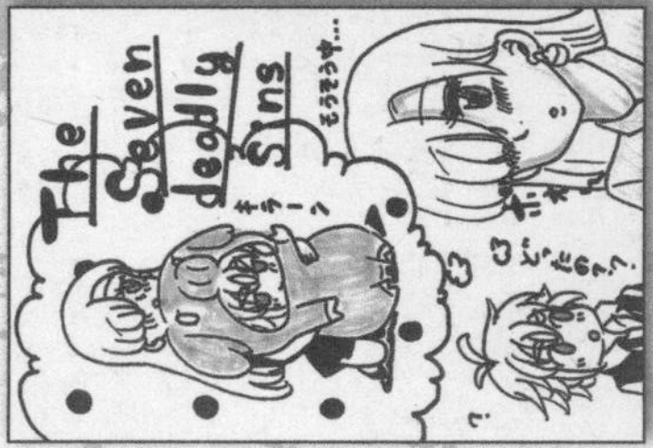
The Seven deadly Sins

H "Elizabeth-chan, when Meliodas gets back, I hope you can snuggle him to your heart's content. I'll allow it!"

Barta "I as well!"

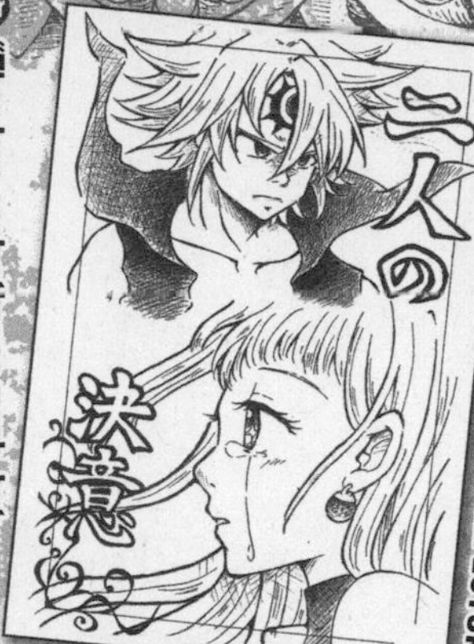
二人の
決意

CHIKA HIRANO-SAN / CHIBA PREFECTURE

Mer **"They love each other so much, but that's also why they must part too... It's tragic."**

D **"It'll be okay! Knowing those two, I'm sure they'll get back to how they were!"**

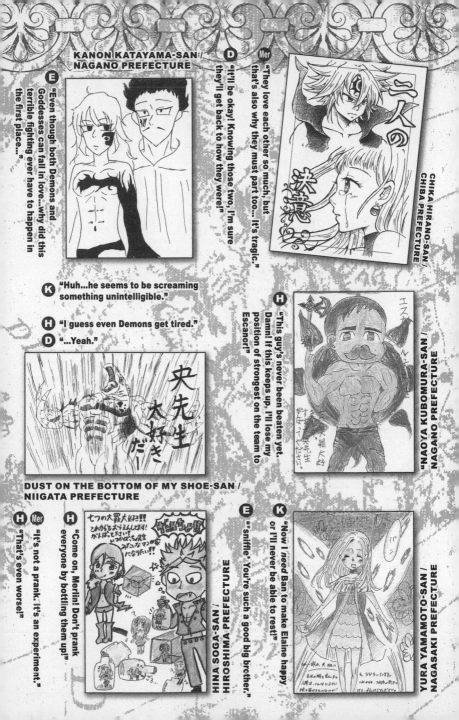

KANON KATAYAMA-SAN / NAGANO PREFECTURE

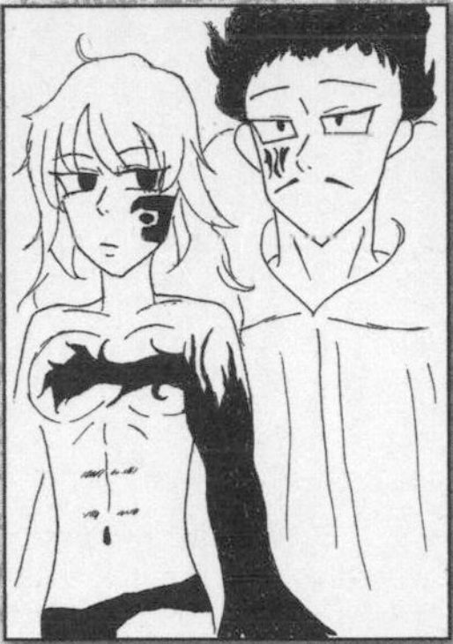

E **"Even though both Demons and Goddesses can fall in love...why did this terrible fighting ever have to happen in the first place..."**

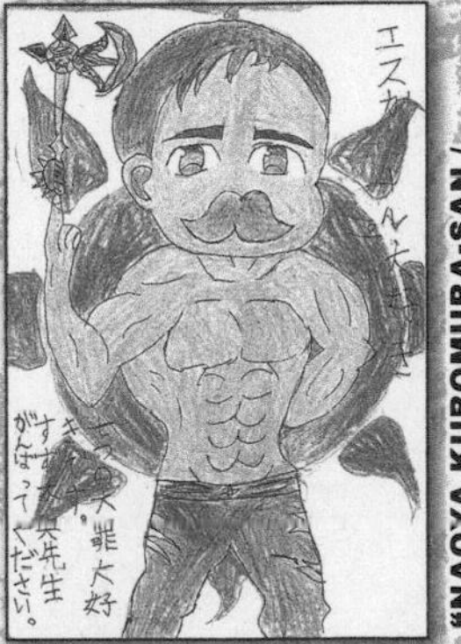

NAOYA KUBOMURA-SAN / NAGANO PREFECTURE

H **"This guy's never been beaten yet. Damn! If this keeps up, I'll lose my position of strongest on the team to Escanor!"**

K **"Huh...he seems to be screaming something unintelligible."**

H **"I guess even Demons get tired."**

D **"...Yeah."**

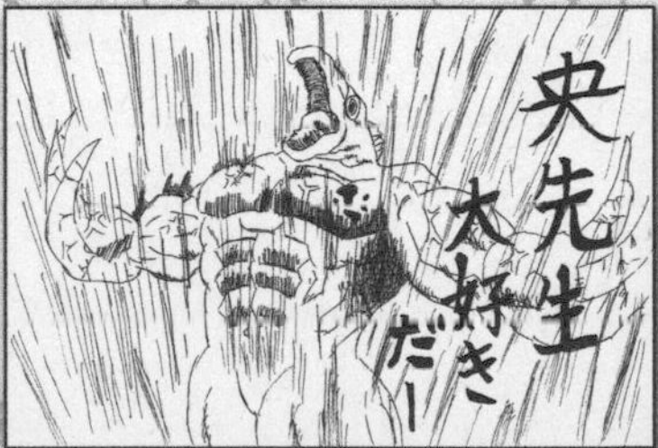
央先生
太好き
だー

DUST ON THE BOTTOM OF MY SHOE-SAN / NIIGATA PREFECTURE

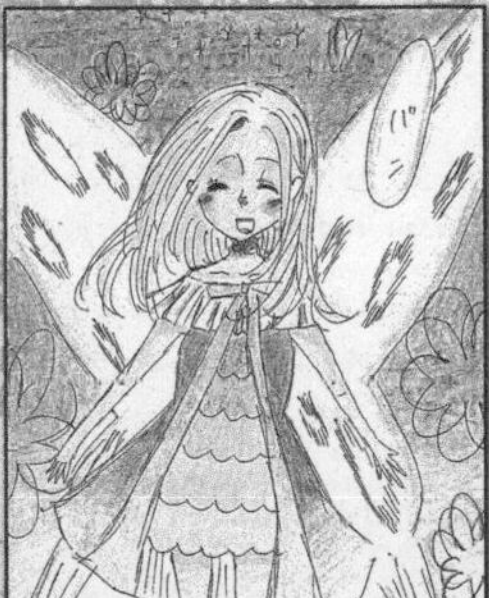

YURA YAMAMOTO-SAN / NAGASAKI PREFECTURE

K **"Now I *need* Ban to make Elaine happy or I'll never be able to rest!"**

E **"*sniffle* You're such a good big brother."**

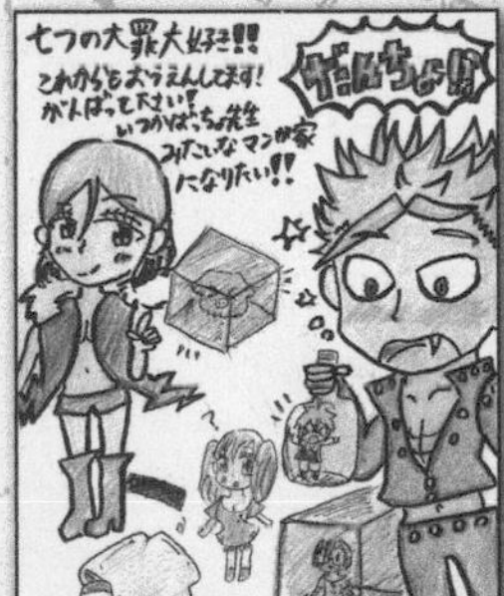
七つの大罪大好き!!!
これからもおうえんしてます!
がんばって下さい!
いつかはっちな先生みたいなマンガ家になりたい!!

HINA SOGA-SAN / HIROSHIMA PREFECTURE

H **"Come on, Merlin! Don't prank everyone by bottling them up!"**

Mer **"It's not a prank. It's an experiment."**

H **"That's even worse!"**

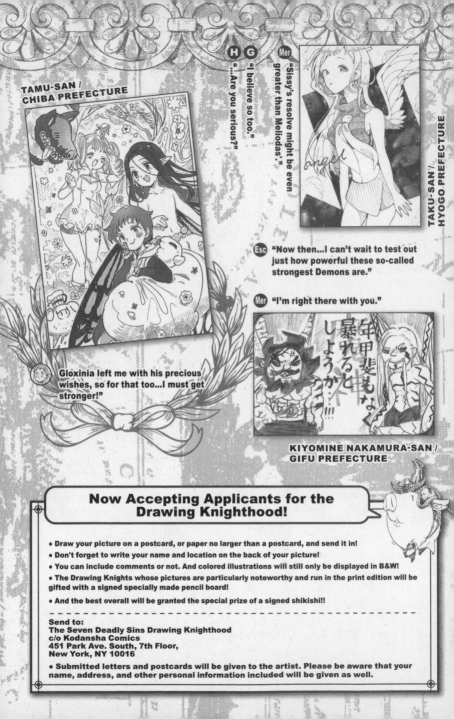

TAMU-SAN /
CHIBA PREFECTURE

TAKU-SAN /
HYOGO PREFECTURE

Mer "Sissy's resolve might be even greater than Meliodas'."

H **G** "I believe so too."
"...Are you serious?"

Esc "Now then...I can't wait to test out just how powerful these so-called strongest Demons are."

Mer "I'm right there with you."

"Gloxinia left me with his precious wishes, so for that too...I must get stronger!"

KIYOMINE NAKAMURA-SAN /
GIFU PREFECTURE

KC
KODANSHA COMICS

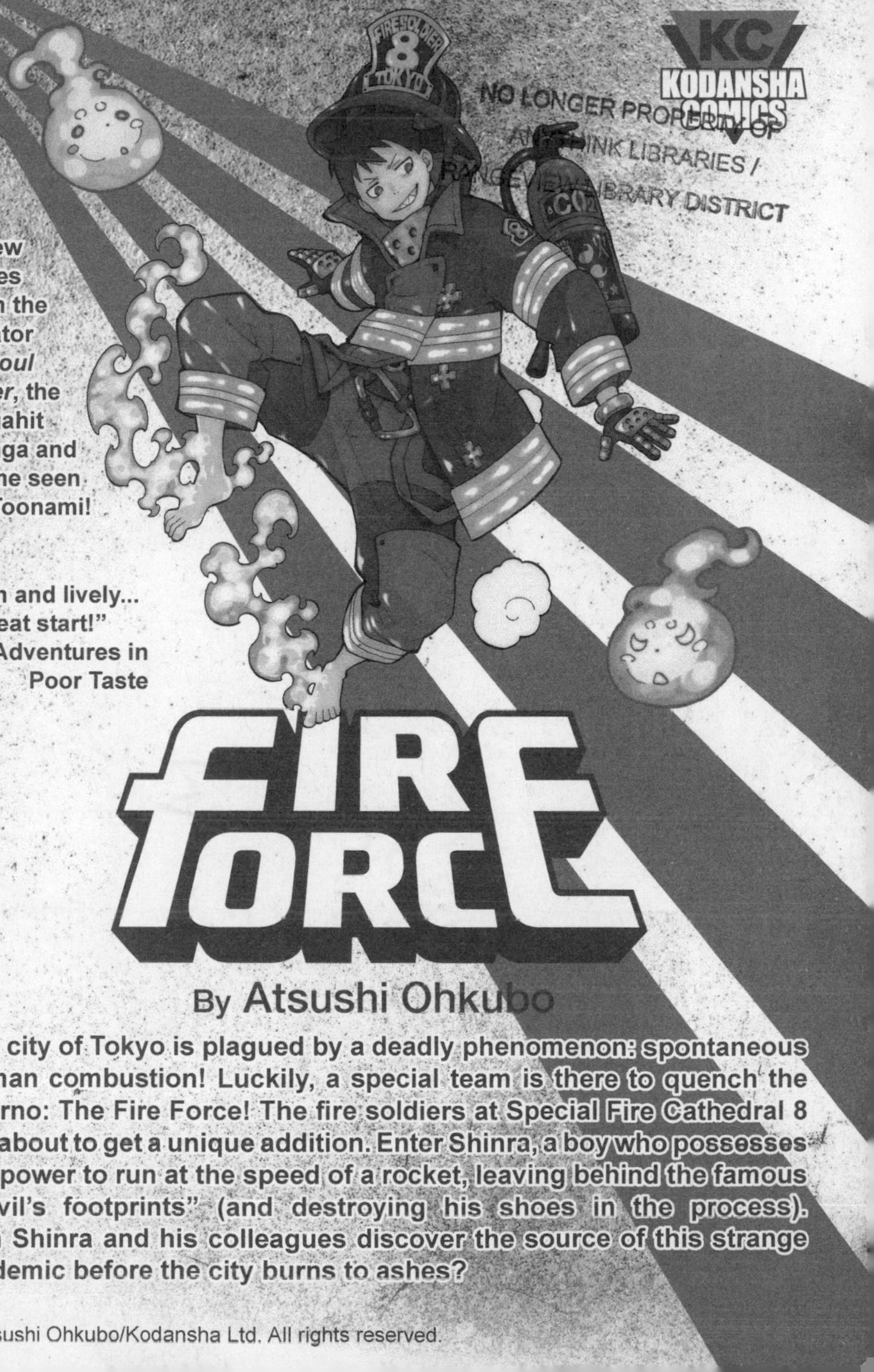

new
eries
om the
reator
f *Soul*
ater, the
egahit
anga and
nime seen
n Toonami!

Fun and lively...
great start!"
-Adventures in
Poor Taste

FIRE FORCE

By Atsushi Ohkubo

he city of Tokyo is plagued by a deadly phenomenon: spontaneous
uman combustion! Luckily, a special team is there to quench the
ferno: The Fire Force! The fire soldiers at Special Fire Cathedral 8
re about to get a unique addition. Enter Shinra, a boy who possesses
e power to run at the speed of a rocket, leaving behind the famous
devil's footprints" (and destroying his shoes in the process).
an Shinra and his colleagues discover the source of this strange
pidemic before the city burns to ashes?

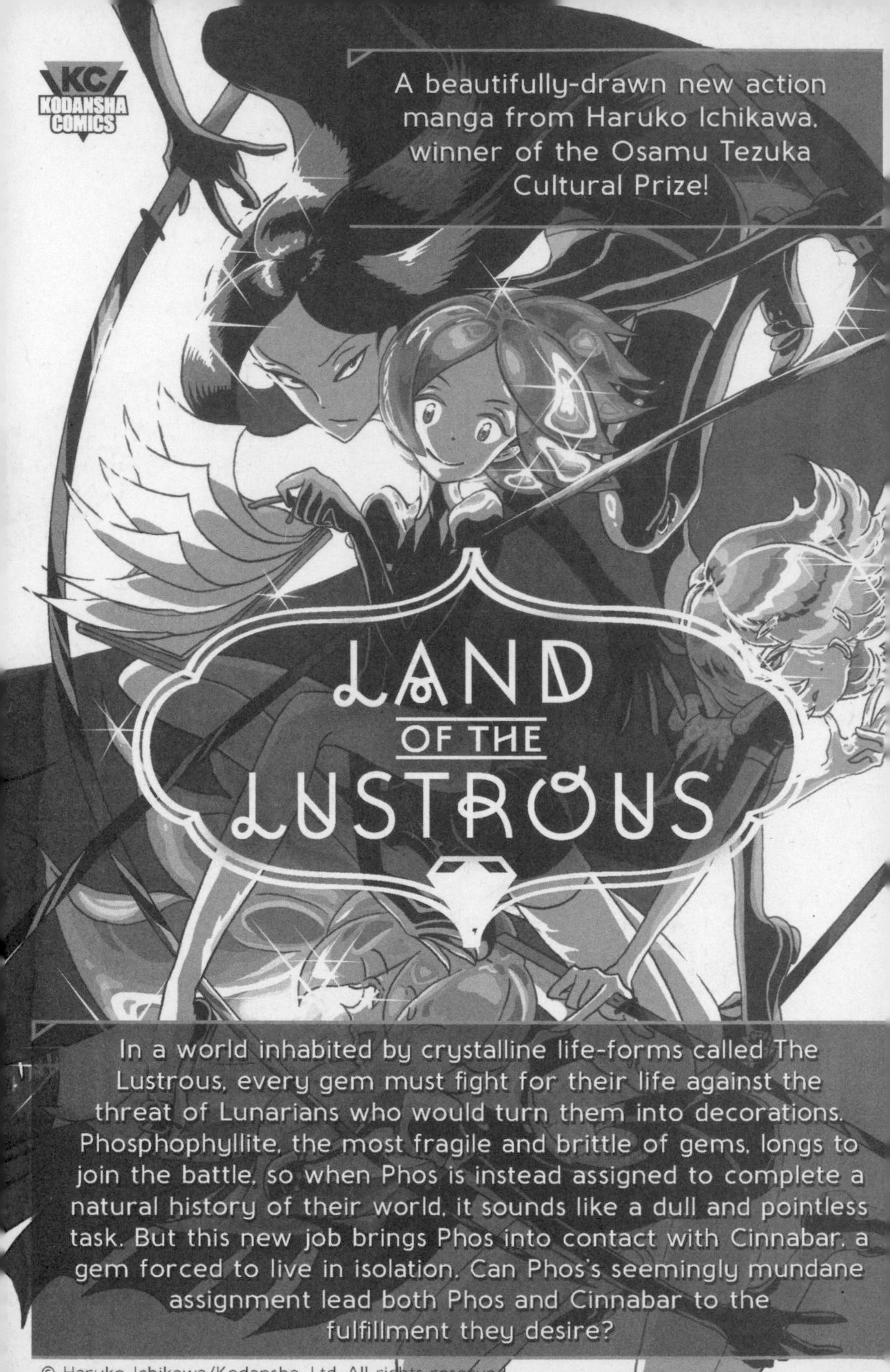
KC KODANSHA COMICS
A beautifully-drawn new action manga from Haruko Ichikawa, winner of the Osamu Tezuka Cultural Prize!
LAND OF THE LUSTROUS
In a world inhabited by crystalline life-forms called The Lustrous, every gem must fight for their life against the threat of Lunarians who would turn them into decorations. Phosphophyllite, the most fragile and brittle of gems, longs to join the battle, so when Phos is instead assigned to complete a natural history of their world, it sounds like a dull and pointless task. But this new job brings Phos into contact with Cinnabar, a gem forced to live in isolation. Can Phos's seemingly mundane assignment lead both Phos and Cinnabar to the fulfillment they desire?

The Seven Deadly Sins volume 32 is a work of fiction. Names, characters, places, and incidents are the products of the author's imagination or are used fictitiously. Any resemblance to actual events, locales, or persons, living or dead, is entirely coincidental.

A Kodansha Comics Trade Paperback Original.

Published in the United States by Kodansha Comics, an imprint of Kodansha USA Publishing, LLC, New York.

Publication rights for this English edition arranged through Kodansha Ltd., Tokyo.

First published in Japan in 2018 by Kodansha Ltd., Tokyo.

ISBN 978-1-63236-732-7

Printed in the United States of America.

www.kodanshacomics.com

9 8 7 6 5 4 3 2 1

Translation: Christine Dashiell
Lettering: James Dashiell
Kodansha Comics edition cover design: Phil Balsman